SATHER CLASSICAL LECTURES

Volume Seventy-Eight

The Poetry of Being and the Prose of the World in Early Greek Philosophy

The publisher and the University of California Press Foundation
gratefully acknowledge the generous support of the
Fletcher Jones Foundation Imprint in Humanities.

THE FLETCHER JONES FOUNDATION

HUMANITIES IMPRINT

The Fletcher Jones Foundation has endowed this imprint to foster innovative and enduring scholarship in the humanities.

A free ebook version of this title is available through Luminos,
University of California Press's Open Access publishing program.
Visit www.luminosoa.org to learn more.

The Poetry of Being and the Prose of the World in Early Greek Philosophy

The Poetry of Being and the Prose of the World in Early Greek Philosophy

Victoria Wohl

UNIVERSITY OF CALIFORNIA PRESS

University of California Press
Oakland, California

Suggested citation: Wohl, V. *The Poetry of Being and the Prose of the World in Early Greek Philosophy*. Oakland: University of California Press, 2025.
DOI: https://doi.org/10.1525/luminos.242

Cataloging-in-Publication Data is on file at the Library of Congress.

ISBN 978–0-520–42264-3 (cloth)
ISBN 978–0-520–41332-0 (pbk.)
ISBN 978–0-520–41333-7 (ebook)

33 32 31 30 29 28 27 26 25
10 9 8 7 6 5 4 3 2 1

For my teachers

CONTENTS

PREFACE

(Meta)Physics for Poets

What men are poets who can speak of Jupiter if he were like a man, but if he is an immense spinning sphere of methane and ammonia must be silent?
—RICHARD FEYNMAN

I took a course in college entitled "Physics for Poets." The class was designed to give students with no scientific or mathematical background a sense of the key questions and concepts of physics, to allow them to appreciate the "poetry" of physics. I could little have guessed then that I would find myself working, several decades later, on the poetry of the first physicists, the early philosophers whom Aristotle calls *phusikoi*. These thinkers, active in ancient Greece in the late archaic and early classical period (roughly 600–400 BCE), were philosophers of *phusis*, nature. Their books, often known by the generic title *Peri Phuseōs* (*On Nature*), deal with the creation and constitutive elements of the cosmos and cover a vast array of topics: the planets and meteorological phenomena; the origins and development of plants, animals, and human beings; the soul and the limitations of knowledge; the gods and their relation to mortals. As this partial list suggests, their inquiries into nature took them beyond what we would think of as physics; they extended into metaphysics and the investigation of the fundamental qualities of reality itself, the "nature" of being as a whole. These thinkers were also poets, and it was their poetry not their physics or metaphysics that first drew me to them: the enigmatic brilliance of Heraclitus's aphorisms, the verbal invention of Democritus, the swirling, rushing verbiage of Empedocles. Even when they did not write in verse, they used language in self-conscious and innovative ways. This poetic language and its relation to their philosophical thought is the topic of this book.

The thinkers I examine here—Parmenides, Heraclitus, Empedocles, Anaxagoras, and Democritus—are members of the eclectic group generally known as the "Presocratics."[1] This label, as we shall see in the Introduction, has come into question in recent years both for its teleological assumptions and for its historical inaccuracies. The term "Presocratic" tells an interesting story about the reception of these writers and the place they have been granted in the history of Western philosophy, but it says almost nothing about these thinkers themselves. They did not know they came before Socrates, nor did they call themselves philosophers. I use the label for convenience, but I do not subscribe to the assumptions it might entail as to the position of these writers in the diachronic sweep of intellectual history or the characteristics that unite them synchronically and differentiate them from other contemporaneous thinkers.

These are intriguing and important questions, but they are not my questions.[2] This study is less historicist or genealogical than literary-theoretical. I approach each author individually, attempting to elucidate the particular qualities of his thought and expression and the dynamic interrelation between them that plays out in his surviving texts. Of course, these texts do not exist in isolation, nor did their authors. The Presocratics were in conversation with one another: Parmenides seems to respond to Heraclitus, and everyone else responds to Parmenides.[3] It would be tempting—and productive—to compare Presocratic thinkers on a given topic in order to paint a picture of the intellectual culture of early Greece and their position within it.[4] Common themes will emerge in the pages that follow: a shared interest in origins and causality; time, fixity, and change; universality and plurality; and the conceptual and spatial geometry of the circle, to name just a few. But my interest is less in such themes per se than in how they take shape in and through each author's unique language. For these purposes it proved more expedient to treat each figure separately.

1. My choice of these five is exemplary, not exhaustive, though it does represent a large percentage of the surviving words attributed to the Presocratics. One notable omission is Xenophanes, who composed elegiac poetry on traditional themes, as well as hexameter poetry on the physical world, epistemology, and the nature of the divine. This heterogeneous output makes Xenophanes an important figure in a broader survey of the relation between philosophy and poetry in archaic Greece. But I find both the philosophy of the "poetic" fragments and the poetics of the "philosophical" fragments less rich than in the authors considered here, and the corpus as a whole offers less purchase for the kind of analysis I am undertaking. For a good recent treatment of Xenophanes's poetics and how they support his philosophy, see Mackenzie 2021a, 24–64.

2. Readers wanting an introduction to the Presocratics as a whole may consult Guthrie 1962, 1965; Kirk, Raven, and Schofield 1983; Long 1999a; Curd and Graham 2008; and the excellent study of Sassi (2018), who situates them well within their historical and sociological, as well as intellectual and literary, context. Hussey 1972; Warren 2007c; and McKirahan 2010 are informative and accessible for those with less background in the field.

3. See especially Curd 1998. Parmenides's decisive influence has been questioned by Osborne (2006).

4. There are many examples of the productivity of this approach, from Stokes 1971 (on the one and the many) to Porter 2010, 121–76 (on aesthetics); Bryan 2012 (on likeness and likelihood); and Tor 2017 (on the divine).

The Presocratics were in dialogue not only with one another but also indirectly, if not directly, with their "nonphilosophical" contemporaries. Focused study of this dialogue, too, would be illuminating and would no doubt support and extend the claims I make here about the porous border between philosophy and poetry in early Greece.[5] My project, however, is more inward-looking and, in a sense, preliminary. While I do hope to shed light on the larger intellectual landscape in which the Presocratics operated, my focus is on the figures, not the landscape. The complexity of these figures in themselves—the intricacy of the theories, their expression, and the relation between the two—precludes drawing easy connections with their contemporaries, philosophical or nonphilosophical, and complicates in advance any totalizing account of their intellectual milieu that might be extrapolated from such connections.

Links might be forged diachronically as well as synchronically. Each of my authors engaged in a sustained and serious way with Homer and Hesiod, thinking both with and against these authoritative figures and reworking not only their epic forms but their entire worldview. We will see examples of this engagement throughout the book, but it is not my emphasis. The creative rewriting of their epic predecessors was never an end in itself for the Presocratic philosophers, and it needs to be understood within the context of their larger poetic and philosophical projects.[6] A diachronic approach might, alternatively, lead forward in time to examine the Presocratics' influence on later thinkers, ancient and modern, philosophical and nonphilosophical.[7] Again, we will observe this influence, especially in chapter 5, which situates Democritus in relation to both Aristotle's reception and the (avowedly anti-Aristotelian) reception of Barbara Cassin and other modern philosophers. But serious consideration of the Presocratics' long philosophical—or poetic—afterlife is beyond the scope of this book, which is, first and foremost, a close analysis of the expressive choices of five Presocratic authors and an attempt to understand how these choices shape—both limit and enable—their philosophical inquiry.

This project is rife with challenges of its own. The philosophical doctrines of each of these figures is the subject of vehement debate and there is often no consensus on the most basic features of their philosophical system nor even on

5. For scholarship in this vein see, e.g., Kouremenos 1993; Egli 2003; Irby-Massie 2008; Seaford 2013; Scapin 2020; Ciampa 2021, 2023; Mackenzie 2022; and Kingsley 2024. Kotwick and Moore (forthcoming) will facilitate this sort of intergeneric study.

6. There are several fine recent studies of the Presocratics' engagement with Homer and Hesiod, including Tor 2017; Iribarren 2018; Mackenzie 2021a; Iribarren and Koning 2022; and Folit-Weinberg 2022.

7. Laks (2018) shows well how the "concept of Presocratic philosophy" was shaped by its later reception. See further, purely by way of example, Stamatellos 2007 on Plotinus and the Presocratics; Porter 2000 on Nietzsche; O'Connell 2005 on Derrida; and Jacobs 1999 and Korab-Karpowicz 2016 on Heidegger. A list of poetic receptions would likewise be lengthy, ranging from Ovid to Hölderlin to T. S. Eliot.

their (highly fragmentary) texts. To attempt to interpret the thought and language of the Presocratics is to work always amid radical uncertainty about both the thought and the language. I remain agnostic on many fundamental points of doctrine. Myriad decisions must be made about each in order to proceed, but my commitment to these decisions is at most provisional. In reaching them, I rely on the work of scholars of ancient philosophy who have labored to reconstruct the texts and the theories of these authors. But while I engage extensively, and I hope responsibly, with the philosophical scholarship, my own hermeneutics are unapologetically literary. This interpretive strategy follows closely on my conviction that in the Presocratics poetics and philosophy are inseparable. Writers—even philosophers!—think in language: their language very simply is their thought (and vice versa), and thus a close reading of their poetics is the only way to fully understand their philosophy.

The primacy of language relative to thought is a generally accepted premise of modern continental philosophy. The same premise is less accepted (when not outright rejected) within the Anglo-American tradition—indeed, this is one of the main differences between the two.[8] For readers in the latter camp this difference in approach may produce misunderstandings, in particular surrounding the evaluation of incoherence and inconsistency, notions that will figure centrally in my readings of the Presocratics. These are serious failings in a philosophical tradition that (starting with Aristotle, as we shall see) prizes clarity of expression, consistency of argumentation, and coherence of thought above all else and presupposes that these are the proper aims of philosophical writing. When I use terms like "incoherence" below, I do so not to denounce the author's shortcomings or suggest that his theories are invalid or worthless—quite the opposite. I proceed from the assumption that no systematic thinking, much less writing, is ever fully coherent, and that its unresolved tensions and unresolvable paradoxes are among the most exciting moments in any text—the richest, the most telling, and the most hermeneutically rewarding. I do not aim to resolve them myself, nor do I require my authors to resolve them. Instead, I examine how each author approaches and thinks through these aporias—including how he tries and necessarily fails to solve them—in order to identify both the theoretical impasses and creative impetuses of his philosophy.

In emphasizing language and its aporias, I put the Presocratic philosophers into conversation with certain modern continental philosophers who, in my view, share their concerns. The book engages throughout with these theorists, in particular Jacques Derrida and Gilles Deleuze, the former for his exploration of language at the "margins of philosophy," the latter for his attempt to articulate a mode of philosophy that expands those margins. My emphasis on this

8. Rowett (2020) notes the challenge the Presocratic philosopher-poets pose to the alliance of scholars of ancient philosophy with analytic philosophy.

nonlinear lineage over more immediate or direct genealogies may incur the charge of anachronism. But the Presocratics, as I hope to show, were preoccupied with the same questions that—in a very different idiom, to be sure, and with different presuppositions and aims—concern these twentieth-century thinkers, and the juxtaposition brings out otherwise obscure aspects of their thought. Part of the merit of drawing these connections is precisely its untimeliness, which can open up new and unanticipated ways of interpreting the texts in their historical specificity—what Barbara Cassin terms "a different way of being pre-Socratic."[9] The strategic anachronism of my theoretical framework also helps counter the different, and more entrenched, anachronism of reading the Presocratics through Aristotle. The modern philosophers (or perhaps "antiphilosophers") with whom I engage operate at a critical remove from the Aristotelian tradition and help us to see beyond his influential but partial (in both senses) definition of philosophy. In this way, too, the anachronism of modern theories can be a means to the end of a more—or at least differently—attuned historicism.

If for some readers my choice of theoretical interlocutors will seem too modern, for others it may feel rather old-fashioned. Why Deleuze and Derrida in preference to approaches with higher current cachet like the various new materialisms, speculative realisms, or object-oriented ontologies? These theories are helpful in understanding the world the Presocratics imagine (in particular that of Empedocles, as we shall see in chapter 3) but less helpful in understanding that imagining itself: they tend to be relatively uninterested in language. But the Presocratics' cosmos is created and preserved in language. This language, as I hope to show, has a materiality and an agency of its own and to overlook it, or attempt to look through it as though it were transparent, is to ignore a fundamental element of that cosmos itself.

Both the cosmos and the poetics of the Presocratics are stunning in their originality and strangeness. I think of the Presocratics as what Deleuze and Guattari call "a minor literature." This has nothing to do with the minuteness of the fragments or the minor place they occupy in ancient literary history, but rather evokes their strangeness in relation to more familiar genres of Greek expression and thought. To write a minor literature is, Deleuze and Guattari say, "to be as a stranger *in* one's own language."[10] The Presocratics are strangers in the Greek language, expanding its possibilities, bending it into new forms, often straining it to the breaking point of syntax and semantics alike. They are also strangers in the language of philosophy passed down from Plato and Aristotle, dialects of which are still spoken by

9. Cassin 2014, 26; cf. 2, 8, 27. See the thoughtful comments on untimeliness in Postclassicisms Collective 2020, 161–81. Michel Serres (Serres and Latour 1995, 60) offers the image of a crumpled handkerchief to figure nonlinear history and the surprising transhistorical proximities it produces. Holmes (2016) adopts this image as a model for the study of classical reception.

10. Deleuze and Guattari 1983a, 26 (= 1986, 16–27).

most professional philosophers today. I attempt to hear this strangeness and to do it justice in my readings.

I cite the fragments by their Diels-Kranz (DK) number, as this is the numbering system most commonly used in the scholarship and in the searchable databases of ancient Greek literature. The Diels-Kranz system refers to authors by number; for ease of reference I will refer to them by abbreviated name (so Heraclitus's first fragment will be Her. B1 instead of Diels-Kranz's 21 B1) and where there is no risk of ambiguity, simply by the fragment number. As Diels-Kranz seems likely to be superseded, at least in the anglophone and francophone worlds, by Laks-Most's Loeb edition, I also give LM numbers for each fragment, separated by a backslash. Where I prefer Laks-Most's text to Diels-Kranz's, I put their number first. The result is some rather ungainly strings of numbers, but I hope the loss in elegance will be compensated by a gain in utility. Translations, also often ungainly, are my own.

. . .

Versions of the following chapters were presented as the Sather Lectures in the Department of Ancient Greek and Roman Studies at UC Berkeley in Autumn 2023. I am grateful to everyone there, and especially to Dylan Sailor, Leslie Kurke, Mark Griffith, Tony Long, Jim Porter, and Mario Telò, for their hospitality and for making my term in Berkeley so fruitful and enjoyable. It was a particular honor to deliver these lectures in the department from which I received my PhD. I feel very sincerely that this project would not have been possible had I not been a grad student in the (then) Department of Classics at Berkeley. The project follows a reading agenda outlined by Leslie Kurke: "a wayward mobile practice that forces us to poach and to trespass—across the boundaries of different fields and subfields; across different texts, both literary and 'sub-' or nonliterary, both canonical and marginal."[11] The program supported such a practice with its exceptional commitment to interdisciplinarity and to breadth, as well as depth, of learning. Berkeley encouraged students to think boldly and not to confine ourselves to received paradigms. I have tried to live up to that lesson in this book.

Doing so has meant often working at, or even over, the limits of my knowledge—of physics, of philosophy, and of poetry. As Bernard Williams, one of the many illustrious previous Sather Lecturers, said, "The truth is that we all have to do more things than we can rightly do, if we are to do anything at all."[12] If I have done more things than I can rightly do in this project, it has been with the help of many generous friends and colleagues. The project began as a graduate seminar on the Presocratics at the University of Toronto in the fall of 2017 and culminated in seminars on the four elements at UC Berkeley in the fall of 2023 and the University

11. Kurke 2011, 49.
12. Williams 1993, x.

of Toronto the following fall. Discussions with students in these seminars helped me develop and refine my ideas. In the intervening years, I presented preliminary versions of this material to many audiences and received invaluable feedback. I am especially thankful to Phiroze Vasunia for organizing an extremely helpful roundtable discussion and to everyone who participated, particularly respondents Shaul Tor and Duncan Kennedy. My thanks to Matt Evans, Tom Mackenzie, Kathryn Morgan, James Porter, David Sider, Charles Stocking, Shaul Tor, and Iakovos Vasiliou for sharing their ideas and (then) unpublished work with me, and to many of these colleagues again plus Phil Mitsis, Jean-Claude Picot, Emmanuela Bakola, and especially Alex Purves for reading and offering valuable advice on drafts of individual chapters. Material related to chapter 2 was published as "Heraclitus Stuttered," in S. Nooter and M. Telò, eds. *Radical Formalisms: Reading, Theory, and the Boundaries of the Classical* (Bloomsbury Academic, 2024), 138–52. I thank the two editors for their improvements to that chapter and the press for permission to reprint the material. I am also grateful to Rebecca Comay for turning me on to the Dolar articles that became the basis of chapter 5 and for her insightful feedback on that chapter.

I am pleased to recognize financial support from the Chancellor Jackman Research Fellowship in the Humanities at University of Toronto and the Social Sciences and Humanities Research Council of Canada. Among other things, these grants enabled me to employ excellent research assistants. For their help in preparing the manuscript I am grateful to Elliott Rosenthal and especially Kat Furtado, who added all the Laks-Most references, an eye- and patience-straining task. Eric Schmidt and Jyoti Arvey shepherded the project through publication, and Catherine Osborne (not the Presocratics scholar!) copyedited the manuscript. I thank them, as well as the two semianonymous readers, who helped improve the book in myriad ways.

Much of this project was carried out under the double lockdown of COVID and chairing. It could not have been completed without three friends—Alex Purves, Verity Platt, and Nancy Worman—who supported me through that time of languishing, and without my family, whose unflagging interest in the project helped sustain my own. Last but always most, no project would ever be completed without Erik Gunderson. He talked through every argument with me, gave me brilliant and challenging feedback on multiple drafts of every chapter, and saved me again and again from the space madness cosmological speculation can induce. In this project even more than others I was continually blown away by his knowledge "concerning all things," from Greek particles to particle physics. Ever since we were at Berkeley, he has helped me to do more things than I can rightly do and I am grateful *aei.*

Introduction

The Poetry of Being

Poetry is the creation of a name-of-being that was previously unknown.
—ALAIN BADIOU

The Presocratic philosophers invented new ways of thinking about life, the natural world, and the structure of reality. In doing so, they also conceived new ways of using language and novel forms of expression. This book examines these two innovations and the productive relation between them. It aims to show that the language of these thinkers not only conveys their thought but shapes and enables it. Experimenting in both poetry and prose, the Presocratics offer a unique laboratory for studying the formative and reciprocal interaction between thought and expression, idea and word, and—a distinction alien to these thinkers themselves—philosophy and literature.

The book examines the work of five Presocratic philosophers: Parmenides, Heraclitus, Empedocles, Anaxagoras, and Democritus. Heraclitus was composing around 500 BCE in Ephesus on the eastern edge of the Greek world; Parmenides at around the same time in Elea, on the western edge. Empedocles lived a generation later (c. 484–424 BCE) in Acragas in Sicily. Anaxagoras, from Clazomene in Asia Minor (c. 500–428 BCE), spent time in Athens and was part of the lively intellectual culture of the democracy. Democritus, born in Abdera in far northern Greece, also came to Athens, although he complains that no one recognized him there (B116/P22). He died some time after 399 BCE, the year of Socrates's trial. These five figures thus span the full length of the fifth century, from the late archaic through the classical period, and the geographical breadth of the Greek-speaking world.

Their thought, too, is striking in its scope and variety. These "first philosophers," as Aristotle termed them (*Metaph.* 1.3 983b6–7), investigated the origins

Epigraph: From *Wittgenstein's Antiphilosophy*, by Alain Badiou, translated by Bruno Bosteels, 109.

of the cosmos and the basic elements of which it was composed. They scrutinized the heavens—stars and planets, clouds and rainbows—and life in all its forms, including human life. They asked about the shape of the earth and what holds it in place, about the cause of eclipses and earthquakes, how magnets work or the eye sees color, how plants grow and whether they can think, what happens to the soul after death. These *phusikoi* (natural philosophers) were also metaphysicians, inquiring into the nature of time and space, causality, identity, and change. Where did everything come from and how? Why is there something rather than nothing? What *is* something and what, if anything, is nothing? The Presocratics were ontologists in the broadest sense of the term, analyzing all the manifold beings (*ta onta*) in the universe and the fundamental nature of being (*to on*) itself.

This new study of being and beings required a new discourse, the *logos* in "ontology." Parmenides was the first Greek we know of to use the verb "to be" as a noun to name being (*to eon*, in his epic dialect). In so doing, he created not only a new word but a new vision of a reality beyond our everyday perceptions and opinions, basically inventing the study of metaphysics. Parmenides's *To Eon* not only denotes that metaphysical vision but enables it to appear, lucent at the very edge of language and thought. Likewise, Democritus invented a new word to name his atom: he artificially dissected the Greek word *mēden* ("nothing") to create the neologism *den*. This new word allowed him to think, as well as to articulate, a new relation between being and nonbeing, beyond the simple binary of atoms and void. As these two examples suggest (and we will see many more), language does not follow passively in the wake of ideas, a vehicle deployed for their communication or a cosmetic added to adorn them. Instead, the word enables and extends the idea, such that without it the idea of the thing and even the thing itself could not exist. Through their innovative poetics the Presocratic philosophers not only describe a new reality; they create one.

This book attempts to demonstrate this claim through a close examination of the poetics of five Presocratic philosophers. By "poetics" I mean simply these writers' self-conscious deployment of the resources of language, including simile and metaphor, visual imagery and acoustic effects, unusual diction and word order, repetition and rhythm, puns, wordplay, and pointed ambiguity.[1] Two of these thinkers were poets in the stricter sense. Parmenides and Empedocles wrote in dactylic hexameter, the meter of epic. Both make extensive and creative use of epic diction and imagery, borrowing Homeric lines or Hesiodic phrases and putting them to uses neither epic poet could have dreamed of; both reimagine the epic Muse as they draw on the cultural prestige of epic poetry to authorize their radical

1. Silk (2010) offers a helpful discussion of poetic style in the ancient Greek context. To the extent that these features of poetry are a heightening of features of language in general, when I refer to the "poetics" of the Presocratics I might equally say their "language." The most comprehensive study of Presocratic poetics is still Most 1999.

intellectual projects.[2] The others wrote in prose, a stylistic choice that was in itself radical at a time when authoritative speech was expressed in verse and poets were divinely inspired "masters of truth."[3] But the choice of prose did not make them less poetic in the broader sense. Heraclitus's intricately structured and densely resonant prose aphorisms have been compared to the odes of his contemporary Aeschylus, and Democritus was praised by no lesser an authority on style than Cicero for the "brilliance of his diction" (*clarissimis verborum luminibus, Orat.* 20.67 < Dem. A34/R6). Even Anaxagoras, the most prosaic of the prose writers, makes artful use of hypotaxis and parataxis.[4]

But that art is never gratuitous nor merely *gratia artis*. Instead, it is profoundly implicated in these writers' vision of the cosmos. That implication is encapsulated in the very word *kosmos*, which, before it came to denote the universe, originally signified an aesthetically pleasing order.[5] In the Presocratics' cosmology, these two meanings can be neither separated nor fully superimposed. When Heraclitus writes of "this cosmos . . . [which] no god nor man created (*epoiēsen*), but it always was and is and will be fire ever-living, kindled in measure and extinguished in measure" (Her. B30/D85), he differentiates the natural cosmos—unauthored and eternal—from the artistry of his own *poiēsis*, but also connects the two, as the balanced rhythms of his prose replicate the rhythmic cycles of the cosmic fire. When Parmenides invites us to hear "the deceptive *kosmos* of my words" (Parm. B8.52/D8.57), he evokes both the natural universe he will describe and the aesthetic ordering of its description. At the same time he suggests a potential tension between the two: the "cosmetic" beauty of human language can conjure a false vision of the world. Even as they forge a new language of being, the Presocratics ask whether that being can be expressed in language. Can *ta onta*—to say nothing of *to on*—really be contained within *logos*, or will some aspect of being always remain in excess of its discursive articulation? Conversely, is *logos* itself securely part of "what is," or must it exceed being in order to express it? As I will argue

2. Cicero remarks that although Parmenides was a bad poet, he was indeed a poet (*Acad.* 2.74 = Xen. A25/R1, Parm. R1). Ancient verdicts on Empedocles were somewhat kinder: Aristotle praised his skillful diction and his use of metaphor and "the other poetic devices" ("On poets," fr. 70 Rose, quoted at Diog. Laert. 8.57 < Emp. A1/R1b). He also, however, insinuated that Empedocles wrote in verse to disguise the fact that he had nothing to say (*Rh.* 3.5 1407a32–33 < Emp. A25/R1c). On these and other ancient assessments of Empedocles's style, see Willi 2008, 197–200; and Rowett 2013.

3. Detienne 1996, 35–88.

4. Diogenes Laertius praises the "brevity and weightiness" of Heraclitus's style (*brakhutēs, baros,* 9.6–7 < Her. A1/R5c), and the Suda remarks that "he wrote many things poetically" (*poiētikōs,* H.472 < Her. A1a/R11). Plutarch comments that Democritus speaks "marvelously and magnificently" (*daimoniōs, megaloprepōs, Quaest. conv.* 683A = Dem. A77/R9). Even Anaxagoras, today largely unappreciated as a stylist, was judged to write "sweetly and magnificently" (*hēdeōs kai megalophronōs,* Diog. Laert. 2.6 < Anaxag. A1/R35).

5. Finkelberg (1998) argues that *kosmos* at this period denoted an order or arrangement, not a world or universe, but Kahn (1960, 219–30) sees the seeds of the latter meaning in the former.

throughout this book, the Presocratics' ontological inquiry is also an inquiry into the possibility or impossibility of ontology as a discursive project.

At first glance, the poetics of the Presocratics may seem an unpromising subject for study. The conditions within which their texts were first produced and circulated are unclear; fundamental questions about their original audience and performance context and how these factors affected each author's choice of expressive medium—verse or prose—are hard to answer decisively.[6] However they originally came into being, these texts survive for us only in fragments, some substantial, like the sixty-six continuous verses of Parmenides B8/D8, but some no more than a single evocative word, like Democritus's "change of world" (*ameipsikosmiē*, Dem. B138/D83b), or a mysterious phrase, like Heraclitus's statement that "souls can smell in Hades" (Her. B98/D121). These shards, moreover, are preserved almost entirely in the works of later authors, making it difficult to determine in any given case which words belong to the original text and which to the surrounding context. Hermann Diels, in his towering edition *Die Fragmente der Vorsokratiker*, differentiated what he believed were the original words of the author (which he labeled B fragments) from the testimonia that preserve them (his A fragments).[7] This practice is followed by André Laks and Glenn Most, whose important new English-Greek edition supplements and is poised to supplant Diels's: they distinguish D fragments (Doctrine) from R texts (Reception).[8] Presenting the fragments like gems on a velvet tray, this separation produces the illusion of solid objects with clear-cut edges, obscuring the way the history of transmission has impacted virtually every remaining word, rendering each individual fragment porous and unstable and the works as a whole less lapidary than labile, sand that shifts continually under our feet.[9]

6. For a good treatment of the issues see Sassi 2018, 64–109. The choice of verse or prose is not insignificant: as we shall see, it is tied to each author's understanding of his own linguistic practice. But the difference is often overstated, sometimes in service of a fallacious distinction between verse's supposed emotionality and the rational objectivity of prose and a historical trajectory from the former to the latter (from *muthos* to *logos*). For discussion of the topic, and the related question of whether the Presocratics composed and disseminated their works orally or in writing, see Havelock 1966, 1983; Kahn 1983, 2003; Robb 1983b; Osborne 1998; Laks 2001; Goldhill 2002; Patzer 2006; Sassi 2018, 81–93; and Bryan 2020. "The poetry of being" and "the prose of the world" in my title should be understood as congruent, not contrastive.

7. Diels and Kranz 1951, 1952, first published in 1903; the sixth edition, edited by Walther Kranz, is currently still the standard edition of the Presocratics. My citational practices are explained in the Preface.

8. Laks and Most 2016. They also have a section of P fragments having to do with the philosopher as a person and the tradition surrounding his biography.

9. Hence the insistence in much recent scholarship that one cannot study the original texts in isolation from the doxographic tradition and a tendency to focus on the latter even to the exclusion of the former. In addition to Diels 1929; Cherniss 1935; Osborne 1987b; Mansfeld and Runia 1997; Laks 2007; and other works surveyed in Baltussen 2005, see the interesting discussion of Cassin (2020, 5–22): "With doxography we are plunged right into a Nietzschean modernity, since it is clear that there are no facts but only interpretations and interpretations of interpretations" (8).

A close literary reading of the Presocratics is thus a precarious project, but I believe it is worth the risks, for despite the many uncertainties they pose, these tiny texts dazzle. I approach them as one would a poem, each rich and complex in itself and resonating complexly with all the others to make up a whole that is never really whole.[10] I view the fragmentary nature of these texts, both individually and in the aggregate, not as a liability but as an asset—or, at a minimum, a genuine opportunity. It demands a different quality of attention and promotes not just a resignation to but a positive valorization of incompleteness and incoherence. In this approach I follow the lead of Page DuBois, who notes that the challenge—and excitement—of studying fragments is merely an extreme version of that involved in the study of antiquity in general, inasmuch as all ancient texts are, to a greater or lesser degree, lacunose and unstable, both deracinated from their original context and overlaid by the history of their reception, and thus any coherent narrative we create from or for them is both tenuous and tendentious, the product of our own desire.[11]

I also take my cue from the Presocratic philosophers themselves, who are not only fragmentary philosophers but philosophers of the fragmentary. Pluralists like Empedocles, Anaxagoras, and Democritus posited the conceptual priority of the part to the whole, which is always contingent and provisional, and valued the productive energy of parts in unstable combination. But even those whose vision was more monistic or holistic (like Parmenides and Heraclitus) recognized the generativity of incoherence and preserved within their texts the gaps and contradictions that simultaneously propel their inquiry and prevent its totalization. Even before they were fragments these texts were not whole, and their internal fractures and aporias, as I will argue, represent moments not of failure, but of a formal and conceptual openness productive for both their poetics and their philosophy.

We will return to the productivity of aporia below. But first the term "Presocratic philosophy" requires some explanation. The label "Presocratic" is a convenient umbrella term for the philosophers who preceded Socrates. But that apparently simple designation is actually quite complicated, and it is surrounded by question marks on all sides.[12] For one thing, the chronology does not hold. Some of these thinkers, like Democritus, were contemporaries of Socrates; others who might be included in the group, like the fourth-century author of the Derveni Papyrus, were actually post-Socratic. One feature often taken to define the Presocratics

10. Compare Blanchot (1993, 153–55) on the "strange pluralism" of the fragment. Blanchot is one of the great modern masters of the fragment. His affinity for Heraclitus is manifest in his preface to Ramnoux 1968.

11. On the study of classical antiquity as a relationship with fragments, see DuBois 1995, 18–30; and on the aesthetics of the fragment (in her case, of Sappho), 31–54.

12. Laks (2018) traces the ancient and modern construction of "the concept of Presocratic philosophy." He notes that the term dates to the end of the eighteenth century and was adopted at the end of the nineteenth under the influence of Nietzsche and Diels (19–34). Cf. Laks 2002a. On the problems and advantages of the label, see Long 1999b, 5–10; and Laks 2018, 28–34.

is their interest in the natural world; but since Socrates himself was a student of nature in his youth (as he confesses), he might himself be considered a Presocratic. In that case, the watershed moment would come not with Socrates but with Plato, whose account of Socrates tells of his development from natural philosopher to metaphysician (*Phd.* 96a–100a). "Presocratic philosophy" would thus be a Platonic conceit and the Presocratics more properly Preplatonic.[13] Alternatively, they might be considered Prearistotelian. This, in fact, is how Aristotle presents them in a key passage of *Metaphysics* I (to which we will return momentarily), a passage instrumental in the construction of these diverse thinkers as a unified group. Regardless of to whom or what one considers the Presocratics prior, many scholars have rightly objected to the teleological implications of the label, the notion that philosophy evolved along a single, unidirectional track.[14] This progressivist narrative figures the Presocratics as primitives, taking the first stumbling steps toward answering questions that would be formulated decisively by Plato and Aristotle and that, in that form, would define the modern discipline of philosophy. "Presocratic" in this narrative would seem to mean simply pre- or protophilosophical.

Others have seen these thinkers not as precursors to Plato and Aristotle but as alternatives to them and to the entire Western philosophical tradition derived from them. This is partly what drew Nietzsche to the study of the Presocratics and has attracted many other modern thinkers, from Martin Heidegger to Alain Badiou. From this perspective, the Presocratics are not prephilosophers but, in Badiou's term, "antiphilosophers," who challenge the premises and truth claims of Western philosophy as a whole.[15]

The label "Presocratic" thus raises questions about the label "philosophy." In what sense were the Presocratics philosophers? Was it the kind of questions they asked? The way they asked them? These early thinkers have been credited with the invention of logical argument, empiricism, rationalism, secularism, the very "art of thinking."[16] But "philosopher" was not a label they gave themselves, and the line that divides their mode of thought from that of their contemporaries is blurry at

13. Laks 2018, 1–18.

14. This teleological narrative can be traced back, via Zeller (1923), to Hegel. Following Nestle (1942), it often takes the form of a trajectory from *muthos* to *logos*. For a good critique of this narrative as part of philosophy's project of self-definition, see Morgan 2000, 30–37; and for a defense of its functional utility, see Laks 2018, 35–52.

15. Badiou (2011, 69, cf. 75; 2005, 15) takes the term from Lacan. He suggests that Heraclitus might have been the "inventor of the antiphilosophical position" later assumed by Nietzsche, Wittgenstein, and Lacan.

16. The "art of thinking" is Barnes's (1982, 3–5) phrase. Laks (2018, 52; cf. Long 1999b, 10–15) stresses the totalizing nature of their inquiry and "a certain type of rationalization"; Sassi (2018, xiv), their "critical stance toward received opinions." As Moore (2019, 2–3) observes, the attempt to determine whether the Presocratics were philosophers in the modern sense inevitably involves cherry-picking and retrojection of anachronistic assumptions.

best.[17] The intellectual terrain of Greece before Plato was varied and contested, and it was unmarked by boundaries we take for granted today between discrete fields and modalities of knowledge.[18] The archaic "wisdom tradition" encompassed *sophia* both practical and theoretical, including (for example) cosmological speculation, lawgiving and political wisdom, medical knowledge, divinatory and ritual expertise, and poetic and artistic skill.[19] The Presocratics reflect this cultural context both collectively and individually in their heterogeneity of topics and methods of inquiry and in the indeterminacy (from our modern perspective) of their self-presentation. Empedocles speaks as a divine prophet whose teachings can cure illness, protect against old age, and even bring the dead back to life (Emp. B111/D43, B112/D4). Whether we call him a philosopher or a religious healer says less about his ideas than about our own modern categories.[20]

Empedocles was also, of course, a poet, who was reported to have defused a crisis by reciting a well-chosen line from the *Odyssey*.[21] Poets had a privileged claim to *sophia* in a period when Homer and Hesiod were repositories of divinely inspired truth and authoritative sources on everything from the nature of moral excellence to proper agricultural techniques.[22] Aristotle includes Hesiod in his survey of the origins of philosophy as the first person to identify an efficient cause in the form of Eros, and he draws a straight line from there to Empedocles's principles of Love and Strife (*Metaph.* 1.4 984b23–985a10). Empedocles supports such an affiliation with his choice of meter and ubiquitous epic diction. Building his theories through sustained dialogue with his epic predecessors, he implicitly recognizes them as fellow philosophers, even as he presents himself as their fellow poet. Heraclitus makes the connection explicit: when he criticizes the wise men who preceded him, he targets not only Pythagoras, Xenophanes, and the geographer Hecataeus (Her. B40/D20) but also Homer, Hesiod, and Archilochus (B42/D21, B57/D25a).[23]

17. Long 1999b, 3. On the origins and adoption of the label *philosophos*, see Moore 2019.

18. Lloyd 2002. Cf. Gemelli Marciano 2002; Sassi 2002, 2018, 29–30; Cambiano 2006; and Kingsley 2024, 1–37.

19. Kurke 2011, 95–158.

20. In B111/D43 Empedocles also claims to teach control of the winds. Diogenes Laertius's account of him saving crops from damaging winds by constructing ass-skin windcatchers (8.60 < Emp. A1/P16) aligns him with the tradition of practical wisdom associated with the Seven Sages, on which see Martin 1998. On the blurry line between philosophy and religion in the archaic period, see, e.g., Cornford 1952; Kingsley 1995; Most 2007; and Tor 2017; between philosophy and medicine, see Longrigg 1963, 1989; Lloyd 1995, 1999, 10–58; and Vegetti 1999.

21. Iamblichus *VP* 113 = Emp. A15/P17. Mackenzie (2021a) takes this anecdote as the starting point for his rich study of the poetry of Empedocles, Parmenides, and Xenophanes, focusing on its emotional impact.

22. Ford 2002, 197–201; Graziosi 2002; and Folit-Weinberg 2022, 72–84.

23. Of course, Xenophanes himself was at once a philosopher and a poet (Lesher 1992). On his role in the "ancient quarrel" within an archaic culture of competitive wisdom, see Ford 2002, 46–66.

In short, the Presocratics were writing at a time before there was a clear consensus (if there has ever actually been one) on the "proper" form philosophical writing should take or a clear-cut distinction between figures we think of as philosophers and those we label poets.[24] It was only toward the end of the fifth century that philosophy came into its own as a discrete and identifiable mode of thought, such that Aristotle, writing in the fourth century, could opine in a way slighting to both that "Homer and Empedocles have nothing in common except the meter, so that it is right to call the former a poet (*poiētēs*) and the latter a natural philosopher (*phusiologos*) rather than a poet" (*Poet.* 1.11 1447b17–19).[25]

Aristotle plots this difference as a historical evolution of which he himself is the *telos*. In his well-known discussion in *Metaphysics* I, he presents his predecessors as groping uncertainly toward the four causes that he will go on to codify, thus both legitimating his theory and marking its originality.[26] As philosophy matures, it takes on its highest object—metaphysics—and also finds its proper form. "The earliest philosophy speaks falteringly (*psellizomenēi*), as it were, about everything, since it was young and just beginning" (*Metaph.* 1.10 993a15–16). The verb *psellizesthai* connotes baby talk and is also used in an earlier passage to characterize the poetic language of Empedocles.[27] Aristotle's developmental narrative figures poetic language as infantile, a phase that philosophy will grow out of as it matures into the serious discipline that it will become precisely with him.

If Aristotle represents philosophy's relation to poetry as a discursive Bildungsroman, Plato (who himself was said to have dallied with poetry in his youth) figures the relation in spatial, not temporal terms. In the *Republic*, he famously banishes poets from his philosophical city (*Resp.* 595a–608b). Elaborating on his spatial metaphor, scholars like Andrea Wilson Nightingale and Kathryn Morgan

24. Laks and Most (2016) include in the purview of "early Greek philosophy" passages of Hesiod and Homer on one end of the chronological spectrum and Attic tragedy and comedy on the other. They mark the former, however, as prephilosophical ("background that is useful for contextualizing the thought of the early Greek philosophers," 2:56), and the latter as reception (in a "Dramatic Appendix" to vol. 9). While Laks-Most's expansion of the ambit of "early Greek philosophy" to include authors we usually think of as poets is salutary, the isolation of particularly "philosophical" passages gives the impression that the poets simply embedded nuggets of philosophy in their work. But poets engaged in philosophical thought in a more sustained way, as Billings (2021) shows for tragedy and as Tor (2017, 52–103) and Iribarren and Koning (2022) show for Hesiod.

25. Whether Empedocles was a natural philosopher or a poet remained an open question, however, throughout antiquity: see Cic. *Orat.* 1.50.217 (< Emp. A25/R2a), Lactant. *Div. inst.* 2.12.4 (< Emp. A24/R3b). On the construction of philosophy as a discipline, see Nightingale 1995, 13–59; and Moore 2019, 221–87.

26. *Metaph.* 1.3–5 983b1–987a28. On the value of this passage for reconstructing Presocratic philosophy, see Cherniss 1935, 218–46; and Sassi 2018, 21–26. For more general analysis of the way Aristotle represents the views of his predecessors, see Cherniss 1935, 347–404; Furley 1987, 177–201; and Clarke 2019.

27. *Metaph.* 1.4 985a4–7. If one pays attention to his meaning and "not to what he says speaking falteringly" (*ha psellizetai legōn*), one can see that Empedocles's Love and Strife are really efficient causes.

have argued that philosophy first defined itself as a discrete discourse in part by policing its boundaries with poetry.[28] Plato's "ancient quarrel between poetry and philosophy" (*Resp.* 606e–608b) was a quarrel philosophy itself picked, both repudiating and appropriating the forms of traditional poetry in order to carve out and legitimate its own discursive terrain.[29] In this account (as in Plato's philosophical republic), the putative boundary between philosophy and poetry is imagined to stand fully within philosophy's control. Philosophy sets the boundary and defends it; if it transgresses, crossing over to steal a potent image or myth, it does so deliberately and strategically, with philosophical ends in mind. All border skirmishes are fought on philosophy's terms and resolved in philosophy's favor, and if problems arise along the way, these are problems philosophy not only anticipates but in fact instigates in order to surmount.[30]

But the border between philosophy and poetry is always porous, and it is never clear whether it lies within philosophy's jurisdiction or beyond it. This indistinct boundary makes it impossible to say where poetry ends and philosophy begins. On the one side, what makes an account philosophical? That it is rational? If so, precisely how rational does it have to be? That it is argued for? But doesn't every simile make an argument? That it is systematic? What could be more systematic than the verbal and visual imagery of Aeschylus's *Oresteia?* That it criticizes received opinion? Surely Pindar's use of myth or the priamel of Sappho 16 does just that.[31] On the other side, what makes something poetic? Since many of the qualities that define poetic speech, such as metaphoricity and ambiguity, are qualities of speech *tout court*, and poetic language is merely an intensification of the features of language as a whole, to commit thought to language is a first step across the frontier. Those attempting to define poetry's borders often appeal to Cleanth Brooks's much-paraphrased "heresy of paraphrase."[32] You know you are on poetic terrain when the mode of expression is as important as the expressed

28. Nightingale 1995, esp. 60–92; and Morgan 2000.

29. Morgan (2000, 46–88) shows that individual Presocratic thinkers (if not Presocratic philosophy as a whole: Nightingale 1995, 20n21) were already engaged in this self-positioning vis à vis the poetic tradition.

30. See, for example, Morgan's (2000, 39–44) discussion of the difference between early Greek philosophers' view of language and that of deconstruction: the instability of meaning that Derrida identifies is a philosophical problem but not a problem *for* philosophy. Thus, "although myth does encapsulate the displacement of philosophical anxiety over language, it does not do so [contra Derrida and De Man] in a moment of self-blindness" (43). The problem of language, even in its irresolution, affirms the intentionality and self-awareness of the philosopher. Cf. 67: "When it [philosophy] undermines its own authority, it does so in a strictly controlled way that preempts a proliferation of undecidable readings." For the philosopher, in short, "the fallibility of language becomes a source of opportunity" (290).

31. On Sappho, see DuBois 1995, 98–126. Laks (2018, 48–49) observes that philosophy is hard to define because of its "particular inherent plasticity": it has no proper object and its disciplinary boundaries are thus intrinsically open. The same might be said of poetry.

32. Brooks 1949, 176–96.

content and the former cannot be altered without fundamentally altering the latter. This criterion risks reducing philosophy to paraphrasable content independent of its formal articulation. But paraphrase, as I hope this book will demonstrate, is just as heretical for philosophy as it is for poetry.[33] To paraphrase the Presocratics is to change the substance of their ideas and the content of their philosophy. Thus we could say that what the Presocratics are "pre-" is precisely the division that originated with Plato and Aristotle and has been maintained ever since between philosophy and poetry. But if that is true, studying the poetics of the Presocratics merely exposes the falsity of the division in general.

Instead of laboring to differentiate philosophy from poetry, then, this book attempts to read the Presocratics rigorously as both at once. It attempts to understand how these writers use language to articulate their thought without subordinating the former to the latter.[34] My central claim is not only that the Presocratics' form is inseparable from their thought but, more strongly, that the form in itself *constitutes* thought. Parmenides's sphere, for instance, is not merely a vivid representation of his abstract notion of being; instead, the simile itself makes an argument about the self-delimiting wholeness of being. The same is true of Heraclitus's chiastic aphorisms, Empedocles's repetitions, Anaxagoras's parataxis, Democritus's neologisms: these formal features are not just pedagogical expedients or aesthetic ornamentation added to a preexisting philosophical theory, means of rendering abstract ideas more accessible or appealing to a reader. Thought does not come first, pure and autonomous, with language added later. Language is on the scene from the very beginning. Poetic form is not just the expression of philosophical content: it is itself philosophical content.[35]

Scholars of Presocratic philosophy have made this point, but the ancient quarrel has sometimes made it difficult for them to sustain it. The Presocratics have benefited from some exceptionally insightful and sensitive exegesis. Yet even the most philologically minded of their philosophical readers ultimately succumb to a desire to strip away the linguistic features they so carefully analyze to get to a primary philosophical essence. In his brilliant study of Heraclitus, Charles Kahn argues for "the intimate connection between the linguistic form and the intellectual

33. An egregious form of this heresy is the tendency to translate the Presocratics into the algebraism of analytic philosophy: see, e.g., Barnes 1982, 155–75, and for a critique of the practice see Rowett 2020.

34. Nor the latter to the former. This is less common in scholarship on the Presocratics, but see, e.g., Gemelli Marciano (1990), who treats the philosophical questions raised by Empedocles's poetry only "per la tangente" (25), or Mackenzie (2021a), for whom "the philosophical claims are used to shed light on how these texts are designed to affect their audiences" (6). Closer to my own approach is the attempt of Folit-Weinberg (2022) to understand Parmenides's deductive reasoning in light of his poetic strategies (in particular his intertextual adaptation of *Od.* 12.55–126), though he makes no claim to explicate the contents of that reasoning (see, e.g., 25, 270–78).

35. Nussbaum (1990) makes an eloquent case for this claim in the service of her philosophical reading of literary texts.

content of his discourse" and draws on the hermeneutics of literary criticism to explicate that bond.[36] Through a series of minutely close readings, Kahn shows how the deliberate ambiguity of Heraclitus's language binds the fragments into a dense network of images that not only represents but directly instantiates his vision of a cosmos in which "all things are one" (B50/D46). But in the concluding paragraph of his methodological introduction Kahn retreats from this position: the identification of multiple meanings, he says, "is only a hermeneutical device" for reaching "one single meaning, which is in fact the full semantic structure of [Heraclitus's] thought as a whole."[37] Thus his readings of the fragments, he concludes, "are best regarded as workmanlike tools for apprehending and reconstructing this global meaning, as a kind of ladder or crutch to be abandoned once the goal of understanding has been achieved."[38]

This final sentence evokes Wittgenstein's famous metaphor at the end of the *Tractatus Logico-Philosophicus* of his own propositions as a ladder to be thrown away once understanding has been reached.[39] The image, cited explicitly or (as here) allusively with remarkable frequency by scholars of early Greek philosophy,[40] makes both the author's language and its interpretation a mere tool: they allow access to a transcendent philosophical content but are ultimately disposable. Viewed in this instrumental light, literary-critical interpretation becomes a source of shame. It is a "crutch" we lean on to correct our crippling inability to immediately apprehend Heraclitus's "thought as a whole."[41] Were we able to apprehend it, the ladder would become a Jacob's ladder leading to a paradise of full philosophical meaning, free from the ambiguous mediation of language.[42]

36. Kahn 1979, 89. He lays out his interpretive principles at 87–95.

37. Kahn 1979, 95. With this move, the text's ambiguities become epiphenomenal, variegated surface effects produced by a unified underlying thought. See also Kahn 1983, 119–21, on the transparency of philosophical discourse: "The audience is invited to look through his words in order to recognize the reality which he describes" (120).

38. Kahn 1979, 95.

39. Wittgenstein 2001, 89 §6.54–7. I return to this metaphor in chapter 1.

40. Most notably Owen 1960, 100; 1974, 275–76. But compare, e.g., Mackenzie 2021a, 124; and Morgan 2022, 236.

41. In the study of ancient languages, aids to reading (like dictionaries, commentaries, and translations) are often referred to as "crutches." Kahn may have this metaphorical sense in mind and may, like Wittgenstein, be advising his reader how to use his text. But the veiled allusion to Wittgenstein and the visual similarity of a ladder and a literal crutch also suggest an anxiety that literary hermeneutics will be taken as a sign of philosophical disability. Moreover, the tight correspondence Kahn draws between the polysemy of Heraclitus's language and the hermeneutic principle attentive to that polysemy (e.g. at 1979, 92) means that the former gets cast aside with the latter/ladder.

42. This paradise is glimpsed in the final sentences of the *Tractatus*, with its ineffable truth beyond speech. Badiou (2011, 73–159) argues that Wittgenstein posits this mystical element not as a positive truth but in order to expose philosophy's limitations and critique its pretensions to truth; hence he considers Wittgenstein an "antiphilosopher." By this definition, philosophy is the discourse that believes in a truth that transcends language.

A similar conception underlies another of the most insightful readings of early Greek philosophy, Alexander Mourelatos's *The Route of Parmenides*.[43] Like Kahn, Mourelatos stresses the inextricability of his author's thought and language. He shows how Parmenides adapts the traditional poetic trope of the journey not merely to communicate but in fact to formulate his vision of being: What Is (*esti*), a word that conveys us to the truth of things through predication, is itself "*essentially* a route; it is not a route by poetic license, or for the purposes of rhetorical effect."[44] This makes the metaphor both indispensable, a "speculative" force that enables thought, and ultimately dispensable, a path that we can abandon once we reach our goal of a metaphysical reality that works like language but, subsuming its expressive function, no longer requires it.[45]

The theoretical separability of the journey from its destination is replicated in Mourelatos's analysis of the relation between the Aletheia (Truth) and Doxa (Belief) sections of Parmenides's poem. In a reading of tremendous sensitivity, Mourelatos argues that the equivocations of human belief, even as they lead us away from Truth, evoke the latent presence of What Is "as an implicit commitment, as a half-forgotten memory."[46] The latency of What Is within *doxa* reduces poetic ambiguity to a "positive veneer" covering without fully obliterating the unequivocal truth of being.[47] In the final analysis, linguistic ambiguity becomes "a case-study in self-deception, indecisiveness, and confusion" both for Parmenides and for his reader.[48] The implicit task, then, is to strip poetic language away so as to get to the "unvarnished" philosophical truth. Kahn's reading of Heraclitus and Mourelatos's of Parmenides demonstrate in fine detail the inseparability of poetic language and philosophical content, both in the production of the work and as a principle of its interpretation. But both ultimately subordinate language to content, imagining language, in the final reckoning, as a crutch to be used and cast

43. Originally published in 1970 by Yale University Press. I cite the revised and expanded 2008 edition.

44. Mourelatos 2008c, 134 (original emphasis); cf. 47–73.

45. Mourelatos 2008b, 330: "Parmenides' argument unmistakably proceeds from reflection on *logos*. . . . And yet the world he discovers *through logos* does not show the characteristic texture of *logos*. In an important sense, *logos* still has no constitutive function; it remains dispensable." On the speculative force of metaphor, see Mourelatos 2008c, 37–41.

46. Mourelatos 2008c, 226. I return to Mourelatos's reading in chapter 1.

47. Mourelatos 2008c, 226.

48. Mourelatos 2008c, 260. Mourelatos proposes that Parmenides's goddess speaks to two audiences at once: the philosophical initiate who senses the presence of What Is behind ambiguous human belief and the ignorant mortal who does not. This "ironic" double address dissolves the ambiguities of the Doxa by distributing their two meanings between two different audiences, for each of which the meaning is univocal (and right, in the case of the philosophical initiate; wrong, in the case of ignorant mortals). This approach makes Parmenides a proto-Plato (his goddess a forebear of the supreme ironist, Socrates [263]), even perhaps a proto-Straussian.

away, a surface effect concealing an underlying truth, part of the philosophical journey but not present at its ultimate destination.

Behind this view of language as secondary and supplementary lies a conviction that philosophy's proper object is univocal meaning and that the task of the interpreter is to uncover or recover that meaning. This conviction is a foundational thesis of philosophy as a discourse and discipline. In *Metaphysics* 4 Aristotle lays out the basic axioms of metaphysics, "the science of being as being" (4.1 1003a21) and the pinnacle of philosophical inquiry. The most secure (*bebaiotatē*) of these is the principle of noncontradiction, which states that "it is impossible for the same thing simultaneously to hold and not to hold for the same thing and in the same respect" (4.3 1005b19–20). This principle is the grounds for any possible claim and is thus the starting point (*arkhē*) for all other axioms. The demonstration of the principle of noncontradiction is the singularity of meaning. The words "to be" (*to einai*) and "not to be" (*mē einai*) or the word "man" (*anthrōpos*) each signify one thing. Their meaning is discrete and determinate: the words can't mean just anything at all.[49] For if they could—if "man" had infinite meanings (*apeira sēmainein*)—"it is clear that there would be no rational discourse" (*logos*, 4.4 1006b6–7).

> τὸ γὰρ μὴ ἓν σημαίνειν οὐθὲν σημαίνειν ἐστίν, μὴ σημαινόντων δὲ τῶν ὀνομάτων ἀνῄρηται τὸ διαλέγεσθαι πρὸς ἀλλήλους, κατὰ δὲ τὴν ἀλήθειαν καὶ πρὸς αὑτόν· οὐθὲν γὰρ ἐνδέχεται νοεῖν μὴ νοοῦντα ἕν, εἰ δ' ἐνδέχεται, τεθείη ἂν ὄνομα τούτῳ τῷ πράγματι ἕν.—ἔστω δή, ὥσπερ ἐλέχθη κατ' ἀρχάς, σημαῖνόν τι τὸ ὄνομα καὶ σημαῖνον ἕν (Arist. *Metaph*. 4.4 1006b7–13).

> For not to have one meaning is to have no meaning; and if words have no meaning this eliminates discourse with others, and in truth even with oneself. For it is impossible to think of anything if one does not think of one thing, and if this is possible, one name would be given to that thing [of which we think]. Well, then, let the word, as was said at the start, have a meaning and let it have one meaning.

The foundation of thought and of *logos* as language, discourse, and reason, univocality is the *sine qua non* of metaphysics and of philosophy in general.[50]

Barbara Cassin has argued that the most vigorous challenge to this axiomatic singularity of meaning came from the sophists, who in their insistence on the sonorous qualities of language and ludic love of homonomy and wordplay

49. Aristotle concedes that "man" may have more than one meaning as long as they are limited in number and could each be defined with its own "proper name" (4.4 1006b5). The relation between the law of noncontradiction and the singularity of meaning is not straightforward. The latter is the primary proof (4.4 1006b30–1007a1) of an axiom that is said to need no proof (4.4 1006a5–8) and seems less a corollary of this first principle than its precondition.

50. Derrida 1982b, 247–48: "Univocity is the essence, or better, the *telos* of language. No philosophy, as such, has ever renounced this Aristotelian ideal. This ideal is philosophy" (247).

decoupled *logos* at once from singularity and from meaning.[51] If the philosopher requires univocality and meaning and the sophist repudiates both univocality and meaning, the poet, as Jacques Derrida says, stands between the two.[52] Polyvocality is the first principle of poetry. Poetry deliberately courts contradiction and promotes ambiguity—not so as to annihilate meaning but in order to generate and proliferate it. Poetry's metaphors import alien elements into the monologism of "proper" meaning and its metonymies produce branching streams of signification around every word.[53] Indeed, this axiom of polysemy is one reason why the paraphrase of poetry is a heresy: it reduces the multiplicity of significations and thus impoverishes sense. For poetry, "not to have one meaning" is not "to have no meaning" but rather precisely what it *means* to have meaning.

In this way too the Presocratics were poets. Parmenides, often credited with inventing the principle of noncontradiction, apotheosizes univocality in his unique and unitary "Is."[54] But as we shall see, the metaphorical language he deploys to secure that singular "Is" binds it to its contrary "Is Not" such that the word "to be" (*to einai*) also entails "not to be" (*mē einai*). Heraclitus, as Aristotle observed (*Metaph.* 4.3 1005b23–25), was known to violate the law of noncontradiction. In his paradoxical and polysemous aphorisms, contradiction and ambiguity are not surface effects of flawed human language (*logos*) but the defining characteristics of reality itself (which, ambiguously, he also terms *logos*). Democritus weaves contradiction into the material fabric of the universe: the neologism *den* makes his atom an "avatar of the void" (in Heinz Wismann's apt phrase).[55] A signifier of both something and nothing, the contradictory *den* introduces a quantum indeterminacy not only into Democritus's physics but also into his ethics, rendering the meaning of "man" as multiple as that of "to be." Far from eliminating discourse, then, as Aristotle predicts, polysemy and ambiguity are defining qualities of the Presocratics' discourse, and they do not disable meaning but generate and ramify it. Moreover, as these examples suggest, it is not just meaning that is multiple in the Presocratics but being as well. Ambiguity is a feature not only of their words but also of their worlds: theirs is a polyvocal ontology. If philosophy is founded

51. See esp. Cassin 2020, 59–92. She sees a similar challenge in Democritus (100–111) and in Lacan. I return to her reading of Democritus in chapter 5.

52. Derrida 1982b, 248n54: "The poet stands between the two [*logos* and sophistry]. He is the man of metaphor." Derrida's investigation of the effect of metaphor within the text of philosophy provides the theoretical impetus for chapter 1.

53. On metaphor as "alien," see Arist. *Rh.* 3.2 1404b8–37: such foreign elements are appropriate to poetry, in Aristotle's view, but must be used sparingly in prose. On Aristotle's critique of metaphor and his own (nonetheless) metaphorical language, see Lloyd 1995, 183–203; 1996, 205–22.

54. Detienne (1996, 130–37) considers Parmenides pivotal in a historical shift from a religious tradition of ambiguous truth to a secular insistence on truth as noncontradiction. Kahn (2009, 150) writes that the principle of noncontradiction was not explicitly formulated until Plato and Aristotle, but it is "on the tip of Parmenides' tongue." I disagree with Morgan (2000, 40) that because the Presocratics established the law of noncontradiction "they cannot therefore have deconstructionist reservations about it."

55. Wismann 2010.

on the axiom of univocality, the Presocratics were thus antiphilosophers *avant la lettre*, and the study of these "first philosophers" suggests that polyvocality was not just a sophistic assault from without but a native feature of philosophy's discursive landscape from its very inception.

This is to say that philosophy never fully controls its own terrain: its text, as Derrida says, always "overflows and cracks its meaning."[56] Poetic language has a force in excess of its words' immediate representative function and each ambiguous utterance opens up many simultaneous "paths of inquiry." Some of these paths proceed directly in line with the philosopher's charted itinerary, leading straight toward the *telos* of a coherent philosophical theory. But others run athwart of such a unidirectional trajectory; wandering off-course or even in the opposite direction, these poetic paths (*poroi*) often lead to aporia, an impasse within the author's thought and incoherence within his theory. The chapters that follow home in on these moments of incoherence, considering them not as failures of the theory but as sources of an internal capaciousness. One characteristic sometimes taken to define Presocratic thought is its totalizing nature: "speaking about all things" (Xenoph. B34/D49), it aims, as A. A. Long writes, "to give a universalist account... to take everything—the world as a whole—as the subject of inquiry."[57] The aporias within their theories are an inevitable byproduct of this totalizing ambition; they mark its limits but also, as we shall see, an attempt to think beyond them. If we linger at these impasses, then, it is not to identify a dead end. Rather, it is to demonstrate that aporia can provide a resource (*poros*) for thought and thus (as Plato and Aristotle would both assert) the instigation to further philosophical inquiry.[58]

The first chapter, "Parmenides's *Logos* of Being," examines this aporia most directly, exploring the paradoxical relationship between language (*logos*) and being (*to on*) at the heart of ontology. The ontological project, it argues, is driven by two competing desires: to contain being within *logos*, fixing it as the object of analysis, and to contain *logos* within being as the faithful servant of a more fundamental reality. Parmenides uses metaphor to think through this ontological paradox. This is itself paradoxical. Metaphor is the trope par excellence of *doxa*, the register of erroneous human belief and of language in all its misleading doubleness and ambiguity. Parmenides deploys metaphor—his famous metaphor of the road—to convey the reader out of the doxic realm; following this path we seem to transcend metaphorical language to a pure aether of "Is" (*esti*) where *logos* and being speak as one. At the same time, Parmenides also exploits metaphor to secure this metaphysical reality in the repeated image of Necessity's bonds. This image is generally taken as merely a picturesque representation of being's innate qualities of fixity, wholeness, and determinate singularity. A close reading will show, however, that

56. Derrida 1982a, xxiii.

57. Long 1999b, 10; cf. Laks 2018, 52; and Sassi 2018, 30. In addition to Xenoph. B34/D49, see Her. B1/D1; Parm. B1.28/D4.28; and Dem. B165/P44.

58. Arist. *Metaph.* 1.2 982b17–21: men began (and still begin) to philosophize out of *aporia* and *thauma* (wonder).

the metaphor of Necessity's bonds, far from a secondary expression of those necessary qualities, is in fact the source of their necessity. Metaphysics cannot escape metaphor, for it relies on it to secure its fundamental truths. At the extreme, being itself becomes a metaphor or simile, "like a well-rounded sphere" (B8.43/D8.48). The sphere figures both the determinate wholeness of being and the circular form of the poem. But its very shape forbids a unidirectional reading of the relation between poetic form and metaphysical substance or any presupposition that the former is a mere mimesis of the latter. Instead, it sets *logos* and *to on* circling one another as in a Möbius strip, each bounding and bonding the other.

The second chapter, "Time, the Cosmos, and the Soul in Heraclitus," aims to show how Heraclitus negotiates the relations among these three terms through his poetic form. It proposes that the exquisite symmetry—and asymmetry—of his aphorisms enables the reader to experience corporeally what she cannot grasp cognitively, the "back-turned harmony" (B51/D49) of the cosmos. Beginning from Bruno Snell's claim that Heraclitus invented "a new concept of soul," it argues that the Heraclitean *psukhē* emerges in its difference from the material cosmos through a temporal schism, a fundamental asynchrony between the eternal always of cosmic time (the *aei*) and the terminal existence of human life (the *aiōn*). That asynchrony is exemplified by the *logos* with which Heraclitus's book begins (B1/D1), which refers simultaneously to the words we are about to read—an ephemeral human product, as its fragmentary status attests—and the eternal *logos* that for Heraclitus names the ordering principle of the cosmos. Heraclitus attempts to synchronize *logos* and *logos, aei* and *aiōn* through the formal structure of his aphorisms: the extreme compression of his paradoxes eliminates time, reproducing the atemporal temporality of the cosmic *aei*; his chiastic structures suspend the reader in that impossible temporality, lulling us into a lucid sleep in which we experience the elemental rhythms of the cosmos. Simultaneously ephemeral and timeless, his fragments thus bridge at the level of sensation a schism that is ineradicable at the level of sense, bringing human comprehension (*xunesis*, B1/D1) together with the "common *logos*" (*xunos logos*, B2/D2) to produce, even as they mimetically reproduce, a cosmos in which "all things are one" (B50/D46). And yet from time to time this metaphysical union is ruptured by odd moments of disequilibrium, slight stutters in both Heraclitus's own *logos* and the cosmic *logos*. These moments hold open the interval between *logos* and *logos* and preserve the asynchrony of cosmic *aei* and human *aiōn* that Heraclitus ostensibly works to close, producing a generative incoherence that, I will argue, is the condition of possibility of both his philosophical project and the human psyche.

Chapter 3, "Empedocles's Autobiography," examines Empedocles's radical experiment in materialist poetics. Narrated in the first person, Empedocles's poems tell a traumatic tale of his reincarnation as a *daimōn*, a divine entity, and share the philosophical wisdom gleaned in his thirty-thousand-year journey of metempsychosis. Reading Empedocles's poems as autobiography in the root sense of the word—as the account (*graphē*) of the life (*bios*) of a self (*autos*)—I consider how Empedocles's materialist ontology destabilizes each of these terms. *Bios*, as Empedocles imagines it, is a dynamic meshwork of mobile and mutually transforming parts, each with its own agency and desire. This labile ontology decenters the human *autos* as a singular entity stable across time: the self is just one thing among an assemblage of things and itself composed of an assemblage of things, which are all constantly changing; none has "a stable lifetime" (*empedos aiōn*, B17.11/D73.242). But where does this leave the authorial *autos*, Empedocles himself? Writing (*graphē*) would seem to presuppose a singular self as the stable origin of enunciation, making Empedocles the aporia in his own ontological theory. Empedocles's radical poetic style is an attempt to negotiate that contradiction, to erase his own authorial *egō* and write life not from above but from within its dynamic midst. On the one hand, words are material things with a will and trajectory of their own; on the other hand, they are carefully wrought representations of things, the artistry of a poet who compares his aesthetic production to cosmogonic creation (B23/D60). Oscillating between the literal and the metaphorical, materiality and mimesis, Empedocles's language produces a schizophrenic poetics and a schizophrenic poet. That internal division (manifested in the schism between Empedocles's two poems) symptomatizes both the challenge and the limits of Empedocles's radical experiment in materialist poetics.

One defining feature of the Presocratics' thought was the search for an *arkhē*, a primary and governing principle. This quest means that their natural philosophy also entailed an implicit vision of politics. Starting from this observation, the fourth chapter ("Paratactic Politics: Anaxagoras and the Things") examines the political thought implicit in the cosmology of Anaxagoras. Anaxagoras begins with a decentralized pluriverse of infinite, equal, and heterogeneous "things" (*khrēmata*), reciprocally interconnected such that "everything is in everything" (B4/D12, B6/D25, B12/D27). Into this original community (described in language of political participation, B6/D25), Anaxagoras introduces Nous (Mind). Ontologically distinct, autonomous and "autocratic" (*autokrates*, B12/D27), Nous initiates the process that will organize the things into the compounds that make up our phenomenal world. In this way he performs the "distribution of the sensible" that Jacques Rancière posits as the founding gesture of the political. Chapter 4 explores this "aesthetic politics" not only in the content of Anaxagoras's cosmological theory but also in the formal structure of his prose. In Nous, I argue, Anaxagoras theorizes sovereign power as autonomous and self-grounding. He sustains this autocratic power by repressing the political contest from which it originates, a struggle between Nous and the things over the distribution of the sensible. But that repressed political struggle rages on in Anaxagoras's prose: even as the author aligns himself closely with Nous's omniscient gaze, his paratactic and polysyndetic style recuperates the political logic of the original community of things and not only sustains but in fact develops its political potential. The contest between these two arrangements of power plays out in the literary form and syntactic structure of the text, illustrating Rancière's thesis that aesthetics are political (and vice versa) and adding a new dimension to this book's central claim that the Presocratics' cosmos is an aesthetic, as well as physical and metaphysical, order.

In a ring composition that imitates a central figure of Presocratic thought and poetics, the final chapter, "Democritus and the Poetics of (N)othing," returns to the ontological paradox of the first chapter and to the relation of language to being and, especially, nonbeing. Democritus famously posits that everything is atoms and void. This theory seems to reify being in the form of the atom and to secure its presence against the negative space of the void. But the binarism of atomic theory overwrites a stranger and more alien ontology, for which Democritus invents the word *den*. This subtraction from *mēden* names the atom not as a positive presence but as the negation of a negation, literally less than nothing. Jacques Lacan speaks of the *den* as a fragment of the Real, that which resists theorization within Western philosophy. It also resists theorization, as we shall see, within Democritus's own theoretical discourse. That discourse is totalizing: it claims to be comprehensive, a theory of everything. It creates a new technical language to articulate that theory, a language that presents itself, in its immediate legibility, as transparent and true. The *den* both exemplifies this new language and marks its limits: it instantiates Democritus's vision of (non)being but cannot signify it, eluding both *onta* and *logos*. Instead, it appears as an exclusion, a blind spot within his philosophy. Untheorizable in itself, the *den* nonetheless exerts a dark force on Democritus's theory, shaping not only his physics but also his ethics and an ethical subject centered around a psychic void. "In reality to recognize what each thing is is in aporia" (*en aporōi*, B8/D19), writes Democritus. *Den* embodies that aporia and the unspeakable, untheorizable knowledge it contains.

As these synopses indicate, ontology for these five authors is a poetic as well as a philosophical project: it is an experiment in uniting language and being. This experiment enacts the truth that for the Presocratics language is not merely expressive or mimetic of reality but continuous with it, governed by its laws and sharing its same fundamental structure. Empedocles's words combine and separate just like his elements, and Democritus's *den* exhibits all the indeterminacy of his material universe. For Heraclitus the word "bow" enacts cosmic unity-in-difference no less than the physical object (B48/D53, B51/D49). Even Parmenides, who sets language against reality, works to forge a pure language of being and a word that *is* in the same way as Is itself. Indeed, the (physical and metaphysical) reality of their language is partly what makes the Presocratics such an exciting object of study: the symbolic, for them, presses up not just against reality but against the Real, precisely that which resists linguistic expression.[59] But if their poetics bring them closer to the Real, theirs was no "naive metaphysics of things," a mythic "before" to

59. This is part of what makes the Presocratics "antiphilosophers," in Badiou's term. It should be noted that the label is not necessarily approbative for Badiou, who defends philosophy's ability to signify the Real via mathematical formulas. I return to the Presocratics' antiphilosophy in the Conclusion.

the "after/beyond" of metaphysics.[60] The Presocratics had no metaphysical metalanguage in which to speak of *logos, to on*, and the relation between them. This is not because they lacked the conceptual sophistication or specialized vocabulary to formulate one but because they attempt to write this relation from within it and thus reproduce it—not mimetically but materially—in the very process of writing.

In so doing, they inevitably also reproduce the limits of that project, for the synthesis between *logos* and *to on*, as we shall see, is never total, and the attempt to bring them together produces a surplus on both sides: a being (or nonbeing) not captured in language; language that, impossibly, exceeds being. Language and being never fully converge, and their nonconvergence sustains a gap or aporia within the author's work and his world. That aporia is not an end in itself, however. The Presocratics' thought does not dead end in the impasse between language and the ineffable truth of a being that language cannot reach. If that were the case, to study their poetics would merely be to watch them throw the linguistic ladder away over and over again. Instead, the aporia between language and being opens generative aporias within language and being themselves. On the one side, being is revealed as not-whole: structured by internal rifts and disjunctions, it is fundamentally incoherent. On the other side, the discourse of being is shown to be nontotalizable, a circle that never fully closes. That lack of closure is the condition of possibility, as well as the condition of impossibility, of the Presocratics' theory of everything, for if it were possible to completely unite *logos* and being—to speak being fully and univocally—there would be nothing to say but "Is." The poetry and prose of the Presocratics in all its astonishing and fragmentary richness is the product of this ineluctable aporia.

60. "Naive metaphysics of things" is the title of Mourelatos 2008b.

1

Parmenides's *Logos* of Being

[Metaphor is] the moment of the detour in which the truth might still be lost.
—JACQUES DERRIDA

METAPHOR AND METAPHYSICS

Ontology is a paradoxical enterprise. The attempt to give an account (*logos*) of beings (*ta onta*) or of being (*to on*) immediately raises questions about the relation between the word's two components. What is the ontological status of *logos* in an ontological account? On the one hand, *logos* (speech, account, or argument) would seem to stand within the ambit of "the things that are" and thus to be included in the set of its own objects: in accounting for *ta onta, logos* must also give an account of itself. On the other hand, *logos* must go beyond *ta onta* and encompass them in order to constitute them as an object of study, in the process subtracting itself from both being and the philosophical account of it. Ontology is thus structured by a fundamental tension between *logos* and *to on*: what bonds connect them and which bounds the other?

These questions go back to the first ontologist, Parmenides, who lived in Elea, a Greek colony in Italy, at the very start of the fifth century BCE. Earlier thinkers, including not only the Ionian natural philosophers but also poets like Hesiod, had meditated on the nature of beings, but Parmenides was the first to explicitly take on being itself. His poem *Peri Phuseōs* (*On Nature*) journeys beyond the limits of the physical world to metaphysics, the study of fundamental reality. That reality—which Parmenides, with stunning simplicity, calls "Being" (*to eon*) or "Is" (*esti*)—lies beyond the myriad ephemeral phenomena of our everyday world. In contrast to them it is ungenerated, indestructible, unchanging, homogeneous, and whole.[1]

1. *To eon* is the epic form of *to on*. I capitalize Being, Is, and Is Not when translating Parmenides's *to eon, esti,* and *ouk esti* in order to mark them as terms of art and to indicate their metaphysical status. As we shall see, the choice of majuscule or minuscule is a question of some philosophical import in

It is also singular: Is is all that truly is, and everything else is merely the false object of human opinions (*doxa*).[2]

How does one write a *logos* of such a Being? To express it in language would seem to entail subjecting it to a logic not only alien but in fact antithetical to its nature. Being is monadic, but language creates meaning through difference: "bound" is not "bond"; "sphere" is neither "here" nor "square." The sense of a word in any given context is determined by the exclusion of other possible senses, a present absence strictly forbidden within Parmenides's ontology, where Is Not is declared impossible, unthinkable, and unspeakable. Its inseparability of presence and absence, sameness and difference, makes language inherently ambiguous, again in contrast to the solipsism of Is, which is completely and only what it is, a pure and perfect orb of presence.

Logos and *To Eon* would appear to have different and incompatible natures. Parmenides explores this paradox with marked self-consciousness; indeed, his every poetic choice seems designed to intensify it. His poem is divided into two sharply delineated sections or, in his dominant metaphor, "routes": the route of Truth that leads to Is and the route of Opinion, which confuses Is and Is Not. The 161 surviving lines of Parmenides's work preserve the bulk of the former (commonly referred to as the Aletheia) but only a small fraction of the latter (the so-called Doxa). These diverging roads are approached via a lengthy proem that describes the journey of the philosophical initiate (an anonymous "I" addressed as *kouros*, young man) to the palace of the unnamed goddess who will be his guide along the way. This opening "road of much speech" (*hodos poluphēmos*, B1.2/D4.2), with its mythical frame and ostentatiously allusive and ambiguous poetic language, anticipates the Doxa, which the goddess introduces as "the deceptive order of my words" (*kosmon emōn epeōn apatēlon*, B8.52/D8.57) and which is the realm of polyvalent speech par excellence. Drawing on a poetic tradition that opposes seductive persuasion to truth, Parmenides goes out of his way to highlight the potential schism between language and reality, *logos* and *to on*.

He widens that schism through his pointed use of metaphor.[3] Describing a thing by means of something it is not, metaphor intensifies the qualities of lan-

---

Parmenides. I prefer the translation "Being" for Parmenides's *esti* and *to eon* to "What Is," which overstresses the nominal at the expense of the verbal. The best translation, "Is," is grammatically unwieldy.

2. Parmenides's monism was already a source of perplexity and object of critique in antiquity. Aristotle took it to be an extreme "entity" and "essence" monism (see Clarke 2019) and characterized it as akin to madness (*mania, Gen. corr.* 1.8 325a2–23). The debate over its nature continues. Palmer's "generous monism" is appealing (2009, 38–50, 181–84); cf. Finkelberg 1999. Tor (2023b) cites other "permissive ontological models" and supports the position. See further Curd 1998, 64–97, and the interesting approach of Robbiano (2006, 129–33; 2016), stressing the unity of Being with knowing and the knower. I assume that Parmenides propounds the singularity of Being (see esp. B8.5–6/D8.10–11) but am not committed to a more precise account of the form that singularity takes.

3. The best discussion of Parmenides's use of metaphor (as of many of his literary techniques) is by Mourelatos (2008c, 37–41, 134–35). He emphasizes its "speculative" nature, whereby existing words

guage in general, calling attention to its predication of meaning on difference, doubleness, and negation. In "White Mythology," Jacques Derrida argues that metaphysics is sustained by metaphor, even as it claims to reach beyond mere rhetoric to reality itself.[4] The ascent from the physical to the metaphysical is attended by a whitewashing of language, as philosophy attempts to efface the rhetorical process by which it produces itself. But this effaced rhetoric persists within the text of philosophy. Even the most blandly abstract philosophical language carries a metaphorical charge: "concept," "theory," "foundation," "idea" are all themselves metaphors. These words bear within them an entire history of philosophy, but one that philosophy itself cannot fully examine, since its instrument of analysis is inseparable from its object. Philosophy may seek to deny this double bind by denigrating metaphor as an extraneous supplement to the thing it describes, a mere "detour" on the path to truth. But in doing so it "would have to posit that the sense aimed at through these figures is an essence rigorously independent of that which transports it, which is an already philosophical *thesis*, one might even say philosophy's *unique thesis*"—the very thesis that metaphor instantiates, that is, the opposition between the idea and its expression, reality and semblances, being and language. Conveying and reproducing this thesis, metaphor is itself, as Derrida says, "a classical philosopheme, a metaphysical concept."[5]

Derrida observes that philosophy is unable to examine its own grounding metaphors because it has no meta-metaphorical metalanguage in which to speak of them.[6] Parmenides labors to invent such a metalanguage. His *Esti* and *To Eon* appear to escape figurative expression and attain to a clarified, objective, almost mathematical denotation of reality.[7] At the same time, Parmenides also uses metaphor to examine the intimate entanglement of language and being. These two modes of discourse proceed in tandem in his poem and neither can be discounted. Parmenides is often depicted as a sublime logician who resorts to metaphor as a communicative necessity: *faute de mieux*, since he must speak in human language to his human audience, he makes use of metaphor to convey more clearly or engagingly the abstract truth of Being.[8] But Parmenides's use of metaphor, while

and images are appropriated to create novel concepts. The distinction between metaphorical and literal was first explicitly theorized by Aristotle (see Lloyd 1995, 172–214; and Gemelli Marciano 2008). But of course Parmenides could have had a practical (and even theoretical) sense of the trope without being able to name it as such. For a sensitive study of metaphor in Greek poetry and criticism and the spatial metaphors through which it was articulated (including that of the road), see Worman 2015.

4. Derrida 1982b. The essay was first published in *Poétique* 5 (1971): 1–52.

5. Derrida 1982b, 229 (original emphasis), 219.

6. Derrida 1982b, 219–20. Thus there would always be one metaphor in excess of the analysis and "the field is never saturated" (220).

7. See Badiou 2014, 18–21, 159–61, 229–59. Badiou (cf. 2007), Lacan (esp. 1998), and Meillassoux (2009) all argue for mathematics as the proper language of ontology.

8. Procl. *In Parm.* p. 665.12–21 (A18/R4): Parmenides was obliged by his poetic form to make use of metaphorical terms and figures. Bryan (2020) offers an astute critique of this assumption of the

extravagant, is never merely ornamental or cosmetic. His metaphors are neither a mere vehicle to the truth, to be abandoned when enlightenment is finally reached, nor just a mode of conveying that exotic truth to the folks back home. Instead, they are themselves ways of thinking about Being and its many perplexities. Heightening the tension between *onta* and *logos*, metaphors both enact the paradoxes of ontology and theorize (though necessarily without resolving) them.

Parmenides thus approaches these questions along two parallel tracks. The first (which is the focus of the next section) is his pathbreaking attempt to journey beyond the bounds of metaphorical language to forge a true language of Being. This novel language would reduce "ontology" to a pleonasm or even a tautology, as *logos* is drawn fully within the charmed circle of *to on*. But this tautology immediately introduces a new conundrum, because Parmenides's singular *To Eon* cannot be the same (*t'auta*) as *logos* or anything but itself. The doubleness of language infiltrates the terrain of Aletheia and divides its object, the unique and indivisible Is (*Esti*). The second track is an attempt to safeguard Is through a series of striking metaphors of Necessity's (or Fate's or Justice's) "bounds of bonds" or "bonds of bounds." These vivid images of containment hold Being together (whole, coherent, and indivisible), hold it apart (in its difference from Nonbeing), and hold it in place (unmoving and unchanging), fixing it in its spherical perfection. They promise simultaneously to secure Being and to secure language for Being. And yet, as we shall see in the third section of the chapter, this strategy is no less contradictory than the first: Necessity's bonds exert a force that destabilizes the very reality they are meant to safeguard, leaving it divided and lacking. Not only does metaphor stand within metaphysics, as Derrida posits; at its limit, the metaphysical itself becomes a kind of metaphor in the simile of the sphere that expresses Being's perfection, but only by comparing it to what it is not, a predicate that has already been precluded as impossible and unthinkable.

Along both of these tracks, Parmenides exposes the aporias of ontology, but he does so necessarily from within them, replicating them even as he subjects them to scrutiny. This recursivity—the fact, as Derrida insists, that there is no metametaphoric position from which to analyze metaphor—renders futile the ongoing debate over whether Parmenides was simply unaware of the paradoxes of his metaphysical theory or whether identifying those paradoxes was in fact his point.[9]

separability of poetic form and philosophical content; see also Osborne 1998; Patzer 2006, 83–85; and Granger 2008.

9. For a trenchant articulation of the debate (and argument for the latter position) see Mackenzie 1982. This debate has often centered around the question of why Parmenides includes the Doxa if he considers it untrue, a question to which we will turn at the end of the chapter. In an excellent recent article on the tension between language and doctrine in Parmenides, Tor (2023b) discusses many of the same features of the poem as I do, arguing for Parmenides's "reflective preoccupation with, and a consistent and self-aware attitude towards, the scope, orientation and limitations of human language" (268) for describing What Is. Similar arguments are made by Morgan 2000, 67–88; Barrett 2004; Gemelli

With his *To Eon*, did Parmenides attempt to escape *logos* and fail, or did he set out to demonstrate the impossibility of a reality that escapes *logos?* The question is, I think, unanswerable, and the two positions are not mutually exclusive: Parmenides would be caught in the paradoxes of language whether he was conscious of them or not. This means, furthermore, that wherever one comes down on the question of his intent, the incoherences we identify in Parmenides's text should be considered not as a failure of his philosophical theory (as if he really could escape language if he tried hard enough) but rather as one of its generative sources, as he attempts to square the circle of contradictions that inhere within ontology as a philosophical project.

These contradictions are ineradicable because they arise from ontology's irreconcilable desires: the desire to subordinate *logos* to *to on* by producing a transparent language of being, and the desire to subordinate *to on* to *logos*, to fix being as an object of discourse and in this way to consecrate what Parmenides calls a "trustworthy *logos* and thought about truth" (B8.50–51/D8.55–56).[10] These competing desires converge in Parmenides in the sphere, which is both the figure of a nonfigurable Being and the structure of Parmenides's poem. The sphere instantiates Parmenides's desire for an autonomous metaphysical reality, a reality that can be truly expressed in *logos* but that exists before and beyond any similes by which we might describe it. At the same time, as the structure of his poem, the sphere represents the dream of a *logos* that encircles that reality in its entirety: both Aletheia and Doxa, Is and Is Not. In the sphere, then, *logos* and *onta* encircle one another in an ontological Möbius strip, each simultaneously the other's outside and inside, neither separable nor synthesizable into a single, homogeneous ontological whole. This chapter will trace the contours of this aporia, marking in Parmenides's metaphors both the path and the impasses of his revolutionary metaphysics.

THE *HODOS POLUPHĒMOS*

Parmenides's poem begins on the road.

> ἵπποι ταί με φέρουσιν, ὅσον τ᾽ ἐπὶ θυμὸς ἱκάνοι,
> πέμπον, ἐπεί μ᾽ ἐς ὁδὸν βῆσαν πολύφημον ἄγουσαι
> δαίμονος, ἣ κατὰ πάντ᾽ ἄστη φέρει εἰδότα φῶτα. (B1.1–3/D4.1–3)[11]

Marciano 2008, 37–41; and Cherubin 2017, 2018. I am in sympathy with this approach, but I remain agnostic on the question of intent. See the discussion of the author function in the Conclusion, below.

10. These competing desires have shaped the entire history of Western philosophy and are manifest in the discipline's current bifurcation between analytic (with its faith in mathematics and formal logic) and continental (Nietzsche and his heirs, including Derrida).

11. Sext. Emp. *Math.* 7.111 tells us this fragment was the opening of the *Peri Phuseōs* (though it is unlikely that these were the first lines: Sider forthcoming, ad loc.). I accept his reading of *daimonos* (referring to the goddess); Diels-Kranz print Stein's emendation *daimones*, referring to the Heliades.

> The mares that are bearing me as far as passion might reach
> were conveying me, when they led and set me upon the goddess's road of
> much speech,
> which bears through all towns a man who knows.

The poem charts a journey of passion (*thumos*), and its first line anticipates its *telos* in that passion's fulfillment. The speaker goes on to detail his adventure. Escorted by the Maidens of the Sun, he comes to the palace of the goddess, who presents him with two routes: the way of Truth, *Alētheiē*, and the path of Opinion, *Doxa* (B1.28–32/D4.28–32, B2/D6). This fork in the road will set the direction for the poem as a whole, which will first follow the path of Truth to describe Is, before moving to the second route and human opinion.

The path leading up to that critical crossroads is described as *poluphēmos*, much speaking or much spoken of. The word is markedly poetic: it occurs repeatedly in epic poetry and once in reference to an epic poet (Hom. *Od.* 22.376). The epic resonance of the adjective is all the stronger if it reminds the listener of the cyclops Polyphemus, establishing the *Odyssey* as the key poetic intertext for this philosophical voyage.[12] *Poluphēmos* is also used of the enigmatic utterances of divine or prophetic speech, like the words of the Pythia, which conceal their true meaning (Hdt. 5.79.4, cf. Hom. *Od.* 2.150), suggesting another contemporary model for Parmenides's enigmatic and divinely inspired poem.[13] But one might wonder about the meaning of *poluphēmos* itself. Does it mean "much spoken of" or "much speaking"?[14] If the former, is it the road that is renowned—a nod to the well-traveled trope of "the path of song"—or the poem that exalts it, an aspirational transfer of epithet that makes the path a proleptic metaphor for the poem itself?[15] If the latter, the word is a daring metaphor, since roads do not literally

12. The word also appears in Pindar (*Isthm.* 8.58) in reference to epic *kleos*. The epic antecedents of the journey motif and Parmenides's adaptation of them are well documented by Mourelatos (2008c, 16–25). Parmenides is in continuous dialogue with Homer and Hesiod throughout his poem. Cassin (1998, 48–64) reads the poem as a palimpsestic rewriting of the *Odyssey* with Being as its hero; cf. Havelock 1958, with Parmenides himself in the role of Odysseus. See further Deichgräber 1958, 15–43; Schwabl 1963; Pellikaan-Engel 1974; Böhme 1986; Floyd 1992; Wöhrle 1993; Mourelatos 2008c, 1–46; Coxon 2009, 7–12; Ranzato 2015; and Mackenzie 2021a, 78–93. Folit-Weinberg (2022, esp. 65–116) argues that *Odyssey* 12.55–126 provided the discursive blueprint for Parmenides's "invention" of deductive reasoning.

13. Tor 2017, 265–66. The choice of dactylic hexameter amplifies both the Homeric and prophetic resonances.

14. Translations differ. Gallop 1984: "the much-speaking route"; Tarán 1965: "resounding road"; Laks-Most: "many-worded"; Diels-Kranz: "vielberühmten"; Mansfeld 1964, 229: "ruhmvoll und Ruhm verleihend," which he takes as a reference to Parmenides's own fame.

15. The road metaphor was well established—perhaps even a cliché—by this time. Homer has paths of song (*Od.* 8.74, 8.481, 22.347); Hesiod, the steep path of justice (*Op.* 216–8, 287–92); and the image is ubiquitous in Pindar (e.g. *Ol.* 6). On Parmenides's models and for the trope in archaic Greek poetry, see Bowra 1937. See also Becker 1937; Nünlist 1998, 228–83; and the detailed study of Folit-Weinberg (2022), who attends to the physical, as well as poetic, affordances of ancient *hodoi* for Parmenides's

speak. This word for polyvocality is itself polyvocal. Proliferating meanings, literal and metaphoric, it sends the reader off on branching paths of poetic allusion.

Performing the verbal multiplicity it names, this *hodos poluphēmos* alerts us to the polysemy of words and their tendency toward metaphor. Sextus Empiricus, who quotes the fragment, reads the entire proem as an extended metaphor, a Platonizing allegory in which each element symbolizes something it is not: the horses are the irrational impulses of the soul; the maidens, the senses; the road, the progression of "theoretical contemplation in accordance with philosophical reason which, like an escorting divinity, leads to knowledge of all things."[16] Sextus's one-to-one correspondence between each signifier and its hidden signified keeps us on the hermeneutic straight and narrow, but once we abandon literal meanings every word points in multiple possible semantic directions, as the divergent allegorical interpretations of the proem demonstrate.[17]

Transporting us from the literal to the figurative, a metaphor of metaphor, Parmenides's route opens onto an ostentatiously poetic terrain. The *hodos poluphēmos* resonates in the polyphony of *polu*: the "much-thinking" mares (*poluphrastoi*, 4), "much-punishing" Dikē (*polupoinos*, 14), the pivots of "much bronze" (*polukhalkous*, 18–19).[18] These pivots (*axonas*) turning in their sockets (*surinxin*, 19) are themselves part of an elaborate verbal patterning. At line 6 the same words describe the chariot as it rushes along its path: "The axle (*axōn*), burning in the axle boxes, emitted the cry of a whistle (*suringos*)." As words are repeated, any notion of a univocal or proper meaning is left by the wayside: does *surinx* mean "whistle" or "socket"? All meaning starts to look metaphoric and multiple. Throughout the proem Parmenides multiplies these multiplicities with a linguistic exuberance that draws us repeatedly away from any singular trajectory such as Sextus's "philosophical reason which . . . leads to knowledge of all things." Rampant Homeric and Hesiodic allusions pull us to one side, tempting us down intertextual digressions.

---

philosophical method. More generally, Gagné (2021, 203–65) demonstrates the importance of travel narratives to ancient poetic world-creation.

16. Sext. Emp. *Math.* 7.112 (ad B1/R8). Sextus's explication of this journey metaphor is itself freighted with journey metaphors, proving Derrida's point that any philosophical exposition of metaphor is bound to replicate its terms.

17. Most agree in reading it as an allegory for the attainment of knowledge, but they differ on the particulars: e.g., for Coxon (2009, 14–18) it symbolizes the journey of the soul toward divinity; for Bollack (2006, 71–96), the drive of language toward truth; for Cordero (2004, 19–35), Parmenides's philosophical method; while Latona (2008) supports Sextus's interpretation. Other allegorical readings are surveyed by Couloubaritsis (2008, 165–77), and the question is treated by Mackenzie (2017). Bowra (1937, 98) notes that allegorizing on this scale is unprecedented in Greek poetry. Arguing against an allegorical reading (in favor of understanding the scene as the literal account of a real religious experience) are Mansfeld 1964, 222–73; Robbiano 2006, 22–23; and Gemelli Marciano 2008.

18. There are later echoes in the Aletheia in the *polupeiron ethos* (much-experienced habit) that might drive one toward *doxa* (B7.3/D8.3) and the *poludērin elenkhon* (much-contested proof) of truth (B7.5/D8.5); and in the Doxa in mortals' *meleōn poluplanktōn* (much-wandering limbs, B16.1/D51.1). The play on *polu* may recall the opening of the *Odyssey* and its *polutropos* hero; if the diction of manyness there alludes to the *Iliad,* as Pucci (1982) proposes, Parmenides's intertextuality proliferates polyphemy.

Repetitions like *surinx* and *axōn* force us to circle back and retrace our steps, while the ornate detail in the description of the palace gates (B1.16–20/D4.16–20) makes us linger, delaying our forward journey. Indeed, despite the best efforts of our divine escorts, the proem's route has an aleatory quality that makes it unclear even whether it is an ascent into the light or a descent to the underworld.[19]

This meandering road, "far from the path of men" (*ap' anthrōpōn ektos patou*, B1.27/D4.27), anticipates the aporia (literally, "pathlessness") of human opinion.[20] The Doxa will chart a terrain of error and errancy. This is the "road of inquiry" (*hodos dizēsios*)

ἣν δὴ βροτοὶ εἰδότες οὐδὲν
πλάττονται,[21] δίκρανοι· ἀμηχανίη γὰρ ἐν αὐτῶν
στήθεσιν ἰθύνει πλακτὸν νόον· οἱ δὲ φοροῦνται
κωφοὶ ὁμῶς τυφλοί τε, τεθηπότες, ἄκριτα φῦλα,
οἷς τὸ πέλειν τε καὶ οὐκ εἶναι ταὐτὸν νενόμισται
κοὐ ταὐτόν, πάντων δὲ παλίντροπός ἐστι κέλευθος. (B6.4–9/D7.4–9)

that know-nothing mortals
wander, two-headed. For resourcelessness in their hearts
guides straight their wandering thought. And they are borne
deaf and blind alike, stunned, indiscriminate races,
by whom to be and not to be are considered the same
and not the same, and the path of all things is backward-turning.

We mortals wander (*plattontai*) through the world in ignorance of the truth, our intellectual resourcelessness directing us straight (*ithunei*) to more wandering

19. *Katabasis:* Morrison 1955, 59–60; Burkert 1969, 1–15; Kingsley 1999, 59, 68–85; 2002, 369–81; and Palmer 2009, 54–55. Ascent: Fränkel 1975, 1–6; Owens 1979; Kahn 2009, 210–15; and Coxon 2009, 275–76. Miller (2006, 18–24); Mourelatos (2008c, 15–16); Bryan (2020, 222–26); and Mackenzie (2021a, 94–97) argue for deliberate ambiguity; cf. Granger 2008; and Gemelli Marciano 2008, 29–32. Tor (2017, 347–59) surveys the various options: his support for a circular journey is appealing in light of Parmenides's ring composition, discussed at the end of this chapter. If *kata pant' astē* is the correct reading in line 3, the road leads "through all cities," an Odyssean wandering. But the text is disputed: see Lesher 1994b; and Sider forthcoming, ad loc.

20. Parmenides does not use the word *aporia; poros* is not among his many synonyms for *hodos*. At this time, *poros* referred primarily to a sea crossing and only later became generalized as a physical or conceptual pathway, and *aporia* as the absence thereof. The closest we get to *poros* is with the *doxai* that at B1.32/D4.32 are said to "pass entirely through everything" (*dia pantos panta perōnta*). The verb *peraō* (etymologically linked to *poros*) also gives us *peras* (limit), which we shall see is a seminal term in Parmenides's ontology. The connections between the proem and the Doxa are detailed by Cosgrove (2011), arguing for an ironic reading of the proem. Note in particular the diction of light and fire (B1.7/D4.7, B1.10/D4.10), and of day and night (B1.8–11/D4.8–11), all prominent in the Doxa.

21. Diels prints the manuscripts' *plattontai*, understanding it as the corruption of a dialectical variant of *plazontai*, from *plazō* (to go astray, wander): see Diels 2003, 72–73. Sider (1985, 363–65, forthcoming, ad loc.) argues for *plassontai* from *plassō* (to fabricate, mold, invent). Laks-Most offer both translations.

(*plakton noon*). Our path leads around in circles (*palintropos*). This mental errancy derives from our lack of discrimination: mortals are an uncritical race, *akrita phula*, unable to discern (*krinein*) the fundamental distinction (*krisis*) between Is and Is Not.[22] We fail to differentiate not only between Being and Nonbeing, but even between sameness and difference. As a result, we falsely distinguish (*ekrinanto*) singularities into opposites (B8.55/D8.60). Double-headed (*dikranoi*, B6.5/D7.5), we see the world in binary terms, dividing male and female (B12.5–6/D14b.5–6, B17/D46), heavy and light (B8.57–59/D8.62–64), night and day, and dark and light (B8.56–59/D8.61–64, B9/D13).

Our erroneous division of singular Being is associated with language. Mortals

> μορφὰς γὰρ κατέθεντο δύο γνώμας ὀνομάζειν·
> τῶν μίαν οὐ χρεών ἐστιν—ἐν ὧι πεπλανημένοι εἰσίν—
> τἀντία δ' ἐκρίναντο δέμας καὶ σήματ' ἔθεντο
> χωρὶς ἀπ' ἀλλήλων. (B8.53–56/D8.58–61)
>
> have established two forms to name their thoughts,
> one of which must not be named—in this they go astray—
> and they distinguished a body into opposites and established signs
> apart from each other.

Through naming we divide what is truly one, creating a false multiplicity, all the myriad nameable things that fill our cosmos. Our world of discrete phenomena and diverse opinions is an illusion sustained by language: "For it [Being] all things will be a name (*onoma*), the things which mortals have established, believing them to be true (*alēthē*), to be born and to die, to be and not to be" (B8.38–40/D8.43–45).[23]

From these false multiplicities mortals construct false unities. Thus when we have named (*onomastai*) all things light and night and divided the world between them, "the whole is full of light and invisible night at once, both equally" (B9/D13). The result is a confused and ambiguous unity, a poetic rather than ontic unity, as in the paradoxical description of the moon as a "night-shining alien light wandering around the earth" (*nuktiphaes peri gaian alōmenon allotrion phōs*, B14/D27). With its vivid compound adjective *nuktiphaes* (a Parmenidean coinage); its

22. "The choice (*krisis*) concerning these things lies in this: Is or Is Not" (B8.15–16/D8.20–21); cf. *kekritai*, B8.16/D8.21; *krinai*, B7.5/D8.5. On *krisis* in the Aletheia and Doxa, see Bryan 2018, 27–35. Curd (1992 [~ 1998, 98–126]) helpfully identifies the false dualities of the Doxa as enantiomorphs, each element of which entails the other.

23. Cf. B19/D62, probably the final lines of the Doxa: "Thus according to *doxa* these things were born and now exist and afterwards, having grown from this, will die. And to each of them mortals have given a distinguishing name (*onom[a] . . . episēmon*)." *Onomazein* is associated with false speech and *doxa*, in contrast to *legein*, *phasthai*, and *phrazein*, which denote true speech: see Tarán 1965, 129–33, 141–43; and Cassin 1998, 153–74. Barrett (2004, 279–87) sees the problem of naming as paradigmatic of the failure of mortal understanding; cf. Mason 1988.

euphonious alliteration (*alō-*, *allo-*) and repetition (*phaes*, *phōs*); its pun on *phōs* (which with one accentuation means "light" and with another, "man") and astronomical repurposing of the epic phrase *allotrion phōs* (which in Homer refers to a stranger), the beautiful line encapsulates the seductive adornment of the language of *doxa*, just as the moon's wandering orbit literalizes *doxa*'s erroneous thought.[24]

Doxa is the realm of words, then, but its words inevitably fail to denominate the singular reality of Being. Parmenides famously introduces the Doxa section of the poem as "the deceptive order of my words" (*kosmon emōn epeōn apatēlon*, B8.52/D8.57).[25] *Kosmos* suggests a rational order but also ornament or adornment. The phrase evokes an entire archaic Greek discourse of poetic speech as *apatē*, persuasive but untrue.[26] This deceptive persuasion is anticipated in the proem, where the Daughters of the Sun persuade Justice to open her gates, "talking her around with soft words" (*tēn dē parphamenai kourai malakoisi logoisin*, B1.15/D4.15). In the *Odyssey*, Calypso uses "soft and wily words" (*malakoisi kai haimulioisi logoisi*, 1.56) to divert Odysseus from his course, a diversion echoed in Parmenides's verb *paraphasthai* (literally, "to speak to the side"), which can mean either to persuade or to deceive.

The duplicitous language of *doxai* and the goddess's *kosmos apatēlos* concerning them thus bring us back to the proem's resonant *hodos poluphēmos*. The ambiguous, polysemous language of the proem anticipates the Doxa and its false dualities. The proem too is full of dualities, as Kathryn Morgan has shown, like the "gates of the paths of Night and Day" (B1.11/D4.11) where the philosophical initiate is led by the Sun-maidens who themselves "seem to oscillate between the worlds of darkness and light."[27] Morgan views this imagery as part of a strategy of "the studied cancellation of dualistic imagery," in which Parmenides sets up in the proem the dualities that will be overcome, in the Aletheia, in the unity of Being. Thus she views the philosopher's path as a kind of Hegelian *Aufhebung* in which doxic

24. Popper (1992) notes the importance of the moon for Parmenides. The line was striking enough that Empedocles copied it, also in reference to the moon (Emp. B45/D139).

25. Cf. B8.60/D8.65 where the Doxa is a *diakosmon eoikota* ("a plausible or fitting order"): the label is well discussed by Bryan (2012, 58–113). See also Cherubin 2005; and Mackenzie 2021a, 70–73. Macé (2019) proposes that Parmenides was the first to apply the word *kosmos* (which in archaic poetry denotes an aesthetic or military ordering) to the universe. On the word's philosophical evolution, see further Kahn 1960, 219–30; and Finkelberg 1998. Nünlist (2005, 75–76) lists the parallels for *kosmos epeōn* and proposes that the poetological metaphor was well established, perhaps even ossified, by Parmenides's time.

26. Detienne (1996) tracks the intimate connection of poetic truth to *peithō* and *apatē* (69–88) and to *doxa* (109–19) in early Greek thought; he presents Parmenides as the culmination of this tradition (130–34).

27. Morgan 2000, 73–81 (the quotation is on 77). The day-night binary is compounded by the gender binary between the *Heliades kourai* (B1.5, 9/D4.5, 9) and the philosophical *kouros* (B1.24/D4.24). The binary of *kouroi* and *kourai* is a feature of human *doxa* (B17/D46); see also B12.4–6/D14b.4–6 on the "hateful mixing" of male and female in childbirth. Cherubin 2019 (extending Journée 2012) examines gender in Parmenides.

duality is canceled in the ascent to a purer unity.[28] This hermeneutic trajectory aligns with readings that take Parmenides to use doxic language in the manner of Wittgenstein's ladder, to be thrown away once it has been ascended.[29] Both readings posit poetic language as something that philosophy must move beyond in order to reach the lucent aether of reality and both suggest that the essence of philosophy lies in this transcendence.

These interpretations follow the path Parmenides sets for us. Indeed, the metaphor of the road seems designed expressly to produce such teleological readings: as Alexander Mourelatos observes and Benjamin Folit-Weinberg emphasizes, in Homer a *hodos* is a one-way road to a specific end.[30] The passion that launches Parmenides's journey sustains its undeviating course until it reaches the sphere of Being, where the goddess terminates (*pauō*) her "trustworthy *logos* and thought about truth" (B8.50–51/D8.55–56). The directive force of the metaphor is reinforced by the several divine escorts of the proem and especially the goddess herself, whose voice soon supersedes that of the first-person narrator and who bossily dictates his (and the reader's) every move.

This unnamed deity embodies the enunciative force of the poem and directs its argumentative trajectory. At her command, our hermeneutic paths narrow from many to two to one.

> εἰ δ' ἄγ' ἐγὼν ἐρέω, κόμισαι δὲ σὺ μῦθον ἀκούσας,
> αἵπερ ὁδοὶ μοῦναι διζήσιός εἰσι νοῆσαι·
> ἡ μὲν ὅπως ἔστιν τε καὶ ὡς οὐκ ἔστι μὴ εἶναι,
> Πειθοῦς ἐστι κέλευθος (Ἀληθείηι γὰρ ὀπηδεῖ),
> ἡ δ' ὡς οὐκ ἔστιν τε καὶ ὡς χρεών ἐστι μὴ εἶναι,
> τὴν δή τοι φράζω παναπευθέα ἔμμεν ἀταρπόν·
> οὔτε γὰρ ἂν γνοίης τό γε μὴ ἐὸν (οὐ γὰρ ἀνυστόν)
> οὔτε φράσαις. (B2/D6)
>
> Come, I will tell you and you listen and convey my speech,
> what are the only roads of inquiry for thought:
> the one, that Is and cannot not be,

28. Morgan 2000, 75. She goes on, however, to cast doubt on the purity of a truth communicated via mythical figures. Morgan does not use the Hegelian term, but see Cassin (1998, 63), who identifies both the poem's transcendence of epic and the Aletheia's transcendence of *doxa* as an *Aufhebung*. Derrida (1982b, 225–26) links Hegel's treatment of metaphor as the *Aufhebung* of the concrete into the conceptual to the grounding distinction of metaphysics: hence "Metaphysics—the *Aufhebung* (*relève*) of metaphor" (258; cf. 268).

29. First proposed by Owen (1960, 100–101) and much cited; cf. above, Introduction, n. 40. Morgan (2022, 236) connects her theory of ascent to the Wittgensteinian ladder in passing. Tor (2023b, 271) observes that the image both overstates Parmenides's argumentative reliance on human language and underestimates language's hold on his listeners.

30. Mourelatos 2008c, 18. Folit-Weinberg (2022, 35–46) notes that the deeply rutted roads of archaic and classical Greece locked travelers into a prescribed route and destination, with significant implications for Parmenides's use of the image (see esp. 258–62).

> is the way of Persuasion (for she attends Truth);
> the other, that Is Not and must not be,
> I tell you this is a path that cannot be learned,
> for you could not know what is not (for that is impossible)
> nor could you speak it.

In a move that will be repeated several times in the poem, the goddess brings us to a fork in the road and seems to offer us a choice only to bar one of the two routes. "The choice (*krisis*) concerning these things lies in this: Is or Is Not" (B8.15–16/D8.20–21), but Is Not has already been judged (*kekritai*) unthinkable and unnamable; not only is it not the road to truth, it is not even a true road (*ou gar alēthēs estin hodos*, B8.17–18/D8.22–23). First the nonroute to Nonbeing is blocked, then the detour to Doxa: "I bar you from this first road of inquiry [Is Not], and then in turn from this one," the wandering path of "two-headed mortals" (B6.3–5/D7.3–5; cf. B7.3–5/D8.3–5).[31] Through this reiterated gesture toward foreclosed alternatives, the field of inquiry is constricted until, as the goddess says at the start of B8/D8, "a single utterance of road is still left: that Is" (*monos d'eti muthos hodoio leipetai hōs estin*, B8.1–2/D8.6–7).

By this single, undeviating road we seem to leave the poetic terrain of the proem and the doxic semiotics it prefigures. The seductive duplicity of "soft words" (B1.15/D4.15) and the "deceptive adornment" (B8.52/D8.57) that characterize human opinion are apparently left behind, as *peithō*—so often opposed to *alētheia* in early Greek thought—joins forces with truth on "the way of Persuasion (for she attends Truth)" leading to Is (B2.4/D6.4).[32] The peculiar locution *muthos hodoio* ("utterance of road") at B8.1/D8.6 marks the culmination of Parmenides's road imagery (which will occur only once more in the extant fragments, B8.17–18/D8.22–23). Metaphor yields to *muthos*, the authoritative speech of ontology.[33] The vague passion (*thumos*, B1.1/D4.1) that initiated the journey now finds its proper object: in place of *muthos* (Simplicius's reading) at B8.1/D8.6, Sextus Empiricus

31. *Eirgō* in B6.3/D7.3 is Diels-Kranz's supplement (defended by Wedin 2014, 53–71; contra, Cordero 1979; Sider 1985, ad loc.), based on the parallel with B7.2/D8.2: "Bar (*eirge*) your thought from this road of inquiry." Again, the choice is no choice, as this barred path will ultimately be traveled. There is much debate as to whether Parmenides imagined two roads or three. More important than the initial number of routes, to my mind, is the way they are insistently reduced to one. Compare Couloubaritsis (2008), who proposes that Parmenides transforms the polysemic theme of the *hodos* into a philosophical method, a *met'hodon* (32–33, 54–55, 57–66, 295, 307, 366–67). See also Folit-Weinberg (2022, 52–63), who shows that purposeful activity was part of the semantics of *hodos* from Homer on.

32. Blank 1982. Cf. *pistis alēthēs* (B1.30/D4.30, B8.28/D8.33) and *Alētheiēs eupeitheos* (Sextus's reading of B1.29/D4.29; Simplicius has *eukukleos*, discussed below, n. 79). On Peithō and *pistis* in Parmenides see further Mourelatos 2008c, 136–63.

33. Cf. B2.1/D6.1. For *muthos* as authoritative utterance, see Martin 1989, 1–42. Cassin (1998, 19–23) takes this ambiguous phrase as the starting point for two divergent readings of the poem: "le mot du chemin" (the word Is, which constitutes Parmenides as the first rationalist) and "le récit de la route" (the epic saga of Being).

tellingly reads *thumos*. In this way Parmenides's guiding metaphor itself guides the reader out of the proem's landscape of metaphoric language as our route narrows from the *hodos poluphēmos* to a singular, authoritative, univocal word: Is.

With this singular word we enter new linguistic territory. *Esti* is the verb "to be" in its present indicative form. The form is third-person singular but has no stated subject: it is being without a specific be-er.[34] Parmenides's audacious use of the word, unprecedented in Greek literature, develops the metaphysics implicit in the Greek verb *einai*. In his exhaustive study of the verb, Charles Kahn argues that the primary sense of *einai* was not existential ("exists") but veridical ("truly is, is the case"). This basic meaning conjoins the notions of existence and predication, reality and truth: *esti* indicates both what is and what can truly be said to be.[35] This conflation is in keeping (as Kahn stresses) with Parmenides's apparent equation of speech, thought, and being: "It is necessary that to speak and to think be what is, for to be is and nothing is not" (B6.1–2/D7.1–2).[36] This equation suggests, on the one hand, that the objects of thought and speech partake of reality and, on the other, that reality is by its very nature thinkable and speakable (which is why Is Not can be neither thought nor spoken, B2.7–8/D6.7–8, B8.8–9/D8.13–14, B8.17/D8.22). *Esti* encapsulates this congruence of language and reality. Collapsing signified and signifier, What Is and what is said about it, into a single lexeme, it bespeaks the speakability of being.[37] At the same time, if "it is necessary that to speak and to think be what is," that lexeme itself shares in the reality of being. *Esti*—the word—is.

With this metaphysical *esti* Parmenides forges an *onto-logos*, a novel language of being. Singular, abstract, and univocal, fully present in its eternal present tense, *esti* seems to escape from the polysemy of ordinary human language as

34. A variety of potential subjects has been mooted; the possibilities are discussed by Finkelberg 1988; Cordero 2004, 44–54, 60–64; and Sider forthcoming, ad B2.3.

35. Kahn 1973, 331–70, 401–9. He presents that study as a "grammatical prolegomenon" to the radical new notion of Being formulated by Parmenides (Kahn 2009, 109–10). See further Kahn 2009, 16–40, 62–74, 170–80. Kahn insists on the veridical sense of the verb in Parmenides (e.g. at 2009, 150–56, 170–80, 198–206) against proponents of an existential reading like Owen 1960; Gallop 1979; and Barnes 1982, 160–61. See also the "definitional" reading of Curd 1998, 34–51; and Bredlow 2011.

36. *Khrē to legein te noein t'eon emmenai; esti gar einai, mēden d'ouk estin.* Cf. B3/D6.8, B8.34–36/D8.39–41. Translation of B6.1–2/D7.1–2 is extraordinarily difficult and there is no agreement on its interpretation. My reading follows Kahn (2009, 163–65), who views the lines as articulating "a correspondence theory of truth." He surveys other interpretations at 189–91. Cassin (1998, 34–38, 144–48) offers a lucid discussion of the syntactical complexities and their ontological implications. See further Mourelatos 2008c, 77n7 (and 164–93 for his own "correspondence theory" of thought and reality) and Long 1996 for a strong argument for the identity of thinking and being. For the counterargument and review of the question, see Cherubin 2001. Badiou (2014) identifies his construction of a "borromean knot" of being, thought, and nonbeing as Parmenides's signal innovation.

37. This is articulated in the strange construction "that Is" (*hōs estin*, B8.2/D8.7; *hopōs estin*, B2.3/D6.3), which emphasizes *esti* as signifier. Contrast B8.16/D8.21, where the decision is *estin ē ouk estin*, a choice between signifieds not signifiers, two alternative realities not two statements about them.

Parmenides characterizes it in the proem and Doxa.[38] Indeed, it seems to escape language altogether. Without subject or predicate, *esti* seems to float in glorious isolation from syntax. In paradigmatic statements like B8.1–2/D8.6–7—"a single utterance of road is still left: that Is" (*hōs estin*)—*esti* is propositional content in and of itself; in fact, it is the only true propositional content. Syntax falls away. Or rather, *esti* absorbs all syntax into itself. Containing within itself its own subject (in the third-person singular form) and its own predicate ("is" = "is real/true"), *esti* is a complete grammatical sentence. Moreover, as Kahn suggests, in its collapsing of existence and predication the verb enacts the ideal correspondence between signifier and signified, word and world, that is the foundation of language as a whole.[39] *Esti* simultaneously transcends language and sublimates it as a pure *logos* of *to on*.

Via this linguistic *Aufhebung*, Parmenides's Is appears to escape the mire of metaphor. Metaphor trades in the slippage between signifier and signified, transferring a signifier (say, *hodos*) from its proper signified (a road) to define something else (like a philosophical inquiry). Thus, as Derrida says, every metaphor conveys "philosophy's *unique thesis*": that reality can be separated from its expression, the signified from its signifier, *einai* from *legein*.[40] With his *esti*, Parmenides refuses the metaphoric thesis. Both expressing and enacting that refusal, *esti* functions as a signifier of Parmenides's dream of a nonmetaphorical or antimetaphorical language of metaphysics. *Esti* is: the ultimate fantasy of *onto-logy*.[41]

But that fantasy is fragile. *Esti* is supposed to name a reality that is unitary, singular, and unchanging, wholly and eternally present. But the verb itself is subject to the same doubling, negation, and polysemy as all language. For one thing, it seems to have a synonym. In five instances Parmenides uses the verb *pelenai* as a substitute for *einai* with no clearly discernible difference in meaning.[42] This substitute not only replaces *esti* but also constitutes one of its necessary qualities:

38. On the temporality of Parmenides's *esti,* see Tarán 1965, 175–88, 1979; Schofield 1970; Stokes 1971, 128–31; Owen 1974; O'Brien 1980; Sorabji 1983, 99–108, 128–30; Gallop 1984, 13–14; Mourelatos 2008c, 103–11; and Couloubaritsis (2008, 297–342), who emphasizes the absolute present of *Eon* (which he translates "What is in the present"); cf. Alcocer Urueta 2023.

39. Kahn 1973, 227.

40. Derrida 1982b, 229. In Mourelatos's understanding of Parmenides's *esti* as "the copula of speculative predication" (X *is really* Y), the verb functions like a metaphor as "the conveyer to the reality of a thing" (2008c, 51–60; the quotation is on p. 59). Thus Is "is *essentially* a route; it is not a route by poetic license" (134). He does not take the further step of connecting *Esti* to metaphor in general, although his idiom of transport and conveyance (2008c, 61, 134–35; 2008a, 349) suggests the connection. Literalized in "Is," not just the metaphor of the route but metaphor *tout court* is left by the wayside.

41. See the suggestive comment of Morgan (2000, 85): "At the heart of the goddess' revelation lies the dream of language denying itself, an unshaken kernel where Being is uniform and there is no distance between the referring word and that to which it refers."

42. For example in the criticism of mortals "for whom to be (*pelenai*) and not to be (*einai*) are considered the same thing" (B6.8/D7.8). Cf. B8.18/D8.23, B8.45/D8.50, and possibly B8.19/D8.24, although the text is disputed. The verb is not used accidentally. *Pelenai* is etymologically connected to *teleō* (to turn) and thus to the perfect completeness of Being as sphere (*tetelesmenon,* B8.42/D8.47; cf.

so we hear of Being that "it is necessary either that it be (*pelenai*) entirely or not [be]" (B8.11/D8.16). Singular Being has a double name: *einai* and *pelenai*. *Esti* is itself *poluphēmos*.

This doubleness divides *esti*. Throughout the poem, forms of *einai* proliferate and the meaning of the verb shifts and slides. As a result, the word's every occurrence is the object of divergent and contested readings.[43] Kahn offers a neat taxonomy of the eighty-nine occurrences of the verb "to be" in Parmenides's extant fragments, dividing them into "the strong or ontological use" and "ordinary uses" (like the copular or predicative).[44] But in every instance "ontological" *esti* is at risk of dissolving back into the "ordinary" verb—not "Is" (reality itself) but just "is," a garden-variety linking verb. The opening lines of B8 are typical.

μόνος δ' ἔτι μῦθος ὁδοῖο
λείπεται ὡς ἔστιν· ταύτηι δ' ἐπὶ σήματ' ἔασι
πολλὰ μάλ', ὡς ἀγένητον ἐὸν καὶ ἀνώλεθρόν ἐστιν,
ἐστι γὰρ οὐλομελές τε καὶ ἀτρεμὲς ἠδ' ἀτέλεστον. (B8.1–4/D8.6–9)[45]

A single utterance of road is still left:
that Is (*estin*). And there are (*easi*) very many signs along this road,
that being (*eon*) ungenerated, it is (*estin*) also indestructible,
for it is (*esti*) whole-limbed and untrembling and without end.

"Is" in the second line is *esti* in Kahn's ontological sense: it is a strong statement of Parmenides's commitment to a reality that can be fully accessed in speech and a speech that can fully access it. But the same verb in the third-person plural (*easi*) inserts *sēmata* between that reality and its expression. Can these signs be said to "be" in the same way that Being itself "is," or does the same verb signify different existential conditions? These *sēmata* show, in the third line, that Is, "being ungenerated, is also indestructible." In the ambiguous grammar of this line, *eon* and *estin* both seem to function as copulae, connecting "Is" to its defining predicates, "ungenerated" and "indestructible." But an alternative reading of the line might take *estin* as predicative and the participle *eon* as ontological ("that being [*eon*, i.e. because it truly is], it is [*estin*] ungenerated and indestructible"); or, more strongly, *estin* as predicative and *eon* as substantive ("that Being [*eon*] is [*estin*] ungenerated and indestructible"); or, stronger still, *eon* as predicative and *estin* as

B8.4/D8.9, B8.32/D8.37). But as Tor (2023b, 266–67) and Alcocer Urueta (2023, 177–78) observe, it also introduces a sense of motion and change at odds with the fixity of What Is.

43. Gallop (1984) registers this aporia: beneath his functional translation, Gallop includes multiple alternative translations of disputed lines, an editorial decision unparalleled in the Phoenix Presocratics series. See also Tarán 1965. The signifier that promises to unify language and being instead throws their relation into crisis.

44. Kahn 2009, 187–91.

45. I print Diels's *monos* in the first line. Sider (1985, 365–66) argues for the epic form *mounos*, which Parmenides uses elsewhere. This would preclude running B8 into B7 (as Laks-Most do in D8).

ontological ("that being [*eon*] ungenerated and indestructible, it Is [*estin*])." Only the will of the translator differentiates the numinous "Is" from an ordinary linking verb, with its different numbers (*easi*, B8.2/D8.7) and tenses (*ēn*, *estai*, B8.5/D8.10). Untrembling *esti* trembles.[46]

This slippage between the ontological and copular is a challenge for the metaphysics of Parmenides's Is. First, copular *esti* is prone to disappear. Since Greek does not need an expressed linking verb in order to convey predication, *esti* can always be omitted. This possibility is illustrated in the final line of the passage above: in Diels-Kranz's text (*esti gar oulomeles*) the repetition of *esti* in the two strongest line positions at the end of line 3 and beginning of line 4 makes an insistent claim for the being of Being, a claim supported by but independent of its various predicates. But an alternative reading of line 4 has *oulon mounogenes* ("whole, single-born") without *esti*.[47] On the former reading, *esti* forcefully asserts Parmenides's ontology as the true signifier of Being. On the latter, *esti* evanesces, absorbed into syntax, and Being itself is replaced by its predicate. This points to a second problem, for even if copular *esti* is expressed, predication doubles the singularity of Being. Being is one (*hen*, B8.6/D8.11), but as Plato already observed, to say this is to say it is two things, Being and one.[48] Plato's observation turns every predication into a metaphor, importing an alien meaning and dividing proper identity: predicated, Being is both itself and something else. This problem is compounded in this passage by the emphatically negative form of the predicates: ungenerated, indestructible, untrembling, and unending. These predicates insinuate the impossible, unspeakable Is Not into the very definition of Is, troubling the word's pure presence and positivity. Is *is not* what it is not.[49]

46. Cassin 1998, 46. She tracks a trajectory in the poem from *esti* to *to eon*, the substantive identity or "proper name" of Being (the participle without the article in this passage marks a medial stage). But *to eon* is subject to the same slippages as *esti*: to doubling and division (B4.2/D10.2), to negation (B2.7/D6.7), to negative predication (B8.32–33/D8.37–38).

47. The former (Diels-Kranz's text) is the reading of Plut. *Adv. Col.* 1114C; the latter (printed by Tarán, Gallop, Laks-Most) that of Clem. Al. *Strom* 5.112.2; Simpl. *in Cael.* p. 556, *in Phys.* p. 29 (DE), p. 120 (D), p. 145 (E). Other emendations are collected by Gallop (1984, ad loc.) and discussed by Tarán (1965, 88–93); and Sider (forthcoming, ad loc.).

48. Pl. *Soph.* 244b–d. Tarán 1965, 193: "To say 'Being is X' would be tantamount to admitting the reality of difference, which difference from Being could be for Parmenides only non-Being and non-Being is for him inconceivable." He sees the negative predicates as denying difference, but if so they reinscribe it in the very process. Tor (2023b, 252–55) offers an intelligent critique of the Platonic objection, which he argues rests on too restrictive an understanding of Parmenides's monism.

49. Again, the problem manifests in the text. At the end of the fourth line Diels-Kranz print *ēd' ateleston* ("and unending"), but this seems to contradict Parmenides's insistence at B8.32/D8.37 that Being is "not unending" (*ouk ateleutēton*), and editors have suggested various emendations including *ēde teleston* ("and complete"), *ēde teleion* ("and perfect"), and *oud' ateleston* ("and not unending"). The predicate destabilizes the text of Being such that its own proper qualities become uncertain and contradictory.

The metaphor of the path seems to carry us decisively out of the poetic proem, with its branching and multivalent *hodos poluphēmos*, and onto the terrain of ontology, where *logos* unites with *to on* in a sublimity of the real and true. Forcefully prohibiting the impossible detour into Is Not and the wandering of Doxa, the goddess insists that we follow the single remaining "utterance of road" (*muthos hodoio*), and readers have generally obeyed her command, traveling a unidirectional ascent from duality to unity, from physics to metaphysics, and from the doubleness and duplicity of human language to the univocal true *logos* of Being. And yet if Parmenides's path does suggest such an ascent, it misleads, because like Hegel's *Aufhebung* it retains what it cancels: negativity, doubleness, polyvalence. Indeed, the new landscape resembles the old so much that we might wonder whether the straight road has merely brought us back to where we began (a circle to which we will circle back at the end of the chapter). Perhaps the authoritative *muthos hodoio* glossed as "Is" is, after all, just a myth consisting of a metaphor. The thesis (or metaphor) of language as a Wittgensteinian ladder supposes that the destination can be separated from the journey, the philosophical *telos* from the linguistic process by which it is reached. This is, of course, the thesis of metaphor itself: that ideas can be separated from the image that "conveys" them. But that metaphorical thesis, itself conveyed metaphorically, merely reproduces metaphoricity *en abyme*, as Derrida proposes.[50] However far it goes and however undeviating the path, then, metaphysics cannot escape metaphor. Parmenides's road is a metaphor of that futile attempt.

BOUNDS OF BONDS

If with his novel language of "Is" Parmenides attempts to sublate *logos* as Being, he also exploits metaphorical language to secure that sublime Being. With the recurring metaphor of Anankē's bonds or bounds, Parmenides strives to subordinate *logos* to *to on*, to ensure that metaphor works in the service of metaphysics, faithfully articulating its essential truths. And yet, as we shall see, these images also have a truth of their own: the metaphor of bonds does not merely describe a preexisting and always-existing substance but instead secures its substantiality, defining its very essence. A necessary supplement to Being's totality, the origin of a Being without origin and limit of a Being with no beyond, the metaphor deployed to stabilize Being consistently destabilizes and deontologizes it, showing again and again that *To Eon* requires *logos* to achieve its innate form. Necessity's bonds of bounds are thus the tie that binds—and unbinds—Parmenides's ontological project as a whole.

The metaphor of bounds/bonds appears multiple times in the poem in slightly different configurations. We find the image first at B8.13–15/D8.18–20 where Dikē (Justice) is said to hold *To Eon* in her fetters (*pedēisin*), not slackening them so as

50. Derrida 1982b, 262.

to allow it to be born or die. The image of bondage recurs at B8.26–33/D8.31–38. There we first get Being "unmoving in bounds of great bonds" (*en peirasi desmōn*) and then, four lines later, mighty Anankē (Necessity) holding Being "in bonds of a boundary (*peiratos en desmoisin*), which confine it all around." There are three more echoes toward the end of the Aletheia in the references to the bondage of Moira (Fate) at B8.37/D8.42 (*Moir' epedēsen*) and the boundaries of the sphere of Being at B8.42/D8.47 (*peiras*) and B8.49/D8.54 (*peirasi*). Finally, in B10.6–7/D12.6–7 the image recurs in the physical world, where Anankē is said to have bound (*epedēsen*) the heavens so that they have "boundaries" (*peirat[a]*) of stars.

This network of images connects binding and bounding, both literal and figurative, physical and metaphysical. *Desmos* is concrete: it denotes an implement for tying or attaching, and in the plural *desma*, bonds or chains or (by metonymy) imprisonment. It is thus semantically close to the *pedai*, fetters or shackles, that appear at B8.14/D8.19 and (in the verbal form *pedaō*) at B8.37/D8.42 and B10.6/D12.6. *Peiras* denotes an end or limit, both in a concrete local sense of a geographical boundary and in a more abstract sense of completion or consummation.[51] The two words are joined in two mirroring phrases: "in boundaries of bonds" (*en peirasi desmōn*, B8.26/D8.31) and "in bonds of a boundary" (*peiratos in desmoisin*, B8.31/D8.36). A. H. Coxon complains that the former makes no sense "since it treats the image as prior and the concept which it illustrates as secondary."[52] Indeed, Parmenides's apparent indifference to the order of the phrase makes it surprisingly difficult to segregate image and concept or to decide which has priority, the metaphysical limits of Being or the metaphorical chains by which it is bound.

On first view, that decision would seem simple. For Parmenides, Being is bounded: this is one of its primordial qualities.[53] Rejecting the indistinct *apeiron* of Anaximander, Parmenides envisions Being as perfect because it is complete (*tetelesmenon*, B8.42/D8.47). It is delimited by nature, although its limit is purely conceptual, not spatial. That limit is internal to it, not something separate or extrinsic; and it is "furthest" or "ultimate" (*pumaton*, B8.42/D8.47), encompassing

51. In Homer it can mean a tackle or rope, and Coxon (2009, 72) translates it so at B8.26/D8.31: "in the coils of huge bonds." But it seems clear from B8.42/D8.47, B8.49/D8.54 that Parmenides uses it at least sometimes in the broader sense, and Coxon (74) takes it thus at B8.31/D8.36: "in the bondage of a limit." I agree with Mourelatos (2008c, 28): "It is probably correct to visualize the polymorph deity as engaged in 'binding' with every occurrence of the word πεῖρας in the text."

52. Coxon 2009, 327. This, as we shall see, is precisely the challenge of this metaphor.

53. Cassin 1998, 55. This is in marked contrast to Melissus, who adopts Parmenides's monadic Being but predicates its singularity on its boundlessness (B2–6/D3–7). The question of Being's spatial extension poses "a puzzling choice between a literal and a metaphorical interpretation of 'limit'" (Kirk, Raven, and Schofield 1983, 253). As they note, if the limits are spatial, Being must have an outside and Parmenides is to be condemned for "his apparently uncritical exploitation of the metaphor of limit (i.e. of what we would take to be a metaphor)" (254). See also Tarán 1965, 115–19; Gallop 1984, 18; and Sedley 1999, 117–19. For Owen (1960, 100) this is where Parmenides's thought comes up against the limits of his expressive resources; cf. Fränkel 1975, 35.

everything that is, a closed sphere with no outside. Thus Parmenides insists on the boundaries of Is but also insists that there is nothing beyond those boundaries—only the impossible, limitless indeterminacy of Is Not.

The binding metaphors in B8/D8 are generally read as a vivid figurative expression of Being's determinate totality, a heuristic device Parmenides uses to convey both this paradoxical boundedness and its ontological necessity. A metaphor wielded by a personification, this conspicuously poetic figure seems to belong to the world of *doxa*. The goddesses Anankē, Moira, and Dikē, who appear—apparently interchangeably—as bearers of the bonds/bounds, are akin to the "much-punishing" Dikē who in the proem holds the keys to the double gate of Night and Day (B1.14/D4.14) and the mysterious feminine *daimōn* who in B12/D14 stands at the center of the cosmos and "directs all things" (*panta kubernāi*, B12.3/D14.3), both of them residents of our physical world. The goddesses' multiple names or identities and even their gender likewise associate them with the binarisms and polysemy of human *doxa*.[54] The deontological deities of B8/D8 also work in close association with the goddess who directs the poem's exposition and embodies its argumentative force: they encircle and constrain Being (*amphis eergei*, B8.31/D8.36) in the same way as that goddess encircles truth (*amphis alētheiēs*, B8.51/D8.56) and constrains (*eirgō*, B6.3/D7.3; *eirge*, B7.2/D8.2) the *kouros* in his journey to it.

Affiliated with the act of poetic enunciation but standing within the pure realm of Being, Anankē and her sisters may be read as personifications of metaphor itself. With their vivid imagery, they help ferry us mortals across the conceptual divide from our everyday world of phenomena, opinions, and names to the abstract register of reality, that mysterious world of *Esti* and *To Eon*. But Anankē not only transports us imaginatively to that metaphysical realm; as we shall see, she also acts in and upon it, imposing her force on it and shaping it from within. Metaphor dwells within the halls of metaphysics, simultaneously preserving Being and contaminating its unadulterated essence, introducing multiplicity and difference.[55]

The image of Anankē's bonds/bounds is connected in B8/D8 to the necessity of Being and of its intrinsic qualities. Binding images are often associated with Anankē in archaic Greek, as Heinz Schreckenberg has shown, as well as with Moira and Dikē.[56] Through the concrete imagery of physical bondage they

54. Aëtius identifies them as different names for the same deity (A32/R55a, A37/D15a), followed by Mourelatos 2008c, 26, 160–63; and Coxon 2009, 280–81.

55. The ontological status of these goddesses is a bedeviled question. Couloubaritsis (2008, 66) puts the problem succinctly: if they are real, then there is something besides Being; if they are fictional, Being risks resting on a fiction. Tor (2023b, 261–65) situates them within a larger tension between Parmenides's doctrine of Being and the human language in which he describes it. Cf. Morgan 2000, 81–87; and Cherubin 2018.

56. Schreckenberg 1964; see also Onians 1951, 310–42. Binding may be part of *anankē*'s etymology: Chantraine (1968, 83) suggests derivation from *anankōn* ("take in the arms"). Cassin (1998, 57, 151) develops this association, connecting *anankē* to the image of the sphere as circle.

represent the constraint of the inevitable. Parmenides reinforces this metaphoric connection by the presence of Anankē, Moira, and Dikē, divine personifications of necessity. These deities are shadowed by their nonpersonified avatars *anankē, moira, themis,* and *dikē* (B8.16/D8.21, B1.26–28/D4.26–28), and are also closely associated with the abstract expression *khreōn estin* or *khrē*, by which Parmenides denotes the necessity or propriety of Being's unqualified existence (B8.11/D8.16) and of its essential characteristics (ungenerated, B8.9/D8.14; thinkable, B6.1/D7.1; homogeneous, B8.45/D8.50).[57] Via the oscillation of majuscule and minuscule, Necessity and her chains would seem to be a simple personification, a poetic elaboration, of the abstract metaphysical necessities of Being.

And yet, the very presence of this personified Necessity might make us wonder about the binding force of Being's supposedly inherent qualities. Consider the first instance of the image at B8.7–15/D8.12–20.

> πῆι πόθεν αὐξηθέν; οὐδ' ἐκ μὴ ἐόντος ἐάσσω
> φάσθαι σ' οὐδὲ νοεῖν· οὐ γὰρ φατὸν οὐδὲ νοητόν
> ἔστιν ὅπως οὐκ ἔστι. τί δ' ἄν μιν καὶ χρέος ὦρσεν
> ὕστερον ἢ πρόσθεν, τοῦ μηδενὸς ἀρξάμενον, φῦν;
> οὕτως ἢ πάμπαν πελέναι χρεών ἐστιν ἢ οὐχί.
> οὐδέ ποτ' ἐκ μὴ ἐόντος ἐφήσει πίστιος ἰσχύς
> γίγνεσθαί τι παρ' αὐτό· τοῦ εἵνεκεν οὔτε γενέσθαι
> οὔτ' ὄλλυσθαι ἀνῆκε Δίκη χαλάσασα πέδῃσιν,
> ἀλλ' ἔχει.

> How did it grow, from what? Not from Nonbeing: I will not allow
> you to say or to think that, for it cannot be said or thought
> that it is not. What need could have impelled it to grow,
> either later or sooner, if it began from nothing?
> Thus it must either be entirely or not be.
> Nor out of Nonbeing will force of conviction ever let
> anything be born beside it [Being]. For this reason,
> Justice has not loosened her bonds and let it be born or die,
> but she holds it.

Just prior to this we were told that Being is unborn and undying (B8.3/D8.8). This is part of its primary essence—indeed, these are its first two defining predicates. That essence is reasserted in this passage as a matter of necessity, both ontological and logical, in accordance with Parmenides's conflation of reality and truth (discussed in the last section). The innate necessity of Being's ungenerated state

57. See Palmer (2009, 360–61) on the challenge of distinguishing common nouns from proper names in Parmenides. *Khrē* also expresses the impossibility of Nonbeing (B2.5/D6.5), as well as the obligatory path toward perceiving the difference between the two (B1.28/D4.28, B1.32/D4.32, B8.54/D8.59). Mourelatos and Pulpito (2018) show that *khrē*- words in Parmenides connote necessity as propriety. Palmer (2009) views the necessity of Is as the essence of its being: it is what is and must be, in contrast to the contingent things of *doxa*.

is sustained by the logical argumentation that is often considered Parmenides's signal philosophical contribution: since one cannot point to a necessity for its generation (*ti . . . khreos*, B8.9/D8.14) it is therefore a necessary conclusion (*houtōs . . . khreōn*) that Being be entirely. Aligned so closely with Being's own necessities, logical reasoning takes on a deontological force of its own, a *pistios iskhus* or "force of conviction" (B8.12/D8.17). The many causal conjunctions form a logical chain around Being.[58] The goddess adds her forceful command to this double necessity: she will not allow us to say or think that Being is generated from Nonbeing, "for it cannot be said or thought." Dikē with her fetters brings up the rear. Her prohibition (*out' . . . anēke*) picks up that of *pistios iskhus* (*ephēsei*), and *tou heineken* ("for this reason") makes her causally subsequent to those prior forms of necessity. If necessity is really necessary, though, then Dikē's fetters would seem surplus to requirement, a tertiary backup to the necessities that inhere within Is as part of its essential nature and the logical exposition of that nature.

We see the same dynamic at B8.26–33/D8.31–38.

> αὐτὰρ ἀκίνητον μεγάλων ἐν πείρασι δεσμῶν
> ἔστιν ἄναρχον ἄπαυστον, ἐπεὶ γένεσις καὶ ὄλεθρος
> τῆλε μάλ' ἐπλάχθησαν, ἀπῶσε δὲ πίστις ἀληθής.
> ταὐτόν τ' ἐν ταὐτῶι τε μένον καθ' ἑαυτό τε κεῖται
> χοὔτως ἔμπεδον αὖθι μένει· κρατερὴ γὰρ Ἀνάγκη
> πείρατος ἐν δεσμοῖσιν ἔχει, τό μιν ἀμφὶς ἐέργει
> οὕνεκεν οὐκ ἀτελεύτητον τὸ ἐὸν θέμις εἶναι·
> ἔστι γὰρ οὐκ ἐπιδευές· [μὴ] ἐὸν δ' ἂν παντὸς ἐδεῖτο.

> Moreover, unmoving in bounds of great bonds
> it is without beginning or end, since birth and death
> have wandered far off: true conviction thrust them away.
> Remaining the same and in the same place it lies by itself
> and thus remains fixed there, for mighty Necessity
> holds it in bonds of a boundary, which confines it all around;
> for this reason it is not right that Being be imperfect.
> For it is not lacking; if it were, it would lack for everything.

At the beginning of this passage, the bonds/bounds belong to Being itself. The phrase seems like an extension of the predicates (*akinēton, anarkhon, apauston*), an expression of Being's unalterable nature. Again this ontological necessity is buttressed by the force of logical argumentation, the *pistis alēthēs* which, like *pistios iskhus* in the previous passage, precludes the logical possibility of birth and death. The bounds/bonds come into Anankē's hands at B8.30–31/D8.35–36. As in B8.7–15/D8.12–20, this divine personification seems to be a mere supplement to Being's

58. Mourelatos (2008c, 3) notes that Parmenides uses *gar* "almost to the point of obsession." He offers a clear explication of the logic of this passage (94–111). See also the detailed analysis of Evans (2021), with careful consideration of the causal role of Dikē/Anankē.

own immanent necessity and the logical conclusions that entails. But again we might ask why Being—or Parmenides—needs this superfluous deity. Are their own necessities, ontological and logical, not binding enough?

A supplement to Being's totality, an extraneous element it requires to be complete and whole in itself, this metaphor calls into question the primacy and force of supposedly metaphysical necessities. Further, the metaphor may even precede and produce those necessities. At B8.13–14/D8.18–19 Dikē's bondage is the consequence of Being's ungenerated state: "For this reason (*tou heineken*), Justice has not loosened her bonds." But at B8.30/D8.35 the causality is reversed: it is because (*gar*) mighty Anankē enchains Being that it is autonomous and unmoving, not the other way around. Further, it is because (*houneken*) Anankē encloses Being on all sides that it is not right (*themis*) for it to be unbounded (B8.32/D8.37).[59] If the deity's bondage is the cause of Being's necessities and not just its consequence, we cannot write the image off as a mere heuristic device or rhetorical elaboration. Instead, the metaphor actively shapes the metaphysical realm; it becomes the origin of the condition without origin that it is enlisted to describe.

If Necessity's bonds are necessary to determine Being's immanent qualities, then those qualities are not actually immanent and Is is not essentially or inevitably what it is. Nor can the ontology of Is be secured by the chain of Parmenides's logic, for not only is that logic contradictory, as we just saw; its persuasive force—*pistios iskhus* (B8.12/D8.17) and *pistis alēthēs* (B8.28/D8.33)—is itself a personification, another poetic fiction that grounds the metaphysical realities it purports merely to express.[60] Anankē's intervention thus challenges the very necessity she seems designed to enforce by raising the unthinkable possibility that Being, in all its autotelic perfection, is the effect—not the cause—of the metaphor that encircles it.

The metaphor of Anankē's bounds/bonds makes *To Eon* what it is and must be. But in the process it deontologizes it, undermining both its necessity and its very being. The goddess's bounds/bonds hold Being together, rendering it whole, coherent, and indivisible. Both Anankē and Dikē are said to "hold" Being (*ekhein*, B8.15/

59. Gallop 1984, 36n50: it is uncertain whether *houneka* means "because" or "therefore," "and consequently whether the subject's not being 'incomplete' is a premiss for the preceding statement or an inference from it." He translates "wherefore" (cf. Mourelatos 2008c, 121n18). *Tou heineken* at B8.13/D8.18 clearly makes the impossibility of something being born of nothing (*tou* refers to the prohibition of *pistios iskhus*) the final cause of Dikē's hold: "therefore" (Coxon, Gallop); "that is why" (Laks-Most). Evans (2021, 3–13) notes the unexpected causal relations in these passages and draws a similar conclusion, that Anankē binds Being itself, not merely trustworthy claims (Mourelatos 2008c, 25–28, 151–62) or inquiry (Cherubin 2004) about it.

60. At B8.12/D8.17 *pistios iskhus* "will not allow" Being's generation; at B8.28/D8.33 *pistis alēthēs* "thrust it away." The former is loosely correlated with Being's ungenerated nature (*oude*), but the latter is the cause (*epei*) of that nature. We might also notice the dramatization of logic in the dialogue of question and answer at B8.7–11/D8.12–16, B8.19–20/D8.24–25. These questions are rhetorical but also continue the dialogue between goddess and *kouros* that structures the poem as a whole.

D8.20, B8.31/D8.36; cf. B10.5/D12.5, B10.7/D12.7).[61] Their embrace would seem to reinforce Being's inherent coherence, literalizing the adjective *sunekhes* that is one of the primary predicates of *To Eon*: "now it is whole all together, one, coherent" (*nun estin homou pan, hen, sunekhes*, B8.5–6/D8.10–11; cf. B8.25/D8.30). Its coherence is a property of its singularity and unity: because Being is one and whole it is "holding together" (*sun-ekhes*), with no internal intervals or disjunction.

But of course the prefix *sun-* and the concept of coherence logically apply only to something with parts, that is, something that is fundamentally *not* one. This paradox is elaborated in B4/D10. This fragment may contain the first occurrence in the poem of the term *to eon*, the substantive participle that Barbara Cassin calls the "proper name" of Being.[62] If so, in its first appearance, unified Being is polyform.

> λεῦσσε δ' ὅμως ἀπεόντα νόωι παρεόντα βεβαίως·
> οὐ γὰρ ἀποτμήξει τὸ ἐὸν τοῦ ἐόντος ἔχεσθαι
> οὔτε σκιδνάμενον πάντηι πάντως κατὰ κόσμον
> οὔτε συνιστάμενον. (B4/D10)

> See these things that though absent are securely present to the mind.
> For you will not sever being from holding onto being,
> neither scattered in every way everywhere throughout the cosmos
> nor gathered together.

Being cleaves to being. The diction of containment elsewhere associated with Anankē is here internal to *To Eon* itself, and its violence is shifted from the force that contains Being to the force that would be required to sunder it: *apotmēgō* is used in Homer of severed body parts. But even as the goddess declares that schism impossible it is happening at the level of grammar, as *To Eon* is split between nominative and genitive, the subject and object of *ekhesthai*. The violent syntactical severance is replicated by semantic severance in the first line's pluralization of Being and its scission into presence (*pareonta*) and absence (*apeonta*). The very denial of disunity bespeaks its possibility. *To Eon* cleaves to itself (*ekhesthai*) precisely against that possibility of cleavage.

We find the same irony at B8.22–25/D8.27–30.

> οὐδὲ διαιρετόν ἐστιν, ἐπεὶ πᾶν ἐστιν ὁμοῖον·
> οὐδέ τι τῆι μᾶλλον, τό κεν εἴργοι μιν συνέχεσθαι,

61. One of the most common verbs in the Greek language, *ekhein* is used relatively sparingly in Parmenides and almost never in the typical sense of "to have." Being cannot have anything, because that would require positing something separate from Being but equally real. Instead, *ekhein* occurs in the context of the image we are examining, in the sense of "to hold," and with the goddess as its subject. The exceptions prove the rule: the verb means "to possess" at B16.1–2/D51.1–2 and B10.7/D12.7, both in relation to the phenomenal world. This bland verb thus encodes a philosophical thesis (as Derrida puts it) about the unity and coherence of *To Eon* and its difference from phenomena.

62. Cassin 1998, 39. She believes this fragment followed B8/D8 (Cassin 1998, 214–17), as do Laks-Most.

οὐδέ τι χειρότερον, πᾶν δ' ἔμπλεόν ἐστιν ἐόντος.
τῶι ξυνεχὲς πᾶν ἐστιν· ἐὸν γὰρ ἐόντι πελάζει.

Nor is it divisible, since it is all similar;
it is not at all more in this place, which would prevent it from cohering,
nor at all less, but it is all full of being.
Therefore it is all cohesive, for being draws near to being.

Being is "all similar" (*pan estin homoion*, B8.22/D8.27): there is no internal difference to prevent it from holding together. As in B4/D10, the act of containment (*sunekhesthai*) is not Anankē's but Being's own, but the goddess's presence is felt in the verb *eirgoi* in B8.23/D8.28: the same verb is used at B8.31/D8.36 of Necessity, who holds (*ekhei*) Being "in bonds of a boundary that confines (*eergei*) it all around." As in the previous passage, force is located not in the bond that holds *To Eon* together but in the futile attempt to sever it. But again, what prevents Being from fully cohering is the language that describes that coherence: *Eon* draws near to *Eon*, it is full of *Eon*. Both subject and object, container and contained, *Eon* is linguistically divided and doubled in a way that undermines its ontological singularity and wholeness. Perhaps it is significant that Anankē is not explicitly present in these two passages. Without her metaphorical chains, Being falls apart. Far from a supplementary articulation of a primary ontological coherence, it starts to look like Anankē's metaphorical chains are all that hold Being together.[63]

If Anankē holds Being together she also holds it apart, segregating and protecting it from Nonbeing. In fact, the preposition *amphis*, which I have been translating "around," can also mean "separate"; thus the same bonds that "confine Being all around" (*amphis eeirge*, B8.31/D8.36) also hold it in sublime isolation. Parmenides, as we have seen, embraces the paradox of determination without negation, a determinate presence unshadowed by absence. Is *is* in its opposition to Is Not: "The choice (*krisis*) lies in this: Is or Is Not" (B8.15–16/D8.20–21). But Is Not *is not*: unthinkable and unnamable, it has no reality (B8.17/D8.22; cf. B2.5–8/D6.5–8). Necessity herself presides over the verdict governing the critical distinction between them (*kekritai d'oun, hōsper anankē*, B8.16/D8.21). And yet in the very process of enforcing this crucial opposition, her bonds sustain and substantiate the negativity to which the poem denies substance. B7/D8 begins:

οὐ γὰρ μήποτε τοῦτο δαμῆι εἶναι μὴ ἐόντα·
ἀλλὰ σὺ τῆσδ' ἀφ' ὁδοῦ διζήσιος εἶργε νόημα
μηδέ σ' ἔθος πολύπειρον ὁδὸν κατὰ τήνδε βιάσθω.

Never let this prevail (*damēi*): that things that are not be.
But you restrain your thought from this route of inquiry,
and do not let the habit of much experience force you down this route.

63. Tor 2023b, 264–65 notes a similar tension in regard to B8.34–41/D8.39–46 between Being's innate indivisibility and the bonds of Moira, whose very name suggests division; cf. Cherubin 2017, 258.

Damēi, to break or tame, subdue or dominate, establishes a hypothetical struggle between Being and Nonbeing over the latter's existence.[64] That potential existence is negated the moment it is thought, yet that thought still needs to be forcibly avoided (*eirge*) and the thinker protected from the "habit of much experience" (that is, *doxa*) that would force (*biasthō*) him to think it. The goddess responds vigorously to the threat of Nonbeing's violence. She does not wield the bonds herself in this passage but commands the *kouros* to constrain himself and resist the very thought that Nonbeing might someday (*mēpote*) dominate so as to claim a being for itself. The violence of the language suggests a contest between the goddess and Nonbeing waged on the field of the philosopher's character (*ethos*) and thought (*noēma*).

But it is not only the philosopher who must be protected from this assault of negativity. At B8.48/D8.53, the sphere of Being is described as "inviolate" (*asulon*) in its internal uniformity and homogeneity:

> οὔτε γὰρ οὐκ ἐὸν ἔστι, τό κεν παύοι μιν ἱκνεῖσθαι
> εἰς ὁμόν, οὔτ' ἐὸν ἔστιν ὅπως εἴη κεν ἐόντος
> τῆι μᾶλλον τῆι δ' ἧσσον, ἐπεὶ πᾶν ἐστιν ἄσυλον·
> οἷ γὰρ πάντοθεν ἶσον, ὁμῶς ἐν πείρασι κύρει. (B8.46–49/D8.51–54)
>
> For neither is there Nonbeing that could stop it from reaching
> its like, nor is there any way that, being, it could be
> more being here and less there, since as a whole it is inviolate.
> For equal to itself from all sides, it reaches likewise to its boundaries.

The verb *sulaō* denotes violation or violent deprivation. If Nonbeing were to exist it would prevent Being from achieving total uniformity and in this way would despoil it of its perfect wholeness. Again Anankē is absent, but we get her telltale diction: Being extends to its limits in all directions (*homōs en peirasi kurei*, B8.49/D8.54), unmixed and uninterrupted up to its ultimate limit (*peiras pumaton*, B8.42/D8.47). Contained within its boundaries, Being is safe against the depredation of Nonbeing. Without those encircling *peirata*, Nonbeing's being would negate the negation (*a-sulon*) that makes Being inviolable and insinuate itself forcibly within the walls of Is. *To Eon* would become a heterogeneous mix of Is and Is Not, something Parmenides declares impossible and unthinkable. But in defending against this horror, the imagery grants Is Not a potential (though negated) force and effectivity that the poem as a whole vehemently repudiates.[65]

64. Used for breaking wild animals, *damnēmi* may connote the same sort of violent constraint as Anankē's fetters: Chantraine (1968, 250) defines it as "réduire par la contrainte"; see also Schreckenberg 1964, 1–6, 106–109. This struggle is reinforced by the phrase *poludērin elenkhon* ("testing with much strife") at B7.5/D8.5, discussed by Lesher (1984).

65. The assault of Nonbeing on Being's integrity is dramatically enacted in the triple repetition of line-initial negations in the passages that assert Being's indivisibility (B4.2–4/D10.2–4, B8.22–24/D8.27–29). The metaphor also forecloses the possibility of Nonbeing's generativity. B8/D8 insists that Is

In this ambivalent fashion, the metaphor mediates Parmenides's paradox of determination without negation, in a single gesture repudiating Nonbeing and reproducing it as Being's constitutive outside. Moira's bonds ensure that *ouden gar <ē> estin ē estai allo parex tou eontos* (B8.36–37/D8.41–42): simultaneously, depending on the translation, that "there is or will be nothing else (*ouden . . . allo*) outside of Being" and that "Nothing (*ouden*) is or will be, something else (*allo*) outside of Being."[66]

The goddess's fetters hold Being together; they hold it apart. Finally, they also hold it in place, preventing movement, alteration, becoming. *Doxai* wander and change; without determinate *peirata*, they "pass (*perōnta*) entirely through everything" (B1.32/D4.32). Being, by contrast, is "unmoving in bounds of great bonds" (*akinēton megalōn en peirasi desmōn*, B8.26/D8.31). *Akinēton*, it can neither change nor move.[67]

> ταὐτόν τ' ἐν ταὐτῶι τε μένον καθ' ἑαυτό τε κεῖται
> χοὔτως ἔμπεδον αὖθι μένει· κρατερὴ γὰρ Ἀνάγκη
> πείρατος ἐν δεσμοῖσιν ἔχει, τό μιν ἀμφὶς ἐέργει,
> οὕνεκεν οὐκ ἀτελεύτητον τὸ ἐὸν θέμις εἶναι·
> ἔστι γὰρ οὐκ ἐπιδευές· [μὴ] ἐὸν δ' ἂν παντὸς ἐδεῖτο. (B8.29–33/D8.34–38)

> Remaining the same and in the same place it lies by itself
> and thus remains fixed there, for mighty Necessity
> holds it in bonds of a boundary, which confines it all around;
> for this reason it is not right that Being be imperfect.
> For it is not lacking; if it were, it would lack for everything.

Parmenides's immobile Being may be modeled on Xenophanes's god, who "always remains in the same place, not moving at all" (Xenoph. B26/D19). But while Xenophanes's *theos* holds himself still—he can make everything tremble without moving (B25/D18)—Parmenides's metaphysical deity is intrinsically *akinēton* yet still requires external constraints. In this regard it more closely resembles the Titan Prometheus, whom in Hesiod's *Theogony* "a great chain

---

can never arise from Is Not, and it is this impossible, unthinkable genesis that first conjures Dikē, who "has not loosened her bonds and let it [Being] be born or die, but she holds it" (B8.13–15/D8.18–20). Eliminated from Being, generation is counterintuitively attributed (under negation) to Nonbeing.

66. Gallop (1984, 24–28) moots the possibility of a connection to the *outis* pun in *Odyssey* 9 (proposed by Hershbell 1972), but finds the idea of an entity called Nothing in Parmenides unlikely. We will return to the language of negation in chapter 5.

67. Mourelatos (2008c, 115–35) understands *akinēton* as the impossibility of Being's "self-alienation," its "dislocation from its own proper place" and nature (118). Cf. Curd 1998, 83–94. Of course, without Nonbeing, movement is impossible anyway (as the atomists realized: see chapter 5, below), rendering the fetters once again logically superfluous.

restrained by necessity" in Tartarus (615–16).[68] The double intertext invites us to ask: if Being is *akinēton* by nature, why does it need to be shackled in place? What would it do if it weren't shackled and "confined all around" by powerful Anankē? Would it go wandering, like the moon with its "alien light" (B14/D27; cf. B10.4/D12.4), or like foolish two-headed mortals stumbling down their "back-turning path" (B6.9/D7.9)? Would it emulate the shimmering, shifting phenomena, eternally altering place and color (B8.41/D8.46)? Or worse yet, would it wander off down the forbidden path of Nonbeing (B8.54/D8.59)? The goddesses curb such ontological errancy.

Its immobility is a condition of Being's perfection and wholeness (B8.32–33/D8.37–38). But if prohibition bespeaks desire, Anankē's chains force the question of Being's desire and insinuate the possibility of its lack. Coxon identifies behind the binding image in this passage a further allusion to *Odyssey* 8.275, where Hephaestus plans to trap Ares and Aphrodite together in bed in "unbreakable, inescapable chains (*desmous*) so that they would remain there unmoving" (*empedon authi menoien*).[69] We know what passion Hephaestus is trying to curb. But what is the passion of Is? What does *Eon* want that the goddess's chains hold it back from obtaining? Even to ask this question is to imagine that Being *does* want, and therefore lacks. It is not "not lacking," *ouk epideues*, as B8.33/D8.38 claims. Furthermore, in the all-or-nothing logic of this line—which is the logic dictated by the *krisis* "Is or Is Not" (B8.15–16/D8.20–21)—if Being lacks for anything it lacks for everything. It not only contains nothing: it becomes nothing.[70]

Thus the metaphorical bonds that make Being perfect make it imperfect: divided, frustrated, lacking. Parmenides's bondage metaphor does not serve Being as a passive supplement to its absolute presence, securing its necessities and faithfully communicating its inherent qualities. Instead, as we have seen, it actively constitutes that metaphysical presence, along with its necessity and qualities. Its chains protect *To Eon* but in the process constrain it, leaving it immobile, isolated, and inert. Its need for these superfluous bonds, moreover, exposes the fragility of Being. Without the bondage of Parmenides's metaphor, Being would come apart;

68. On the parallels with Xenophanes's god, see Long 1996, 143, 148; Coxon 2009, 327–29; Bryan 2012, 97–100; and Tor 2017, 313–17; and with Hesiod's Prometheus, Coxon 2009, 327–28; Ranzato 2015, 166–70; Morgan 2022; and Tor 2023b, 262.

69. Coxon 2009, 329. At *Od.* 8.340 the bonds are "boundless" (*apeirones*), a Parmenidean collocation *avant la lettre. Empedon* further evokes Odysseus's marital bed (*Od.* 23.203; Zeitlin 1996, 29–31; Cassin 1998, 55n2; and Folit-Weinberg 2022, 281–300). Eros plays a prominent role in the Doxa (B13/D16) but enters the Aletheia only via the Homeric intertext.

70. There is a textual crux in B8.33/D8.38 involving (tellingly) the intrusion of an extrametrical negation: see Coxon 1968, 72–73; and Sider forthcoming, ad loc. The final verb of the passage ties together this nexus of themes: *edeito* could be from *deō* "to bind" or from *deō* "to lack," the verb that also supplies the impersonal form *dei,* "it is necessary." The two verbs are apparently unrelated etymologically but they overlap aurally and share many forms in common.

violated by Nonbeing, wandering like *doxai*, it would be revealed as precisely *epideues*—lacking its own proper identity as *To Eon* and requiring a metaphor to make good that lack.

LIKE A WELL-ROUNDED SPHERE

The metaphor of Anankē's bonds, and indeed the Aletheia as a whole, reaches its limit in the simile of the sphere.

> αὐτὰρ ἐπεὶ πεῖρας πύματον, τετελεσμένον ἐστί
> πάντοθεν, εὐκύκλου σφαίρης ἐναλίγκιον ὄγκωι,
> μεσσόθεν ἰσοπαλὲς πάντηι· τὸ γὰρ οὔτε τι μεῖζον
> οὔτε τι βαιότερον πελέναι χρεόν ἐστι τῆι ἢ τῆι.
> οὔτε γὰρ οὐκ ἐὸν ἔστι, τό κεν παύοι μιν ἱκνεῖσθαι
> εἰς ὁμόν, οὔτ' ἐὸν ἔστιν ὅπως εἴη κεν ἐόντος
> τῆι μᾶλλον τῆι δ' ἧσσον, ἐπεὶ πᾶν ἐστιν ἄσυλον·
> οἷ γὰρ πάντοθεν ἶσον, ὁμῶς ἐν πείρασι κύρει. (B8.42–49/D8.47–54)

> Moreover, since there is a furthest boundary,
> it is perfected from all sides, like the bulk of a well-rounded sphere,
> equal everywhere from its center. For it must be neither greater
> nor smaller at all in this place or that.
> For neither is there Nonbeing that could stop it from reaching
> its like, nor is there any way that, being, it could be
> more being here and less there, since as a whole it is inviolate.
> For equal to itself from all sides, it reaches likewise to its boundaries.

Parmenides's Being gets its spherical shape from its metaphorical limits: it is in reaching for its furthest boundary (*peiras pumaton*, 42/47) and maintaining itself inside its boundaries (*en peirasi kurei*, 49/54) that Is becomes perfect and spherical. With the repetition of *peiras*, the bounding metaphor neatly encircles the sphere, defining it "from all sides" (*pantothen*, 43/48, 49/54).[71] These *peirata* are strictly speaking unnecessary, since a sphere is a figure whose limits are intrinsic: they are not imposed from without but defined from within by a determinate relation to the center, as Parmenides emphasizes (*messothen*, 44/49).[72] In this sense, the sphere in and of itself is a geometric representation of the finite nature of *To Eon* and the fulfillment of Parmenides's dream of a bounded entity with no beyond. In

71. On the link between *peirar, telos,* and the circle, see Onians 1951, 426–66; Detienne and Vernant 1978, 279–326; Cassin 1998, 59; and Mourelatos 2008c, 31, 123–29. It makes little difference to my argument whether we understand the *sphaira* as a sphere (shape) or a ball (object), as it is taken, e.g., by Sedley (1999, 121); and Iribarren (2018, 142–53).

72. The *meson* renders Parmenides's sphere three-dimensional but is not otherwise a significant reference point: it is not a stop on the goddess's itinerary, much less its *telos*. One can circle around (*amphis*) Being, but never penetrate to its center.

pointedly encircling this self-delimiting sphere with the superfluous metaphor of limits, Parmenides demonstrates the point I argued in the last section: that this metaphor is not in fact superfluous nor peripheral to the project of defining Being. Instead, it constitutes the center, the *meson*, of Parmenides's ontology, the poetic core from which it radiates out until it reaches its furthest limit.

At that limit, Being itself becomes a metaphor, or more precisely, a simile. Simplicius tells us not to be surprised (*mē thaumasēis*) by this simile "because Parmenides is writing poetry, so he applies a sort of fictional invention (*muthikou tinos . . . plasmatos*)."[73] Nonetheless, it is surprising. Being has many predicates in the poem, but this is the only simile. Predicates are problematic enough, as we have seen: if you say that Being is one, you are saying it is two things, Being and one.[74] A simile magnifies and draws attention to this problem, and Parmenides's simile does so pointedly with the striking four-syllable epic adjective *enalinkion*. Describing through difference, similes overtly double the identity of the thing they describe. Parmenides's monism becomes a weird dualism, Being plus sphere. And this, moreover, in a passage that emphasizes Being's perfect homogeneity, its internal uniformity (*isopales*, 44/49; *ison*, 49/54) and self-sameness (*homon*, 47/52; *homōs*, 49/54), in short, its absolute identity. At the very moment that Being becomes fully and only itself, it is like something else.

The simile that doubles Being is itself doubled in the near-pleonastic adjective "well-rounded" (*eukuklou*). Calling the same object by two different names (*kuklos* and *sphairos*), the adjective evokes the polyonomy of the Doxa, to which Parmenides alludes a few lines earlier in speaking of the name (*onoma*) mortals give to phenomena "believing them to be true" (B8.38–39/D8.43–44). As a simile, the sphere belongs to the register of *doxa*, that "deceptive *kosmos* of words" (B8.52/D8.57). The simile thus insinuates Doxa's false appearances into the realm of Being and makes those appearances a defining supplement to Being's wholeness. The weight of this doxic supplement can be felt in the noun *onkos* in line 43/48, "like the bulk (*onkōi*) of a well-rounded sphere." This superfluous dative maintains a distance between the immaterial *comparandum* and its bulky *comparans*. That bulk is itself surprising, since, as we have seen, Parmenides is capable of conceptualizing sphere as an abstract mathematical figure. He goes out of his way, then, to give it physical heft. Its physicality links the sphere of Being to the various spheres

73. Commentary on Arist. *Phys.* 146.29 (< A20/R5b). Bollack and Wismann (1974, 204) take the simile of the sphere as "the decisive moment" when Being accedes to representation. Cf. Iribarren (2018, 142–53), taking it as the pivot between ontology and cosmology.

74. We might respond that the predicate is just another version of Being, as Coxon (2009, 20–21) does, apparently unconcerned about what this polymorphism means for Being's identity. But even if we are satisfied with that solution, the simile flagrantly advertises the problem. Likewise, the simile troubles Mourelatos's (2008c, 57) notion of a "speculative *esti*" which conflates predication and identity such that "on the side of the predicate, the subject fully explains itself, and in terms of itself." Simile turns that self-explication into alterity.

of the phenomenal world, such as the "circuit of the circle-eyed moon" (*kuklōpos . . . periphoita selēnēs*, B10.4/D12.4) and the "garlands" (*stephanoi*) of fire and night and flame that make up the cosmos (B12/D14b, A37/D15). Scholars generally suppose that these repetitions make the mundane orbs doubles of the metaphysical sphere and signs (*sēmata*, B10.2/D12.2) of its deeper reality.[75] But if the "circle-eyed" moon replicates Being's "well-rounded" sphere, the reverse also seems to be true, as the massy physicality of *onkos* suggests. Being, in its spherical perfection, is like the phenomenal orbits that are like it, a cycle of simile and similitude to which we will return momentarily.[76]

Parmenides's entire poetics is implicated in this tropic geometry. In the ring composition that encircles the simile of the sphere with the metaphor of the bounds (B8.42/D8.47, B8.49/D8.54) the poem formally reproduces its contents. That miniature ring is itself reproduced in the composition of the poem as a whole. The *Peri Phuseōs* moves around (*peri*) its subject in an annular pattern that belies the linear trajectory of its road metaphor. The road reaches its apparent *telos*—"as far as passion might reach" (*hikanoi*, B1.1/D4.1)—where Being reaches (*hikneisthai*, B8.46/D8.51) its limits in the sphere. "At this point I stop (*pauō*) my trustworthy *logos* and thought about truth" (*amphis alētheiēs*, B8.50–51/D8.55–56). The linear route is now revealed to be a circuit that loops around (*amphis*) the Aletheia.[77] It then continues on—the goddess's *pauō* is in fact merely a pause—toward the Doxa: "From this point, learn mortal opinions, hearing the deceptive order of my words" (B8.51–52/D8.56–57). From there it will circle back, reaching its end in the return to its starting point, as the goddess expressly announces: "In common for me is the point from which I begin, for I will reach it once again hereafter" (*palin hixomai authis*, B5/D5).

This annular structure inscribes the poem's ultimate wisdom in its opening images: return invests these cryptic symbols with the force of revelation, thereby turning them into allegories or metaphors. In the proem's many prolepses, details take on greater resonance—or only make sense to begin with—in light of later truths. Thus the road on which the philosophical initiate sets out is said to "bear a man who knows" (*pherei eidota phōta*, B1.3/D4.3), an auspicious beginning

75. Mourelatos 2008c, 222–63; and Coxon 2009, 356. The ambiguous doubling of Being in phenomena is signaled by Parmenides's description of the Doxa as a *diakosmon eoikota* (B8.60/D8.65): *eikōs* evokes similarity but also speciousness. See Bryan 2012, 66–74; Johansen 2016; and (on *eikos*) the essays in Wohl 2014.

76. This explains the urgency of the debate over whether Parmenides imagined Being as "like a sphere" or as literally spherical. Scholars who argue against the latter (on the grounds that it makes the metaphysical physical) rarely acknowledge the risks of the former (which makes the metaphysical metaphorical). The question is closely linked to the question of whether Being's spatial extent is to be understood as literal or metaphorical: see Tarán 1965, 150–60; Sedley 1999, 121; McKirahan 2008, 210–14; and n. 53 above.

77. Mourelatos 2008c, 191–93: all thought and language are "round about" (on account of, with reference to) reality; "mind revolves around, or pivots on, the real" (193).

that anticipates the journey's end in the final attainment of wisdom.[78] Several of these prolepses themselves take the form of a circle, like the "untrembling heart of well-rounded Truth" (*Alētheiēs eukukleos atremes ētor*, B1.29/D4.29), a phrase that anticipates both the untrembling wholeness of Is (*atremes*, B8.4/D8.9) and the "well-rounded sphere" to which it is ultimately likened (*eukuklou sphairēs*, B8.43/D.48).[79] Circles spiral around one another, as the circular images reiterate the poem's circular structure, which itself reiterates the sphere of Being.

This troping on turning is generally understood as an artful mimesis: as a *logos* "about truth" (*amphis alētheiēs*, B8.51/D8.56) the poem imitates the spherical form of its subject.[80] In this sense the poem enacts its own correspondence theory of language, in which reality is accessible to speech and true speech participates in reality. Through this mimetic artistry, the poem seems to redeem both the "back-turning path" (*palintropos keleuthos*, B6.9/D7.9) of deluded human *doxai* and the deceptive language that describes them. This is how Mourelatos understands the many "similarities-with-a-difference" between the Aletheia and the Doxa. In the latter's verbal equivocations mortals "cannot help feeling the presence of the ἐόν [*eon*]: as a goal, as an intention, as an implicit commitment, as a half-forgotten memory of the ancient covenant with reality."[81] We indiscriminate mortals wander around in circles (*palintropos*). But if we can discern the true meaning behind the ironic ambiguities of the goddess's speech, we will intuit the true unity of Being behind the multifarious phenomena and recognize the singular sphere behind the revolutions of the "circle-eyed" moon. The poem's own annular form thus seems to align the mundane circles of mortal existence with the totality of Being in a metaphysical harmony of the spheres. At the same time, it redeems poetic language as both the medium and one element of that harmony. For a man who knows/has seen (*eidota phōta)*, the lush poeticism that describes the moon

78. *Eidota phōta* may carry initiatory overtones which contribute to the prolepsis: the initiate has already attained the light that is often the *telos* of initiation (*eis phaos,* B1.10/D4.10) and is passing it on (hence the present tenses in the verbs of the first lines: Sider forthcoming, ad loc). The initiatory structure of the poem is stressed by Tor 2017, 267–73; Kingsley 1999, 80–85, 2002, 369–81; and Ranzato 2015, 57–123. See also Derrida (1982b, 257) on revelation as metaphor's "twisting return toward the already-there of a meaning."

79. *Eukukleos* is the reading of Simplicius, followed by Diels-Kranz (see Diels 2003, 55–56) and defended by Mansfeld 1995, 232; Bollack 2006, 99–100; Couloubaritsis 2008, 363, 370–76; Palmer 2009, 90, 378–80; Ranzato 2015, 114–18; and Sider forthcoming, ad loc. Plutarch's reading *eupeitheos* (*Adv. Col.* 1114D) is adopted by Gallop 1984; Coxon 2009; and Laks-Most, and defended by Jameson 1958; and Mourelatos 2008c, 154–57. Other prolepses include the "double circles" (*kuklois*) of wheels, whirling on both sides (*amphoterōthen,* B1.8/D4.8) of the chariot, the wise (*poluphrastoi,* B1.4/D4.4) horses, the presence of *themis* and *dikē* (B1.14/D4.14, B1.28/D4.28) and of *pistis alēthēs* (B1.29–30/D4.29–30), and the lintel and threshold that surround (*amphis ekhei*) the gates of Night and Day (B1.12/D4.12). In B1.3/D4.3, *asinē* (unharmed) has been conjectured (in lieu of *astē*) in anticipation of the inviolate (*asulon*) sphere at B8.48/D8.53.

80. Starting with Diels 2003, 56; and Reinhardt 1959, 60. See further Ballew 1979, 45–50.

81. Mourelatos 2008c, 226.

as a "night-shining alien light (*allotrion phōs*) wandering around (*peri*) the earth" (B14/D27) is no mere "deceptive ornament of words" but a lucent vision of the true effulgence of Being.[82]

And yet that harmony immediately introduces a new discord, for the artful reduplication of the sphere sets the poem's mimetic form against its monadic content. The singular totality of Is is doubled in its likeness to a sphere, as we have seen, which is then doubled again in the spherical *logos* that describes it and again in the spherical poem that expounds that *logos*. This mimetic proliferation opens the door to all the problems Plato sought to solve with his theory of the Forms (a theory built on the back of Parmenides). Plato's ontology of the Forms dictates a unidirectional relationship between the original Form and its phenomenal copy. When Mourelatos speaks of the latent presence of *To Eon* within *doxa* "as a goal, as an intention," he presupposes the same single directionality: the philosophical journey moves from ambiguous phenomena to the univocal truth of the metaphysical.[83] In this way Mourelatos reconciles the geometry of the road and the circle by imagining the route as a return to a forgotten truth, a philosophical *nostos*.[84] But Odysseus, we should remember, gets only one night back in his own bed before setting off again. Circles are by their nature nonteleological: they go round and round without end, and the relations they plot are necessarily reciprocal. Thus if the moon is like the sphere, the sphere is also like the moon, and we cannot read the poem as a mimesis of Being without also entertaining the reverse possibility: that Being is a mimesis of the poem, produced in its own spherical image.

The poem's annular form thus debars us from reading it as a unidirectional ascent from ignorance to enlightenment, or *doxa* to truth, for all that the metaphorical path may encourage us to do so. The ambiguities of the proem anticipate the revelations of Aletheia but also preview the duplicities of Doxa: the goddess's *logos*, as she says, comes full circle, ending where it began, in the human world.[85]

82. Mourelatos (2008c, 224–25) takes this fragment as the starting point for his exegesis of the ambiguities of the Doxa. Cf. B15/D28, which describes the moon "always looking toward the rays of the sun." "White Mythology" concludes with a discussion of heliotropism as a trope of metaphor's return to proper meaning (Derrida 1982b, 245–71).

83. Mourelatos 2008c, 226. The route is, as he says, "definitely one-way" (18). This unidirectional relation imbues our false opinions with a hidden substrate of truth, but does not trouble truth with the equivocations of *doxa*. Compare Johansen (2016), who argues that Parmenides relates the phenomenal world to Being as likeness to model in a way that anticipates Plato's *Timaeus*.

84. This return is predicated on his argument that Parmenides understands "an implicit quasi-subconscious 'ontological commitment'" of thought to truth (Mourelatos 2008c, 180). On Parmenides's route as a *nostos*, see also Robbiano (2006, 133–45), for whom its circular movement ultimately comes to rest in the traveler's unity with immobile Being.

85. Thus the "circles" of the chariot wheels (*kuklois*, B1.8/D4.8) anticipate both the Aletheia's "well-rounded" sphere (*eukuklou*, B8.43/D8.48) and the Doxa's "circle-eyed" moon (*kuklōpos*, B10.4/D12.4); Dikē's surrounding lintel (*amphis ekhei*, B1.12/D4.12) prefigures both Necessity's hold on Being (*amphis eergei*, B8.31/D8.36) and the surrounding heavens of the cosmology (*amphis ekhonta*, B10.5/D12.5). Even the *eidōs phōs* prefigures the appearances of Doxa (as Cosgrove 2011 argues) as well as the

In the endless circuit that takes the philosopher from *doxa* to *alētheia* and back again, no *Aufhebung* is irreversible. This means that the poetic language of *doxa* can never be transcended once and for all. It may serve as a metaphorical ladder that helps the philosopher ascend to the sublime reality of Is, but since that ascent is never final, the ladder can never be kicked away. The *eidōs phōs* will be needing it again and again.

Moreover, if the philosophical route is an interminable loop, then every retreading of the path will encounter the same temptations to detour and errancy. The goddess says she will come back (*palin*) to where she began (B5/D5). But the point to which she returns is not identical to the one from which she started, a fact revealed by the very prolepses that instantiate the poem's circularity, as the proem's enigmatic symbols take on distinctly new meanings the second time around. Repetition introduces difference, and the same path repeated is a potentially different path.[86] Maybe this time the *eidōs phōs* will head off in another direction, not up into the sunlight of truth (*eis phaos*, B1.10/D4.10) but toward the "alien light" (*allotrion phōs*, B14/D27) of *doxa*. Maybe he will wander off the path altogether into that pathless expanse of Is Not. Maybe a detour will become the destination, this time with no return, and instead of a *logos* about (*amphis*) truth we will get a *logos* apart from (*amphis*) truth. These possibilities turn the goddess's circular (*palin*, B5.2/D5.2) road of inquiry into a *palintropos keleuthos* in all the senses of *palin*: backwards, again, contrary.[87]

Derrida's "White Mythology" concludes with a discussion of philosophy's determination to return metaphor to univocal meaning. Metaphor as "the wandering of the semantic"—"the moment of the detour in which the truth might still be lost"—is brought home in a "circular reappropriation of literal, proper meaning."[88] But Parmenides's return refuses such reappropriation. The repetition built into its structure means that the poem's circle, unlike the metaphysical sphere, never fully closes. Its end and beginning may be "in common" (*xunon*, B5.1/D5.1), as the goddess says, but it lacks the hermetic cohesion (*sunekhes*, B8.6/D8.11) of

enlightenment of Aletheia. Deichgräber (1958) stresses the close link between the proem and both the Aletheia and the Doxa.

86. See Deleuze (1994), especially his comments (à propos of Nietzsche's eternal return) about the circle of difference (65–69, 156).

87. Parmenides's *palintropos keleuthos* (B6.9/D7.9) may evoke the *palintropos harmoniē* of Her. B51/D49 (if that reading is correct) and the goddess's return to a common (*xunon*) starting point in B5/D5 recall the common (*xunon*) beginning and end of the circle in Her. B103/D54. I agree with Graham (2002) (cf. 2006, 131–40), against Mansfeld (1964, 1–41) and Stokes (1971, 109–27), that the parallels are too strong to be coincidental. Indeed, there is something symptomatic about them, as if Parmenides needed to reach beyond himself in order to square the circle of his text, opening the circuit even as he closes it. See further Tarán 1965, 69–72; Nehamas 2002; and Bollack 2006, 134–36. The theory of Reinhardt (1959, 155–230) that Heraclitus followed Parmenides chronologically has been rejected by recent scholars (a notable exception being Hölscher [1968, 161–69]).

88. Derrida 1982b, 241, 270. Cf. 271 on the operation of metaphor as the opening of a circle.

Being. We saw in the first section how, under the goddess's command, the "road of inquiry" narrows from the branching *hodos poluphēmos* to a single word: Is. But Parmenides's poem contains within its ambit not only the road of "Is" but also all those forbidden detours glimpsed along the way. The road to Doxa is a false direction that the goddess exhorts the initiate to avoid (B6.3–5/D7.3–5). Yet, although "there is no true credence" in the *doxai* of mortals, she tells the *kouros*, "nonetheless you will learn these things too" (B1.30–31/D4.30–31).[89] Indeed, her account of the "deceptive order" of the Doxa originally filled some 300 lines.[90] Why Parmenides included this extended treatment of a topic he labels false and fraudulent is one of the most debated questions in Parmenides scholarship and with good reason: the contradiction seems to render the goddess's *logos*—if not Parmenides's very thought—incoherent.[91]

But perhaps this is precisely the point. Being is a closed circle, singular, unitary, and homogeneous, sealed within its autotelic bounds. But *logos* is unbounded. It speaks of the false as well as the true, deluded *doxa* as well as *alētheia*. It even speaks the unspeakable Is Not, conjuring its impossible presence again and again and inviting us to think its unthinkability. Encompassing not just the true path to Being but also the forbidden detours to Doxa and Nonbeing, the goddess's *logos* encircles (*amphis*) Being but is larger than it. And the poetic account is larger than her *logos*. This is easy to forget, since the first-person narrator who opens the poem soon becomes the goddess's silent interlocutor, his poetic persona replaced by her strong didactic voice. But the insistence of the first-person perspective at the start of the poem (and the continual reminder of it in the goddess's direct address), as well as the complex framing of the goddess's speech in the proem, indicates the difference between her *logos* and the *kouros*'s narrative and alerts us that the latter exceeds the former. The poem, moreover, exceeds both. Parmenides, probably reciting his verses to a large audience at a public festival, is not identical to the young initiate, although the first-person

89. The paradox that the goddess takes the route that she bars is encapsulated in the textual crux of B6.3/D7.3, where (depending on the supplement one accepts) she either "begins" (*arxō*) from the road of Doxa, after the road to Truth, or "bars" (*eirgō*) the road of Doxa, after the road to Nonbeing: see Cordero 1979, 2004, 108–24. Parmenides's equivocal treatment of the way of Doxa makes the textual debate undecidable.

90. Diels (2003, 25–26) believes the extant fragments represent 90 percent of the original Aletheia and 10 percent of the Doxa. That would mean that the Doxa was originally some 300 lines, twice as long as the Aletheia.

91. Nietzsche's biographical thesis, that Parmenides turned from *doxa* to *alētheia* as the result of a midlife conversion experience but never lost his "paternal good-will toward the sturdy and well-made child of his youth" (Nietzsche 1962, 70), registers the severity of the split. Among the seminal contributions to the debate are Owen (1960), for whom the cosmology serves a dialectical purpose as a case study in self-deception (similarly Long 1975) and Mackenzie (1982), who proposes that the contradiction deliberately renders the Aletheia self-refuting. Tor (2017, 163–221) offers a good recent presentation of the problem and an attempt to solve it; see also Curd 1992; Rosetti 2010; and Bryan 2018.

voice may invite us to mistake the one for the other.[92] The goddess's speech surrounds Being, the *kouros*'s account surrounds her speech, and the poem itself surrounds them both in a series of concentric circles.

Parmenides presents Being as all, a totality with no outside. But in fact, it is his poem that is all, that contains not only the totality (*pan*) of Being but all the things (*panta*) of the phenomenal world, not only the determinate sphere of Is but the unbounded, infinite expanse of Is Not.[93] Parmenides wants to sublate *logos*, to purify it so that it disappears in the dazzling presence of *Esti*. But he also wants his *logos* to exceed *To Eon* so as to encompass it and contain it as one (but only one) of its objects. These competing desires express a paradox built into the very project of ontology. Encircling both desires at once, Parmenides's poem binds *logos* and being, metaphor and metaphysics, in the aporetic geometry of a Möbius strip, each simultaneously inside and outside the other, passing into the other, separate but inseparably implicated in an endlessly twisting loop that can never be unwound into a singular closed circle. Following the impossible path of this figure, this chapter has circled around the central aporia of ontology itself, showing that from the very start the question of *to on* has always been a question of *logos*, defined—to the extent that it can be—by the wandering route of metaphor.

92. This is true even if, with Mansfeld (1964, 222–73), Kingsley (1999, 2003, 9–306), Robbiano (2006, 22–23), and Gemelli Marciano (2008), we imagine Parmenides as recounting his own mystical experience. Morgan (2000, 74) remarks on the "uneasy tension" between Parmenides as author, the *kouros* as narrator, and the goddess. On the performance context of Parmenides's poem, see Mackenzie 2021a, 67.

93. In the singular, *pan* is a predicate of Being in its totality (B8.5/D8.10, B8.22/D8.27, B8.24–25/D8.29–30); in the plural it belongs to *doxa* (B1.32/D4.32, B6.9/D7.9, B8.38/D8.43, B8.60/D8.65, B10.1/D12.1, B12.3–4/D14b.3–4, B13/D16, B16.4/D51.4). The poem's compass is broadened to infinity if we suppose, following Mourelatos, that Parmenides conceived of Nonbeing not as nonexistent but as indefinite, "that wholly unencompassable space of indeterminacy that lies outside the thing" (2008a, 347–48; cf. 2008c, 74–93; and Bollack 2006, 106–13).

2

Time, the Cosmos, and the Soul in Heraclitus

It is not possible to step into the same river twice, according to Heraclitus.
—PLUTARCH

All aphorisms must therefore be read twice.
—GILLES DELEUZE

HERACLITUS'S PSYCHOCOSMOLOGY

We saw in the last chapter how Parmenides forges a metaphorical "route of inquiry" to true knowledge and uses language to bind and bound metaphysical reality. For Heraclitus, by contrast, both the route and its destination are boundless.

> ψυχῆς πείρατα ἰὼν οὐκ ἂν ἐξεύροιο, πᾶσαν ἐπιπορευόμενος ὁδόν· οὕτω βαθὺν λόγον ἔχει. (B45/D98)
>
> Going to the limits (*peirata*) of the *psukhē* you could not discover them, although you travel (*epiporeuomenos*) every road, so profound is the account (*logon*) it holds.

In this fragment it is as if the Parmenidean traveler falls off a cliff: the *poros* becomes aporia as the road opens beneath our feet onto an abyss.[1] *Logos* is the measure of that abyss. Simultaneously the principle of coherence of Heraclitus's cosmos and the site of a necessary and generative incoherence, *logos* is a bottomless paradox and the expression of a reality that is itself profoundly paradoxical.

Epigraph: From *Nietzsche and Philosophy*, by Gilles Deleuze, translated by Hugh Tomlinson, 31.

1. Betegh (2009) explicates well the textual and interpretive difficulties of B45/D98. *Bathus* usually connotes marine depths, but it can also indicate height. See Porter (2016, 531; 2020, 231) on the spatial disorientation of a metaphysical perspective, and compare B60/D51: "The road up, down: one and the same." The metaphor of the road recurs at B18/D37 and B71/R54; in both cases it figures aporia.

In the depths of this aporia Heraclitus locates the *psukhē*. In *The Discovery of the Mind*, Bruno Snell, citing this fragment, credits Heraclitus with devising a "new concept of the soul."[2] No longer just a spectral emanation of the dead (as it was in Homer), with Heraclitus, Snell claims, the *psukhē* becomes properly psychological: an autonomous entity within the individual that presages (in Snell's teleological account) the modern subject.[3] But Heraclitus's *psukhē* is far from the modern psyche, as we shall see. Closely associated with breath and vitality, it denotes the life of the individual and is intimately bound up with the life of the cosmos.[4] Heraclitus's cosmology describes a dynamic cycle of elemental transformation, from fire to water to earth and back again. A material element like fire, water, or earth, the *psukhē* is part of this cosmic process, and if it has no ends (*peirata*, B45/D98) that is because it revolves in an elemental circle of which "the beginning and end (*peras*) are in common" (B103/D54). To seek the limits of the *psukhē* is thus to explore the profundity of the cosmos as a whole.[5] This assimilation of the *psukhē* to the physical universe would seem to leave no room for Snell's autonomous soul as the site of individual experience, memory, and self-consciousness. The *psukhē*'s measure (*logos*) would seem to be identical to that of the cosmos, and Heraclitean psychology to be cosmology by another name.

And yet, boundless as it is, the *psukhē* is not precisely coterminous with the cosmos. Its divergence, I shall propose, arises in relation to the experience of time. The measure of the cosmos is boundless, but the human journey is finite, and while the cosmic cycle revolves forever, our lives are brief and delimited by death. The difference between cosmic eternity (*aei*) and the finite human life span (*aiōn*) means that the human subject is always out of step with the rhythm of the universe. This chapter examines the asynchrony between *aei* and *aiōn* and its ramifications for Heraclitus's cosmology and his psychology. Heraclitus attempts to align human understanding with the unchanging structure of the cosmos and in this way both to reveal and to secure the cohesion of a universe in which opposites merge and "all things are one" (B50/D46). Yet even as he sings that "unseen harmony" (B54/

2. Snell 1953, 17. Cf. Reinhardt 1959, 201.

3. Snell 1953, 17–22. Snell's linear trajectory from the physical *psukhē* of Homer to the psychological soul of Socrates is followed by Furley (1956); Nussbaum (1972a); and Robb (1986), and critiqued by Claus (1981); Holmes (2010, 5–9, 29–30); and Sassi (2018, 113), who nevertheless follows its general lines, (110–38). Many scholars identify in Heraclitus a new conception of the *psukhē* but they differ on its precise nature. Some, like Kahn (1979, 107, 127–29), stress rational cognition; others, like Laks (2018, 253–54), the controlling function (cf. Nussbaum 1972a); others still the capacity for self-consciousness or self-transcendence (Long's [1992] "objective self").

4. As forcefully argued by Porter (2023, 2024). I agree with Porter that these two are thoroughly intermeshed for Heraclitus, but am also interested here in the difference he preserves between them, the slight interval between individual life and life in general or between *psukhai* and *psukhē* (B36/D100).

5. Kahn 1979, 14–15, 116, 118, 119, 122–23, 127–30, 252; Hussey 1982; and Long 1992, 271. Many adopt Reinhardt's (1959, 196–201) microcosm-macrocosm homology of self and cosmos, e.g. Dilcher (1995, 90–98); and Sandywell (1996, 267–75).

D50), Heraclitus also sustains a note of dissonance in the interval between human time and cosmic. This asynchrony is felt as an occasional disruption, a stutter or syncopation, in his fragments' formal symmetry. In these moments, I propose, Heraclitus preserves a space for the emergence of the individual psyche in its difference from the material cosmos and for the flourishing—ephemeral though it may be—of human life.

These opposing lines of force toward coherence and incoherence form the "back-turned harmony" (B51/D49) that characterizes Heraclitus's *kosmos* both as a unified physical and metaphysical order and as an aesthetic order the integral beauty of which is manifested in Heraclitus's writing.[6] Heraclitus is the most brilliant stylist of the early Greek philosophers. Although he composed in prose, "he wrote many things poetically (*poiētikōs*)," as one ancient commentator observed, and indeed his fragments are markedly poetic in their vivid imagery, rich internal resonances, riddling ambiguity, and intricate verbal patterning.[7] These effects are not merely cosmetic. Instead, they both mimetically represent and materially instantiate the *logos* that is the deepest structure of reality. Unlike Parmenides, for whom (as we saw in the last chapter) language and being circle one another in a tense intimacy, for Heraclitus language is a manifestation of and model for the systemic order of the cosmos.[8] Speaking in unison with what he calls the "common" (*xunos*) *logos* (B2/D2), Heraclitus's own *logos* seems to enact the concord that binds the universe, the principle that "what differs with itself agrees with itself" (*homologeei*, literally "speaks the same *logos*," B51/D49).[9] But if what differs with itself agrees, what agrees with itself also differs, and these two *logoi* never fully harmonize. Further, as we shall see, the cosmic *logos* never fully harmonizes with itself. This metaphysical discord, even as it creates a rift in Heraclitus's unified cosmos, also produces the space in which his philosophical inquiry unfolds. *Logos* thus emerges as both a principle of coherence and a principle of incoherence, both

6. As noted above, chapter 1, n. 25, the word *kosmos* originally meant an aesthetic or military ordering and only later came to refer to the universe, perhaps first in Heraclitus. On Heraclitus's use of *kosmos*, see further Kirk 1954, 311–16; Kahn 1960, 224–27; Finkelberg 2017, 58–64; and Schofield 2019, 70–72.

7. Suda H.472 (< A1a/R11). Ancient judgments on his style are collected at Laks-Most R5–11; cf. Mouraviev 2002, 9–26. Kahn (1979, 7–9) compares his style to the odes of his contemporaries Pindar and Aeschylus; his commentary emphasizes the ambiguity and linguistic density of Heraclitus's fragments and the resonances between them (see esp. 87–95). On Heraclitus's poetic style, see further Deichgräber 1963; Lilja 1968; Hölscher 1974; Dilcher 1995, 133–44; Most 1999, 357–59; Bernabé 2009; Sassi 2018, 98–109; and the exhaustive poetological study of Mouraviev 2002, 2006.

8. Kahn 1979, 107, 123–24, 131.

9. On the unity of Heraclitus's own *logos* and *logos* as the structure of the cosmos, see e.g. Verdenius 1966, 93; Robinson 1991, 2009; Voigtländer 1995; Hülsz 2013, 292; Johnstone 2014; and Lebedev 2017. Mourelatos (2008b) terms this a "*logos*-textured world" and sees Heraclitus as the first to articulate it. Ramnoux (1968), by contrast, emphasizes the uncertain relation between words and things in Heraclitus's thought (e.g. 67–99).

the condition of possibility and the condition of impossibility of his philosophy—a *bathus logos* indeed!

The paradoxical nature of *logos* suggests that dissonance and difference are not incidental to Heraclitus's philosophical discourse but ineradicable, necessary, and productive. Aristotle, as we saw in the Introduction, identifies univocity—the singularity of meaning, the law of noncontradiction—as the foundational principle of philosophical inquiry (*Metaph.* 4.4 1006b7–13). But Heraclitus delights in flouting the law of noncontradiction: the way up is the way down (B60/D51); day and night are one (B57/D25a, B106/D25b); mortals are immortal, immortals mortal (B62/D70).[10] Perhaps we might imagine that, if we ponder them long enough, his paradoxes will yield to some sort of *doxa* or univocal good sense and his riddles resolve into a more fundamental and unitary meaning. Heraclitus's own metaphors of depth and concealment might lead us to expect that beneath the puzzling surface of things we may discover the singular truth of a nature that "tends to hide itself" (B123/D35).[11] But "those who search for gold dig much earth and find little" (B22/D39), and paradox, as we shall see, is not a mere surface effect of Heraclitus's discourse but part of the deepest structure of his cosmos: it is paradox all the way down.[12] If the *xunos logos*—the rational structure of reality—is itself paradoxical, then Heraclitus's riddles will never yield a common sense (*xunos logos*). Instead, they produce sensations, effects more corporeal and affective than cognitive.[13] Through these sensations, Heraclitus allows us to experience the coherence of

10. See further B8/D62, B10/D47, B48/D53, B51/D49, B59/D52, B67/D48, B80/D63, B88/D68. Bernabé (2009) provides a taxonomy of such polar expressions. Aristotle reports that "some think" Heraclitus breaches the principle of noncontradiction (*Metaph.* 4.3 1005b23–26, 4.7 1012a24–26, 11.5 1062a30–b11). Aristotle does not say whether he is among these (Rapp 2017); but Barnes (1982, 69–81) clearly is. Heraclitus's unity of opposites has been variously understood: see, e.g., Emlyn-Jones 1976; Hussey 1999, 93–98. Stokes (1971, 89–100) lays out the interpretive possibilities clearly. For Mackenzie (1988) the frustration such contradictions produce is designed to establish the law of noncontradiction elenchically; cf. Cook 1975. In the unity of opposites, most scholars lay the stress on the former term, seeing oppositions as merely apparent. Notable exceptions are Bollack and Wismann 1972; and Porter 2024.

11. Cf. B54/D50, B93/D41, B18/D37. Heraclitus was compared in antiquity to a "Delian diver" (Diog. Laert. 2.22 < A4/R5a), and his homey similes suggest an underlying reality latent within everyday objects, from bows and lyres (B51/D49, B48/D53) to carding combs (B59/D52) and even lice (B56/D22). Note also the language of *lēthē* (B1/D1, B16/D83, B71/R45), which Heidegger (1975, 102–23) examines as a trope of concealment; concealment and emergence are central to his reading of Heraclitus (Heidegger 2018, 35–135). The paragon of the hermeneutics of concealment is Mouraviev (2002), for whom Heraclitus's poetics constitutes a "code" (401) that, once reconstructed, allows the scholar to decipher his vision of reality.

12. In Hölscher's oft-quoted words, "His language, too, must be one of paradox, simile, and riddle, precisely insofar as it seeks to proclaim the essence of what is. . . . His speech is paradoxical because his truth is paradoxical" (1974, 233–34). Cf. Hölscher 1968, 136–41; Gallop 1989; and Porter 2024.

13. I am playing on Deleuze's (1990, 74–81) concept of paradox as non-sense that reverses both good sense and common sense and of sensation as affective and corporeal apperception (Deleuze and Guattari 1994, 163–99).

the cosmos but also its incoherence, a gap not only between human reason and the cosmic *logos* but within that metaphysical *logos* itself. Heraclitus does not fully close that gap but instead holds it open as the asymptotic limit of the philosophical journey: "Going to the limits of the *psukhē* you could not discover them . . . so profound is the *logos* it holds."

Incoherence is thus a significant feature of Heraclitus's fragmentary text as a whole. Probably originally disseminated in written form, Heraclitus's work has come down to us only in fragments, of course.[14] This is true of all early Greek philosophers, but in Heraclitus this historical accident seems to reiterate a deliberate aesthetic choice. The philosopher's famed "brevity" and a relative lack of connective particles suggest that the fragments were never part of a continuous stream of connected prose and thus that the enigmatic aphorism was not a byproduct of preservation but the primary expressive unit of Heraclitus's thought.[15] Aphorism is by definition incoherent, "separated off" (*aphorizein*). This generic incoherence is emphasized in Diels-Kranz's edition by the pointedly arbitrary arrangement of the fragments: exceptionally, Diels gave up on logical ordering and simply listed fragments alphabetically by source author, from Aëtius to Tzetzes (with the exception of the first two, which ancient sources place at the opening of the book). Repeated images—fire, rivers, sleep—and marked verbal and structural resonances bind the dispersed fragments, promising to make the book an instance of the principle that "all things are one."[16] "Like a sweeping at random of things scattered (*hōsper sarma eikē kekhumenōn*) is the most beautiful *kosmos*," says Heraclitus (B124/D60). But just as Heraclitus's paradoxes never resolve into a univocal *doxa*, so his fragments never cohere into a singular doctrine or dogma. To say this is not to chastise Heraclitus for failure to rectify his inconsistencies, but rather to posit incoherence as a positive and productive feature of his thought.[17] The ambiguous placement in this fragment of the adverb "at random" (*eikē*)—a

14. Diog. Laert. 9.6 (< A1/P13) reports that Heraclitus deposited his book in the temple of Artemis, and the complex structure of his writing seems to require a text that can be read and reread: see Kahn 1983; Sassi 2018, 98–109. But as Robb (1983b, 182–201) notes, his prose is full of aural effects, and I agree with Deichgräber (1963, 5–13) that the text was meant to be read aloud, and more than once (cf. Havelock 1966, 55; and Robb 1983b, 183).

15. Hölscher 1974, 236–38; Kirk, Raven, and Schofield 1983, 184; Robb 1983b; Hussey 1999, 88; and Most 1999, 357; contra, Barnes 1983, 97–105; and Finkelberg 2017, 33–38. Diogenes (Diog. Laert. 9.7 < A1/R5c) praises the "brevity and dignity" of his style, while Demetrius (*Eloc.* 191–92 < A4/R7) condemns the obscurity produced "when the whole is asyndetic and dispersed." Theophrastus's diagnosis of "melancholia" (i.e. inconsistency) may speak to the same qualities (Diog. Laert. 9.6 < A1/R5c). There were contemporary models for Heraclitus's discontinuous style in the maxims of the Seven Sages and the enigmatic pronouncements of the Delphic oracle: see Granger 2004; and Sassi 2018, 103–6.

16. Kahn 1979, 90.

17. *Pace* Barnes 1982, 57–81. The text of B124/D60 is uncertain, and *sarma* ("sweeping") is Diels's emendation.

stylistic quirk to which we will return—preserves randomness within the beautiful order of the cosmos and suggests that it is precisely that randomness that accounts for its beauty. In reading the fragments of Heraclitus we come to appreciate the *kosmos* of incoherence as a philosophical as well as a poetic principle and to sense the productive force of asynchrony both for philosophy and for human life.

AEI AND *AIŌN*

The non-synchrony of human time and cosmic time is established in the very first fragment.

> τοῦ δὲ λόγου τοῦδ' ἐόντος ἀεὶ ἀξύνετοι γίνονται ἄνθρωποι καὶ πρόσθεν ἢ ἀκοῦσαι καὶ ἀκούσαντες τὸ πρῶτον· γινομένων γὰρ πάντων κατὰ τὸν λόγον τόνδε ἀπείροισιν ἐοίκασι, πειρώμενοι καὶ ἐπέων καὶ ἔργων τοιούτων, ὁκοίων ἐγὼ διηγεῦμαι κατὰ φύσιν διαιρέων ἕκαστον καὶ φράζων ὅκως ἔχει. τοὺς δὲ ἄλλους ἀνθρώπους λανθάνει ὁκόσα ἐγερθέντες ποιοῦσιν, ὅκωσπερ ὁκόσα εὕδοντες ἐπιλανθάνονται. (B1/D1)

> Of this *logos* that is always (*aei*) mortals are always uncomprehending, both before they have heard it and when they have first heard it. Though all things come about in accordance with this *logos* they are like people without experience even when they experience such words and deeds as I expound, distinguishing each thing according to its nature and saying how it is. But other men are not aware of what they do when they are awake, just as they forget what they do when asleep.

This book begins with the word, *logos*. Appearing at the opening as a kind of authorial *sphragis*, "this *logos*" seems to refer to the work we are about to read, the "words and deeds" the philosopher will expound.[18] But in its eternal being this *logos* also signifies the structure of the physical and metaphysical universe of which Heraclitus's own *logos* will be an account. A single word operating on two different planes at once, this equivocal *logos* makes for a perfect Heraclitean opening. But does its ambivalence unite opposites—"all things are one"—or does it bespeak a schism within the fundamental structure of the universe?

This question unfolds as a matter of time. The *logos* occupies a temporality of eternal being: it is always (*eontos aei*). By contrast, humans live in the time of becoming (*ginontai*). This is a temporality of before and after, of transformation (from inexperience to experience and incomprehension to comprehension) and temporal rhythms (sleeping and waking). But the ambiguous placement of *aei*

18. Kahn (1979, 97) notes that an introductory reference to the author's own *logos* is typical of Ionian prose. Sextus Empiricus (*Math.* 7.132–133), who quotes the fragment, tells us that it came at the opening of the book; see also Arist. *Rh.* 3.5 1407b15–16 (< A4/R6). The passage was likely preceded by a statement of the author's identity, such as Diels-Kranz suggest ("Heraclitus son of Bloson of Ephesus teaches the following"). Dilcher (1995, 11–13) discusses the parallels.

raises a question, noted already by Aristotle.[19] Is it the existence of the *logos* that is eternal or the ignorance of mortals or both? "Always" is a point of continuity between cosmic realm and human but also a point of divergence. The adverb binds the two grammatically even as it signals their eternal separation at the level of content: mortals will always fail to understand the always-existent *logos*. Maybe we are dealing with two different kinds of "always" here. Maybe we should understand *aei* as "eternally" on the cosmic level but something more like "usually" or "typically" for humans. But this zeugma would merely perpetuate the separation of humans and cosmos, which exist in fundamentally different temporalities. That means that even if there is only one *aei* there are always two (human and cosmic), and even if there are two there is only one (an eternity in which people fail to understand the *logos*). This paradoxical adverb leaves open the question of whether humans can change over time from *axunetoi* to *xunetoi*, or whether their incomprehension truly is eternal, *aei*.

The stakes of this question are high, both for Heraclitus and for his cosmos. *Axunetoi* alludes via negation to *to xunon*, Heraclitus's term for the unity and coherence of the cosmos.[20] In our ignorance, humans are separated from this cosmic whole: "Although the *logos* is in common (*tou logou d'eontos xunou*), most people are living as if they have their own private thought" (B2/D2). Isolated in their private world, unable to commune with the common *logos*, they "do not understand (*ou xuniasin*) that what differs with itself agrees with itself" (B51/D49). As a result mortals are asleep when they think they are awake, they hear with deaf ears, they are absent while present (B34/D4; cf. B17/D3, B19/D5, B71–73/R54, B89/R56). This alienation is humanity's tragedy. But it is also a cosmic tragedy, for how can the *logos* be truly common if it does not include the understanding of mortals? Out of tempo with the common *logos*, human *axunesia* risks negating (*a*–) *to xunon*, creating a break in the circle whose beginning and end are in common (*xunon*, B103/D54).[21]

This possibility puts pressure on Heraclitus's own *logos* to transform ignorance (*axunesia*) into shared wisdom and in this way to secure the *xunos logos*. Heraclitus would thus seem to undertake to put together (*xun-hiēmi*, the root of *xunesis*)

19. Arist. *Rh.* 3.5 1407b11–18 (< A4/R6). I translate the adjective twice in an attempt to capture the ambiguity. I will return to this *apo koinou* construction at the end of the chapter. On the syntactical structure of B1/D1, see Gigon 1935, 1–11.

20. Lesher (1983, 163–67) stresses the novelty of Heraclitus's use of *xunesis* as genuine understanding, not mere perceptual contact. But we will see in the next section that the haptic sense ("putting together") remains active in the word. On Heraclitus's epistemological theory, see Hussey 1982; Lesher 1983; Curd 1991; Wilcox 1991, 631–33; and Graham 2009.

21. That the *xunos logos* requires human *xunesis* is hinted in the grammar of the opening clauses of B1/D1: the eternal being of the *logos* that on first glance might seem to be a genitive absolute is revealed, as one reads on, as the object of mortals' (lack of) understanding. The *logos* is at once independent and dependent, not just grammatically but ontologically, on human understanding. The same grammatical ambiguity structures B2/D2, where *tou logou d'eontos xunou* could be absolute or the object of human *phronēsis*. On the grammar, see Tarán 1986, 7–8.

our private thinking (*idia phronēsis*) with the *xunos logos* (B2/D2), on the assumption that "to think (*phroneein*) is common (*xunon*) to all" (B113/D29).[22] This *xun-* can be imagined in spatial terms—a fitting together of different parts—but it can also be taken temporally, as the first fragment's temporal idiom suggests. Heraclitus's challenge, then, as he establishes it at the opening of his book, is to bring human understanding into synchrony with cosmic eternity, to make the two temporalities simultaneous.

Let's consider these two temporalities more closely, beginning with the cosmic *aei*. Scholars differentiate between two senses of eternity: timeless eternity and an eternity of everlasting duration.[23] Does Heraclitus's *aei* fill all time or fall outside of time altogether? As we might expect from the philosopher of paradox, it seems to do both at once. The ambivalence is evident in fragment B30/D85.

> κόσμον τόνδε, τὸν αὐτὸν ἁπάντων, οὔτε τις θεῶν οὔτε ἀνθρώπων ἐποίησεν, ἀλλ' ἦν ἀεὶ καὶ ἔστιν καὶ ἔσται πῦρ ἀείζωον, ἁπτόμενον μέτρα καὶ ἀποσβεννύμενον μέτρα.
>
> This cosmos, the same of all, no god nor man created, but it always (*aei*) was and is and will be fire ever-living (*aeizōon*), kindled in measure and extinguished in measure.

This fragment places cosmic eternity (*aei*) within time, but it is a time without limit, neither beginning nor end. Like human time, it can be conceptualized in terms of past, present, and future, but it also renders that chronology meaningless as it fills all three temporalities with its eternal life (*aeizōon*).[24] Extending its present-tense being into past and future, this is eternity as limitless plenitude and presence, an eternal now. And yet like human time it is also subject to change, as it is kindled and extinguished in an alternation marked out by regular measures (*metra*) in a metronomic beat.

The cosmic *aei* thus seems to be simultaneously within time and beyond it, susceptible to its measures but not subject to its limits. To understand this paradox, we need to understand the nature of the Heraclitean cosmos. The universe Heraclitus imagines is dynamic and cyclical, ever-changing but always staying the same. Like the circle whose beginning and end are in common (B103/D54),

22. Cf. B114/D105, where Heraclitus seems to pun on "common" (*xunōi*) and "with mind" (*xun noōi*). Benjamin (2010, 29–53, 57–63) examines Heraclitus's *xunos* as a primordial "being-in-common."

23. Sorabji 1983, 98–130; and Wilberding 2016, 14–15. Ramelli and Konstan (2007, 5–35) survey the vocabulary for eternity in classical Greek literature.

24. Parmenides describes the eternity of Being similarly (*oude pot' ēn oud' estai, epei nun estin,* Parm. B8.5/D8.10), but there is debate over whether by this he envisions Being as interminable (Schofield 1970; O'Brien 1980; and Wilberding 2016, 16–21) or timeless (Owen 1974; and Sorabji 1983, 99–108). See further the references in chapter 1, n. 38 and the similar formulations of Melissus B1/D2; Emp. B16/D63, B21.9/D77a.9; Anax. B12/D27. The tripartite formula goes back to Homer (*Il.* 1.70) and Hesiod (*Th.* 38): see Šćepanović 2022. Benjamin (1988) offers a stimulating reading of the *aei* in B30/D85 as signaling a "temporal realm which is neither transcendental nor empirical" (121). Cf. Snell 1926, 374; and Heidegger and Fink 1993, 49–70.

it cycles forever, and its sequential transformations are circumscribed within a timeless repetition of sameness.[25] This cycle is reiterated at every level of the cosmic order. At the highest level, it describes the cycles (*tropai*) of elemental transformation: fire becomes sea, sea becomes earth (B31/D86, cf. B36/D100, B90/D87, B76/R54); the eternal fire is kindled and extinguished in endless alternation (B30/D85). At the human level, the same cycle describes the seasons of the year (B100/D90), the cycle of birth and death over human generations (B20/D118, A19/D69), and the alternation of day and night (B6/D91a, B94/D89c). At every level the rhythm of this cyclical transformation is regular and isometric: change is marked by *metra* (B30/D85, B31/D86, B94/D89c, A8/≠LM), the constant beats or measures that allow us to perceive change (and thus time) by themselves remaining unvarying.[26] This rhythmic revolution constitutes Heraclitus's *kosmos* in both senses of the word. It describes the structure of physical and metaphysical reality but also provides a paradigm of aesthetic order, one reflected in the artful symmetry and balance of Heraclitus's aphorisms, including B30/D85 with its isometric antithesis (*oute tis theōn oute anthrōpōn*), tricolon polyptoton (*all' ēn aei kai estin kai estai*), and balanced repetitions (*haptomenon metra kai aposbennumenon metra*). The fragment formally enacts the *kosmos* it describes.

Inasmuch as it undergoes—or in fact simply is—transformation, the Heraclitean cosmos is fully temporal, even if it has no beginning or end. Its transformations are not simultaneous but sequential, and they move at a steady tempo and on a fixed circuit.[27] This is clear, for instance, in fragment B31/D86, which describes the "turnings" (*tropai*) of the elements.

> πυρὸς τροπαὶ πρῶτον θάλασσα, θαλάσσης δὲ τὸ μὲν ἥμισυ γῆ, τὸ δὲ ἥμισυ πρηστήρ. . . . ⟨γῆ⟩ θάλασσα διαχέεται, καὶ μετρέεται εἰς τὸν αὐτὸν λόγον, ὁκοῖος πρόσθεν ἦν ἢ γενέσθαι γῆ.
>
> Turnings of fire: first sea, but of sea half is earth, half lightning storm. As earth sea is poured out, and it measures up (*metreetai*) to the same amount (*ton auton logon*) as it was before becoming earth.

The cosmic *tropai* have a temporal sequence (*prōton, prosthen*) that can be counted off in *metra* (*metreetai*). As in B30/D85, the metronomic repetition of the *metra*

25. *Aei* would be the appropriate adverb for this cyclical eternity if, as Chantraine (1968, 42) posits, the word often had the nuance of "each time" or "again and again." Fragments like B103/D54 suggest that the process is a closed circle, not an open rectangle, as proposed by Kirk (1954, 102–3), followed by Vieira (2013). As we shall see, however, it does not close completely. On the circle in Heraclitus and in Greek thought, see Ballew 1979.

26. Cf. B94/D89c: "Helios will not overstep his *metra*. If he does, the Erinyes, guardians of Dikē, will find him out." The plural (*metra*) may suggest multiple tempos; the point is regularity not singularity. See Kirk 1974; Long 2013; and on the semantic range of *metron*, Van Berkel 2013.

27. This is disputed. Kahn (1979, 139, 147–53) argues for periodic, sequential transformation; contra, Bollack and Wismann 1972, 134–36; and Porter 2024. Cf. Gigon (1935, 20–31) on the tension between a succession and unity of opposites.

measures change in a cosmos that is itself unchanging. In B30/D85 that cosmos is "the same of all" (*ton auton hapantōn*); it is the same order for all (people or things) and it remains the same through all time.[28] Likewise, the sequential "turnings" of the elements in B31/D86 revolve within a cycle that is itself timeless inasmuch as its transformations always preserve the same amount, *ton auton logon.*

Logos is this principle of sameness amid change, like the *logos* in B1/D1, which governs phenomenal becoming—"all things come about (*ginomenōn*) in accordance with this *logos*"—but itself is fixed in its unchanging being, "the *logos* that is (*eontos*) always." Flickering fire is one vivid example of this sameness-in-difference, like the cosmic fire that in B30/D85 is "ever-living" (*aeizōon*) even when extinguished.[29] But perhaps the best-known example is the river: "Upon those stepping into the same rivers different and different waters flow" (*potamoisi toisin autoisin embainousin hetera kai hetera hudata epirrhei*, B12/D65b, cf. B49a/D65a, B91a/≠LM). Different water is always flowing, but the river is always the same.[30] Like the cosmic *tropai*, the river exists both in time, as the *hetera kai hetera hudata* mimetically reproduce the rhythm of water flowing sequentially downstream, and out of time in the rivers' eternal self-sameness.

Plato characterized Heraclitus as a philosopher of flux, a constant and multidirectional transformation that destabilizes any fixed meaning or truth. He is followed in this by Nietzsche, who claims that Heraclitus knows only becoming, not being.[31] But that becoming flows regularly within fixed banks, and its flux operates within a logic of sameness regulated by a singular and constant—if ever-changing—element, whether we call it *logos* or *kosmos* or fire. This element functions as a cosmic universal equivalent, lending the coherent order to the

28. In B30/D85 Kahn and Laks-Most translate "the same for all." The genitive is odd, though, and may be a Stoic interpolation (Reinhardt 1959, 170n1; and Kirk 1954, 307–10; contra, Vlastos 1955, 344–47; and Marcovich 1967, 269–70).

29. On the choice of fire, see A5/R45; Wiggins 1982, 13–18; Furley 1987, 34–36; and Goldin 1991. Cf. B67/D48: "God: day night, winter summer, war peace, satiety hunger. He alters like fire when it is mixed with incense, and is named according to the flavor of each one." Other images of sameness amid change include Helios (B6/D91a, B16/D83, B94/D89c, B100/≠LM), Zeus (B32/D45), and war (B53/D64, B80/D63). Perhaps Nehamas (2002) is right (following Arist. *Metaph.* 1.3 984a7–10) that this makes Heraclitus an odd sort of monist.

30. Or perhaps those who step into it: *toisin autoisin* could go with "rivers" or "steppers," an ambiguity to which we will return at the end of the chapter. On the authenticity and interpretation of the river fragments, see Kirk 1954, 366–84; Tarán 1999; Dilcher 2005; Graham 2006, 129–37; and Mouraviev 2008.

31. Pl. *Cra.* 402a, 411b–c, 439c–440d; cf. Arist. *Metaph.* 4.5 1010a7–15, 13.4 1078b12–17; and Nietzsche 1962, 51 (on which Deleuze 2006, 23–25). On Plato's (mis)reading of Heraclitus, see Kirk 1954, 366–80; Kirk, Raven, and Schofield 1983, 194–97; and Colvin 2007. For Kahn (1979, 167–68) and Kirk (1974, 189–91), following Reinhardt (1959, 206–7), the river exemplifies the preservation of structure or regularity amid change; for Guthrie (1974) and Barnes (1982, 65–69), universal flux. Graham (2006, 113–47) offers a useful synopsis of the scholarly schism between "Heraclitus the Constancy Theorist" and "Heraclitus the Flux Theorist" and an intelligent attempt to bridge it; cf. 2008b, 172–76, 2013. See also Porter (2024), arguing for multidirectional flux.

transformations of becoming that allows us to speak of a cosmos at all. So Heraclitus suggests in B90/D87: "All things are exchange for fire and fire for all things, just as goods for gold and gold for goods" (*puros te antamoibē ta panta kai pur hapantōn hokōsper khrusou khrēmata kai khrēmatōn khrusos*). Far from a directionless flux that nullifies meaning, the universal signifier secures meaning. Its constant value enables substitution and hence exchanges of all sorts: commerce, communication, law.[32] As the equivalent of everything it also underpins the equation that describes Heraclitus's philosophy of paradox—all things are one.[33] Day is night, mortal immortal, sleeping waking: grounded on the universal *logos*, paradox is not the antithesis of this logic but its most general form. This singular entity, preserved in some way throughout the "turnings" of the elements, enables change, and therefore time,within the cosmos but is itself timeless, and it is because of this that the cosmic *aei* can be simultaneously timeless and time without end.

Against that cosmic *aei* Heraclitus sets the human *aiōn*: a life span, a period of vitality that ends in death. Although the two terms are related and later become synonymous, in early Greek *aiōn* was connected to the life force, the *zōē* or *psukhē*. As the animacy lost at the moment of death, *aiōn* denotes the duration of a life seen from the perspective of its end.[34] It is presumably to this terminal human temporality that Heraclitus alludes in B52/D76 when he says "*Aiōn* is a child playing, playing checkers. Sovereignty belongs to the child," although we will return to this fragment and to this presumption below.[35] *Aiōn* serves as a shorthand for a long tradition of Greek thought on mortal temporality. Long before Solon warned Croesus to "look to the end" (Hdt. 1.32.9), human existence was defined for the Greeks by its finitude: we are *thnētoi*, creatures whose lives will end in death. Heraclitus evokes this conception when he comments that mortals don't even know the

32. This singular economy grounds law (B33/D108, B114/D105); justice (B16/D83, B66/D84, B102/D73); ethics (B29/D13, B43/D112, B85/D116, B102/D73); social hierarchy (B39/D11, B49/D12); politics (B121/D14); war (B53/D64, B80/D63). See Kurke (1999, 50–52) for gold as sameness over time (and 58n36 on gold in Heraclitus). Seaford (2004, 231–42) connects Heraclitus's *logos* to the rise of money as both universal equivalent and transcendental abstraction.

33. Papamichael-Paspalides (2005) stresses the role of the One in Heraclitus's thought, but at the risk of reifying what is always for him a dynamic process.

34. Arist. *Cael.* 1.9 279a24–26: its *aiōn* "is the end (*telos*) encompassing the time of the life (*zōēs khronon*) of each creature, which nothing can exceed in accordance with nature." Hesychius A2216 defines *aiōn* as "the life (*bios*) of mortals, the time of living (*zōēs*)." The word could also denote the spinal marrow, perhaps as a vital fluid (*Hom. Hymn Hermes* 42, 119; Hipp. *Epid.* 7.122). The evolution of *aiōn*'s meaning from "life span" to "eternity" is traced by Lackeit 1916; Benveniste 1937; Festugière 1949; Chantraine 1968, 42; Couloubaritsis 1989; and Keizer 2000. Deleuze's conception of Aion as the empty nonpresent of the event, influenced by Stoicism, is hard to square with Heraclitus's usage: see Deleuze 1990, 62–65, 162–68 (with a veiled allusion to Heraclitus at 64).

35. Wohlfart (1991, 33–55) discusses in detail the meaning of the word in this fragment. See also Couloubaritsis (1989), stressing the link to both time and vitality.

things they encounter every day (*kat' hēmeran*, B72/R54, cf. B17/D3), an allusion to the Homeric designation of mortals as *ephēmerioi*, creatures of a day.[36]

This traditional conception of mortal existence afforded two traditional forms of immortality: biological reproduction through children and symbolic reproduction through *kleos*. Heraclitus alludes to these familiar ideas but adapts them to his cosmological scheme. He slights the former, as Clement notes in his introduction to B20/D118:

> Ἡ. γοῦν κακίζων φαίνεται τὴν γένεσιν, ἐπειδὰν φῆι· γενόμενοι ζώειν ἐθέλουσι μόρους τ' ἔχειν, μᾶλλον δὲ ἀναπαύεσθαι, καὶ παῖδας καταλείπουσι μόρους γενέσθαι.
>
> Heraclitus apparently reproaches generation when he says 'once born, they want to live and to have their destiny (*morous*), [or rather, to pause] and they leave behind them children to be their doom' (*morous*).

The fragment's play on the double meaning of *moros* figures reproduction as a cycle of morbidity, as the "destiny" promised by generation (*morous genesthai*) obliterates not just the hope for immortality but the modest desire to live out one's allotted life span (*morous t'ekhein*). In the fragment's punning and ring composition, birth (*genomenoi*) generates death (*morous genesthai*); life (*zōein*) becomes a mere "pause," as Clement says, between *moros* and *moros*.[37] In the idiom of B52/D76, *aiōn* is a game quickly over, and the "sovereignty" of the child is nothing but mortal finitude.

To hope for immortality through one's children is thus a fool's game. But "greater deaths (*moroi*) are allotted greater destinies (*moiras*)" (B25/D122b), and the best men seek immortality by other means:

> αἱρεῦνται γὰρ ἓν ἀντὶ ἁπάντων οἱ ἄριστοι, κλέος ἀέναον θνητῶν· οἱ δὲ πολλοὶ κεκόρηνται ὅκωσπερ κτήνεα. (B29/D13)
>
> The best men choose one thing in exchange for everything: glory ever-flowing (*kleos aenaon*) among men. But the many are sated like cattle.

Again, the idea is familiar: Kahn reads the fragment as an allusion to Achilles's choice in the *Iliad* between undying *kleos* and a long but finite life.[38] Heraclitus integrates the theme into his cosmology. The adjective *aenaon* ("ever-flowing")

36. Fränkel (1946) argues that *ephēmerioi* refers not to the brevity of human existence ("creature of a day") but to its instability (changing from one day to another); Dickie (1976) defends the former definition. The close connection between the two qualities in archaic thought (cf. Parmenides's Doxa) makes it hard to decide between them in any given context. See further Nooter 2023, 17–24.

37. *Mallon de anapauesthai* is presumably Clement's interjection, but note the suggestive parallel at B84a/D58: *metaballon anapauetai.* Plutarch reports that Heraclitus called a period of thirty years a generation (A19/D69), a mere drop in the bucket compared to the 10,800 years it takes for a full cycle of the cosmic rotation (A13/R64).

38. Kahn 1979, 233–34. Nussbaum (1972b) connects immortality through *kleos* to the Heraclitean *psukhē*'s novel (in her view) affinity for *logos.*

connects *kleos* to the "ever-living" (*aeizōon*) fire of B30/D85 and the *logos* that exists *aei* of B1/D1, as well as the ever-changing, ever-the-same river of B12/D65b, while the choice of "one thing in exchange for everything" recalls the *antamoibē* of all things for fire in B90/D87. Through these echoes, *kleos aenaon* connects the mortal *aiōn*—a brief life ending in death—to the cycle of material transformation that constitutes the cosmic *aei.*[39]

In the *Phaedo*, in a passage full of Heraclitean echoes, Plato argues for the immortality of the *psukhē.*[40] For him it is because the *psukhē* is immaterial, unlike the perishable body, that it is immortal. For Heraclitus, by contrast, the *psukhē*'s immortality derives from its materiality, a materiality that binds the animating breath of the individual to the physical elements that make up the cosmos. The human *psukhē* is one of those elements, though whether we should imagine it as fire or air or some combination of the two is much debated.[41] A physical substance, it is degraded by contact with liquid (B77/D101, B117/D104): "A dry *psukhē* is wisest and best" (B118/D103). As part of the physical stuff of the cosmos it participates in the *tropai* of elements. "Breathed out" at death in the form of an airy exhalation (*anathumiasis*), it becomes water. It is drawn into the endless flow of the cosmic river, both metaphorically and literally: the river metaphor of B12/D65b may in fact describe the *psukhē* and refer to this very process.[42] Fragment B36/D100 tells us where it goes from there: "For *psukhai* it is death to become water, for water it is death to become earth; from earth water is born, from water *psukhē*."[43] *Psukhai* die and are reborn in an unending cycle of material transformation and in this way become immortal. The fragment both describes and enacts this eternal cycle in its almost perfectly circular form (we will return to that "almost").

Heraclitus's "psychophysics" radically reconfigures the traditional nature of the *psukhē*. Etymologically linked to the breath, the *psukhē* in Homer figures the animating force of the living individual.[44] It appears at death as a ghostly double of the

39. The phrase *kleos aenaon* also appears in Simonides's epitaph for the Spartan dead at Thermopylae (531.8–9 *PMG*), to which Heraclitus may be alluding (Sider 2013, 326–27). See also Pind. *Ol.* 14.12: *aienaon timan.*

40. *Phd.* 70d–72d. On the *Phaedo*'s "reminders" of Heraclitus, see Rowett 2017. For Plato, the immortality of the *psukhē* means the survival of the individual, an idea alien to Heraclitus's eschatology.

41. The best recent discussion is by Betegh (2013), who splits the difference by associating *psukhē* with air in a variety of states, from moist to fiery.

42. So, at least, we are told by Arius Didymus, citing Cleanthes citing Zeno (with support from Arist. *De an.* 1.2 405a27: *reon aei*): see Mouraviev 2008. It is doubtful that Heraclitus himself mentioned *anathumiasis* (Kirk 1954, 367–72) and the entire exhalation theory may be a Stoic superimposition: see the discussion by Dilcher (1995, 62–65), who defends it as original to Heraclitus; likewise, Buchheim 2005.

43. Marcovich (1967, 362–64) takes this fragment to describe a process within the human organism not the destiny of the *psukhē* after death. Contra, Schofield (1991, 15–21), for whom it epitomizes the principle that the *psukhē* is subject to the same processes as the cosmos. See further Betegh 2006.

44. Rohde 1925, 3–54; Snell 1953, 8–17; and Chantraine 1968, 1294–95. Claus (1981) argues that it never fully lost that Homeric meaning. The term "psychophysics" is Hölscher's (1968, 156); cf. Kahn 1979, 238.

dying hero; breathed out with his final breath, it flutters away to the underworld. We might think of it as a posthumous quasi-personification of the *aiōn*, which evaporates when life ends.[45] Pindar calls this evanescent remainder "the still-living image of a lifetime" (*aiōnos eidōlon*, 131b S-M). But for Heraclitus the *psukhē* does not evanesce at death. Instead, it becomes a gleam (*augē*, B118/R101) of the ever-living fire. In this way, through its mutable materiality and not (as for Plato) through its immateriality, the *psukhē* becomes eternal.[46] Snell may be correct, then, to credit Heraclitus with "a new concept of the soul"—not, however, as a spiritual substance within the individual but as a material substance that exceeds her. If the limit of the *psukhē* is unreachable, as B45/D98 proclaims, it is not because "the soul, as contrasted with things physical, reaches into infinity," as Snell says, but because it participates *as a physical thing* in a physical process that is infinite.[47]

Through the material afterlife of the *psukhē*, we enter the eternity of the cosmic *aei*. Trading "all things for fire," we gain immortality in the fire ever-living (*aeizōon*). But in doing so we must relinquish the *aiōn*, our ephemeral life and all it contains. In the Achillean choice of B29/D13, "the best men" choose one thing in exchange for all, "glory ever-flowing among men." In the *Iliad* that choice affirms the value of a human life: *kleos aphthiton* is the only thing worth the sacrifice of one's *aiōn* (9.415) or the loss of one's *psukhē*, which can never be regained once "it has passed the barrier of the teeth" (9.408–9). Heraclitus asks us to make a more radical choice: he offers us immortality at the price not just of an individual life but of human life as a whole, which is reduced to a base animal existence, the satiety of the herd ("But the many are sated like cattle"). Joining in the eternal cycle of fire, water, and earth, we become immortal but only, as Kahn writes, by "the overcoming of everything personal, partial, and particular, in the recognition and full acceptance of what is common to all."[48] *Aiōn* and *aei* are thus mutually exclusive not just in the trivial sense that death is the prerequisite for immortality, but in the more absolute sense suggested by the exchange of everything for one thing. We may gain the blaze of eternity, but we lose our lives in the fire.

45. Thus the death of Sarpedon is described as the departure of the *psukhē te kai aiōn* (Hom. *Il.* 16.453). The Sarpedon episode is the setting for the earliest visual depictions of the *psukhē*: see Wohl 2020, 128–31. We will return to one image of the scene (without *psukhē*) below.

46. Thus if for Homer the *psukhē* is material and therefore perishable and for Plato the *psukhē* is immaterial and therefore imperishable, Heraclitus's *psukhē* is imperishable because material. Finkelberg (2009) offers a Platonic reading of the Heraclitean *psukhē* as divine until embodied.

47. Snell 1953, 17. For Snell, Heraclitus occupies a key moment in a historical trajectory of spiritual transcendence, as the soul liberates itself from the corporeal and moves toward ever greater abstraction, rationality, and self-consciousness. The Hegelian orientation of this trajectory is signaled by the word *Geist* in Snell's title. Compare Hegel's parenthetical discussion of Heraclitus at Hegel 1975b, 132–33.

48. Kahn 1979, 253; cf. 1979, 222–27, 238–40, 245–54. Kahn is sanguine about this exchange of the private self for "something better" (253), but as we shall see in the next section, Heraclitus invites us to doubt (as Achilles himself did) whether immortality at this cost is such a good deal.

This brings us back to the ambiguous "always" of fragment B1/D1. That fragment opens a vista onto eternity. But as soon as we contemplate that *aei* we begin to lose sight of our mortal *aiōn*.[49] "Of this *logos* that is always (*aei*) mortals are always uncomprehending, both before they have heard it and when they have first heard it." The *logos* is the marker of time for mortals, but the chronology it produces is confused: not quite before and after. Human temporality is blurred and with it the change (*ginontai, ginomenōn*) that defines our existence. Experience is no different from inexperience: "They are like people without experience even when they experience such words and deeds as I expound." Memory slides into *lēthē*, the oblivion of a sleepwalker: "Other men are not aware (*lanthanei*) of what they do when they are awake, just as they forget (*epilanthanontai*) what they do when asleep." Fragment B1/D1 offers us a vantage on cosmic eternity, the *logos* that exists always. But from that eternal perspective time, change, experience, memory, the rhythms of the day—all the things that make up an individual *aiōn*—dim and fade from view.

The *aei* of B1/D1 thus marks an irreducible asynchrony between cosmic temporality and human. Human life cannot be brought into rhythm with the cosmic cycle without the loss of its defining *metra*, its unique tempos and temporality. We may come to understand that day and night are one (B57/D25a, B106/D25b), but that understanding renders our existence as *ephēmerioi*, creatures of a day, meaningless. This would seem to indicate the limits of Heraclitus's synthetic project—his hope of transforming *axunetoi anthrōpoi* into *xunetoi*—and of his synthetic vision of a *xunos logos*, for a *logos* that excludes human life is not truly *xunos*. The eternal circle of Heraclitus's cosmology would seem to be a bad infinity, returning always to the "common (*xunon*) beginning and end" (B103/D54) of noncoincidence between the cosmic and the human. Out of tempo with the cosmic cycle, human life is an eternal hole in the cosmic whole.

APHORISM LULLABY

And yet Heraclitus does manage to bring together *aei* and *aiōn*. He effects this synthesis or *xunesis* (literally, "putting together") through the form of his aphorisms.[50] Aphorism has its own particular formal temporality. On the one hand, its brevity makes aphorism the most ephemeral of forms.[51] Delimited by definition

49. Long (1992, 272) speaks of "Heraclitus's view from nowhere." *Aei* and *aiōn* form a parallax, two closely related perspectives that can nonetheless never be synthesized: see Žižek 2006 and chapter 5 below.

50. This section title is a nod to Derrida's essay "Aphorism Countertime" (1992a). Derrida proposes that the aphoristic form precludes synchronicity or simultaneity (both of which are implied by his term *contretemps*). While the same can be said of Heraclitus's aphorisms (as we shall see in the next section), this section shows that his aphorisms can also eliminate asynchrony by eliminating time altogether.

51. For Grant (2016, 45), aphorism's apparent instantaneity "produces an immediate and striking effect, like a flash of lightning." The lightning strike recurs in discussions of aphorism including

(*ap-horizein*), the aphorism exists apart from the temporal flow of continuous narrative or extended exegesis; like the individual *aiōn*, it occupies but a brief and terminal moment. On the other hand, inasmuch as it claims to encapsulate an essential truth, the aphorism is timeless: Nietzsche (himself one of the great aphorists) called aphorism one of "the forms of 'eternity.'"[52] "In this smallness," writes Ben Grant in his study of aphorism, "our short human life and eternity come together, for the timelessness of the truth that the aphorism encapsulates can only be measured against our own ephemerality, of which the brevity of the aphorism serves as an apt expression."[53]

Simultaneously fleeting and eternal, the aphorism brings together *aiōn* and *aei*. Heraclitus exploits and develops this paradoxical temporality with the skillful rhythms of his prose.

> ταὐτό τ' ἔνι ζῶν καὶ τεθνηκὸς καὶ [τὸ] ἐγρηγορὸς καὶ καθεῦδον καὶ νέον καὶ γηραιόν· τάδε γὰρ μεταπεσόντα ἐκεῖνά ἐστι κἀκεῖνα πάλιν μεταπεσόντα ταῦτα. (B88/D68)

> The same within: living and being dead and being awake and sleeping and young and old. For these things, changing, are those and those, changing again, are these.[54]

Through its formal structure, this fragment replicates the rift between human and cosmic time. The first sentence measures out the finite arc of a human life span. The leisurely polysyndeton (and . . . and . . . and) counts off its discrete *metra*, the sequential moments that make up an *aiōn*. But "the same within" erases these *metra* and compresses the human narrative into an atemporal simultaneity of "the same." That paradoxical instant is extended in the second sentence; changing and changing back in an unchanging circuit, its chiasmus reproduces the timeless time of the cosmic cycle and sustains us, as we read it, within that impossible temporality. Through its form, this aphorism allows us to feel the different tempos of human and cosmic time; even as it reproduces the split between *aiōn* and *aei* it enables us to experience both simultaneously and thus bridges at the level of sensation a gap that is ineradicable at the level of sense.

Morson 2012, 46; and Marsden 2006, 29. It also figures in both Nietzsche's and Heidegger's reading of Heraclitus (Nietzsche 1962, 50; Heidegger 1975, 78; and Heidegger and Fink 1993, 10).

52. Nietzsche 1998, 75. On Nietzsche's aphorisms, see Blanchot 1993, 151–70; Marsden 2006; and Grant 2016, 97–98. Heraclitus emphasizes this gnomic timelessness with his evocations of the Delphic oracle (B92/D42, B93/D41) and the abiding truth of divine speech; see Grant 2016, 7–8.

53. Grant 2016, 4.

54. The opening as Diels-Kranz print it is probably corrupt, and scholars are divided on how to understand *t'eni*: see Laks 2015, 43. Some editors attribute the second sentence to Ps.-Plutarch, who quotes the fragment. But the same pattern of paradoxical unity of opposites followed by chiasmus is also found in B10/D47, B62/D70, and B67/D48, and I am inclined to think it is original. Bollack and Wismann (1972, 261) offer a subtle analysis of the temporality of the fragment; Deichgräber (1963, 31–33) parses its meter, remarking on the structural similarity to B10/D47 (35). Cf. Mouraviev 2006, 124–25, and for detailed analysis of Heraclitus's prose rhythms, both metrical and syllabotonic, Mouraviev 2002, 219–64.

Nietzsche posited that Heraclitus knows no present moment of being between coming-into-being and passing-away.[55] This non-time is what Aristotle calls "the now" (*to nun*), an instantaneous division between past and future with no temporal duration of its own.[56] Heraclitus's aphorisms hold us in this impossible now, a paradoxical present that is the human experience of cosmic time. As in "the same within," Heraclitus's union of opposites both produces and is produced by an extreme temporal compression that renders the sequential simultaneous.[57] Consider fragment B60/D51: "The road up/down is one and the same" (*hodos anō katō mia kai hōutē*). If understood in static spatial terms, the fragment is a truism: it is one and the same road whether one is heading up to the Acropolis or down to the Piraeus. The truism becomes a paradox only when motion, direction, and change are introduced: laws of physics make it impossible to walk the road from north to south and south to north at the same time. The paradox is produced, in other words, by removing the element of time, by imagining sequential movement (going up *then* going down) as simultaneous: up/down, *anō katō*.[58] There is not even the interval of an "and" in which to switch directions. Instead, that "and" is introduced in the pleonastic "one and the same" (*mia kai hōutē*). That pleonasm allows us to linger, paradoxically, in the instantaneity of the paradox, extending its atemporal "now" into a brief but perceptible duration of human experience.[59]

Or consider another famous fragment, B51/D49.

> οὐ ξυνιᾶσιν ὅκως διαφερόμενον ἑωυτῶι ὁμολογέει· παλίντροπος ἁρμονίη ὅκωσπερ τόξου καὶ λύρης.
>
> They do not comprehend how what differs with itself agrees with itself: back-turned *harmoniē* as of a bow and a lyre.

The compressed phrase "what differs with itself agrees with itself" (*diapheromenon heōutōi homologeei*) encapsulates Heraclitus's unity of opposites and raises it to the meta-level as the unity-in-opposition of unity and opposition themselves. The paradox is elaborated through a simile that introduces further paradox. The linking of instruments of death and music illustrates the abstract claim that "what

55. Nietzsche 1962, 51. Plutarch (*de E* 392A10–E6) says much the same thing, quoting B91/≠LM and B76/R54.

56. Arist. *Ph.* 4.10 218a3–8. On Aristotle's *to nun*, see Coope 2005, 17–30, 125–39.

57. Long 1992, 269: "Remove all temporal distinctions, and you get the identity of living and dead." The first series of Deleuze's *Logic of Sense* (1990) stresses the temporality of paradox: "the simultaneity of a becoming whose characteristic is to elude the present" (1).

58. As Deleuze (1990, 74–81) argues, paradox does not simply reverse the direction of *doxa* but challenges the very notion of directionality by pointing in two directions at once. It is possible that Heraclitus's contrary roads refer to the cosmic cycle, which the doxographers sometimes speak of as a *hodos epi to katō* (from fire to water to earth) and a *hodos epi to anō* (from earth to water to fire): see Diog. Laert. 9.9 (< A1/R46b).

59. The pattern of paradox followed by pleonasm may recur in B59/D52 and B118/R101, but the text of both fragments is uncertain.

differs with itself agrees with itself," as does each instrument in itself if we imagine its string tensed between two parts straining in opposite directions, or the hand of the user pulling back to project the arrow or sound forward.[60] That tense simultaneity of opposite lines of force is perhaps what Heraclitus means by *palintropos harmoniē*. But the temporality of these words is complicated. *Harmoniē*, from *arariskō*, is originally a metaphor from construction: the fitting together of different parts to form an integrated whole (for instance, a building or wall) designed to remain fixed through time. By Heraclitus's day the word had also taken on a musical sense, though one rather different from our own. For the Greeks, *harmoniē* meant not the simultaneous sounding of different notes but a pattern of attunement, that is, the sequential ordering of different pitches into a tonal system.[61] So *harmoniē* is both simultaneous (the enduring structure of a well-fitted wall) and sequential (musical patterns that unfold in time). The same temporal ambiguity is perhaps reflected in the textual uncertainty around *palintropos. Palintropos* comes from *trepō*, turning back. Kahn relates it to the cyclical revolutions of the *puros tropai.*[62] But there was an ancient variant: *palintonos*, from *teinō* (to stretch, strain). While *palintropos* entails movement and therefore temporality, *palintonos* suggests the static state of strings held in tension.

Superimposing simultaneity and sequentiality, the fragment jams time in a tense and intense instant. This reading of the fragment's temporality finds confirmation in Plato's *Symposium*, when Eryximachus loosely quotes B51/D49 in the course of his argument that eros reconciles opposites (Pl. *Symp*. 187a5–6). He finds the image nonsensical: when opposite things are brought into harmony, they are no longer opposite; conversely, as long as they are opposite, they are not in harmony. "Perhaps," he suggests, "Heraclitus meant that out of an initial (*proteron*) opposition of sharp and flat notes, harmony is produced subsequently (*epeita husteron*) after they have been made to agree through the musical art" (187a8–b1).[63] He resolves the paradox by reintroducing a clear chronological sequence. In this way he shows that it is precisely time—or rather its elimination—that makes the paradox so paradoxical.

60. The latter interpretation is proposed by Vlastos (1955, 351 and n32).

61. Gurd 2016, 116 (with further references in n125).

62. Kahn 1979, 199–200. The reading *palintropos* is defended forcefully by Vlastos (1955, 348–51), against Kirk (1954, 211–14) and Marcovich (1967, 125–26). Mackenzie (2021b) discusses the textual alternatives in light of a possible allusion to Odysseus's stringing of the bow in *Odyssey* 21. *Palin* itself can be both spatial ("backward") and temporal ("again"). Cf. B88/D68, where *palin* expresses the simultaneous temporality ("once and again") and timelessness ("again and again") of the elemental cycle.

63. Compare Plutarch's comment on B91/≠LM ("they scatter and come together again *[palin]* . . . and are present and absent"); he interjects, "Rather, it is not again (*palin*) and later (*husteron*) but at the same time (*hama*) that they combine and cease and 'are present and absent,'" *de E* 392B10–C1). *Palin* introduces temporal sequence (*husteron*); the paradox, as Plutarch recognizes, lies in the simultaneity (*hama*).

But Heraclitus not only eliminates time but, as we saw with the road up/down, allows us to linger in that paradoxical instant. Fragment B10/D47 also uses *harmoniē* to figure the concordance of opposites:

> συνάψιες ὅλα καὶ οὐχ ὅλα, συμφερόμενον διαφερόμενον, συνᾶιδον διᾶιδον, καὶ ἐκ πάντων ἓν καὶ ἐξ ἑνὸς πάντα.
>
> Conjunctions (*sunapsies*): wholes and not wholes, converging diverging, consonant dissonant, and from all one and from one all.[64]

The aphorism is structured similarly to fragment B88/D68. The first part compresses opposites to their asyndetic extreme: without the temporality of a finite verb or even the tiniest conjunction of space or time between *sun*- and *dia*- (not even the *kai* that distinguishes whole and not whole), Heraclitus's *sunapsies* come together in a timeless instant.[65] But the second part unfolds these tightly packed oppositions into a more commodious chiasmus, "and from all one and from one all." The double *kai* ("and") slows down the tempo and the double *ek* ("from") reintroduces the temporal duration of cyclical transformation, the before and after that Plato's Eryximachus wanted in order to make sense of Heraclitus's dissonant harmony. Circling between one and all, this chiastic clause holds us suspended within the eternal now of atemporal conjunction.

The chiasmus is, in fact, one of Heraclitus's favorite forms and it structures many of his aphorisms.[66] The trope enacts at the aesthetic level the *tropai* of the elements that constitute Heraclitus's cosmos, as in B36/D100 where the description of the cosmic cycle is replicated in the chiasmus of *psukhai*-water-earth-water-*psukhē*. Through this mimetic effect, Heraclitus's own *logos* joins with the *xunos logos*, performing the unity it describes.[67] That unity is effected less through the logical sense of the propositional content than through the sensory response elicited by the aphorism's form. In her insightful discussion of Nietzsche's aphorisms, Jill Marsden describes aphorism as a kind of sensory paradox. Because of their

64. *Sunapsies* is disputed, and some editors read *sullapsies* ("graspings"). I like the former for its resonance with *haptomai* in B26/D71 and B30/D85, but *lambanō* is also a good Heraclitean word (B28/D28, B56/D22, B66/D84). Dilcher (1995, 112–14) offers a careful reading of the fragment's structure.

65. The paradoxical temporality of this fragment is intensified by the participles, which have aspect but not tense: the present aspect turns action within time into the timeless present of an ongoing condition. Asyndeton reproduces the disjointedness of aphorism within the aphorism. As Dilcher (1995, 134) points out, it characterizes many of Heraclitus's aphorisms (e.g. B10/D47, B60/D51, B67/D48, B111/D56, B126/D67). Demetrius notes the feature and blames it for the author's obscurity (A4/R7).

66. Most conspicuously in the final sentence of B1/D1, and B10/D47, B21/D72, B25/D122b, B26/D71, B36/D100, B88/D68, B90/D87, B126/D67. For a detailed taxonomy and discussion see Mouraviev 2002, 334–49.

67. This mimetic effect has often been noted. For a recent discussion see Vieira 2013. Graham (2009, 79) advances an argument similar to my own, that "Heraclitus does not just tell us about reality, but he *shows* us. . . . He expects us not simply to read his words but to *experience* them," although he describes that experience in terms of cognition, not corporeal sensation.

rapidity, their "rhythmic necessity—prior to comprehension," aphorisms shake us out of our doxic assumptions and open us to a new way of knowing, one that is less cognitive than corporeal and affective. "What is momentarily glimpsed or made tangible in the aphorism," she writes, "is a mute affective vitality."[68] Marsden's formulation neatly encapsulates the effect of Heraclitus's chiastic aphorisms. Suspending the reader in a timeless present, they make tangible the eternal rhythm of the cosmic *aei*, allowing us to sense its *metra* in our bodies.

We grasp this rhythm in a state of receptivity akin to a waking sleep. Sleep is a recurring theme in Heraclitus's fragments.[69] We encountered it in B1/D1 as a metaphor for the condition of mortals before hearing the *logos*. These people "are not aware (*lanthanei*) of what they do when they are awake, just as they forget (*epilanthanontai*) what they do when asleep." Sleepwalking through life, they are wrapped in oblivious isolation: "Heraclitus says that the cosmos is one and in common for those who are awake, but each sleeper turns to his own private cosmos" (B89/R56).[70] To "act and speak like sleepers" (B73/R54) is to "forget (*epilanthanomenou*) where the road is leading" (B71/R54). For such people "those things they encounter every day seem to them alien" (B72/R54). Sleep is thus a paradigm for human incomprehension, our alienation from knowledge of the cosmic whole, a metaphysical *lēthē*.

But Heraclitus transforms this *lēthē* into a mode of embodied *alētheia* through the chiastic lullaby of his aphorisms.

> ἄνθρωπος ἐν εὐφρόνηι φάος ἅπτεται ἑαυτῶι ἀποσβεσθεὶς ὄψεις, ζῶν δὲ ἅπτεται τεθνεῶτος εὕδων, ἐγρηγορὼς ἅπτεται εὕδοντος. (B26/D71)
>
> A man kindles (*haptetai*) a light for himself in the night when his eyes are extinguished. While he is alive, he touches (*haptetai*) the dead in his sleep; waking, he touches (*haptetai*) the sleeper.[71]

This intricately patterned fragment, with its interlocking double chiasmus, both juxtaposes and interweaves life and death, waking and sleeping. The first clause

68. Marsden 2006, 27, 29. Among its physiological effects, Marsden notes, aphorism denaturalizes the act of reading. We will see this effect of Heraclitus's aphorisms at the end of the chapter. Clarifying the affective force of Heraclitus's formal structure allows us to develop the often-quoted insight of Verdenius (1966, 90) that "die Einheit der Gegensätze, nicht zu beweisen, sondern nur intuitiv zu erfassen ist." Nietzsche (1962, 52) likewise stresses Heraclitus's intuition.

69. I examine the philosophical perplexities of sleep in Wohl 2020. Carson (1999, 55–60) writes eloquently on sleeping and waking in Heraclitus. See also Mansfeld 1967; Kahn 1979, 213–16; Rankin 1995; and Laks 2015, 40–45.

70. Only the first clause seems to be Heraclitus's own words; the second is a paraphrase of B2/D2. Laks-Most (R56) take the whole quotation as paraphrase.

71. I omit Clement's explanatory annotations, printed in Diels-Kranz. The fragment is well analyzed by Schofield (1991, 27–28). Mansfeld (1967) provides the history of its emendation and interpretation; see also Rousseau 1970. Laks (2015, 44) stresses sleep as a simultaneous experience of life and death but reads the fragment as referring to dreams; likewise Kahn 1979, 214–15.

shades imperceptibly from the literal to the metaphoric and from the everyday to the existential, as the darkness of night deepens into the blindness of death. The second clause returns to life (*zōn de*), which it figures as an alternation of sleeping and waking. But instead of viewing these as opposed states, this fragment figures them as a haptic continuum. The kindling (*haptetai*) of a light in the night of death is repeated in the touch (*haptetai*) of that dead self. Sleep is the condition of that "touch," which is then carried over into waking life. The waking man touches his sleeping self, who touches his dead self, who touches the light of an eternal life-in-death. The language of the fragment, with its balanced clauses, repetitions, and interlacing word order, replicates that continuum, weaving life and death, sleeping and waking, into a synthetic state that serves as a virtual definition of *anthrōpos.*

In this somnolent state the individual grasps (*haptetai*) her connection to the cosmos: her body becomes a physical register of its wholeness and cohesion. The language of kindling and quenching links this fragment to B30/D85 and the cyclical transformation of the cosmic fire, "kindled (*haptomenon*) in measure and extinguished (*aposbennumenon*) in measure." Waking and sleeping are figured as a quotidian experience not only of life and death but of the underlying dynamics of the physical universe, marking out in our bodies the regular *metra* of its elemental beat. But the fragment lets us feel not only the sequential alternation of the cosmic kindling and quenching but also the simultaneity of these opposite states, kindling the light of life in the night of death and touching death while alive. The fragment's chiasms lull us into a lucid lethargy in which we can apprehend corporeally, if not comprehend intellectually, the concordance of opposites that Heraclitus calls "conjunctions" (*sunapsies*, from *sun-haptomai*, B10/D47).[72]

I have been translating the verb *haptetai* in the first clause of B26/D71 as a middle voice: "kindles for himself." But that usage is unparalleled, and it is equally possible that the verb is passive.[73] That would make the *anthrōpos* himself the light kindled in the dark. Elsewhere Heraclitus describes the *psukhē* as a gleam or flash of light (*augē*, B118/R101).[74] Lit up in death, the *psukhē* becomes a literal spark of the ever-living fire. Leaving our extinguished bodies, that *psukhē* will join in the cosmic chiasmus of elemental birth and death: "For *psukhai* it is death to become water, for water it is death to become earth; from earth water is born, from water

72. See n. 64 above on the textual question surrounding *sunapsies.* B26/D71 also plays on an opposition of touch and vision. When our eyes are quenched, touch gives us access to the "invisible harmony" that is better than the visible (B54/D50). Ellis (2020b, 129–39) emphasizes the haptic nature of cognition for Heraclitus.

73. In the active *haptō* means to fasten or join, as well as to kindle; in the middle it usually means to touch or to grasp, both physically and (by extension) conceptually, and takes a genitive. The construction here, a middle with the accusative, is thus doubly atypical: see Rousseau 1970. Heidegger and Fink (1993, 127–49) worry at some length over the meaning of *haptetai* in Heraclitus B26/D71.

74. The text is uncertain. On the fire of the *psukhē,* see Kahn 1979, 245–54; and Betegh 2013. Cf. Macrob. *In Somn.* 1.14.19 (= R48c/≠DK): "Heraclitus the natural philosopher [calls the *psukhē*] a spark of the stars' substance (*scintillam stellaris essentiae*)."

psukhē" (B36/D100). It is this ever-living/ever-dying *psukhē* that we touch in sleep, feeling its presence within us as a "mute affective vitality."

In this way, fragment B26/D71 enables us to sense both the eternal fire and the spark that is our own part in it. But that immortal spark appears only in the night of our own lives and can be seen only with extinguished eyes. Where does this leave the *aiōn?* The aphorism figures living as an alternation of sleeping and waking, evoking the alternating *metra* that measure out our quotidian existence. But touch reaches across this defining antithesis in a morbid contiguity. The balance of life and death is lost, and living becomes no more than a pause (*zōn*) between the night of death and a sleep from which we never fully wake.

The fragment thus allows us to touch the cosmic *aei* but at the risk of losing our grip on the *aiōn*. That risk is realized in the fever dream of fragment B21/D72.

> θάνατός ἐστιν ὁκόσα ἐγερθέντες ὁρέομεν, ὁκόσα δὲ εὕδοντες ὕπνος.
>
> Death is whatever we see when awake, whatever [we see when] sleeping is sleep.

The aphorism promises a perfect chiasmus between death and life, waking and sleeping. At the level of form, its structural symmetry and the soft alliteration of initial aspirations lull us into the same somnolent state as B26/D71. At the level of content, the aphorism poses a literal paradox in the untraditional association of waking with death. But paradox becomes aprosdoketon when we reach the final term of the chiasmus: the symmetry is broken and in place of the expected *bios* we get *hupnos. Thanatos* is whatever we see when we are awake, whatever we see when we are asleep is . . . sleep. The fragment stands, as Kahn says, "at the climax of Heraclitus's riddling."[75] The association of waking with death may be understood in terms of the unity of opposites that in B88/D68 declared "the same within: living and being dead and being awake and sleeping." But the second clause seems tautological on the face of it, not a unity of opposites but a repetition of the same. In place of a balanced alternation of life and death, waking and sleep, or even a sustained tension between these opposite states, this chiasmus collapses in on itself. Waking and sleeping circle back on one another, leaving no room for life, only for death.

The effect can be measured by reading this fragment against another contemporary meditation on sleep and death: Euphronios's krater depicting the death of

75. Kahn 1979, 213: "Does Heraclitus mean after all to identify life with the private, half-conscious, phantom experience of the dream world? Apparently not, and that is why the sentence does not end as symmetry would require." Similarly, Schofield 1991, 30. Ramnoux (1968, 36–38) asks the same question as Kahn but answers in the affirmative. Diels emphasizes the asymmetry with his proposed supplement: *hokosa de tethnēkotes zōē*. It is worth noting that Heraclitus never uses the noun *zōē* in the extant fragments, only verbal forms of the word (B2/D2, B20/D118, B26/D71, B62/D70, B30/D85, B63/D123, B88/D68). He does use the noun *bios* (B48/D53, B62/D70) and of course *thanatos*, but life (*zōē*) is for him an activity not a state.

FIGURE 1. Calyx-krater by Euphronios showing the body of Sarpedon lifted by Hupnos and Thanatos. From Ceveteri, ca. 515 BCE. Museo Nazionale Etrusco di Villa Giulia, Rome. Photo: Scala/Ministero per i Beni e le Attività culturali / Art Resource, NY.

Sarpedon (fig. 1).[76] Like Heraclitus's fragment, this vase forms a perfect chiasmus between death (Thanatos, labeled on the right) and Hupnos (on the left). That chiastic structure is underlined repeatedly: by the X formed at the top by Hermes's rhabdos and raised hand, and at the edges by the gods' wings and legs, echoed by Sarpedon's own arms and legs. Form follows content as the image, like the gods, holds Sarpedon in suspension between life and death. That perfect equilibrium lasts but a moment, though. The image's lines of action draw the eye up from the bottom left corner, with its overlapping feet of god and men (both dead and living), across Sarpedon's body, to the wingtip of death.[77] The image is an instant of suspension in a larger narrative trajectory that leads from life to death. Although Hupnos and Thanatos work together to bear Sarpedon from the battlefield, you can see that Hupnos's grip is already slipping: soon the hero will belong entirely to

76. The vase is dated to 515, so almost exactly contemporary with Heraclitus. Neer (2002, 44–66) analyzes Euphronios's style as an instantiation of Heraclitus's "backsprung tension." He posits a chiastic relation in the vases between the object depicted and the technique of its depiction, between flatness and depth, that creates a "visual paradox" (61).

77. Many of these lines flow downward (the blood from Sarpedon's wounds, his dropping arm and leg, the fold of Hermes's cloak), but visually the way down and the way up are one.

Thanatos. This trajectory offers a narrative exemplum of the other major structural component of the image, the T formed by Sarpedon's supine body and Hermes's upright figure. Superimposed over the X of Sleep and Death, this T figures the binary opposition between gods and mortals. Even as the hero approaches divine status through what J.-P. Vernant (1991) terms "the beautiful death," the cross of his abdominal muscles reinforces the distinction that is the fundamental point of this mythic episode: mortals and immortals are as different as vertical and horizontal. Their point of contact is also their point of greatest difference: the moment of death depicted on this vase.

The Sarpedon krater and the Homeric episode behind it immortalize the ephemeral human *aiōn* at the moment of its loss ("when the *psukhē* and *aiōn* left him," *Il.* 16.453). The image holds you for a moment in its chiasmus and then lets you go, as all mortals must go, to Death. It is, in this sense, a perfect image of human temporality. The Heraclitean aphorism, by contrast, never lets you go. It holds you suspended, as I suggested above, in a timeless interminable present that is mortals' experience of the cosmic *aei*. That static present does not eternalize human life. Instead, it ellipses it, just as fragment B21/D72 replaces the expected final term *bios* with *hupnos*. Life is present only as an absence. If for Pindar *psukhē* is an *aiōnos eidōlon*, in Heraclitus's sleep fragments *aiōn* is itself a mere phantom, a vanishing dream vision.

At the extreme, even that ghost of an *aiōn* is lost.

> ἀθάνατοι θνητοί, θνητοὶ ἀθάνατοι, ζῶντες τὸν ἐκείνων θάνατον, τὸν δὲ ἐκείνων βίον τεθνεῶτες. (B62/D70)
>
> Immortals mortals, mortals immortals, living the others' death, dying the others' life.

In this fragment the chiasmus implodes, voiding the difference between life and death, mortals and immortals. With a symmetry of form that mirrors its content, it negates the very idea of negation (*a-thanatoi*) in an intensely pointed paradox. The paradox is perhaps comprehensible if we situate it within the temporality of cosmic transformation: its union of opposites would then allude to the sequential devolution and evolution of the elements, described in fragment B36/D100 as a cycle of death and birth.[78] But this aphorism nullifies that sequentiality. Instead of a cycle of life and death, each discrete and following one upon the other in even measure, we find life and death condensed into a single static condition, a condition that (in the absence of a finite verb) is interminable. This paradox thwarts the propositional logic of signification: negation, predication, and demonstration buckle under its weight, unable to produce sense.[79] In its asyndetic juxtaposition

78. Betegh 2013, 253–54. Cf. B76/R54, which is likely a gloss on B36/D100.

79. The alpha privative does not negate; the demonstrative pronouns fail to differentiate and identify; the internal accusatives strain against their verbs; predication produces nonsense. Bossi (2009)

of opposites, the signifiers that define human existence lose their meaning. That existence itself loses its meaning. Mortals and immortals alike are robbed of their proper being as each lives/dies the death/life of the other. Death is gone but so too is the *aiōn*, the concept of human existence as a duration of life punctuated by death. Both duration and punctuation are lost. Instead, we go around and around forever in a nightmarish spiral of life-death.

In his chiastic mimesis of the cosmic cycle, Heraclitus's *logos* speaks in unison with the *logos* that exists always; aesthetic form harmonizes with the structure of the universe, *kosmos* with *kosmos*. Through this mimetic synthesis, Heraclitus synchronizes human and cosmic tempos in a timeless eternal now. He brings human *xunesis* together with the common *logos*, making us feel this unity in our own bodies as a common rhythm, the shared *metra* of the cosmic revolution, and in this way secures the wholeness and unity of a cosmos in which "all things are one." But in fragments B26/D71 and B62/D70 that unity is experienced as annihilation. The chiasms' embrace becomes a death grip, holding us in the cosmic *aei* but at the cost of our mortal *aiōn*.

Fragment B21/D72 holds us in this same eternal chiasmus between *thanatos* and *hupnos*: "Death is whatever we see when awake, whatever we see when sleeping is sleep." Life appears here only as a distressing imbalance in the aphorism's perfect symmetry. And yet perhaps that is enough to wake us from our morbid lethargy. Asymmetry breaks the chiastic stranglehold of *athanatoi thnētoi thnētoi athanatoi* and opens a space for that which we do not see either in sleep or awake: *bios*.

STUTTER, SYNCOPATION

In the symmetry of his aphorisms Heraclitus both produces and reproduces a cosmos of such unity and coherence that it leaves no space for human life. But every once in a while, as in B21/D72, we find a subtle but pointed asymmetry, a syncopation generated by the convergence of different tempos. These moments are expressed as a kind of stutter in the text, a "grammar of disequilibrium" within both Heraclitus's *logos* and the cosmic *logos*.[80] This stutter introduces an incoherence into the perfect order of Heraclitus's *kosmos*, but a productive and necessary one, for it is here, I will suggest, in this briefest interval, that we find a space (or time) for human life, as well as the paradoxical origins of Heraclitus's own philosophical discourse.

offers the fullest treatment of B62/D70; see also Porter's (2024) explication of the fragment's paradoxes. For a very different interpretation see Hussey (1991), who takes immortals and mortals to mean minds with and without understanding.

80. Deleuze 1997, 112: the stutter is "a syntax in the process of becoming, a creation of syntax that gives birth to a foreign language within language, a grammar of disequilibrium." Cf. Deleuze and Guattari 1987, 98, and on the generativity of asymmetry, Deleuze 1994, 22–24.

We saw how the *psukhē* takes part in the elemental transformations of the cosmos, following the path down to water and earth and back up through the same changes.

> ψυχῇσιν θάνατος ὕδωρ γενέσθαι, ὕδατι δὲ θάνατος γῆν γενέσθαι, ἐκ γῆς δὲ ὕδωρ γίνεται, ἐξ ὕδατος δὲ ψυχή. (B36/D100)
>
> For *psukhai* it is death to become water, for water it is death to become earth; from earth water is born, from water *psukhē*.

That cycle of transformation "measures up to the same amount" (*metreetai eis ton auton logon*, B31/D86), preserving the eternal sameness of Heraclitus's cosmos, its circular perfection replicated in the annular form and verbal symmetry of the fragment. But there is one small but significant asymmetry: a change from *psukhai* to *psukhē*. Does this difference indicate the merging of particular individual souls into a universal "world-soul," as some ancient readers thought? Or does it mark the transmutation of spirit into matter, as the life-breath of individuals becomes a physical element of the universe?[81] Perhaps. But the circular form complicates such a linear reading: if individual souls become singular through this process ("from all one"), how do we get from that singular back to the plural ("from one all," B10/D47) to start the process again? *Psukhai*/*psukhē* emerges as a point of difference that disrupts the cosmic cycle. The circle does not come full circle: its beginning and end are, very literally, *not xunon* (B103/D54). The aphorism's broken symmetry introduces a syncopation in the cosmic rhythm right at the moment when the *psukhē* is absorbed into the elements. The human is not fully synchronized with the cosmic and the interval between them preserves the *psukhē* in its individual plurality and difference from the universality of "this cosmos, the same of all" (B30/D85).

A similar interval opens around the *aiōn*. We can return to fragment B52/D76.

> αἰὼν παῖς ἐστι παίζων, πεσσεύων· παιδὸς ἡ βασιληίη.
>
> *Aiōn* is a child playing, playing checkers. Sovereignty belongs to the child.

Heraclitus, as we saw, rejects the traditional notion of immortality through reproduction: the child's sovereignty is the parent's doom. Instead, we become immortal through our participation in the cycle of cosmic transformation. Kahn reads the checkers metaphor as an image of the alternating *metra* of the eternal fire as it is kindled and quenched, and identifies the *basilēiē*—the kingdom or maybe the king

81. The former is implied by Aët. 4.3.12 (< A15/R48a) and supported by Finkelberg (2013, 149–50; 2017, 84–103); while Betegh (2013, 227–34, 245–57) defends the latter; cf. Kahn 1979, 238; Sassi 2018, 118. Vieira (2013) labels this construction, in which the first and last term are related but in tension, "bow composition," and sees it as a mimetic description of the union of opposites within a cosmic process that he takes to be rectilinear not circular.

piece in the game—with the governing force of the cosmos.[82] Just as the human *psukhē* follows the cyclical path of the elements, so the human child plays the eternal game, and thus swaps his mortal *aiōn* for the kingdom of *aei*. The fragment encourages this reading with its chiastic form, which connects it to the *tropai* of the cosmos and their measured beat.[83]

But in the central ring of this chiasmus there is an odd stutter: *paizōn, pesseuōn*. This repetition is often read as a pointed self-correction: human life seems at first, from our limited human perspective, like random play, but is actually a game with clear and orderly rules. This would suggest the shift of perspective that we encountered (apropos of B1/D1) at the end of the second section, where a view from eternity obfuscates human life: from that sovereign vantage point our *aiōn* appears as mere child's play.[84] But if the latter vision corrects the former, it doesn't fully erase it, and *paizōn* is repeated in *paidos* (to which it is etymologically related) and in the alliterative play of plosives that continue right to the end of the line. So the orderly rule-bound *pesseuōn* does not fully overwrite the random, ludic *paizōn*. The equivocation introduces a vacillation precisely where the *aiōn* meets the *aei*. This momentary vacillation—the mere interval of an asyndeton—interrupts the closure of the chiasmus and maintains a gap between human existence and the cosmic game. *Aiōn*, the human lifespan brief as youth itself, persists in that gap, and not only persists but rules. *Aiōn*, like *psukhē* and *bios*, flourishes in asynchrony.

In this vital interval we feel the presence of the author within his own text. In general Heraclitus, like nature (B123/D35), "tends to hide himself." His book begins with a strong assertion of the authorial voice, implicitly in the opening announcement of "this *logos*" and explicitly in the *egō* who proclaims it ("such words and deeds as I [*egō*] expound, distinguishing each thing according to its nature and saying how it is").[85] But for the most part his aphorisms are autonomous and

82. Kahn 1979, 227–29; cf. Dasen 2020; Schädler 2020; Macé 2020; and Pl. *Leg.* 903d6 for the creator of the cosmos as a *pessoi* player. Kurke (1999, 254–75) examines *pessoi* as a civic metaphor in early Greek thought (including that of Heraclitus). In its only other occurrence in Heraclitus, *basileus* is associated with *polemos* as the order of the cosmos and the unity of opposites: "War is the father of all and the king (*basileus*) of all; it reveals these as gods and those as men, it makes these slaves and those free" (B53/D64). That fragment's linking of paternity and sovereignty makes the sovereignty of the child in B52/D76 all the more striking.

83. It is reiterated too in the acoustic structure of the aphorism. *Aiōn* is repeated in the *ai-* of *pais, paizōn, paidos,* and the *-ōn* of *paizōn, pesseuōn,* only to be absorbed into the *aei,* the vowels lengthened, in the final two syllables of *basilēiē*. On the acoustic effects in this fragment, see Ramnoux 1968, 399; Mouraviev 2006, 79–80; Année 2020; and for the history of the fragment's interpretations, Wohlfart 1991, 124–49. I discuss this fragment and Deleuze's stutter in Wohl 2024.

84. Cf. B70/D6 where *ta anthrōpina doxasmata* are compared to child's play and B79/D75: "A man is called childish (*nēpios*) by a god, just as a child by a man." Ellis (2020a) offers a stimulating Deleuzian reading of child's play in Heraclitus; cf. Ellis 2020b.

85. On the opening authorial *sphragis*, see n. 18 above. Lloyd (1995, 56–70) notes a persistent connection between egotism and innovation in early Greek thought; see also Sassi 2018, 70–73. Grant

self-validating. There is no personal narrative or autobiographical fiction to validate them, such as we saw in Parmenides and shall see in Empedocles, and their truth is not anchored to an authoritative "I." Indeed, as we shall observe shortly, Heraclitus disavows his personal voice and presents his aphorisms as direct expressions of the cosmic *logos* itself.[86] In their compressed and riddling form, these aphorisms are reminiscent of and may be modeled on the enigmatic pronouncements of an oracle. Heraclitus's references to the Delphic oracle have been read since antiquity as self-conscious models for his own style. Likening him to the "Sibyl with the raving mouth" (B92/D42), the mouthpiece of the divine *logos*, they figure his paradoxes as the mysterious semaphore of a god who "neither speaks nor conceals but signifies" (*oute legei oute kruptei alla sēmainei*, B93/D41).[87]

But if Heraclitus does liken his *logos* to the oracular speech of the Delphic oracle and present himself as the obscure spokesman of the cosmic word, he also differentiates himself in one important respect. The Pythia's riddles were delivered in dactylic hexameter. This was the meter of divine speech and social authority alike in Heraclitus's day, as we have noted, and it would have been the natural form for his presentation of cosmic verities, sometimes couched in religious terms.[88] His rejection of dactylic hexameter is thus a marked choice, a formal break not only from the Greek tradition of veridical speech but also from his own oracular metaphor. This break draws attention to the author's distinct human voice. That authorial voice is amplified by the poetic quality of Heraclitus's prose. The highly stylized, carefully wrought sonorous and structural effects we have been examining remind us continually of the presence of the *poiētēs* behind this representation of the cosmos that "no god nor man created" (*epoiēsen*, B30/D85). *Kosmos* as ornamentation denaturalizes the description of *kosmos* as natural universe, for if the chiastic form of the aphorisms reproduces the cyclical order they describe, that very artifice reveals a poetic origin that disrupts the mimetic effect.

In this way, the author preserves a gap between his own *logos* and "the *logos* that is always" and situates himself at the asyndetic juncture between the two. The

(2016, 67–71), however, proposes that the aphorism disperses the authority of the proper name; cf. Marsden 2006, 28. Its very iterability undermines any mastery the author claims in repeating it.

86. This effect may be augmented by the history of preservation: Heraclitus may have been cited in such a way as to heighten the vatic feel of his text. Forms of the first person occur in B1/D1, B49/D12, B50/D46, B55/D31, B101/D36, and B108/D43; but as Garin (2017) proposes, authorial presence can take other forms than the first person.

87. The connection is often commented on. See, e.g., Hölscher 1968, 136–41, 1974; Cook 1975, 444–46; Kahn 1979, 123–26; Tor 2016; Gianvittorio 2017; and Sassi 2018, 104–6. Maurizio (2012) calls Heraclitus "a Pythia manqué" (116). Bollack (2016, 238–41) rejects the idea of Heraclitus as prophet of the *logos* and the transparent relation to language it implies; cf. Bollack and Wismann 1972, 270–74.

88. Most (1999, 353–57) notes that in archaic Greece dactylic hexameter "functioned as an unmistakable sign that the ultimate source of the text it articulated was not human but divine" (353). See further Osborne 1998. Norden (1915, 44) finds "fairly frequent" hexametric sentence endings in Heraclitus but cites only four examples, and the occasional rhythmic line ending is a far cry from composing entirely in hexameter.

opening words of B1/D1 hold out the promise that the two *logoi* may speak in unison, the rational structure of the universe replicated perfectly in the structure of the book. But that promise is immediately belied and the ambiguity of the opening "word," instead of an identity between work and world, bespeaks an ironic distance between them. That irony is played out in the first fragment in a tone of pedagogical frustration and epistemological despair. *Anthrōpoi* will always be *axunetoi*. Heraclitus's words, falling on deaf ears, will always fail to communicate the *logos*, a schism signaled in the vocabulary he uses to characterize his own speech: not *legein* or *logos* but a variety of synonyms (*epeōn, phrazōn*) and precisions (*diēgeumai, diaireōn*). The repetition of the prefix *dia-*, which often indicates differentiation or separation, sets Heraclitus's diegesis against the integrating force of *xun*–, aligning him with *axunetoi* mortals and their individual idiocy against the *xunos logos* (B2/D2). This is an epistemological failure but also an ontological one, as we have seen, for a *xunos logos* that cannot be communicated in language is neither *xunos* nor truly a *logos*. Always inaccessible to human comprehension, the *xunos logos* is not *xunos* with itself.

This means that it is not just Heraclitus who stutters. The *logos* itself stutters. The "grammar of disequilibrium" felt in Heraclitus's work also structures his world.

> οὐ ξυνιᾶσιν ὅκως διαφερόμενον ἑωυτῶι ὁμολογέει· παλίντροπος ἁρμονίη ὅκωσπερ τόξου καὶ λύρης. (B51/D49)
>
> They do not comprehend how what differs with itself agrees with itself (*diapheromenon heōutōi homologeei*): back-turned *harmoniē* as of a bow and a lyre.

The cosmos is a *logos* in agreement (*homologeei*) with itself. The fragment encapsulates Heraclitus's synthetic project, as he sets it out in fragment B1/D1: by remedying their lack of comprehension (*ou xuniasin*) he will bring *axunetoi* mortals into accord with the metaphysical concord. But "itself" introduces a note of discord. The ambiguous placement of *heōutōi*, which can be read with both "differs" and "agrees," locates difference and agreement in the same place and asserts their fundamental copresence.[89] Stumbling on "itself," the *logos* agrees in differing and differs in agreeing. Difference (*dia*–) is not a regrettable feature of imperfect human speech or of limited human comprehension, as B1/D1 might lead us to believe. The difference between *logos* and *logos* is a difference within the cosmic *logos*, an intrinsic quality of its identity (*homologeei*) that ensures that it will never sound fully in unison with itself.

Recognizing this perpetual dissonance in the cosmic harmony is wisdom, a wisdom Heraclitus not only speaks but himself embodies.

89. The dative with *diapheromai* in B51/D49 indicates difference *in* not difference *from*, that is, internal variance not differentiation of one thing from another. Cf. B10/D47: *sumpheromenon diapheromenon, sunāidon diāidon*. Blanchot, in the preface to Ramnoux 1968, stresses the "sovereignty of mysterious Difference" in Heraclitus's writing, "cette différence qui fait que, parlant, nous différons de parler" (xvii). Cf. Porter (2024), emphasizing "disorderly and disordered (dis)harmony."

οὐκ ἐμοῦ, ἀλλὰ τοῦ λόγου ἀκούσαντας ὁμολογεῖν σοφόν ἐστιν ἓν πάντα εἶναι. (B50/D46)

Having listened not to me but to the *logos*, it is wise (*sophon*) to agree (*homologein*) that all things are one.

Along with B51/D49, B50/D46 would seem to epitomize Heraclitus's philosophy of unity. Wisdom, *to sophon*, consists in chiming with the cosmic harmony, speaking in agreement (*homologein*) with the *logos* that agrees with itself and proclaiming that all things are one. What is wise is itself one, as Heraclitus says elsewhere (*hen to sophon*, B32/D45, B41/D44).[90] B50/D46 would perform its own propositional content, as all things become one in the *homologia* that is wisdom. All things, that is, but one: Heraclitus himself (*emou*). The phrase "having listened to the *logos*" harkens back to B1/D1 and its ambivalent opening "word," and would seem to resolve that ambivalence by simply bypassing Heraclitus and his speech to offer unmediated access to the cosmic *logos*. But this move merely compounds the ironies of that equivocal *logos*. On the one hand, the instruction is impossible. The command to ignore Heraclitus is Heraclitus's own utterance. The accord of wisdom thus becomes a liar's paradox: to listen to the *logos*, not Heraclitus, is also to listen to Heraclitus, not the *logos*. On the other hand, if it were possible to separate Heraclitus's *logos* from the cosmic *logos* it would negate the wisdom that *logos* offers, the *homologia* that all things are one.

In the ironic tension between the performative and the propositional, the philosophical *egō* appears as a difference not only *from* the *logos* but *in* the *logos*, and the wisdom he offers is not the simple concord with a reality itself in concord, but instead a philosophical discourse characterized by dissonance and discord.[91] Fragment B1/D1's question as to whether mortals can become *xunetoi* through Heraclitus's teaching or whether they truly are *aei axunetoi* is not resolved but rather complicated beyond any possible resolution: what would it mean to be one with a *logos* that both is and is not one with itself? Heraclitus lays claim to this aporetic *sophia*. The difference that is the condition of impossibility of his philosophy is also the condition of its possibility. This paradox entails a bidirectional causality. On the one hand, because Heraclitus's *logos* is not identical to the cosmic *logos*, the latter is not identical to itself. "This cosmos, the same of all" is riven by difference. On the other hand, it is because the *logos* does not speak only and always the same as itself (*homologeei*) that Heraclitus's own *logos*—the philosophy he is expounding and the text we are reading—can be heard. The stutter that

90. See also B32/D45, B41/D44, B108/D43. On the unity of wisdom, see Long 2007. Heraclitus accordingly repudiates the shallow polymathy of those with a reputation for wisdom (B40/D20, B57/D25a, B106/D25b, B108/D43). It seems that Heraclitus may have coined (or been the first to use) the word *philosophos* to describe these pretenders to wisdom: see B35/D40 and Moore 2019, 37–65.

91. *Polemos* (war) and *eris* (strife) are two of Heraclitus's terms for the unity of opposites: B53/D64, B80/D63.

disrupts the perfect cohesion of his universe enables the discourse of that universe, Heraclitus's cosmology.

It also enables his psychology. When Heraclitus breaks from the cosmic *homologia* to say "I," he takes up a complex and self-conscious relation not only to the *logos* but to himself: do not listen to Heraclitus, says Heraclitus. In this utterance he gives voice to the psychological subject whose origin Snell detected in his fragments. This subject is not to be identified, as Snell proposed, with the *psukhē*, which for Heraclitus, as we have seen, is that spark that joins us to the fire of the physical cosmos. But neither is it, as Kahn argues, wholly identical with that cosmos, such that to go in search of oneself is "to lose one's self but to find something better: the unity of all things in the wise one."[92] Instead, it is precisely the difference from that unity; not the *psukhē* itself but the interval between *psukhai* and *psukhē*. If Heraclitus discovers "a new concept of soul," then, as Snell would have it, that concept appears neither as a fully autonomous subject nor just as one element among others in a constantly changing universe, but as a rupture or arrhythmia in the cosmic unity, a moment of difference in the interminable cycling of the same.

That arrhythmia, I have proposed, arises from the asynchrony between the human *aiōn* and the cosmic *aei*. As a mortal "I" who speaks the immortal word, Heraclitus himself embodies this asynchrony without mastering or transcending it. He also reproduces it for his reader in the act of reading. The riddling form of his aphorisms, their "obscure" thought and deliberately enigmatic expression, ensures that for us comprehension will never be instantaneous. The time of understanding will always lag behind the time of encounter. This temporal lag enacts the epistemological failure of *axunetoi anthrōpoi*, who "do not think about those things they encounter" (B17/D3) and are strangers to those things they encounter each day (B71/R54). But it also enacts the difference within the *logos* that prevents it from complete *homologia*. Opaque on first reading, "all aphorisms," as Deleuze writes, "must therefore be read twice."[93] And the aphorism is different on each rereading: "It is not possible to step into the same river twice, according to Heraclitus" (Plut. *De E* 392B = B91/≠LM).

Heraclitus forces such rereading not only through his obscurity but also through what we could think of as a stutter at the point of reception. In fact, the book opens with such a stutter: "Of this *logos* that is always mortals are always uncomprehending" (*tou de logou toud' eontos aei axunetoi ginontai anthrōpoi*, B1/D1). Stumbling

92. Kahn 1979, 253; cf. B101/D36: "I went in search of myself" (*edizēsamēn emeōuton*). To the extent that Kahn allows for an individual subject, it is as the consciousness that grasps its oneness with the cosmos and thus embodies difference only to resolve it at a higher level (253–54). Laks (1999, 253–54) and Long (1992) propose something similar.

93. Deleuze 2006, 31. He is speaking of Nietzsche's aphorisms and ties this necessity of rereading to the eternal return. Cf. Marsden 2006, 28. Fragment B91/≠LM, quoted by Plutarch, is probably a paraphrase of B12/D65b, not Heraclitus's own words (Marcovich 1966, 19–22; Graham 2013, responding to Tarán 1999).

over the placement of *aei* (as Aristotle already did), I must read it twice. If I read aloud, as an ancient reader would have, reading becomes literal stuttering: *aei aei*. In this repetition I reproduce physically the metaphysical schism the line opens up, the gap between the *logos* that exists forever (the first reading) and my own mortal incomprehension (the second). Another example: "What differs with itself agrees with itself" (*diapheromenon heōutōi homologeei*, B51/D49). Stumbling over the ambiguously placed pronoun, the reader must stop and read again: "Differs with itself"? "Agrees with itself"? Even as I speak the metaphysical *homologia* I reproduce the difference within it. In rereading, the same aphorism differs from itself, and the reader becomes the corporeal manifestation of its paradoxical (dis) harmony. She does not come to understand the *xunos logos* but, like Heraclitus, to embody it precisely in its lack of unity and self-sameness.

This stutter in reading reproduces the cosmic asynchrony that, I have suggested, is the space of human life. "Upon those stepping into the same rivers different and different waters flow" (*potamoisi toisin autoisin embainousin hetera kai hetera hudata epirrhei*, B12/D65b). Above we considered this fragment as an expression of the stability of the cosmos amid its continuous transformation: the waters are always other but the river remains the same. But this fragment contains another ambiguously placed word: *toisin autoisin* ("the same") could be read with either *potamoisi* or *embainousin*. Cleanthes, who quotes the fragment, takes the river as an image of the *psukhē* exhaled as a moist vapor. This is the posthumous material *psukhē* that "dies" as water and is eventually reborn from water in the eternal revolution of the elements (B36/D100). This transformation would erase any border between steppers and rivers: we become one with the river in the course of this spiritual flow.[94] But the ambiguity of *toisin autoisin* obstructs that confluence and introduces difference into the very image of sameness. The same rivers? The same steppers? The moment of hesitation produces an almost imperceptible syncopation, a tiny breathing space that prevents our individual lives from being washed away entirely in the cosmic flux.[95]

That figurative breathing space is literalized in the breath of the reader as she reads. This breath is the *psukhē* not as a posthumous exhalation but as a vital presence and presence of vitality within the living subject. Consider one final

94. As Kahn (1979, 253) proposes: "The psyche is only one elemental form among others, a bubble that bursts and is forgotten in the continual steaming up of new vapors from the waters ever flowing on in the river of the cosmos." Graham (2006, 134–37), by contrast, reads the ambiguity of *toisin autoisin* in B12/D65b as reaffirming the identity of the individual through interaction with a changing world. Cf. Graham 2013, 313–17; and Dilcher 2005, 212–16.

95. Graham (2002, 35–37; cf. 2008b, 179–81) considers other instances of this *apo koinou* construction, including B119/D111 *ēthos anthrōpōi daimōn*. See also Graham 2009; Sider 1989; and Mouraviev 2002, 352–55. This construction works as a "speculative grammar," even a "speculative punctuation mark," like Hegel's dash, brilliantly analyzed by Comay and Ruda (2018, 53–61): an ambiguous mark that necessitates rereading, it instantiates their proposal that philosophy "teaches us to stumble" (58).

example, fragment B48/D53: "The bow's name is *bios* but its work is death" (*tōi oun toxōi onoma bios, ergon de thanatos*). The wordplay on *biós* (bow) and *bíos* (life) encapsulates the unity of opposites. As in B51/D49, what differs with itself agrees with itself, and the bow offers an image of the back-turned harmony between life and death that (as we saw in the last section) shrouds life in the *lēthē* of a morbid slumber. Thus life becomes a mere name (*onoma*), erased by the fact (*ergon*) of death. But the word that holds together this tautly strung aphorism also disrupts its unity, for as soon as I recognize the pun, I must go back and read the word a second time: *biós-bíos.*[96] In that stutter on the word "life," my voice resists the equation of life with death that the fragment proposes and bodies forth a *bios* made possible only by the difference between my *logos* and the cosmic *logos*. Rooted in the body and in time, that *bios* is not a waking dream of death and immortality in the cosmic *aei*, but the living, breathing experience of an ephemeral *aiōn*.

Bios, psukhē, aiōn: life in its difference from the elemental cosmos flourishes in the syncopation between the regular rhythm of the cosmic cycle as it is "kindled in measure and extinguished in measure" and the tempos of our finite mortal existence. Asynchrony is the condition of possibility of human life. This asynchrony is itself *aei*: it can never be resolved into a single tempo. The interminable journey to the limits of the *psuhkē* with which we began thus directs us not toward a vanishing point on the horizon where *psukhē* and *logos* will finally converge, but to the eternal rift between them. If that rift means that the *logos* will never be completely *xunos*—that all will never, in fact, be one—this incoherence does not spoil the beauty of Heraclitus's universe, the *kosmos* of his philosophical and poetic *kosmos*. After all, it is syncopation that turns a simple pulse into music.

96. Most (1999, 358) notes the significance of reading the fragment aloud but interprets it differently: "The reader cannot help but accentuate either the one vowel or the other . . . thereby inevitably reducing a complex truth to a one-sided, and hence partially erroneous, oversimplification." Cf. Dilcher 1995, 129–33; and Sassi 2018, 102. As B1/D1 predicts, by reason of her very embodiment the *axunetos* reader would seem doomed to forever fail to comprehend the *xunos logos;* she can only live its paradoxes.

3

Empedocles's Autobiography

It's not easy to see the grass in things and in words.

—DELEUZE AND GUATTARI

AUTOBIOGRAPHY OF A *DAIMŌN*

Empedocles's *Purifications* begins with an extraordinary statement. Greeting his fellow citizens of Acragas, the narrator proclaims, "I come to you, an immortal god, no longer mortal (*egō d'humin theos ambrotos, ouketi thnētos*), honored among all, as I seem, crowned with ribbons and flourishing crowns" (B112.4–6/D4.4–6). This astonishing first-person assertion launches an extended account of this *egō*'s thirty-thousand-year saga of exile as what he calls a *daimōn*, a personal and highly emotional narrative likewise recounted in the first person.

This insistent first-person voice invites us to read Empedocles's poem as an autobiography. By this I do not mean an autobiography of the historical Empedocles, although he is a fascinating figure with a colorful ancient biographical tradition.[1] I mean instead an autobiography in the root sense of the word: the written account of the life of a self. Empedocles's philosophy explodes each component of the word—self (*autos*), life (*bios*), and writing (*graphē*)—and challenges the basic syntax of autobiography, which is also the syntax of natural philosophy.

Epigraph: From *A Thousand Plateaus: Capitalism and Schizophrenia*, by Gilles Deleuze and Félix Guattari, translated by Brian Massumi, 23. English-language copyright © 1987 by The University of Minnesota Press. Reprinted by permission of The University of Minnesota Press (North America) and Bloomsbury Academic, an imprint of Bloomsbury Publishing Plc (Worldwide, excluding USA, Canada and Philippines). Original published as *Mille Plateaux*, volume 2 of *Capitalisme et Schizophrénie* © 1980 by Les Éditions de Minuit, Paris. Reprinted by permission of Georges Borchardt, Inc. on behalf of Les Éditions de Minuit.

1. Autobiography was not a recognized genre in antiquity, and I am not proposing that Empedocles invented it, nor am I trying to insert him into its history; instead, I use the structure of autobiography as a heuristic device for explicating the complex relation between self, life, and writing in Empedocles's philosophy. For Empedocles's ancient biography, see Diog. Laert. 8.51–77; and Chitwood 2004, 12–58. As with all ancient biographical traditions, the philosopher's life is largely reconstructed from his works.

Empedocles's cosmos is composed of four roots (*rhizōmata*)—earth, water, fire, and air—that combine under the force of Love (Philotēs) until they form an undifferentiated Sphere, then separate out again under the force of Strife (Neikos), in the process producing worlds and destroying them again. This system of elemental transformation undermines the notion of the *autos*, a discernible identity stable over time. As the daimonic *egō* of the *Purifications* will go on to recount, "I was once already a boy and a girl and a bush and a bird and a sea-leaping, voyaging fish" (D13/B117). Who, or what, is this *egō* who survives elemental transformation to recall its past incarnations? Changing form, this *autos* is not self-identical over time. Nor is it distinct from the world around it: it perceives external elements by way of those same elements within (B109/D207) and is composed of matter that was recently part of other beings. This elemental connection to all other things suggests that Empedocles's autobiography will be not the story of an individual self's life but the story of life itself and the place of the *egō* within it.

How does one write a *graphē* of this expanded *bios?* What is the relation of writing to the *autos* that writes and the *bios* that is written? Empedocles's poetic style is as exceptional as his first-person account: with its swirling structure of repetitions and half-echoes, its repurposed Homericisms and tangled metaphors, its idiolect of unfamiliar usages and unexpected coinages, this *graphē* is itself rather demonic. For Empedocles, as we shall see, writing too is alive. Composed of the same elements as every boy or girl or bush or bird, *graphē* is not a mimesis of life but a vital part of it, sharing in its process of endless transmutation.

This dynamic theory poses a challenge to the traditional metaphysics of autobiography. Autobiography both presupposes and produces an autonomous *egō* as the origin of an account of a life the author thereby claims as her own. The autobiographical *egō* must extract herself from the flow and activity of life in order to write it; in doing so, she declares her control over it. Autobiography is structurally homologous to the idealist mode of science that Nietzsche often criticized, the science that extracts itself from the "immediately perceived world" so as to conceptualize and represent it, that elevates the idea of the thing over the thing itself and in this way betrays life.[2] Language is key in this process, as Nietzsche argued: even before the concept, the word marks a first step away from life.[3] Both autobiography and natural philosophy are predicated on a syntax of subject-verb-object—"I write (my) life"—that elevates *autos* over *bios* by means of *graphē* and secures the former

2. This idealism is lambasted throughout Nietzsche's work but see especially 1989a. He traces it back to Parmenides (1962, 80–81, 86–87). In a similar vein, see Ingold (2011, 75): "Science as it stands rests upon an impossible foundation, for in order to turn the world into an object of concern, it has to place itself above and beyond the very world it claims to understand. The conditions that enable scientists to *know* . . . are such as to make it impossible for scientists to *be* in the very world of which they seek knowledge" (original emphasis).

3. Nietzsche (1989a, 251) writes that the concept is "the *residue of a metaphor,*" and our entire relation to reality is metaphoric.

as subject by reducing the latter to a tractable object. James Olney describes the dynamics of autobiography in terms that are apropos: in writing, he proposes, the autobiographer seeks to snatch his or her *bios* from a Heraclitean stream of becoming and fix it in the permanent present of Parmenidean Being.[4] Idealist philosophy, Nietzsche would add, does the same for life as a whole.

Empedocles refuses such fixity, even if he cannot fully avoid it. Responding to and reacting against Parmenides's attempt to cordon off Being from the things of the world, Empedocles insistently roots metaphysics in physics. For him thought and language are matter, made up of the same elements and subject to the same forces as all other matter. Thus there is no separation of words from things or thought from life. *Graphē* does not rise above *bios* to represent it in the idealized form of an objectifying mimesis; instead, *graphē* is enmeshed within *bios*, one vital being among countless others, each engaged in its own process of becoming. Likewise, the *autos* is not the autopoietic author of his own *graphē* and master of his *bios*, but rather coexists with them in a sympoietic network that sets *autos, graphē*, and *bios* on the same ontological ground.[5] Flattening the ontological hierarchy and scrambling the subject-verb-object syntax of autobiography, Empedocles undertakes a radical philosophical and poetic project—radical in the root sense of the word: it is an attempt to formulate a "root language," a philosophical language that is not abstracted from life but that spreads rhizomatically in its midst, like grass, down in the dirt of things.

But as Deleuze and Guattari say, "it's not easy to see the grass in things and in words."[6] Empedocles's experiment in writing a material ontology—in which the writing is as audacious as the ontology—produces certain incoherences in his work, even beyond those produced by the fragmentary state of his text. Empedocles presents his theories in the first person, as the teachings of an authoritative *egō*. But the theories themselves, as we shall see, place pressure on that *egō*. The *egō* tells a life story—or rather, a story of countless lives—that renders him unstable and fragmented, simply one mobile material part of a biosphere made up entirely and exclusively of mobile material parts. Even as he is submerged in this vital meshwork, the *egō* must rise above it to represent it. Empedocles's natural philosophy unsettles the philosophical *autos*, but it also requires and reproduces it as

4. Olney 1980, 237–38. Of course, much (post)modern autobiographical writing and criticism is animated by repudiation of such subjective mastery and fixity: see, e.g., De Man 1979; Derrida 1987, 292–337; and Herbrechter 2012.

5. I take the terms autopoietic and sympoietic from Haraway (2016, 33, 58–98). Empedocles's autobiographical subject is presumptively masculine.

6. Deleuze and Guattari 1987, 23. In labeling Empedocles's philosophy "radical" I mean to evoke Deleuze and Guattari's (1987, 3–25) theory of the rhizome. They differentiate the multiple interconnecting networks of rhizomes from roots, which they characterize as singular and hierarchical. For Empedocles the four roots themselves are singular and ontologically fundamental, but the cosmos they produce through their combinations is rhizomatic. Macauley (2005) develops the connection between Empedocles's *rhizōmata* and Deleuze and Guattari's rhizomatics.

its legitimating source. The author himself embodies this paradox: Empedocles—he of "stable glory" (*empedon kleos*)—will emerge as the singular exception to the volatile ontology he expounds and a productive point of aporia within his own philosophy. In this respect, Empedocles's text resembles Heraclitus's; as we observed in the last chapter, Heraclitus's own *logos* becomes audible at the very moment it splits from, and thus articulates a split in, the unitary cosmic *logos*.[7]

This chapter traces the tangled lines of *autos*, *bios*, and *graphē* across the fragments of Empedocles's text. In doing so, it does not aim to reorder these terms into a hierarchy that would secure both philosophy and philosopher as stable and coherent, vouchsafing their *empedon kleos*. Instead, it embraces the incoherences in Empedocles's work and persona as the inevitable byproduct of his ambitious experiment in rhizomatic thinking—his attempt to articulate a philosophy and poetics of the roots. The *autos* that writes this dynamic philosophy also lives it, but the life undoes the writing and the writing the life. In the schizophrenic autobiography and philosophy this paradox generates we can see both the radical nature of Empedocles's project and its limits.[8]

AUTOS

Questions about the relation between autobiography and natural philosophy and the place of the *egō* in each are central to the study of Empedocles. Two titles come down to us from antiquity attached to Empedocles's name, *Katharmoi* (*Purifications*) and *Peri Phuseōs* (*On Nature*). The long-standing assumption that these two titles refer to two different poems has been challenged in recent decades, and scholars have argued for reading the fragments as part of a single poem.[9] This position received support from the identification in the 1990s of a papyrus in Strasbourg containing substantial new fragments of Empedocles's poem.[10] These

7. We will return to the aporia of the author function in the Conclusion.

8. Deleuze and Guattari label their materialist psychiatry "schizoanalysis" and posit the schizophrenic as the decentered subject of their rhizomatic ontology (1983b, 2, 14, 56–57; Holland 1999, 1–24). Their exemplum is Freud's Judge Schreber, "who sought to remain at that unbearable point where the mind touches matter and lives its every intensity" (1983b, 19–20). The hero of an autobiographical narrative of metempsychosis, persecutory transformations, and purification both individual and cosmic, materially connected to all other beings through nerves and rays, and communicating in a special "root language" (*Grundsprache*), Schreber offers a fertile comparandum to Empedocles's daimonic *autos*.

9. The one-poem thesis was argued forcefully by Osborne (1987a), extending the rearrangement of the fragments by Van der Ben (1975), and is followed by Inwood (2001, with justification at 8–21); Trépanier (2004, 1–30); and Mackenzie (2016, 2021a, 104–7). Without subscribing to a distinction between the esoteric and the exoteric (Kingsley 2002, 344–50; Bollack 2005; and Patzer 2006, 92) I find the two different addressees and imagined performative contexts hard to reconcile from a formal standpoint. But I remain open-minded on the issue and nothing in my argument rides on it: in fact, the tension I examine between the physical theory and the daimonic *autos* is all the more pointed if the two are part of the same poem.

10. The fragments of the Strasbourg papyrus have been edited by Martin and Primavesi (1999). As they point out, however, the papyrus neither proves nor disproves the one-poem theory (118–19). On

new papyrological fragments show that even if (as I believe) Empedocles did write two separate poems, his natural philosophy and religious thought are deeply interconnected.

One apparent point of difference, however, is the authorial voice.[11] The doctrine of *On Nature* is validated to a degree unparalleled in early Greek philosophy by the personal authority of the poetic voice. This work is not structured as an autobiography, but its physical theory is expounded by an *egō* who maintains a strong presence throughout. *On Nature* is staged as a one-on-one pedagogical relationship between this *egō* and his student interlocutor Pausanias. The *egō* asserts himself through repeated imperatives: he urges Pausanias to listen and to hear, to see, to imagine, to pay attention, to know.[12] Demanding that the reader, as well as the fictional interlocutor, attend to his words, this *egō* commands authority. If the student obeys his command, he personally guarantees him extravagant and exclusive benefits: cures for sickness, control of the winds and rains, power over life and death, "since to you alone I ordain (*kraneō*) all these things" (B111.2/D43.2). In the language of divine and oracular fulfillment (*kraneō*, a verb virtually unparalleled in the first-person singular), the *egō* declares the performative efficacy of his teaching: to understand his *On Nature* is to impose one's will on nature.[13]

That personal authority alone validates the truth of the doctrine. Empedocles follows Parmenides in donning the mantle of Homer and laying claim to the bard's traditional authority. His choice of dactylic hexameter in itself announces that double (Parmenidean and Homeric) filiation, as do his appeals to "the assurances of our Muse" (B4.2/D47.2; cf. B3.3–5/D44.3–5, B131/D7). But though Empedocles asks his Muse to stand by his side as he presents his account (B131/D7), she is not manifestly the source of that account.[14] Whereas Parmenides's goddess initiates the young man into the mysteries of Being, Empedocles's Muse assists him as he

---

the impact of the papyrus on our understanding of Empedocles, see Inwood 2001, 75–79; and Ferella 2024, 26–31.

11. Long 1966, 258; Primavesi 2013, 667–68; and Sassi 2018, 167.

12. Listen and hear: B1/D41, B6.1/D57.1, B17.14/D73.245, B17.26/D73.257, B62.3/D157.3; see: B3.9/D44.9, B21.1/D77a.1; imagine: B17.21/D73.252; pay attention: P. Strasb. a(ii) 21–22/D73.291–2; know: B4.3/D47.3, B110.10/D257.10.

13. This is, as Ferella (2024, 246–306) argues, to obtain the mind of a god. The performative force of the teaching in B111/D43 is reiterated in the echo *peusēi/pauseis* (you will learn/you will stop [the winds]), which also resonates with Pausanias's name. *Krainō/kraneō* occurs in prayers to the gods (e.g. Hom. *Il.* 1.41, *Od.* 17.242, 20.115) and in reference to oracles (Pind. *Ol.* 3.11, Eur. *Ion* 464). The prominence of the first-person voice fits with Obbink's (1993, 79n61) observation of the uncommon frequency of second-person address, which he sees as an aspect of "sphragidization," "the embedded assertion of the identity of the poet with his narrative persona."

14. In B3/D44 he calls on her to ensure the piety of his words but does not suggest that she is responsible for their content. As Mackenzie (2021a, 115) nicely puts it, the Muse is metonymic of his own poetic authority. See further Hardie 2013, 216–20; Gheerbrant 2017, 99–218; and Sassi 2018, 164. On Empedocles's creative use of Homer and Hesiod, see Traglia 1952, 11–29; Bollack 1965, 283–86; Gemelli Marciano 1990, 29–60; Picot 1998; and Willi 2008, 193–229, and on his flexible hexameter, see Bollack 1965, 313–20; and Gheerbrant 2017, 161–64.

initiates Pausanias by commanding (*keletai*) the student to trust and learn from his master (B4/D47).[15] Moreover, Parmenides supplements divine inspiration with the logical argumentation that constitutes the persuasive force of his poem. Empedocles, by contrast, offers virtually no logical argumentation.[16] Instead, the truth value of his poem and doctrine rests on the insistence of the *egō*. When the poet (in an overt allusion to Parmenides) demands that Pausanias "hear the not-deceptive expedition of argument" (*su d'akoue logou stolon ouk apatēlon*, B17.26/D73.257; cf. Parm. B8.52/D8.57), the same personal authority that enforces the command also supports the claim that the *logos* is "not deceptive": to obey the command and listen to the poem is to accept the veracity of its account. Thus this *egō* inserts himself frequently into the poem to verify its claims: I will speak, I will show, I will tell.[17]

If the *egō* of *On Nature* is a philosophy professor, the "I" of *Purifications* is a demon.

> ὦ φίλοι, οἳ μέγα ἄστυ κατὰ ξανθοῦ Ἀκράγαντος
> ναίετ' ἀν' ἄκρα πόλεος, ἀγαθῶν μελεδήμονες ἔργων,
> ξείνων αἰδοῖοι λιμένες, κακότητος ἄπειροι,
> χαίρετ'· ἐγὼ δ' ὑμῖν θεὸς ἄμβροτος, οὐκέτι θνητός
> πωλεῦμαι μετὰ πᾶσι τετιμένος, ὥσπερ ἔοικα,
> ταινίαις τε περίστεπτος στέφεσίν τε θαλείοις. (B112.1–6/D4.1–6)
>
> Oh friends, who dwell in the great city along the golden Acragas
> upon the city's heights, you who are concerned for noble deeds,
> harbors respectful of strangers, inexperienced of evil,
> greetings! I come to you, an immortal god, no longer mortal,
> honored among all, as I seem,
> crowned with ribbons and flourishing crowns.

15. Bollack 1969, 18; and Ferella 2024, 266–73. *Peri Phuseōs* as initiatory: Kahn 1974, 431–32; and Kingsley 1995, 230–31, 359–70.

16. As noted by Van Groningen 1960, 201–6; and Barnes 1982, 310–11. For more detailed assessment of Empedocles's argumentative strategies see McKirahan 2005. The only extended deductive reasoning is at B17.30–33/D73.261–64, arguing for the eternal and unchanging existence of the four elements: the argumentative style there, with its rhetorical questions and counterfactual conditions, seems to be a deliberate nod to Parmenides (Wright 1981, 170). On Empedocles's philosophical response to Parmenides, see Solmsen 1975; Curd 1998, 155–71; Graham 1999; Inwood 2001, 24–33; Trépanier 2004, 129–44, 152–70; and Palmer 2009, 271–317; and on his stylistic response, Traglia 1952, 101–16; Nünlist 2005; and Mackenzie 2021a, 108–16.

17. B8.1/D53.1, B9.5/D54.5, B16/D63, B17.1/D73.233, B17.16/D73.247, B35.1/D75.1, B38/D122, P. Strasb. a(ii) 23/D73.293, P. Strasb. d 8/D76.8. On the stylistic features of Empedocles's didactic persona, see further Willi 2008, 231–35. Calame (1995, 1–73) charts the increasing autonomy of the enunciating *egō* over the course of the archaic period and its decreasing reliance on the Muse; he does not discuss Empedocles. Rosenfeld-Löffler (2006, 77–100) fills that gap with her (Calame-inspired) study of the "Je-énonciateur" in *On Nature*.

This fragment, which Diogenes Laertius says came at the beginning of *Purifications*, sets the poem's scene. In contrast to the intimate pedagogical setting figured in *On Nature*, the fictional mise en scène of this poem is public and ceremonial. We are in Acragas, the city Empedocles was from: the poem is anchored in time and place by the author's own biography.[18] But if the setting is "historical," the speaker is outlandishly mythical. Who, or what, is this divine *egō* who has arrived in the city? The peculiar phrase *hōsper eoika* ("as I seem") highlights the perplexity: is he actually a god or does he just seem one?[19] Is he a stranger (*xenos*), as his praise of the audience's hospitality suggests (3), or a friend, a *philos* among *philoi?* The scene is at once a religious epiphany and a glorious homecoming: decked in garlands and ribbons, the *egō* returns to his polis with godlike honor, the benefit of which he will share with us in the form of profit, prophecies, cures for "all sorts of diseases" (10–11).

This triumphant *nostos* marks the end of the *egō*'s long exile, a saga no less baffling than the subject who recounts it. In B115/D10, the speaker tells of "an oracle of Necessity, ancient decree of the gods, eternal, sealed by wide oaths" (1–2). This oracle commands that any god who spills blood or swears false oaths be banished from the divine community to wander for thirty thousand years. These exiled divinities are "*daimones* who have been allotted a long life" (5). The speaker details the misery of the *daimones* as they are driven from air to sea to earth to aether, and "one after another welcomes them and all detest them" (12). The fragment ends with another first-person epiphany: "Of these I too am now one (*tōn kai egō nun eimi*), a fugitive from the gods and a wanderer, trusting in mad Strife" (13–14).[20]

The narrative this daimonic "I" goes on to tell is like nothing else in Greek literature.[21] He recounts his wanderings through strange and dismal lands: an

18. Diog. Laert. 8.54 (< A1/P7). The performance context of the poem is debated, but I follow recent scholars like Mackenzie (2021a, 106–7) in supposing that both poems were originally disseminated through rhapsodic performances at public festivals, such as the Olympic games (as reported at Diog. Laert. 8.63). On the poem's performance and addressees, see further Zuntz 1971, 186–92; Rösler 1983; Obbink 1993, 76–80; Stehle 2005; Gheerbrant 2017, 595–641, 2022; and Mackenzie 2021a, 126–56.

19. The Palatine Anthology correction of B112.5/D4.5 to the third-person singular marks the oddity of the form. The phrase is common in the second and third person but the only other occurrence of the first person is in the pleonastic construction at Pl. *Alc.* 116d6 (*phainomai, hōs eoika*), where it is also "odd" (Denyer 2001, 151 ad loc.). Interpretation of B112/D4 is also affected by how we construe the dative in line 4: "I come to you as god" or "I come as a god to (or for) you."

20. Plutarch reads *eími* ("I go") instead of *eimí* ("I am") and *tēn* for *tōn* in this line (*tēn kai egō nun eími*), i.e., "I too now go this way." For him, the *daimōn* is an allegory for each of us inasmuch as we are all "migrants here [on earth] and strangers and fugitives" (*De exil.* 607D2–3). Plutarch's reading is favored by Wilamowitz (1929, 634); Zuntz (1971, 198); Rashed (2008, 24–25); and Picot (2022, 585, 596–612), against that of Hippolytus, printed by Diels-Kranz. B115/D10 is riddled with textual and interpretive uncertainties: see Rashed 2008, 2018, 213–43. There is no consensus on the precise nature of the *daimones*. Picot 2022, 665–88 helpfully collates views on the question.

21. Even the speaker recognizes that this account may be hard to believe (B114/D6; cf. B113/D5). Mackenzie (2021a, 127–42) identifies the mythical and literary antecedents of the exile-purification narrative.

underworld cave, the vortex of Strife, the dark meadow of delusion (B118–123/D14–24). The narrative is told from the first-person perspective and with intense emotion: "I cried and wailed seeing this unfamiliar place" (B118/D14); "I wet my cheeks . . . I came into the furthest place . . . with a scream and a shout . . . reaching the meadow of Atē" (P. Strasb. d7–17/D76.7–17). This anguished travelogue is a tale of guilt, punishment, and ultimate redemption. Banished from the gods for "staining his own limbs with murder" (B115.3/D10.3), the daimonic narrator undergoes countless reincarnations, "growing over time into various forms of mortal things that exchange the terrible paths of life" (B115.7–8/D10.7–8). These transformations too he recounts in the first person: "I was once already (*ēdē gar pot' egō genomēn*) a boy and a girl and a bush and a bird and a sea-leaping, voyaging fish" (D13/B117). After thirty thousand years of suffering, by adhering to moral laws that include abstaining from animal sacrifice (and possibly from sexual activity) he will finally expiate his crime.[22] Purified—hence the title of the poem—he will ultimately rejoin the divine community: "In the end they [the *daimones*] become seers and singers and doctors and leaders among earthly humans; from there they grow to be gods (*theoi*), highest in honors" (B146/D39). The happy *telos* is recounted in B147/D40: "Sharing a feast with the other immortals (*athanatois*), being at the same table, with no share in the sufferings of men, indestructible." It is in this final, divine form that the *egō* makes his triumphant return to Acragas, "an immortal god (*theos*), no longer mortal" (B112.4/D4.4), and divulges the wisdom he has acquired in his long wanderings.

What are we to make of this metempsychotic autobiography, the first-person account of the life—or lives—of an exiled *daimōn*? Who—or what—is this narrator, and what is his relation to the authoritative narrator of *On Nature?* Ancient readers took the daimonic *egō* as an allegory for the philosophical (and particularly Platonic) soul and his otherworldly adventures as a tale of moral and intellectual *askēsis*. For these readers, the *daimōn*'s saga is a tale of philosophical redemption, in which the individual ascends from the meadow of delusion to apotheosis and a seat at the banquet of the wise.[23] "Purifying" the *daimōn* as a philosopher-to-be,

22. Animal sacrifice is clearly prohibited at B135–139/D27a–D35. Eating beans is also proscribed at B141/D31: "Wretched, entirely wretched men, keep your hands away from beans (*kuamōn*)!" Aulus Gellius, who cites this line, says that *kuamoi* means not beans but testicles (4.11.9–10) and thinks this refers to sexual abstinence. For other evidence for an injunction to sexual abstinence and discussion of the rationale, see Inwood 2001, 64–66.

23. Clem. Al. *Strom.* 4.150 ad B146/R82: "Empedocles says the souls of *sophoi* become gods"; cf. Hierocles, Synesius ad B121/D24; Aët. 1.7.28 (A32/≠LM). Plut. *De exil.* 607C–D, quoting B115/D10, takes the *daimōn*'s journey as a "gentle euphemism" for the tribulations of the human soul. He probably has the Platonic soul in mind, a connection Plato himself invites when he reuses Empedocles's "unfamiliar cloak of flesh" (B126/D19) at *Phd.* 87c–88b (Inwood 2001, 55–59). Plotinus and Porphyry likewise compare the cave visited by the fallen *daimōn* (B120/D16) to the cave in Plato's *Republic* (Plotinus *Enn.* 4.8.1, Porph. *De antr. nymph.* 8). Laks-Most collect other allegorical readings of the *daimōn*'s exile at Emp. R47–57. A number of modern scholars take the *daimōn* as a proto-Platonic *psukhē*, the enduring

this interpretation assimilates the outlandish *egō* of *Katharmoi* to his pedagogical counterpart. Criticizing a similar tendency in modern scholarship, Peter Kingsley views Empedocles not as a rational philosopher but as a magician and inspired mystic, whose teaching—cosmology no less than demonology—is divine revelation. For him, the *daimōn*'s story is effectively Empedocles's own autobiography, the account of his shamanic initiation, and the cosmology is an esoteric vehicle of spiritual salvation.[24] While early readers assimilated the daimonic *egō* to *On Nature*'s philosopher, Kingsley unites the two authorial personae by assimilating the natural philosopher to the divinized *daimōn* and identifying that divinity with Empedocles himself.

Werner Jaeger famously characterized the historical Empedocles as "a philosophical centaur . . . a prodigious union of Ionian elemental physics and Orphic religion."[25] This dichotomy between Empedocles the natural philosopher and Empedocles the mystic obviously collapses if *Peri Phuseōs* and *Katharmoi* were a single poem. But even if there were two separate poems, scholars have demonstrated the deep interconnection between the material theory of the cosmology and the religious thought of the daimonology.[26] Moreover, the two authorial personae are not just mutually entangled but in fact mutually dependent if, as some have argued, the autobiography of the *daimōn* reflects or enacts the physical theory expounded in *On Nature*. The oracle of Necessity that dictates the *daimōn*'s punishment in B115/D10 has been taken since antiquity to refer to the alternation of Love and Strife, and the speaker himself attributes his torments to his trust in "mad Strife" (B115.14/D10.14).[27] Thus Oliver Primavesi reads the journey of the *daimōn*, shunted from one element to another, taking on different ephemeral forms as these "exchange the terrible paths of life" (B115.8/D10.8), as a "mythological mirror" for the combination and dispersion of the root elements, themselves apparently called *daimones* at B59/D149.[28] Furthermore, the *daimōn* not only suffers this physical

element of the individual: Inwood 2001, 56; Trépanier 2004, 129, 2017; Curd 2005, 142; and Kahn 2014. Contra, Zuntz 1971, 270–71; Wright 1981, 273–74; Bollack 2003, 65–66; Laks 2004, 35–37; Sassi 2018, 134; Picot 2022, 535–664; and Ferella 2024, 138–84.

24. Kingsley 2002; cf. 1995, 217–391; 2003, 309–559.

25. Jaeger 1945, 295. This dichotomy was strongly articulated by Zeller (1881, 171–207); it is instantiated in Diels-Kranz's edition of the text and argued for in Diels 1969.

26. See especially the important contribution of Kahn (2014). Most scholars now accept the continuity of Empedocles's thought, even if they believe it was articulated in two separate poems: Bignone 1916, 11–21; Long 1949; Wright 1981, 57–63; Osborne 1987a; Inwood 2001; Laks 2004; Curd 2005; Trépanier 2014, 2017, 132; Mackenzie 2021a, 104–7; and Ferella 2024. O'Brien (2001); Kingsley (2002); and Bollack (2003, 14–17, 62–66, 2005), however, warn against conflating the two.

27. Hippol. *Haer.* 7.29. Both are sealed with a "broad oath" (B30.3/D94.3; cf. B115.2/D10.2). Laks (2005) offers a lucid analysis of the different nature of necessity in the two accounts and its implication for their relation (cf. Laks 2004, 42–44, 2010).

28. Primavesi 2008, 252. A variant of the phrase "exchanging paths" (*metallassonta keleuthous*, B115.8/D10.8) is used of the elements at B35.15/D75.15 (*diallaxanta keleuthous*). Scholars have seen the

process but may even, as Catherine Rowett (Osborne) has argued, actively contribute to it.[29] The *daimōn* is exiled for "staining his own limbs with murder" (B115.3/D10.3), presumably by sacrificing and eating animals. The prohibition on animal sacrifice, vividly described in other fragments of *Purifications*, is a universal law based on the common kinship of all living beings (B135/D27a), a kinship likely predicated on their shared elemental composition as described in *On Nature.*[30] In a fragment presumed to belong to *Purifications* the *daimōn* cries out with remorse for his crime: "Alas that the pitiless day did not destroy me first, before I contrived wicked acts with my lips for the sake of food!" (B139/D34). The same *cri du coeur* occurs, with slight variation, in a fragment of the Strasbourg papyrus describing the vortex of Strife (P. Strasb. d 5–6/D76.5–6). This fragment indisputably links the daimonology to the cosmology and suggests that the *daimōn*'s crime not only brought on his personal punishment but also contributed to the sway of Strife in the cosmos, and that his moral purification will, conversely, help to bring about the cosmic reunification under Philotēs.

Read in this way, the *daimōn* is an allegory not for a Platonic soul but for Empedoclean matter. The *daimōn*'s saga becomes the autobiography of the roots as they undergo their cosmic transformations, and the daimonic *autos* is the living (and dying and living . . .) proof of the doctrine. This would suggest in turn that the didactic *egō* who propounds this doctrine in *On Nature* derives his philosophical credibility at least in part from the experience of his daimonic counterpart. Further, that daimonic experience may in fact be his own. Like Heraclitus, Empedocles scorns mortals who "see only a small share of life in their lifetimes" and mistake that fraction for the whole (B2.3–6/D42.3–6). In contrast, B129/D38 describes a "man of extraordinary knowledge": "Whenever he reached out with all his mind, easily he saw each of all the things that are in ten or twenty lifetimes of mortals" (B129.4–6/D38.4–6).[31] Is the poet of *On Nature* claiming to be such a man, passing on to his student the wisdom gained over his many incarnations? This fragment is generally assigned to *Purifications*, but fragment B23/D60, which expounds cosmological doctrine, concludes: "Let no deception overcome your mind that the font of mortal things . . . is from anywhere else [than the mixing of roots], but know these things clearly, having heard a speech from a god" (*theou para muthon*

daimōn variously as the embodiment of a specific force, element, or compound of elements: Mackenzie (2020, 118–21) surveys the different positions.

29. Osborne 2005, anticipated in Osborne 1987a, 35–41; cf. Inwood 2001, 59–68; Ferella 2024, 348–60. Rowett (Osborne) and Inwood both believe the crime that causes the *daimōn*'s exile is not animal sacrifice but the breakup of Sphere and precipitation of Strife. On the *daimōn*'s transgression, see further Tor 2023a.

30. Iambl. *VP* 24.108: "The shared kinship of animals, which arises from sharing life and the same elements and the mixture that arises from these, yoked them to us as if in brotherhood." On the kinship of all living beings in Presocratic philosophy, see Zatta 2017, esp. 9–44.

31. The fragment was taken by its sources to refer to either Pythagoras or Parmenides: see Zuntz 1971, 265–66; Wright 1981, 256; and Bollack 2003, 88–90.

akousas, B23.9–11/D60.9–11). If that *theos* is the speaker himself, the whole *Peri Phuseōs* becomes a kind of epiphany through which the philosopher declares, like the revenant of *Katharmoi*, "I come to you, an immortal god, no longer mortal."[32] This identification would be all the stronger if, as some believe, fragment B115/D10, which recounts the *daimōn*'s exile, came at the opening not of *Purifications* but of *On Nature*.[33] According to this reading, the poet can describe the physical processes of the cosmos truthfully because he has suffered through them himself over the course of his own myriad lifetimes. His natural philosophy in and of itself thus becomes an implicit autobiography, supporting Nietzsche's observation that every philosophy is, at base, "a kind of involuntary and unconscious memoir."[34]

This daimonic experience, finally, would justify the exorbitant benefits the poet claims for his teachings in *On Nature*. Like a god, the teacher "ordains" (*kraneō*, B111.2/D43.2) for his pupil exclusive mastery over the elements, the winds and rains and earth. In addition, he promises, "you will lead the might of a dead man back from Hades" (B111.9/D43.9).[35] Mastery over life and death may be the ultimate benefit of comprehending the physical doctrine, with its teaching that "there is no birth of any living thing nor any end of dire death, but only mixing and interchanging of things mixed" (B8/D53; cf. B9/D54). But reading the fragments of *On Nature* and *Purifications* closely together, it may also be seen as a power derived from the *egō*'s own biography and thanatography, his thirty thousand years of reincarnation.[36]

Far from heterogeneous creatures—the man and horse of Jaeger's "philosophical centaur"—the didactic *egō* of *On Nature* and the daimonic *egō* of *Purifications* appear, then, to be two faces of the same authorial *autos*, and the philosophical authority of the former seems to depend on the mad autobiography of the latter. And yet the two cannot simply be assimilated, and their mutual implication produces certain tensions within each and within Empedocles's oeuvre as a whole. For if the daimonological *autos* validates the physical theory, the theory invalidates that *autos* as the stable source of his own autobiography. In B117/D13, the *daimōn*

32. Some think he is referring to the Muse: Wright 1981, 181; Palmer 2013.

33. Sedley 1989, 274–76; Sassi 2018, 165 (following Van der Ben 1975, 16–26); and Ferella 2024, 24–61. Plutarch says only that Empedocles "uttered it as a preface at the beginning of his philosophy" (*De exil.* 607C). Inwood 2001 places it near the start of the combined single poem; see also Osborne 1987a, 29–31; contra, O'Brien 2001. For Ferella (2024) the reallocation of this and other fragments traditionally assigned to *Katharmoi* to the proem of *Peri Phuseōs* is part of a larger argument that Empedocles's physics is "premised and structured" (22, 307–62) on his theory of reincarnation.

34. Nietzsche 1989b, 13, quoted by Kronick 2000, 997.

35. The biographical tradition reports that Empedocles himself brought a dead woman back to life. The story is recounted by Diogenes Laertius (8.61), who cites as evidence the epiphany of B112/D4. This feat of reanimation is closely linked in Diogenes's account to Empedocles's own mysterious death: see n. 95 below.

36. Ferella 2024, 95–107. Later readers may have believed this power to inhere in the physical text: the Strasbourg papyrus was originally found folded into a crown on the head of a corpse in a sarcophagus in Egypt: Martin and Primavesi 1999, 27–51.

narrates his past lives as boy, girl, bush, bird, and fish. These reincarnations are part of the punishment of the criminal *daimones*, "growing over time into various forms of mortal things that exchange the terrible paths of life" (B115.7–8/D10.7–8). As stages of his "purification" they form the chapters of the *daimōn*'s life story and his path to eventual apotheosis. *On Nature* teaches that all living things—exemplified by this same list of creatures—are compounds of the four elements and as such will eventually dissolve entirely in the general dispersion at the peak of Strife.[37] But if compounds disperse entirely with every cosmic cycle, how can there be an "I" who survives over the longue durée to remember and recount those past lives? Even on a shorter time frame, if the elemental composition of the individual is constantly changing in reaction to the elements of the environment (B106/D243, B109/D207), and "to the extent that they become other (*alloioi*), to that extent it always happens to them also to think otherwise (*to phronein alloia*)" (B108/D244), then every new "unfamiliar (*allognōti)* cloak of flesh" (B126/D19) renders the self's mind (*gnōmē*) and thinking (*phronein*) unfamiliar, unrecognizable from one moment to the next, much less from one life to the next.[38] The same elemental mixing makes it hard even to differentiate absolutely between such beings as a boy and a girl and a bush and a bird and a fish: each is just a temporary reorganization of the components of the other, its identity porous and provisional at best.

The physical theory would thus seem to destabilize not only the *autos* of this exceptional daimonic autobiography but the *autos* in general, the very possibility of a self, stable over time and separate from other beings. Kirk, Raven, and Schofield put the issue well:

> The psychology of *On Nature* is not purely reductive, although it leaves in obscurity what is the 'I' which thinks and perceives *with* the elements. It remains similarly obscure what the continuing identity of a *daimon* consists in, as it is tossed from element to element and transformed from plant to beast to man. What is clear is the force of Empedocles's conviction *that* there is an 'I' which survives such changes, whose perspective on life and death and everything else can never be entirely subsumed within a cosmic perspective. . . . 'I' is ineliminable.[39]

37. B9.2–3/D54.2–3, B20.6–7/D73.307–308, B21.10–12/D77a.10–12, B23.6–8/D60.6–8, P. Strasb. a(i)9–a(ii)2, c7–8/D73.270–272, 307–8. They will also be fused beyond recognition in Sphere at the peak of Philotēs.

38. Kahn 2014, 439–40. This is true of all autobiography, inasmuch as we are all continuously changing and becoming different; the fixity of the authorial position is always a fiction and is often revealed to be so by the life it writes. Mackenzie (2020) stresses the multiplicity and porousness of individual identity in Empedocles's physical system and believes that the daimonology is designed to encourage his audience to accept this expanded conception of selfhood.

39. Kirk, Raven, and Schofield 1983, 321. See further Inwood 2007; and Kahn 2014, 435–42. How much the *egō* remembers of his past lives is (like so much else about Empedocles's daimonology) an open question. I assume, based in part on his emotionally charged memories of exile (B118–123/D14–24), that he recalls the experience, not just the fact, of past lives (with Tor 2017, 332–33; contra, e.g.,

The union of the cosmology and daimonology thus opens new schisms within Empedocles's autobiography and his philosophy. On the one hand, the narrative "I" whose emotional tale of transformation enacts the elemental theory is (literally) disintegrated by that theory: in this contradictory autobiography the *autos* is unwritten by the *bios* he writes, leaving the author (and thus authority) of that life story uncertain. On the other hand, if the pedagogical "I" depends on the daimonic autobiography to substantiate his physical theories, then he, too, is in jeopardy, as is the theory he teaches: the doctrine would be validated by the account of a life that the doctrine itself renders untellable. These contradictions trouble not only the narrative "I," both daimonological and cosmological, but also the authorial "I," the persona projected by the text that allows us to speak of "Empedocles's philosophy" at all.[40] For "Empedocles" as well as his narrators, "I"—as the stable and authoritative source of his philosophy and guarantor of its stability and authority—is at once impossible and, as we shall see, ineliminable.

Recognizing the interdependence of Empedocles's two (if they are two) poems and personae thus merely reproduces a fundamental schism in the position of philosophical enunciation, as the philosophical *autos* is shown to be both divided in itself and in tension with the doctrine it expounds. This schizophrenia is not the effect of a historical split between scientist and sorcerer awkwardly sutured into a mythical hybrid, nor can it be resolved by a reading that turns the daimonic *autos* into an allegorical philosopher or the natural philosopher into a god. Instead, I will suggest, it is the symptom of Empedocles's radical new theory of life and the fundamentally ambiguous place of the self within it.

BIOS

We have seen that Empedocles's autobiography destabilizes the *autos*: the idea of a singular autonomous self, knowing and writing his own life, is undermined by that life itself. In fact, Empedocles shifts the relations among these terms. In his fragments, autobiography is not the writing of the life of a self, the *bios* of an *autos*, but the writing of life itself, *bios ho autos*. And the protagonist of this story is not the singular self but instead a swarming multiplicity of lives, human and nonhuman, each with its own agency and desires.

For Empedocles, the story of an individual life is contained within and inseparable from the story of life as a whole. Most people, Empedocles writes, "see only a small share of life (*biou*) in their lifetimes (*zōēisi*), and swift-fated like smoke they rise and fly, believing only this, what each happens to encounter as they are driven everywhere, but he boasts that he has discovered the whole" (B2.3–6/D42.3–6).

Wright 1981, 276). The latter view would diminish, but not eliminate, the tension between the physical theory and the concept of an identity that persists across reincarnations.

40. Foucault 1984, 105–13. I return to the author function in the Conclusion.

The individual's *zōē*, singular and limited, is contrasted to *bios*, life as a whole. But each ephemeral existence opens onto that whole: the phrase "what each happens to encounter" will appear in another fragment in reference to the elements.[41] Each concrete individual life span, *zōē*, is fundamentally connected to *bios*, life as such.[42]

Bios, in turn, takes on an expanded meaning in light of Empedocles's cosmic theory. "A wise man would not divine such things in his mind, that as long as they live what they call their life (*biōsi to dē bioton kaleousi*), for so long do they exist (*eisin*) and experience bad things and good, but before mortals were formed and after they have dissolved, they are nothing" (B15/D52). Mortals use the word *bios* for their own brief biological life span: they do not realize that their being extends beyond their own birth and death. In truth, there is no birth and death for "mortal things" but only mixing and separation of elements, which we name *phusis* and *thanatos* (B8/D53, cf. B9/D54, B11/D51). This is true for human beings but also for every other being in Empedocles's cosmos, including the gods, who are "long-lived" but not immortal (B21.12/D77a.12, B23.8/D60.8, P. Strasb. a (ii) 2/D73.272). Only the four root elements and the two forces are eternal. Everything else is merely a temporary combination of roots as they merge and separate under the forces of Love and Strife.[43] *Bios* encompasses the entire cycle, as B20/D73.302–308 shows: both the coming together of limbs to form bodies "in the acme of flourishing life" (*biou thalethontos en akmēi*, B20.3/D73.304) under Love and their desolate wandering "each apart in the breakers of life" (*andikh' hekasta perirrēgmini bioio*, B20.5/D73.306) under Strife. The emotional tone of this fragment recalls the autobiographical account of *Purifications*'s *daimōn*. But what is presented there as the saga of a singular *egō*, this fragment shows to be shared with every other mortal creature: "And in the same way for bushes and water-dwelling fish and beasts who sleep in the mountains and doves on the wing" (B20.6–7/D73.307–308).

The life of the individual is thus an intrinsic part of the life of the cosmos, and the story of the *autos* is part of the story of *bios* as a whole. This is because

41. B59.2/D149.2; cf. B53/D105, B98.1/D190.1, B104/D107. Likewise in the first line of B2/D42 the "narrow devices (*palamai*) poured over the limbs" that constrain mortal understanding also link it to the *palamai* of Kupris (B75.2/D200.2) that fashion living things. If he "looks with every device (*palamē*)," as the speaker urges in B3.9/D44.9, the student will come to understand that "the whole" is nothing but myriad "shares of life." Similarly, *aiōn* is used of the life span of individuals (B110.3/D257.3, B129.6/D38.6, P. Strasb. a(ii) 6/D73.276), of the ever-changing existence of the roots (B17.11/D73.242, B26.10/D77b.10), and of the perpetual cycling of Love and Strife (B16/D63).

42. Thus Agamben's distinction, drawn from Aristotle, between *bios* (political life) and *zōē* (natural or bare life) is not helpful for Empedocles, for whom both terms are unstable. As Holmes (2019) points out, Greek usage in general does not support Agamben's dichotomy. Gheerbrant (2017, 74–82) surveys archaic usage of the two words apropos of B2/D42.

43. For my purposes it does not matter whether Empedocles envisioned one creation or two. O'Brien (1969) argues for two (cf. Sedley 2005; 2008b, 31–52, 62–71); Long (1974) for one. Furley (1987, 98–102) rejects any cyclical schema in favor of a linear evolution. Graham (1988) offers a clear synopsis of the issue.

the whole for Empedocles is fundamentally composed of parts. In contrast to Parmenides's unitary metaphysical Being, Empedocles's *arkhē* is plural and material. The word he chooses for his four elements, *rhizōmata*, is concrete and earthy: no abstract components (*stoikheia*) or indivisibles (*atoma*) for him.[44] The four roots combine to produce everything that is and was and will be, all the phenomena of our world and any other possible world. This bottom-up ontology prioritizes material parts over conceptual wholes. Thus we hear less of bodies than of limbs (*melē*, *guia*).[45] We hear of human limbs (B2.1/D42.1, B3.13/D44.13, B63/D164, B100.22/D201a.22). There was a time when body parts wandered alone (B57/D154), isolated limbs that were themselves "single-limbed" (*mounomelē eti ta guia*, B58/D153), and met to form monstrous combinations with "shadowy limbs" (*skierois . . . guiois*, B61/D156). But even in our current form human beings are just a massy collocation of limbs. "This [the alternation of Love and Strife] is conspicuous in the bulk of mortal limbs (*broteōn meleōn arideikton onkon*); sometimes we come together into one through Philotēs, all the limbs which have been allotted a body" (*hapanta guia, ta sōma lelonkhe*, D73.302–4/B20.1–3 = P. Strasb. c 2–4).[46] Not only do we have limbs: we are nothing but limbs, combining by chance (*lelonkhe*) to form ephemeral wholes. And it is not only us. Trees have limbs, as do birds and fish (B82/D198) and gods

44. Ancient commentators often call the roots *stoikheia*, but Empedocles himself does not use the word in the extant fragments. See e.g. Arist. *Metaph.* 1.4 985a32, crediting Empedocles with being the first to speak of four *stoikheia*. Sedley (2008b, 33n7) believes the idea that *rhizōmata* was Empedocles's regular term for the elements is a misleading impression produced by the fragmentary state of his text; he is right that it would have been more characteristic for Empedocles to use a variety of terms.

45. In addition to generic limbs (*melē, guia*) there are a plethora of specific body parts: heads, foreheads, and temples (*kephalē*, B134.1/D93.1; *korsai, metōpoi*, B57.1/D154.1; *prōira, krana, prosōpa*, B61.1–2/D156.2, B44/D123); necks (*aukhenes*, B57.1/D154.1), chests (*sterna*, B61.1/D156.1, B96.1/D192.1) and backs (*nōta*, B29.1/D92.1, B83.2/D197.2, B134.2/D93.2, B76.1/D74.1); arms and shoulders (B3.3/D44.3, B57.2/D154.2); hands (B23.3/D60.3, B100.10/D201a.10, B133.2/D9.2, B141/D31) and palms (B2.1/D42.1, B3.9/D44.9, B75.2/D200.2); knees (*gouna*, B29.2/D92.2, B134.3/D93.3) and feet (*podes*, B29.2/D92.2, B101.2/D232.2, B134.3/D93.3); bones (*ostea*, B96.3/D192.3); flesh (*sarx*, B98.5/D190.5, B99/D226, B100.2/D201a.2, B126/D19; *khrōs*, B100.17/D201a.17, B76.3/P. Strasb. b 2/D74.3); joints (*arthra*, B17.22/D73.253) and pores (*poroi*, B3.12/D44.12); mouths (*stomata*, B3.2/D44.2, B39.3/D113.3, B100.3/D201a.3), tongues (*glōssa*, B3.1/D44.1, B3.11/D44.11, B39.2/D113.2), nostrils (*rhinoi*, B76.2/P. Strasb. b 4/D74.5, B100.4/D201a.4,), ears (*ouata*, P. Strasb. a(ii) 21/D73.291; cf. B99/D226); and eyes (*ophthalmoi*, B133.1/D9.1, *ommata*, B17.21/D73.252, B86/D213, and their components, B84/D215); diaphragms (*phrenes*, B5/D258, B15.1/D52.1, B17.14/D73.245, B23.9/D60.9, B114.3/D6.3, B133.3/D9.3, B134.4/D93.4; *prapides*, B110.1/D257.1, B129.2, 4/D38.2, 4, B132.1/D8.1), and "shaggy genitals" (*mēdea*, B134.3/D93.3, B29.2/D92.2), to name only the most obvious. *Sōma* appears at B20.3/D73.304 (= P. Strasb. c 4), where it is defined in relation to its limbs (cf. B100.2/D201a.2). Trépanier (2014; see also 2017, 139–43) stresses the priority of part to whole in Empedocles.

46. I follow Laks-Most in reading *sunerkhometh'* ("we come together") in preference to Diels-Kranz's *sunerkhomen'* ("coming together"). The first-person plural form is adopted by most recent editors, but rejected by Algra and Mansfeld (2001); and Trépanier (2003). See the discussion in Laks 2002c. At stake in the textual choice is the identification of "us" with the limbs. The grammar of the lines also leaves it open whether a body is allotted limbs or vice versa: the relation between part and whole is reciprocal and purely fortuitous. Cf. below, n. 48.

(B115.3/D10.3) and the sun (B27.1/D89.1). The root elements are basic, but they too have parts (*merē*, B22.1/D101.1, B35.10–11/D75.10–11, B96.2/D192.2). Only Sphere, as the perfect unity of Love, lacks limbs. But that lack is located precisely in his limbs: "There is no civil war nor unseemly battle in his limbs" (*en meleessin*, B27a/D91). In marked contrast to Parmenides's sphere of Being (on which it may be modeled), for Empedocles the perfect whole is just a temporary agglomeration of parts that dispersed again when Neikos, "nurtured in [Sphere's] limbs" (*eni meleessin*, D94/B30), emerged, and "all the limbs (*guia*) of the god were shaken in succession" (B31/D95).[47] These scattered members are destined to form provisional bodies, but their nature is not determined by this destiny: the parts do not exist for the sake of wholeness (as Aristotle complains), and any whole they produce is not their final *telos* but merely one chapter in the life story of its component members.[48]

Empedocles's is thus a universe of material parts. All those parts, moreover, are in constant motion. Things rush and run. They flow and fly. They rise up and leap and whirl and wander.[49] The elements are always on the move, coming together and separating (B17.1–12/D73.233–243), wandering (*plankhthent(a)*, P. Strasb. a(ii) 16/D73.286), running through one another (*theonta*, B17.34/D73.265,

47. Cf. B29/D92, B134/D93: "His limbs are not furnished with a man's head; two branches do not dart from his back; no feet, nor swift knees, nor shaggy genitals." It is not even clear that Sphere could be unitary, since if it contains all things it must contain Strife.

48. Arist. *Metaph.* 1.4 985a21–29 (<A37/R11a). For a helpful comparison of Empedocles's and Aristotle's causes see Inwood 2001, 68–75. There are finalities in Empedocles's cosmology, but they are all local and provisional. B62/D157 describes how, as like elements were drawn together, rough outlines (*oulophueis . . . tupoi*) of human beings sprang up from the earth, "not yet (*oute ti pō*) revealing the lovely frame (*eraton demas*) of limbs nor a voice nor the limb that is native to men." The inchoate joining of limbs is governed by a goal of wholeness, "the lovely frame" of the complete human body. The noun *tupoi*, outlines or models, may suggest that this frame is the work of a demiurge, and Philotēs is presented as a demiurge in other fragments (B23/D60, B59/D149, B86/D213, B87/D214, B95/D217). But here these *tupoi* "were springing up" (*exanetellon*) spontaneously from the earth, and evolution seems driven less by a final form immanent within each creature (as in Aristotle) than by the finality of the poet's own perspective, which is "not off-the-mark nor ignorant" (B62.3/D157.3). It is the poet who is aiming at the mark of complete humans, not nature itself. Cf. B20.3/D73.304 where the limbs are "allotted" a body (*sōma lelonkhe*), a verb that implies random selection, and B53/D105: at the creation of the cosmos air "happened (*sunekurse*) to be running in this way then, but often in a different way." On Empedocles's "curious cocktail of artistic creation and sheer accident," see Sedley 2008b, 52–62.

49. In addition to forms of *bainō* and *erkhomai*, some of Empedocles's favorite verbs of motion include *aissō* "shoot" (B29.1/D92.1, B134.2/D93.2, B100.6–7/D201a.6–7, B134.5/D93.5, P. Strasb. a(ii) 3, 8, 12/D73.273, 278, 282), *theō* "run" (B17.34/D73.265, B21.13/D77a.13, B26.3/D77b.3, B53/D105, P. Strasb. a(ii) 13, 15/D73.283, 285), *thrōiskō* "leap" (B84.5/D215.5, B100.8, 25/D201a.8, 25, B105.1/D240.1), *ornumi* "arise" (B2.9/D42.9, B30.2/D94.2, B111.4/D43.4), *helissō* "whirl" (B17.25/D73.256, B45/D139, B46/D137), *plazō, planaō* "wander" (B20.5/D73.306, B22.3/D101.3, B57.2, 3/D154.2, 3, B58/D153, P. Strasb. a(ii) 16, c6/D73.286, 306), *piptō* "fall" (B59.2/D149.2, B100.13, 21/D201a.13, 21, B104/D107, B133.3/D9.3), *blastanō* "grow" (B21.10/D77a.10, B57.1/D154.1, B146.3/D39.3, P. Strasb. a(i) 9/D73.270). See also below on flowing and pouring and on augmenting. Often words conveying motion are piled up as at B100.7/D201a.7: "aether rushes down seething in a furious swell" (*aithēr paphlazōn kataissetai oidmati margōi*).

B21.13/D77a.13, B26.3/D77b.3, *theesken*, P. Strasb. a(ii) 15/D73.285). So are the forces: Aphrodite whirls among the roots (*helissomenēn*, B17.25/D73.256); Neikos leaps up from Sphere (*anorouse*, B30.2/D94.2). The celestial bodies likewise whirl (*helissetai*, B45/D139, B46/D137) and run (*theei*, P. Strasb. a(ii) 13/D73.283). Human bodies move but are also alive with internal movement as blood "darts back" (*apaixēi*, B100.6/D201a.6), "leaps up" (*anathrōiskēi*, B100.8/D201a.8), and "surging through the limbs rushes backward into the interior" (*kladassomenon dia guiōn . . . palinorson apaixeie mukhonde*, B100.22–23/D201a.22–23; cf. B105.1/D240.1). Thought too is in motion: mind (*phrēn*) "darts (*kataissousa*) with swift thoughts through the entire cosmos" (B134.4–5/D93.4–5); cleverness (*mētis*) arises (*orōren*, B2.9/D42.9) and increases (*aexetai*, B106/D243); belief (*pistis*) assaults the heart (*hormē*, B114.3/D6.3). The poem itself "rushes through" the innards of its listener (B4.3/D47.3).[50]

This motion produces all the phenomena of the cosmos as things "happen upon" one another in their rushing (B104/D107, B59.2/D149.2, cf. B98.1/D190.1). Aristotle objects to the contingency of these encounters and takes Empedocles to task for relying on chance, *tukhē*, in his cosmogonic theory.[51] It is true that these combinations are not governed by Anankē (as is the alternation of Love and Strife, B115.1/D10.1), but neither are they completely random. Instead, these encounters are motivated by the parts' own will and desire. In Empedocles's ontology there are no inanimate things. All things feel desire and move under its impetus. Limbs wander alone (B20.5/D73.306), solitary arms "bereaved" of shoulders (*eunides*, B57.2/D154.2) and eyes "begging" for foreheads (*penēteuonta*, B57.3/D154.3). Plants too desire, perceive, feel joy and sadness, and have mind (A70/D250a, c). Earth, water, fire, and air have their own natural affinities: those most suited to mixing "love one another (*allēlois esterktai*), made similar by Aphrodite" while "enemies [are those that] keep most distant from one another . . . in every way strangers to unification and terribly sad" (*pantēi sunginesthai aēthea kai mala lugra*, B22.4–8/D101.4–8).[52] In this they follow the root elements, which are not passive matter shaped by the divine agency of Love and Strife but, as Rowett has stressed, meet those forces with their own active desire.[53] They "come together

50. "Know, with the argument having rushed through into your innards" (*gnōthi, diassēthentos eni splankhnoisi logoio*). *Diassēthentos* is Diels's suggestion in place of Clement's *diatmēthentos* (retained by most editors). I will return to language's motion below. For *logos* as Empedocles's own argument cf. B17.26/D73.257, B35.2/D75.2, B131.4/D7.4.

51. Arist. *Ph.* 2.4 196a17–24; cf. *Gen. corr.* 2.6 334a1–7 and the discussion at Inwood 2001, 68–75. Simplicius, in his commentary on the *Physics* passage, lists examples of *tukhē* in Empedocles: B53/D105, B59.2/149.2, B98.1/D190.1, B85/D191, B75.2/D200.2, B103/D242. On the nature of necessity in Empedocles, see Osborne (2005): she argues that it is arbitrary but not determinist. Cf. Laks 2005.

52. This is Laks-Most's translation of B22/D101, which brings out the emotional tone of the Greek. Cf. B91/D69: water has a natural affinity with wine but "does not wish" (*ouk ethelei*) to mix with oil. At B115.12/D10.12 all the elements hate (*stugeousi*) the *daimōn*.

53. Rowett 2016, expanding on Osborne 1987a, 46. Cf. Wright 1981, 233–34. Curd (2016) emphasizes the structuring force of Love and Strife's thoughts and emotions.

in love and long for one another" (*sun d'ebē en Philotēti kai allēloisi potheitai*, B21.8/D77a.8); they come together willingly (*thelēma*, B35.6/D75.6), even ardently (*epokheito*, B90/D68), and are reluctant to be separated (*aekazomenoisin*, P. Strasb. d 2/D76.2; cf. B62.6/D157.6). Everything in Empedocles's cosmos is animated by will and intent, from the individual roots all the way up to Sphere as he "rejoices in his circular solitude" (*moniēi periēgei gaiōn*, B27.4/D89.4, B28/D90). "Know that all things have thought and a share of mind" (*panta gar isthi phronēsin ekhein kai nōmatos aisan*, B110.10/D257.10; cf. B103/D242).

In her discussion of this animated world, Rowett rejects what she calls "a reductive materialist analysis" that sees the elements as inert matter naively described with anthropomorphizing metaphor. Taking Empedocles's language literally, she views the elements as "divine agents, with the capacity to make decisions and act on them."[54] I provisionally follow her in reading this language literally (although we will return to the problem of metaphor in the next section). However, I believe the dichotomy between inert matter and divine agents poses a false alternative, one that brings Empedocles's world to life only by extending to matter the liveliness of a hypostasized (indeed, divinized) human agency. Arguing against such a dichotomy, Tim Ingold proposes that matter does not need to be anthropomorphized or divinized to become animate: it is intrinsically animate. It interacts continuously with the world around it, changing in response to its environment and changing its environment in the process.[55] Every thing, human and nonhuman, organic and inorganic, is engaged in its own process of becoming, "pursuing the line of its own movement" in a complex weave with other beings in motion, each of them "bent upon the tasks of life."[56] *Bios*, in his view, is not the exclusive possession of an anthropomorphic agent but simply the "meshwork" of such interwoven lines of flight. Each of those lines is, in a sense, an autobiography, the trajectory of a being in the process of becoming. But it writes the life not of a singular, discrete *autos* but of a tightly interconnected assemblage of mutually transforming parts.[57]

Ingold's meshwork well describes Empedocles's ontology, an ontology neither of inert material objects nor of divinized agential subjects but of lines of flight. In B17/D73.233–66, in a passage full of Parmenidean resonances, the poet asserts the

54. Rowett 2016, 93, 82.

55. Ingold 2011, 28–29.

56. Ingold 2011, 13, 6; see also 71. "Lines of flight" is also a term of art for Deleuze and Guattari (e.g., 1987, 24–25, 222–23, 277). Ingold does not distinguish his concept from theirs, although he says he came to it independently (13–14). He develops the idea in Ingold 2007 and 2015.

57. Ingold 2011, 160: "For the things of this world *are* their stories, identified not by fixed attributes but by their paths of movement in an unfolding field of relations." "Assemblage" (*agencement*) is Deleuze and Guattari's term for a provisional and contingent collocation of heterogeneous elements (individuals and things but also lines of motion, intensities, signifiers) in relations of mutual transformation with unpredictable emergent properties (1987, 4, 22–23 et passim).

eternal and unchanging being of the root elements. Like Parmenides's Being, these elements fill all time and space, without beginning or end (B17.30–33/D73.261–64). They can be neither augmented nor diminished,

> ἀλλ' αὐτ' ἔστιν ταῦτα, δι' ἀλλήλων δὲ θέοντα
> γίγνεται ἄλλοτε ἄλλα καὶ ἠνεκὲς αἰὲν ὁμοῖα. (B17.34–35/D73.265–66)[58]

> but these very things are, and running through each other
> they become different at different times and are always continuously the same.

These lines contain Empedocles's strongest ontological language. The demonstrative pronoun (*tauta*) is Empedocles's usual way of referring to the root elements, but here it is reinforced, exceptionally, by the intensive adjective *auta* ("these things themselves, these very things") and the existential form of the verb "to be."[59] Emphatically themselves, *auta*, the elements are eternally and unfailingly the same as themselves (*ēnekes aien homoia*). This identity, this self-same selfness, constitutes their being (*estin*) and being in general.

But that being is itself in motion: the elements are "running through each other." Heraclitus (as we saw in chapter 2) stabilized becoming within an eternal circle of sameness. Empedocles, with his alternation of Love and Strife, may seem to do something similar. Earlier in fragment B17/D73 we were told that the elements, brought together in Philotēs and dispersed in Neikos, are continually transformed from one to many and many to one, and

> τῆι μὲν γίγνονταί τε καὶ οὔ σφισιν ἔμπεδος αἰών·
> ἧι δὲ διαλλάσσοντα διαμπερὲς οὐδαμὰ λήγει,
> ταύτηι δ' αἰὲν ἔασιν ἀκίνητοι κατὰ κύκλον. (B17.11–13/D73.242–44 = B26.10–12/D77b.10–12)

> in that way they are becoming and they have no stable lifetime,
> but to the extent that they never cease changing continually,
> to that extent they always are, unmoving in a circle.

In these lines, the unsteady life of constant becoming seems to be stabilized, even immobilized, in the cycle of Love and Strife. Situated within that circle, becoming (*gignontai*) and changing (*diallassonta*) are transmuted into eternal, invariable being (*aien easin akinētoi*). But the poem's insistence on motion places

58. Simplicius's *de* in the first line seems to me preferable to the papyrus's *ge*, which creates an atypical asyndeton. See Martin and Primavesi (1999, 172–75), who defend the latter. On the Parmenidean echoes, see Bollack 1969, 76–77; Curd 1998, 156–58; and Inwood 2001, 32–33.

59. See Martin and Primavesi (1999, 171–72) on the force of *estin* here. They translate: "Il n'existe que ces choses elles-mêmes." Laks-Most (D73.265–66) translate *estin* as connective and *auta* as predicate: "But these are themselves." Inwood (2001, 36) compares *aut' estin tauta* to Platonic Forms, as well as Parmenides's Being. See further O'Brien 2016.

the emphasis not on the unchanging rotation of the whole but on the endless transformation of the parts, and the circle of immobile being in B17.13/D73.244 caps twelve lines in which the elements are described only by—indeed, simply *as*—unceasing motion: they are their augmentation (*ēuxēthē*, B17.1/D73.233) and dispersion (*diephu*, B17.2/D73.234; cf. B17.5, 10/D73.237, 241), their transformation (*allassonta*, B17.6/D73.238; *diallassonta*, B17.12/D73.243) as they come together (*sunerkhomen'*, B17.7/D73.239) and are borne apart (*dikh' hekasta phoreumena*, B17.8/D73.240).[60] On a molar level, the frenetic activity of the roots may look like a stable and motionless circle. But Empedocles's eye is trained on the molecular level, down among the darting elements and rushing limbs. Viewed from this angle, being resolves into chaotic becoming: it is only to the extent (*hēi . . . tautēi*) that the roots are always changing that they eternally *are*. Parmenides created his radical ontology by transforming a verb into a noun, *To Eon*. Empedocles articulates an ontology of verbs. His *auta tauta* – the things themselves in their eternal identity—*are* only in their interlaced and mutually transformative running. Empedocles's is a metaphysics *of* motion and *in* motion.

If autobiography, as Olney suggests, is the stabilization of life's Heraclitean becoming into a singular Parmenidean Being, Empedocles refuses that process. *On Nature* tells a story not of a fixed and monadic *autos* but of plural *auta* and ultimately of *allēla*, "each others." Running through each other, each driven by its own individual will and wishes, the elements intersect and combine in unforeseen ways to create a biosphere of infinitely varied and intimately connected phenomena: "From these all things that were and are and will be, and trees grew and men and women, beasts and birds and water-nourished fish and long-lived gods greatest in honors. For these very things are, and running through each other they become different in shape" (B21.9–14/D77a.9–14; cf. B26.3–4/D77b.3–4). In place of phylogenetic trees, things proliferate like weeds, with a crazy rhizomatic fertility that jumps the boundaries between phyla, materially connecting humans, animals, and plants: "The same things become hairs and leaves and the thick wings of birds and scales on stout limbs" (B82/D198; cf. B83/D197). Thus plants bloom (B77/D251, B78/D253; cf. B21.10/D77a.10), but so do humans and animals and gods (*eblastēse*, B21.10–12/D77a.10–12; cf. A72/D151, B99/D226). Trees "lay eggs" that are olives (B79/D254), and exude wine from their bark (B81/D256).

The result is a virtual Amazon of biodiversity: "from these [the elements] mixing flowed out countless races of mortal things, fit together in all sorts of forms, a marvel to see" (B35.16–17/D75.16–17). These forms include the often-mentioned "trees and men and women and beasts and birds and sea-nurtured fish and long-lived

60. The phrase "they never cease changing continually" (*diallassonta diamperes oudama lēgei*, B17.12/D73.243) is itself in motion. It is a repeated refrain in this section of the poem (B17.6, 11–13/D73.238, 242–244, B26.11–12/D77b.11–12). It also occurs in a variation with "darting" (*aissonta*) in place of "changing" (*allassonta*) to describe existence under Strife at P.Strasb. a(ii) 3, a(ii) 8/D73.273, 278.

gods, greatest in honor" (B21.10–12/D77a.10–12; cf. B20.6–7/D73.307–308, B23.6–8/D60.6–8, P. Strasb. a(i) 9–a(ii) 2/D73.270–272, B117/D13) but also "sea-dwelling heavy-backed" mollusks, "stony-skinned trumpet-shells and tortoises" (D74/B76/P. Strasb. b), "late-born pomegranates and succulent apples" (B80/D255), hedgehogs bristling with "sharp-pointed hairs" (B83/D197), "mild-shining," "grey-eyed moon" (B40/D125, B42/D132), and "blind-eyed, lonely night" (B49/D228).[61]

Tracing the rampant productivity of elemental combination, Empedocles writes a biography that ramifies the *autos* in all directions. The divine *egō* who tells with such pathos of his suffering in exile and the philosophical *egō* who insists on the veracity of his teachings are just parts of a vast mesh of interconnected parts, each with its own self-willed trajectory and thus each with its own autobiography. But these autobiographies are always *allēlobiographies*, stories of life together, running through one another.

Instead of rising above life to write it, then, the human subject is simply one thing in this teeming assemblage of things. Indeed, that subject is itself an assemblage, a rushing relay of parts whose lines of flight traverse the boundaries between inside and outside and dissolve any notion of the individual. I end this section with an extended example, B100/D201a's famous comparison of respiration to the working of a clepsydra.[62] The analogy seems clear enough on the surface, but rather than compare two discrete phenomena, one biological and one mechanical, the simile merges the two into a weird hybrid of the organic and inorganic. In the process, it not only displaces the human agent. It also foregrounds the agency of Empedocles's language, which describes respiration with tremendous detail and artistry even as it participates actively in its working. This dual function points to the challenges of writing a material ontology that will be taken up at greater length in the next section.

First there is the body, made up of "pipes of flesh" (*sarkōn suringes*, 2) that extend to the body's surface and "are pierced with thick furrows at their mouths (*stomiois*), right through the lowest ends of their nostrils (*rhinōn*)" (3–4). Respiratory channels are fleshy pipes: a *surinx* is a shepherd's pipe or anything shaped like it. The word evokes the breath required to play the flute, but these flutes are inside the body, as if the breath of the creature is reproduced in fractal form by his

61. Porter (2010, 151–58, 2025) stresses the aesthetic beauty of this world and the sublimity of its "irrepressible vitality" (2016, 416–21). While heterogeneous, this cosmos is not egalitarian. Gods have more honor and survive longer than other beings; lions are superior among animals, laurels among trees (B127/D36). It is also worth noting that Empedocles is relatively uninterested in inanimate beings and sometimes seems to conflate *panta* with *thnēta*.

62. The clepsydra in this fragment is not the water clock but a copper utensil for conveying small quantities of water. Last (1924) explains how it worked; Bollack (1969, 476) provides nice illustrations. The breathing subject of the fragment is not necessarily human. Its opening line—"in this way all things inhale and exhale"—situates its analysis within a common *bios*, since "all things have a share of breath" (B102/D231). The mechanics of the clepsydra, Empedoclean respiration, and the comparison between them are thoroughly discussed by O'Brien (1970, 146–54, 176–79) and Gheerbrant (2017, 343–83).

internal parts, which themselves have parts, "mouths" and "nostrils."[63] At the same time, as a technical artifact the *surinx* already crosses the boundary of the analogy to the clepsydra: the body is a pipe even before it is compared to one. The fragment goes on to describe the violent process by which blood and air fill these pipes in alternation: blood "rushes out" and "leaps up" (*apaixēi*, 6; *anathrōiskēi*, 8); air "rushes down, seething in a furious swell" (*paphlazōn kataissetai oidmati margōi*, 7). In this churning activity, the roots mingle: aether rushes like water (*oidmati*, 7); earth is present in the furrows (*aloxin*, 3) of the veins. The interior of the body is a complex and dynamic cosmos.

An anacoluthon marks a shift to the analogy: "as when a child playing with a clepsydra of gleaming copper" (8–9). This *pais klepsudrēi paizousa* may recall Heraclitus's *pais paizōn* (Her. B52/D76): for both philosophers, innocent actions and everyday objects not only symbolize but instantiate the fundamental workings of the world and bind the individual tightly to them. Empedocles's clepsydra is an assemblage of diverse bodies—copper pipe (9), human hand (10), "thick flow" of water (14), and "bulky" air (13)—each going about its own "task of life" within this intricate meshwork of metal and skin (17). Dipping the pipe in water, the girl sets the mechanism in motion, but her actions are just a part, and not the most active part, of the drama.[64]

> αἰθὴρ δ' ἐκτὸς ἔσω λελιημένος ὄμβρον ἐρύκει,
> ἀμφὶ πύλας ἠθμοῖο δυσηχέος ἄκρα κρατύνων,
> εἰσόκε χειρὶ μεθῆι, τότε δ' αὖ πάλιν, ἔμπαλιν ἢ πρίν,
> πνεύματος ἐμπίπτοντος ὑπεκθέει αἴσιμον ὕδωρ. (B100.18–21/D201a.18–21)
>
> Air from outside, longing to enter, prevents the rainstorm
> around the portals, commanding the heights of the harsh-echoing sieve,
> until she releases it from her hand, and then again in turn, the reverse of before,
> as the breath falls upon it, the water runs out from beneath in equal measure.

In this miniature Homeric battle scene the clepsydra becomes a besieged citadel, with the elements waging war for control of the instrument.[65] As the elements

63. The word *surinx* becomes common in medical writing to refer to the channels of the body (LSJ II.4), but as is often the case, Empedocles seems to be the first to use it in this way. *Rhinōn* may be from *rhinos* (skin) instead of *rhis* (nostril): Bollack 1969, 481; and Wright 1981, 245–46. On the "transfusion" of tenor and vehicle in this simile, see Garani 2007, 111–14.

64. Her agency is strongly marked at the beginning (*paizousa*, 9; *theisa*, 10; *apostegasēi*, 14) but as the passage goes on Empedocles's tendency to leave grammatical subjects unexpressed makes it difficult to tell which actions are hers. She is generally supplied as the subject of *ekhēi* (16) and *methēi* (20). At 17 she appears in the instrumental form of "human flesh" (*broteōi khroi*). The human agent is submerged within the process she sets in motion. The child's gender may link her to Aphrodite (Bollack 1965, 244). Rashed (2018, 183–204) associates her with Persephone, whose presence he detects throughout the fragments.

65. *Aithēr* strives to get in with the zeal of an attacking warrior (*leliēmenos: Il.* 4.465, 5.690, 12.106, 16.552) and the portals are likened to city gates (*pulas*). *Dusēkhes* is a common epithet of war in Homer, with *polemoio dusēkheos* frequently occurring in the same line position as *ēthmoio dusēkheos* (*Il.* 2.686,

engage, each driven by its own heroic impetus, the human agent becomes all but irrelevant. Language too enters the fray: in the plosive repetition of its back-and-forth (*palin empalin ē prin, pneumatos empiptontos hupektheei*, 20–21) words become the sound of the "harsh-echoing sieve," resounding through the implement and contributing to the chaos of battle.

The battle then shifts from the clepsydra to the breathing body. "Just as the delicate blood surging through the limbs when it rushes backward into the interior, a raging flow of air comes out in a wave and when it [the blood] leaps up, it exhales again an equal amount backward" (22–25). These lines closely echo those that preceded this extended simile, forming a ring composition that separates the mechanical vehicle from its biological tenor. Between the "delicate blood" (*teren haima*, 6, 22) of the latter and the "delicate body" (*teren demas*, 11) of the former, however, the line between literal and metaphoric becomes hard to discern: the language literally overflows the bounds of the simile. Further, as Empedocles's words rush and flow across the divide, merging flesh and metal, body and machine, we also lose the clear lines that would define a self, united in itself and distinct from its environment. With every breath we witness a clash of elements that besiege the walls of the *autos*, exposing it to an outside that is already within. Meanwhile the little girl plays, oblivious to the complex physics she is enacting.

And yet, the *autos* lost within Empedocles's materialist theory can be rediscovered behind it, at its origin. This fragment is one of the most celebrated examples of Empedocles's skill with metaphor, a skill recognized already in antiquity.[66] The ostentatious artistry of the fragment recalls the poetic *egō* even where he is not overtly present: the scene is focalized through his eyes, not through the girl's. Empedocles's physics displaces the *autos*, dispersing its qualities across a universe of lively, intentional things (*auta tauta*) and the mutual relations among them (*allēla*). But *graphē* imports an authorial *autos* even where the first-person voice is absent. There is thus one *autos* Empedocles cannot eliminate: himself as author. In this biosphere of constant movement and random joinings, where everything is always in the process of becoming and nothing has a "secure lifetime" (*empedos aiōn*, B17.11/D73.242), one thing does appear to be *empedos*: the poet, Empedocles himself. "'I' is ineliminable."[67] This places Empedocles in tension with his own ontology and reiterates at the metalevel of poetic production

7.376, 7.395, 11.524, 13.535, 18.307). *Aisimon hudōr* perhaps recalls the *aisimon hēmar* that signifies imminent defeat in Homer (*Il.* 8.72, 21.100, 22.212, *Od.* 16.280).

66. Arist. fr. 70 Rose (< A1/R1b): "being skilled at metaphor (*metaphorētikos*) and making use of the other poetic devices." For appraisals of Empedocles's use of metaphor and simile, see Kranz 1938, 100–9; Snell 1953, 214–18; Bollack 1965, 295–302; Van Groningen 1971, 182–84; Garani 2007, 95–220; and Gheerbrant 2017, 271–386. The language in the lines introducing the analogy (9–11) draws attention to its own aesthetics: the pipe is of "bright copper" (*dieipeteos*, a rare word, if the reading is correct); the girl's hand, "well-formed" (*eueidei*); the water, "silvery" (*argupheoio*).

67. Kirk, Raven, and Schofield 1983, 321, quoted above. Obbink (1993, 87–88) notes Empedocles's allusion to his own name at B17.11/D73.242 and in the *empedophulla kai empedokarpa* trees of B77–78/D251–52. Cf. Rashed 2018, 197–98.

the split in the *autos* we witnessed in the last section: the contradiction between an *egō* who narrates his past lives and a physics that vitiates such a narration. Empedocles cannot write *bios* without extracting himself from it, even against his will, and positing himself as both the stabilizing origin of and the sole exception to his dynamic ontology.

GRAPHĒ

Empedocles's innovative poetic style is an attempt to evade this contradiction: to get over himself, as it were, and to write *bios* not from above but from within. It is an attempt "to see the grass in things and in words" and to articulate those rhizomatic connections between words and things. In fact, for Empedocles words *are* things. This means that language does not imitate the world any more than a falling rock imitates gravity. Instead, it enacts its fundamental physical principles. Empedocles's unique poetics are an attempt to activate this immediate, nonmimetic relation between language and the world. But this experiment in radical linguistics is inherently contradictory, as we saw already in the last section, for in the very act of writing Empedocles inevitably reasserts his own authorial *egō*, and the more so the more innovative his style.

Empedocles is self-conscious about his poetics. In B9/D54 he comments explicitly on the difficulty of expressing novel ideas in traditional language. What people call birth and death are actually the mixing and separation of elements: "It is not right, the way they speak of it, but I myself too comply with the norm."[68] To the extent that he does follow linguistic norms, however, he does so in a supremely inventive and idiosyncratic way that calls constant attention to his authorial presence. Phrases like "late-born pomegranates and succulent apples" (*opsigonoi te sidai kai huperphloia mēla*, B80/D255) or the hedgehog's "sharp-pointed hairs" (*oxubeleis khaitai*, B83/D197) are conspicuous in their artistry, adopting Homeric vocabulary to new ends and combining it in novel ways.[69] On the one hand, these innovations illustrate Empedocles's linguistic materialism. Words come into being in the same way as everything else in the cosmos. Lexical limbs combine in surprising forms, and Empedocles's many *hapax legomena* (some sixty-three of

68. Following the text proposed by Wilamowitz (1930, 246) in the (corrupt) last line. On the problem of correct speech, see further B3.4/D44.4, B8/D53, B17.24/D73.255. Empedocles also remarks on his own practice of repetition ("it is good to say twice what is necessary," B25/D45; cf. B17.1, 16/D73.233, 247) and his nonlinear argumentative structure (B24/D46).

69. Mackenzie 2021, 174. *Opsigonoi* in Homer refers to "late-born" humans. *Huperphloia* is a hapax. Plutarch, who quotes B80/D255, wonders over its meaning and notes that Empedocles "was not in the habit of beautifying things with the most attractive epithets, like flowery colors, just for the sake of stylistic elegance, but composed each thing as an illustration of some essence or force" (*Quaest. conv.* 683E). *Oxubelēs* ("sharp-pointed," B83/D197) is used by Homer of an arrow (*Il.* 4.126); at B40/D125 it describes the rays of the sun. *Khaitai* ("hair") denotes human hair, animal manes, and the foliage of trees (LSJ s.v.).

them in the extant fragments) are the material product, not just the description, of this creative process.[70] By the same token, his constant Homeric quotations, allusions, and echoes instantiate the fundamental principle that there is no birth or death, only the mixing and remixing of elements.[71] To that extent, as we shall see, language is simply part of life, subject to the same physical forces and natural laws as everything else. On the other hand, these artistic devices are obviously the invention of a masterful poet who stands outside the world to represent it, indeed, who creates that world in representing it. Inscribing the authorial *autos* at and as the origin of his *biou graphē*—the origin not just of the *graphē* but even of the *bios*—Empedocles's poetic style risks falling back into the idealist metaphysics of autobiography that his materialist physics repudiates.

Language is one part of the assemblage of parts that make up Empedocles's biosphere and like every other part it is material and lively. *Logos* produces knowledge by entering the listener's innards (*diassēthentos eni splankhnoisi logoio*, B4.3/D47.3). It invades the listener (*logou stolon*, B17.26/D73.257), entering his mind in an "onslaught of persuasion" (*pistios hormē*, B114.3/D6.3). An unpersuasive argument is said to be materially defective, *lipoxulos*, literally "lacking wood" (B21.2/D77a.2, B71.1/D61.1). That Empedocles means this literally is suggested by his theory of cognition, which works via the principle of elemental attraction: "By earth we perceive earth, by water water, by air shining air, and by fire destructive fire, Love by love, and Strife by terrible strife" (B109/D207; cf. B107/D241, A86.10/D218). Thinking is a physical process not unlike breath in B100/D201a, a mutually transformative interchange between elements within us and those in the environment. Thus "cleverness (*mētis*) will augment for humans in relation to what is present" (B106/D243). Empedocles's words participate directly and reciprocally in this productive interchange: "Come, listen to my words (*muthōn*): for learning (*mathē*) will augment your mind (*phrenas*)" (B17.14/D73.245). In the aural echo *muthōn/mathē* language is transformed into knowledge before our eyes through contact with the *phrenes* (the mind but also the diaphragm), which will in turn be transformed through the encounter.[72]

Words move and flow and change. B35/D75 begins "I will come back to this path of songs (*es poron humnōn*) which I spoke before, channeling off (*exokheteuōn*)

70. The figure for *hapax legomena* is derived from the index verborum of Wright (1981, 319–46): the majority of these are unparalleled compounds of familiar words, comprehensible but unexpected. On Empedocles's lexical innovation, see Gemelli Marciano 1990, 83–164; and Willi 2008, 202–20.

71. For examples see the index entries at Bollack 1965, 385–86, 1969, 616–17; and Wright 1981, 359.

72. Gheerbrant 2022, 274–75. The poet's words will enter Pausanias's body through the ears and eyes (B3.12–13/D44.12–13). They penetrate, passing beyond the sense organs (P. Strasb. a(ii) 21–22/D73.291–92) until they reach the heart, "for the blood around the heart is thought (*noēma*) for mortals" (B105/D240). Cf. B129/D38, B133/D9. Empedocles's physiology of thought is well explained by Long (1966). For a different view, see Kamtekar (2009), who believes knowledge by likeness means analogical reasoning.

argument from argument" (B35.1–2/D75.1–2). The "path of song," as we noted in chapter 1, is a virtual cliché in archaic poetry.[73] Traveling this path, Empedocles, like Parmenides, would seem to assert control over the trajectory of his argument. But even as he does, the road dissolves under his feet: the path turns liquid (a *poros* is also a channel or stream) in the fluid imagery of *exokhetueōn*, and the poet-traveler finds himself bailing as he heads into the whirling depths of Neikos (*benthos dinēs*, B35.3–4/D75.3–4). A "pure stream" channeled from a holy mouth (*katharēn okheteusate pēgēn*, B3.2/D44.2), Empedocles's language joins the flow of other things in the cosmos: the tribes of creatures "poured out" from the mixed elements (*kheito*, B35.7, 16/D75.7, 16), the seed "poured into pure places" to form embryos (*ekhuthē*, B65/D172), the seas of blood that splash around the heart to produce thought (B105/D240) or that ebb and flow in respiration (B100.6–7, 22–24/D201a.6–7, 22–24). Even "dense and solid things flow forth from the earth" (*ek d'aiēs prorheousi thelemna te kai stereōpa*, B21.6/D77a.6).

Moving and flowing, Empedocles's language, like the roots themselves, has no *empedos aiōn*. This produces some extraordinary linguistic slippages, both syntactic and semantic. We might note, for example, Empedocles's frequent shifts of subject and casual fluctuation between singular and plural, grammatical irregularities that render sense itself slippery.[74] Or the way the meaning of words fluctuates such that, for instance, *theoi* are sometimes immortals, sometimes long-lived mortals, destabilizing not just the semantics of this common word but the entire theology and anthropology it entails.[75] "Running through each other," words lose their stable semantic being.[76] Or think of Empedocles's constant repetitions with

73. Cf. chapter 1, n. 15, and on Empedocles's use of this image, Nünlist 2005, 78–80; and Gheerbrant 2017, 215–42. Empedocles's path is not linear but aleatory and branching so as "joining some peaks of words to others, not to complete a single path" (B24/D46). The poet follows this path but also takes detours and returns (B35.1/D75.1); he doubles back and repeats portions (B17.14–16/D73.245–47).

74. See, e.g., B17.6–13/D73.238–244 and B17.27–35/D73.258–266, where the neuter plural elements alternate between singular and plural verbs (and apparently take a masculine plural adjective, *akinētoi*, in 13/244), or the switch between singular and plural subjects at P. Strasb. d 3–15/D76.3–15 and B115.3–8/D10.3–8, or the odd duals at B23.2–5/D60.2–5 and B137.6/D29.6. See too B3.5/D44.5 where the unmarked change of addressee is so jarring that some editors print this as two separate fragments, and B35.10–12/D75.10–12 where the subject of each verb is uncertain.

75. On *theoi*, see Inwood 2001, 55–59. Sometimes Empedocles seems to use the word in its standard sense, as when he refers to Necessity's oracle as "ancient decree of the gods" (B115.1/D10.1; cf. *makarōn*, B115.6/D10.6, and the list of gods at B128.1/D25.1). But "long-lived gods highest in honors" also appear alongside birds and bushes and men and women in the lists of *thnēta* produced under Strife (P. Strasb. a (ii) 2/D73.272, B21.12/D77a.12, B23.8/D60.8). Since for the Greeks *theoi* were by definition immortal, a mortal *theos* is a contradiction in terms. But immortality too is volatile, for we are told that only the roots are immortal (B17.30–35/D73.261–266) but they can become mortal (B35.14/D75.14), while the poet claims to be immortal (B112.4/D4.4; cf. B147/D40). Long (2017) thus proposes that for Empedocles immortality means continuity not endless duration. See further Ferella (2024, 185–216) on the poet's understanding of divinity.

76. Perhaps the most extreme example of this semantic slippage is the word *zōra* at B35.15/D75.15: the adjective usually means "pure" but in this context must mean "mixed" (Solmsen 1967). Even proper

variation, among which are the very lines that describe his ontology: "But these very things are, and running through each other they become different at different times and are always continuously the same" (B17.34–35/D73.265–66) recurs as "these very things are, and running through each other they become different in shape; to such an extent does mixture transform them" (B21.13–14/D77a.13–14) and "these very things are, and running through each other they become men and the races of other beasts" (B26.3–4/D77b.3–4).[77] The language in which Empedocles articulates his mobile ontology is itself in motion, returning in different forms, transformed by what it encounters.

This language does not stand outside of things but instead is rooted in them. Indeed, it *is* the roots of things, spreading among them with its weird fertility and entangling them in the meshwork of *bios*. When Empedocles writes "the same things become hairs and leaves and the thick wings of birds and scales on stout limbs" (B82/D198), he is not only positing a fundamental equivalence among all beings; his language actively forges that equivalence through its syntax: "and . . . and . . . and." This syntactic construction occurs again and again and again in Empedocles's fragments. It yokes boy and girl and bush and bird and voyaging sea-leaping fish (D13/B117; cf. B9.2–3/D54.2–3, B20.6–7/D73.307–308, B21.10–12/D77a.10–12, B23.6–8/D60.6–8, P. Strasb. a(i) 9–a(ii) 2/D73.270–272). The four elements are introduced in this form (B6/D57), as are their phenomenal instantiations, "sun and earth and heaven and sea" (B22.2/D101.2, cf. B17.18/D73.249, B21.3–5/D77a3–5, B38.3–4/D122.3–4, B71/D61, B115.9–11/D10.9–11). This polysyndetic syntax joins the diverse beings of the cosmos, neither conflating them in a relation of identity nor subordinating them in a relation of hierarchy but binding them in a multidirectional mesh of horizontal connections.[78] Meanwhile, vivid

names, the most rigid of designators, are flexible in Empedocles's poetics: in B6/D57 he introduces the root elements as "bright Zeus and Hera bringer of life and Aidoneus and Nestis, who moistens mortal springs with her tears." Which god corresponds to which root was a matter of debate already in antiquity; see Diog. Laert. 8.76 < A1/R91, A33/R90–92; Picot 2000; and Picot 2022, 419–95, 497–533. So too Aphrodite, Kupris, Philotēs, Philia, Gēthosunē, Storgē, and Harmonia are used synonymously. On Empedocles's polyonomy, see Bollack 1965, 287–88, 292–93.

77. Cf. P. Strasb. a(ii) 15–16/D73.285–86: "In just this way all these things were running through each other and, having wandered off, each reached different places." See Bollack (1965, 322–23) on the repetition of these lines: "Les vers qui relient si étroitement l'Être et le Devenir reproduisent, dans leurs modifications successives, l'acte même de la vie" (323). On Empedocles's repetitions, see further Van Groningen 1960, 201–22; Hershbell 1968; Graham 1988; Rosenfeld-Löffler 2006, 144–58; and Gheerbrant 2017, 493–592, 819–24.

78. This is the construction Deleuze and Guattari (1983b, 5) call the "connective synthesis of production." Other examples of polysyndeton occur at P. Strasb. a(i) 8–a(ii) 2/D73.269–272, P. Strasb. b 3–5/D74.4–6, B21.9/D77a.9, B67/D158, B76/D74, B90/D68, B121/D24, B122/D21, B123/D22, B128.4–7/D25.4–7, B130/D26, B146/D39. Cf. polysyndetic negation (*oute . . . oute . . . oute*) at B2.7–8/D42.7–8, B26.10–12/D77b.10–12, B29.1–2/D92.1–2, B128.1–2/D25.1–2, B134.1–3/D93.1–3; and alternatives (*ē . . . ē . . . ē*) at B9.2–3/D54.2–3, and the paratactic structure of B111/D43. Another of Empedocles's preferred syntactical constructions is the comparative clause with coordinating conjunctions, his countless variations on "as X . . . so Y": e.g., *tēi . . . hopēi* (B12.3/D48.3); *ophra . . . tophra* (B15.2–3/D52.2–3); *tote men*

diction reinforces this dynamic weave: thus, as we saw, trees "lay eggs" (B79/D254) and have "beautiful hair" (B127/D36), while humans and animals blossom like plants (B21.10–12/D77a.10–12). Arms are "branches" that "sprout" from the back (B29.1/D92.1, B134.2/D93.2); ears are "a sprig of flesh" (B99/D226); men and women come into being as "nocturnal saplings drawn up by fire" (B62.2/D157.2).[79] Transforming and being transformed in an exuberant polysyndetic proliferation, language is not an imitation or representation of life; it simply *is* the linguistic texture of life.

Empedocles thus creates a radical poetic style to express his radical vision of the world. This vision displaces the autopoietic *autos* of autobiography and mires the self and its *graphē* in the symbiotic, sympoietic meshwork of *bios*. But the attempt to capture this vital vision also exposes the limits of such a project, for the very language Empedocles uses to express his dispersed ontology reinscribes the presence of the authorial *autos*. The striking images of the last paragraph remind us that Empedocles's language is not a transparent window on the cosmos but the highly wrought aesthetic product of the poet. "'I' is ineliminable," and around it Empedocles's materialist ontology of language comes into tension with itself. On one side words are things, joined at the roots; on the other they are artistic metaphors for things.

This tension accounts for much of the excitement (and frustration) of reading Empedocles's poetry. In every word and phrase, his language oscillates between the literal and the metaphoric, between materiality and mimesis. For Nietzsche it is language's metaphoric nature that sets it apart from and against life: the linguistic concept of a leaf is merely the (dead and deadening) image of the thing itself. But Empedocles's metaphors remain so rooted in matter that it can be difficult to say whether they are metaphors at all. When we read in the programmatic fragment B2/D42 "narrow are the *palamai* poured through the limbs" (*steinōpoi men gar palamai kata guia kekhuntai*, B2.1/D42.1), is the word *palamē* metaphoric (device, art, resource) or concrete (palm of the hand)?[80] At first glance the intellectual context, as well as the liquid action, would seem to require a figurative

. . . *tote de* (B17.1–2, 16–17/D73.233–234, 247–248); *allote men* . . . *allote de* (B17.7–8/D73.239–240; cf. B20.2–4/D73.303–305, B26.5–6/D77b.5–6); *hēi* . . . *tautēi* (B17.12–13/D73.243–244; cf. B26.8–12/D77b8–12); *touto men* . . . *touto de* (P. Strasb. a(ii) 26–27/D73.296–297); *hoson* . . . *toson* (B35.12/D75.12; cf. B71.4/D61.4, B108/D244a); *tēi men* . . . *tēi de* (B61.3–4/D156.3–4); *hōs d'hote* . . . *hōs de tote* (B84.1–7/D215.1–7; cf. B73/D199). This construction connects two items without giving one causal or explanatory priority over the other: instead, it ranges them along a flat plain of equivalence in which the two communicate as heterogeneous equals. We will return to the affordances of a horizontal syntax in chapter 4.

79. For very different interpretations of these images, see Rosenfeld-Löffler 2006, 14–25; Bollack 1965, 295–302; and Picot 1998, 2022, 337–75.

80. The same questions can be asked of B3.9/D44.9 ("look with every *palamē*") and B75.2/D200.2 ("in the *palamai* of Kupris"). Lloyd (1995, 172–214) questions the general validity of the distinction between literal and metaphoric before Aristotle's polemical application of the dichotomy. As I observe in chapter 1, n. 3, the categories remain heuristically useful for interpreting archaic poetry.

reading, and so most translators render it. But if sense perception is the literal confluence of elements outside the body with those inside, then the senses are not merely like palms: they functionally *are* palms. Aristotle criticized Empedocles for calling the sea "the sweat of the earth" (B55/D147a), "for in speaking in this way he has perhaps spoken sufficiently for poetry (since metaphor is a poetic device) but not sufficiently for understanding nature."[81] But is this unequivocally a metaphor? Many things that at first seem like mere metaphors turn out, once we understand the theory more fully, to be literal. The "seas of blood" (B105/D240) that wash around the human heart may seem figurative until we realize that blood is literally composed of elements, "earth . . . and Hephaistus and rainstorm and all-shining aether anchored in the perfect harbors of Aphrodite" (B98.1–3/D190.1–3).[82] If in the wild symbiogenesis of Empedocles's cosmos "the same things become hairs and leaves and the thick wings of birds and scales on stout limbs" (B82/D198), then the earth can literally sweat sea.

Thus at every moment the reader must decide between matter and mimesis: is Empedocles's language a part of life or an imitation of it? When Empedocles speaks of Aphrodite's "loving pegs" (*gomphois . . . katastorgois*, B87/D214), is the phrase a daring transfer of epithet that highlights the artistry of a poet who we will soon see compare his own creative production to the work of Aphrodite? Or is it a literal enactment of Aphrodite's influence on matter, as the adjective is "attracted" to the noun?[83] B61/D156 describes the hybrid creatures produced under the waxing influence of Love:

> πολλὰ μὲν ἀμφιπρόσωπα καὶ ἀμφίστερνα φύεσθαι,
> βουγενῆ ἀνδρόπρωιρα, τὰ δ' ἔμπαλιν ἐξανατέλλειν
> ἀνδροφυῆ βούκρανα. (B61.1–3/D156.1–3)
>
> many things grew double-faced and double-chested,
> cow-race man-faced, and again they sprung up
> man-natured, cow-headed.

The language seems designed for mimetic effect: the monstrous compound adjectives, with their neologistic mixing and matching of species and body parts, reproduce on the level of language the phenomena that language denotes. If words are

81. Arist. *Mete.* 2.3 357a24–28, on which see Bremer 1980; and Zatta 2018. Elsewhere he suggests that Empedocles's style is not just unclear but deliberately obfuscatory (Arist. *Rh.* 3.4 1407a31–35). For reassessment of Aristotle's critique of Empedocles's style see Rowett 2013.

82. Those "harbors of Aphrodite" are presumably metaphorical; cf. the "meadows of Aphrodite" in an embryological fragment (B66/D159). But perhaps not: the harbors of Acragas (B112.3/D4.3) and the meadow of Atē (B121/D24) are literal places in the topography of the *daimōn*'s exile.

83. Cf. B17.22–24/D73.253–55, discussed in the Conclusion, where the description of Philotēs's effect enacts that unifying effect. Singing of Love, Empedocles's poem becomes a love song (*oarōn,* B21.1/D77a.1). Rosenfeld-Löffler (2006) reads the poem as a whole as an instantiation of the creative work of Love (see esp. 35–76, 169–78).

material things, however, then they, like all other things, are subject to the combinatory force of Philotēs. "Cow," "man," "face," "chest," "race," "nature": these words wander just like the errant body parts, searching for what Simplicius calls, in quoting the fragment, "their own proper *logos.*"[84]

The attempt to write a root language thus produces a schizophrenic poetics, in which language hovers undecidably between metaphor and matter. It also produces a schizophrenic poet, who himself stands in an undecidable relation to both his writing and his philosophy. On the one hand, the authorial *autos* is a divine demiurge. B23/D60 compares the creation of phenomena through the mixing of elements to artists mixing paints to produce "forms resembling all things" (*eidea pasin alinkia*, 5). The painters "mixing [the colors] in harmony" (*harmoniēi meixante*, 4) are figures for Aphrodite, herself depicted as an artisan (B86/D213, B87/D214) as she "harmonizes" the elements (*sunarmosthent'*, B71.4/D61.4; cf. B27.3/D89.3, B96.4/D192.4, B107/D241), but also for the poet himself. Emphatically identified as men (*aneres*, 2), these artisans are characterized by their cleverness and learning (*mētios eu dedaōte*, 2), vocabulary used elsewhere for the poet's teaching (B2.9/D42.9, B17.25/D73.256), and their many-colored "potions" (*polukhroa pharmaka*, 3) anticipate the "cures for evils" that will be one benefit of that teaching (*pharmaka . . . kakōn*, B111.1/D43.1). This double analogy, with its overt diction of mimesis, equates the poet with Aphrodite and his poetic "forms" with the phenomena she creates—"trees and men and women and beasts and birds and water-nurtured fish and long-lived gods highest in honors" (6–8). It simultaneously analogizes his poetic production to cosmogonic creation and posits it as a meta-creation through its self-referentially mimetic language.[85] It is little surprise, then, that the fragment ends by declaring this demiurge a god: "Know these things clearly, having heard a speech from a god" (*theou para muthon akousas*, 11). On the other hand, however, if that authorial god is the source of creation he is also one of its creatures, for "long-lived gods" are among the "forms resembling all things" the artist men (*aneres*) produce—as, for that matter, are men (*aneras*, 6). Even as he lifts himself above the world to paint it, the author-as-demiurge is shadowed by a daimonic double that stands within the world he paints, down among its very roots.[86]

84. Simpl. *in Phys.* 371.33 ff. (ad B61/D152); Bollack 1969, 423. Compare B109/D207: "By earth we perceive earth, by water water, by air shining air, and by fire destructive fire, Love by love, and Strife by terrible strife." Is the repeated polyptoton here mimetic of the principle of like-to-like or do the words literally exemplify that principle? Cf. the polyptoton of forms of *allos* (B17.6–8, 28/D73.238–240, 259; B26.2–6/D77b.2–6; B35.6/D75.6; B108/D244; B115.12/D10.12).

85. On the artist as a figure for the poet, see further Bollack 1969, 122; Iribarren 2018, 178–98; and on the parallels between the poet and Love as "master carpenters," Mackenzie 2021a, 119–24. Porter (2025) emphasizes the creative force of Strife. The dual painters are often taken to allude to Love and Strife.

86. Osborne (1987a, 41) notes that in the real world (as opposed to the simile) Empedocles does not ascribe the process of mixture to an agent. The antecedent of *allothen* in line 9 is unspecified; thus even this highly wrought simile leaves it unclear whether the "font of all mortal things" is the painters themselves or their paints. Perhaps we may detect some anxiety about the divine author function in the

The contradictions inherent in the attempt to enunciate his rhizomatic ontology thus split the position of enunciation, leaving the *autos* himself divided. Consider B17/D73.233–66, the single most philosophically significant fragment in *Peri Phuseōs*. In a careful reading of the opening lines, Daniel Graham shows that the cosmic symmetry the fragment describes is mirrored in its artful form. He notes a repeated pattern of couplets pairing motifs of unification and separation. Through this repetition, he argues, the couplets "not only describe the process but *imitate* it. . . . Thus B17 must be read as more than an argument or a programme for an argument: it is also a *mimetic structure* which *portrays* the world condition which it describes."[87] This masterly mimesis is the work of a masterful *egō* who declares his presence at the opening of the fragment:

> δίπλ' ἐρέω· τοτὲ μὲν γὰρ ἓν ηὐξήθη μόνον εἶναι
> ἐκ πλεόνων, τοτὲ δ' αὖ διέφυ πλέον' ἐξ ἑνὸς εἶναι.
> δοιὴ δὲ θνητῶν γένεσις, δοιὴ δ' ἀπόλειψις. (B17.1–3/D73.233–35)

> I will speak double. For at one time they augmented to be one alone
> out of many, at another time they diverged again to be many from one.
> Double is the creation of mortal things, double their failing.

The poet self-consciously promises to reproduce the world in his words. *Dipla* characterizes both the content of this account, the double cycle from many to one and from one to many, and its form, with each clause starting with coordinated temporal adverbs (*tote men . . . tote de*) and ending with the verb "to be" (*einai*). That double process is repeated in the dual birth, dual death of mortal things (*doiē de . . . doiē de*). This doubling is in turn doubled when the first two lines are repeated verbatim a dozen lines later (16–17/247–48): "I will speak double. . . ." The poetic *egō* lays forceful claim to his own speech by drawing attention to its mimetic artistry.

But that artistry does not secure the poet as the singular origin of his discourse, for in the very process of describing it, the *egō* is itself doubled and redoubled. The future tense *ereō* in line 1 divides the first person between the present moment in which he is promising to speak and the future moment in which he will speak. To this present and future *egō* is added a third who looks back on them even as he himself fragments into past, present, and future:

> ἀλλ' ἄγε μύθων κλῦθι· μάθη γάρ τοι φρένας αὔξει·
> ὡς γὰρ καὶ πρὶν ἔειπα πιφαύσκων πείρατα μύθων,
> δίπλ' ἐρέω. (B17.14–16/D73.245–47)

> But come, listen to my words, for learning will augment your mind.
> For as I said before, declaring the bounds of my words,
> I will speak double.

---

adjective *aspeta* ("unspeakable"), which marks a limit to the reach of language, and the "uncharacteristically stilted" (Wright 1981, 180) arrangement of line 10, on which see Diels-Kranz ad loc: "schlechter Vers!"

87. Graham 1988, 305–6 (original emphasis); cf. Reinhardt 1959, 51–55.

The poetic voice divided in time is also divided in space, split between the first person who speaks and the second person who listens: the words (*muthōn*) of the former are effectuated as the learning (*mathē*) that augments (*auxei*) the mind of the latter (14/245). That process in turn repeats the action of the elements as they "learned to grow into one from many" (*memathēke*, 9/240a) and were "augmented (*ēuxēthē*) to be one alone from many" (1, 16/233, 247).[88] In this passage, the *autos* raises himself above *bios* in order to re-present it through the mimetic artistry of his *graphē*. But that *graphē* does not maintain its mimetic distance from *bios*, and both it and its author are drawn back down into the transformative rush of things. In the process the poetic *autos* himself oscillates. Empedocles loses his glorious stability: simultaneously outside of and immersed in his own ontology, he has no *empedos aiōn*.

Finally, this schism in the authorial *autos* produces a schizophrenic philosophy. B110/D257 details the effects of Empedocles's teaching and probably came near the end of *Peri Phuseōs*.[89]

> εἰ γάρ κέν σφ' ἀδινῇσιν ὑπὸ πραπίδεσσιν ἐρείσας
> εὐμενέως καθαρῇσιν ἐποπτεύσῃς μελέτῃσιν,
> ταῦτά τέ σοι μάλα πάντα δι' αἰῶνος παρέσονται,
> ἄλλα τε πόλλ' ἀπὸ τῶνδ' ἐκτήσεαι· αὐτὰ γὰρ αὔξει
> ταῦτ' εἰς ἦθος ἕκαστον, ὅπῃ φύσις ἐστὶν ἑκάστωι.
> εἰ δὲ σύ γ' ἀλλοίων ἐπορέξεαι, οἷα κατ' ἄνδρας
> μυρία δειλὰ πέλονται ἅ τ' ἀμβλύνουσι μερίμνας,
> ἦ σ' ἄφαρ ἐκλείψουσι περιπλομένοιο χρόνοιο
> σφῶν αὐτῶν ποθέοντα φίλην ἐπὶ γένναν ἱκέσθαι·
> πάντα γὰρ ἴσθι φρόνησιν ἔχειν καὶ νώματος αἶσαν. (B110/D257)
>
> For if, pressing them under your dense thought organs,
> you keep kindly watch on them with pure practices,
> all these things will be present for you throughout your lifetime
> and you will acquire many other things from these. For they themselves augment
> into each character (*ēthos*), according to the nature (*phusis*) of each.[90]

88. Line 9, missing from the citations and supplied by Diels on the basis of the parallel with B26.8/D77b.8, is generally accepted.

89. All editors place B110/D257 at or near the end of the poem except Inwood (2001), who locates it in the preamble to the single poem.

90. The sense of this line is contested. *Auxanō* is usually transitive in the active in this period, and some take *hekaston* as its object. This yields a proto-Aristotelian process in which teachings actualize the potential, or *phusis*, of each thing into its final *ēthos*. But it seems to me more natural to take *hekaston* with *ēthos*, and to take *auxei* as intransitive (as it often is in later Greek): it would not be the only time that Empedocles supplies our earliest attestation of a word or usage. Compare Inwood (2001, 219): "For these things themselves will expand to form each character." See further the discussion by Long (1966, 269–70): if he is correct that *auta taut'* refers to external elements and *hekaston* to the internal, then the difference between a transitive and intransitive reading of the verb is not so great.

But if you reach for a different sort, such as those wretched thousands
that are among men and that blunt their thoughts,
then in truth they will quickly abandon you, as time cycles around,
desiring to come to their own dear (*philēn*) race.
For know (*isthi*) that all things have thought and a share of mind.

The conditional structure of the fragment and its initiatory diction place emphasis on the student's ethical agency: he must choose which path to take and will reap the consequences.[91] The fragment thus appears to be the first chapter in the autobiography of a philosophical *autos*: the student who chooses to follow Empedocles's teaching and thereby gains (*ektēseai*) knowledge that will last throughout his lifetime (*di' aiōnos*) is taking the first step in a journey that will culminate in the extraordinary wisdom of the man described in B129/D38 who possessed (*ektēsato*) such a wealth of learning that it filled "ten or twenty lifetimes" (*aiōnessin*).

The young philosopher stands like Heracles at the crossroads. But instead of a spiritual *askēsis*, his intellectual adventure will enact Empedoclean physics. For if the student presses Empedocles's teachings into his thought organs, they press back. The agency of the thinker (in the protasis of each conditional sentence) is matched by the actancy of the thoughts (in the apodoseis). Thoughts move and grow, pursuing their own line of flight. If accepted hospitably, they will stay with the student throughout his life (or maybe their own, *di' aiōnos*, 3). There they will increase, an expansion that will benefit the student but also themselves. Like the roots, thoughts grow and change through their interconnections with other things.[92] The student's mind is one such thing. His thick diaphragm (*prapidessin*) provides a convenient abode for this growth: *ēthos* means disposition or character (in reference to the ethical student-initiate) but also a haunt or habitual

91. Cf. B111.5/D43.5 *ēn etheleistha* and similar conditional constructions in B2/D42, B3/D44. I follow Diels (in his translation) in understanding the antecedent of *sphe* in the first line as "die Lehren des Meisters," and not the elements (as Schwabl 1956 does; cf. Bollack 1969, 577–85), but as Long (1966, 269) comments, "for this context, as for every other, thoughts and elements are one and the same entity." The verb *epopteuein* is initiatory. The "positive attitude" (*eumeneōs*) and "pure practices" (*kathareisin meleteisin*) also evoke initiation: see Bollack 1969, 578–79; and on Empedocles's mystic language more broadly, Traglia 1952, 161–86. The "you" addressed here is presumably Pausanias.

92. In B106/D243 we hear that human cleverness (*mētis*) will increase (*aexetai*) in relation to what is near it. That fragment probably imagines the thoughts within us encountering the world outside us (as in B109/D207, where our internal earth, water, and fire allow us to see those elements in the phenomenal world). B110/D257 reverses the perspective, showing thought in the outer world encountering and growing through its encounter with the inner world. *Auxanō* is used of the roots at B17.1, 16/D73.233, 247, B26.2/D77b.2; cf. B37/D67. Multiple verbal parallels link the words/thoughts of B110/D257 to the elements: e.g. *periplomenoio khronoio* (8) is used of the elements' cycling at B17.29/D73.260 and B26.1/D77b.1; *aisa* (10) is used at B26.2/D77b.2 of the alternating cycle of unification and dispersal; and *aiōn* (3) for the changeable life span of the elements (B17.11/D73.242, B26.10/D77b.10). Cf. B17.9/D73.240a, B26.8/D77b.8: the elements "learned to grow into one from many."

abode (from the perspective of the incubating knowledge).[93] Likewise, in the next clause, *phusis* is simultaneously the student's ethical "nature" and the thoughts' self-generating "growth."

Two independent lines of motion thus intersect in the mutually augmenting encounter of mind and words. If that encounter is hostile, Empedocles's teachings will continue along their way, pursuing their "desire to come to their own dear race." We saw that Empedocles's daimonic autobiography is structured as a story of exile and reintegration, capped with the joyful greeting to his *philoi* in B112/D4. His words have their own *nostos* saga: they too suffer nostalgia and long to return to their *philoi*. Each of them is itself a self (*auta . . . tauta*, B110.4–5/D257.4–5) with its own journey and its own story to tell: "I was once already. . . ."

This shared experience of travels and homecoming motivates the final line. "For know that all things have thought and a share of mind" (cf. B103/D242). Taken out of context this line seems to assert the kinship of all living things, the "law of all things" (B135/D27a) that makes eating animals an act of murder and cannibalism (B137/D29, B136/D28, B128/D25). But the idea is more radical than that. The causal connection (*gar*) between lines 9 and 10 suggests that the "all things" that have thought include thoughts themselves, as they go about seeking a congenial abode, journeying to reach their longed-for home, augmenting themselves. Thought is not a possession of the student, the profit of his ethical agency. Instead, it is a sympoietic coproduction of word and mind, as each pursues its own trajectory "bent upon the tasks of life."[94] This generous understanding of *phronēsis* breaks down the division between matter and thought, thing and concept. Thought is a thing, and like all things, it has thought.

The familiar imperative *isthi*—"know!"—reminds us of the pedagogical *egō* who throughout this poem asserts himself as the origin of philosophical teaching and knowledge. This fragment sidelines that philosophical *egō*. In place of a predictable path starting from the *autos* and proceeding via his *graphē* to the goal of wisdom, we find *egō* and *graphē* working autonomously for themselves and reciprocally on one another. Philosophy is the happy side effect of their fortuitous intersection. Thought, unmoored from the self, takes on a life of its own. It authors itself. It's worth remembering that the English word "author" is derived not from *autos*, but from *augere*, "to increase." In Empedocles, things increase by "running through" other things; they author themselves in a mutually augmenting sympoiesis. The author himself is not above this process, secure (*empedos*) in his autopoietic glory (*kleos*), but simply some thing among "all things" as they rush and collide and change. And *sophia*, finally, is not the product of the authoritative

93. The latter meaning occurs more commonly in the plural, but the singular would not be such a stretch for Empedocles. Kingsley (2002, 400–404) takes *prapidessi* as an esoteric reference to shamanic breathing practices.

94. Ingold 2011, 6. In this fragment, in particular, Empedocles heeds Ingold's (Nietzschean) call: "Knowing must be reconnected with being, epistemology with ontology, thought with life" (75).

autos, an object he creates like a divine demiurge and gives as a gift to his dedicated student. Rather it is an emergent property of the assemblage of moving parts that constitutes *bios*. Philosophy does not master life from above; it wells up in its midst, in the grass of "things and words." This is Empedocles's radical philosophy, a root philosophy in every sense.

The final line of B110/D257—"know that all things have thought and a share of mind"—encapsulates the tensions inherent in that radical philosophical project. The attempt to write this rhizomatic ontology sets the authorial *autos* ("know!") in tension with the world he authors, a world that displaces his authority and authorship. This tension renders the philosophical *autos* himself incoherent, split between the subject and object of his own *graphē*: the enduring *egō* who recounts the story of his life—"I was once already a boy and a girl . . ."—cannot be reconciled with the provisional, unstable being who lives this life nor with the life itself, a life in which every being has such a story to tell. This incoherence in turn ensures that Empedocles's own demiurgic "I"—the "I" that commands us to listen to his poem and learn its philosophy and guarantees the veracity and value of both—will always be shadowed by a daimonic double. That daimonic *egō* is precisely the *autos* we have seen emerge within Empedocles's ontology, one of the myriad heterogeneous *auta tauta* that run through and transform *allēla*. In Empedocles's philosophical discourse, the "I" is both impossible and ineliminable. Fixing the rush of life around a stable self-same subject, the *empedos autos*, it risks petrifying his mobile metaphysics. Empedocles resists such petrification, even if he cannot fully escape it. His schizophrenic autobiography is the symptom of this effort.[95]

95. The oscillation between stability and instability in Empedocles's name is echoed in the well-known biographical tradition concerning his death: ancient sources report that he leapt into Aetna either to confirm his identity as a god (Diog. Laert. 8.67–69, 70) or to dissolve himself in the elements (Tzetzes, quoted by Inwood [2001, 82]). Both gestures are self-defeating, for if the act was meant to prove him immortal it proved him mortal, and if it was meant to disperse his person it also fixed it as a myth. Either way, in this act Empedocles writes a fittingly ambivalent final chapter to his autobiography.

4

Paratactic Politics

Anaxagoras and the Things

Our being-with, as a being-many, is not at all accidental, and it is in no way the secondary and random dispersion of a primordial essence. It forms the proper and necessary status and consistency of originary alterity as such. The plurality of beings is at the foundation of Being.

—JEAN-LUC NANCY

POLITICAL COSMOLOGY

This chapter examines the relation between politics and aesthetics in the fragments of Anaxagoras. This may seem a doubly unpromising topic. First, politics. The Presocratic philosophers examine the origin of the sun and moon, the generation of embryos, the optics of rainbows; they seem to be interested in everything but politics. But in fact, the fragments are full of political language. To start, the natural philosophers seek an *arkhē*, a first element, but also a ruling principle, said to dominate (*kratein*) or steer (*kubernan*) the other elements. The dynamic relations between elements and *arkhē* constitute the *kosmos*, which is thus a political as well as a cosmic order. Ancient critics noticed this homology between physics and politics. Diogenes Laertius passes on a report that Heraclitus's cosmology was entitled not *Peri Phuseōs*, as usually assumed, but *Peri Politeias*, and that his physical doctrines served merely as illustrations of political principles.[1]

Epigraph: From *Being Singular Plural* by Jean-Luc Nancy, translated by Robert D. Richardson and Anne E. O'Byrne, 12.

1. Diogenes Laertius (9.15) attributes this theory to the Hellenistic grammarian Diodotus. Cf. Diog. Laert. 9.5: Heraclitus's book was divided into three *logoi: peri tou pantos, politikos,* and *theologikos.* There is some evidence for such a reading (e.g., Her. B44/D106, B114/D105, B33/D108 on *nomos*; Raaflaub 2017; and Schubert 2017); but Diogenes is known to speculate on his subjects' politics even in the absence of such evidence. On the notion of Heraclitus as the first political philosopher, see Kahn 1979,

Reading natural philosophy politically is particularly tempting with Anaxagoras, an intimate of Pericles, whom many have seen as the real-life model for or manifestation of his cosmological prime mover, Nous (Mind). In undertaking such a reading, though, we must be on guard against the reductive instrumentalization that often attends analogic thinking. There is the risk, on the one hand, of reducing politics to a pedagogical tool for explaining the more serious philosophical questions of nature and being; and, on the other hand, of viewing cosmological speculation as a displacement of more urgent political questions.[2] Instead of subordinating either politics to physics or physics to politics, the task is to consider them as two independent but interconnected ways of conceptualizing the relations of power that structure the cosmos, a cosmos that is natural but always implicitly political too.

That cosmos was also, as we have seen, an aesthetic order. This brings us to aesthetics, the second seemingly inauspicious topic of this chapter. Anaxagoras is not known for his style. His prose is eminently prosaic: the diction is ordinary and repetitive, as is the syntax; imagery is scarce, aural effects few, metaphor and simile virtually nonexistent.[3] His writing is so unadorned as to appear style-free, even styleless. But simplicity too is a style, one Anaxagoras achieves in part through the frequent use of parataxis, the stringing of ideas or statements side by side without syntactical subordination or, in some cases, explicit logical connection. This construction was a characteristic of early Greek style (it is especially common in Homer) and may have already felt archaic by the time Anaxagoras was composing in the early fifth century.[4] Parataxis was thus a stylistic choice. That choice,

---

15, and on the Presocratics' quest for an *arkhē*, Arist. *Metaph.* 1.3 983b1–84a16; Algra 1999; and Sassi 2018, 19–26.

2. The former tendency can be seen in Lloyd 1992, 222, 224; the latter in Vernant: see below, n. 10. Farrar's (1988) rejection of a simple analogy between cosmic and political order (38–43) paves the way for a subtle reading of Democritus as a political thinker (192–264); I engage with that reading in chapter 5.

3. Diogenes, however, calls it "sweetly and magnificently expressed" (Diog. Laert. 2.6 < A1/R35). Anaxagoras's prose is not devoid of stylistic effects: there is a chiasmus in B8/D22 (with parallelism and visual imagery), alliteration (e.g. in B9/D14); the jingle *iskhei kai iskhuei* at B12.10/D27; and frequent polyptoton. But these tropes are not ostentatious or elaborate. Anaxagoras's style has been harshly judged by modern scholarship (e.g. Van Groningen [1960, 231]: "Le souci de variété stylistique est très médiocre") when it has been judged at all. Detailed studies are few: see Schofield 1980, 6–10, 97–99; Ugolini 1985; and Sider 2005, 23–32. Sider (2005, 14–15) estimates that Anaxagoras's book was originally the equivalent of fifteen to twenty-eight OCT pages, of which we have about four, roughly one-seventh to one-fourth of the whole.

4. Aristotle labels the "strung-together style" (*lexis eiromenē*) "archaic" and notes that it was common in the past but no longer much used in his day (*Rh.* 3.9 1409a27–29). On parataxis and the supposed evolution (stylistic and psychological) from parataxis to hypotaxis, see Norden 1915, 36–40, 48–50; Perry 1937; Fränkel 1955, 40–96; Trenker 1960; Havelock 1963, 71–72, 182–86; Immerwahr 1966, 46–51; and Noutopoulos (1949), who sees the Presocratic philosophers (and Anaxagoras in particular, 4)

as I hope to show, not only supports Anaxagoras's political thinking but in fact advances it: political possibilities that remain latent—undeveloped and ostensibly undevelopable—at the level of content are articulated in the paratactic form of his prose.

In developing this thesis, I draw on Jacques Rancière's definition of politics as the "distribution of the sensible" (*le partage du sensible*). The primary political act for Rancière, the political *arkhē*, is the distinction between what is perceptible and what is not: who can be seen as a political subject, what claims can be heard as political claims. Prior to any distribution of rights or goods, the first question is *who counts*: which parts are parts of the whole and which parts stand apart and have no part? For Rancière, politics are aesthetic in the root sense of the word. They are a structuring of the perceptible, "the system of *a priori* forms determining what presents itself to sense experience."[5] Rancière's aesthetic politics resonate closely with the ancient Greek notion of cosmos as a beautiful order and suggest that the Presocratics' cosmogonies and cosmologies, which attempt to explain this order through their own formal ordering, can—and should—also be read as studies in political aesthetics.

I am not the first to read the Presocratics politically. The most influential study is Jean-Pierre Vernant's "Geometric Structures and Political Ideas in the Cosmology of Anaximander."[6] Vernant identifies in the scanty fragments of Anaximander a new configuration of cosmological space that he argues reflects the new division of social space in the polis. The Greek polis, Vernant writes, was organized geographically and conceptually around the center, *to meson*, which represents "all that is common, the collectivity as such." Politics begin when power (*kratos*) is placed *es meson*, accessible to and contestable by all members of the community. This centralized *kratos* produces "egalitarian and reversible relationships, according to which all citizens are defined in relation to one another, as politically identical. Insofar as they have access to the circular space centered on the agora, citizens enter a political system governed by equilibrium, symmetry, and reciprocity." Vernant finds this symmetrical social world reflected in the new cosmology of Anaximander. Anaximander imagined the cosmos as a sphere that is stable and self-sustaining because power resides not with any individual element but in the middle, in the *apeiron*, the boundless. In positing the *apeiron* as his *arkhē*, Anaximander places *kratos* in common and thus guarantees "the permanence of

---

as pivotal in that evolution. As Dover (1997, 73) notes, however, there is no straightforward historical progression from parataxis to hypotaxis, and authors of any period can choose between the two constructions as suits their needs. See further Dewald 1987, 2005.

5. Rancière 2006, 13: "It is a delimitation of spaces and times, of the visible and the invisible, of speech and noise, that simultaneously determines the place and stakes of politics as a form of experience." Cf. Rancière 2010, 36.

6. Vernant 2006a (first published in *Eirene* 7 [1968], 5–23), with the key ideas repeated in Vernant 2006b and 1982, 119–29.

an egalitarian order in which opposing powers are balanced against one another."[7] This cosmic *isonomia* was "made possible by," "modeled on," or even a projection of the new social geometry of the polis.[8]

This is a compelling vision—both of archaic Greek philosophy and politics and of the relation between them. But it raises two immediate methodological issues. First, for Vernant, historical realities are determinative: the city is the prototype for the cosmos. This privileging of the historical limits political theory to reflecting the realia of political practice and underrates the imaginative freedom that is one of the virtues of cosmological speculation as a mode of political analysis.[9] Second, Vernant's polis often sounds specifically like the democratic polis, and his historical narrative is structured by an implicit political teleology culminating in fifth-century Athens.[10] Teleology is a general problem when dealing with the Presocratics, as we saw in the Introduction, and political teleology no less so than philosophical. The Presocratics were writing in a period of great political experimentation. A democracy like the one Athens would develop in the mid-fifth century was not the only kind of political organization, not even in Athens itself. To collapse the political with the democratic thus sets familiar and anachronistic boundaries on the Presocratics' boundless cosmos and circumscribes from the start the exciting creativity of their political thought.

Anaxagoras, in particular, complicates any straightforward democratic *telos*. Born in Clazomenae circa 500 BCE, Anaxagoras moved to Athens in around 456. He was part of Pericles's inner circle and (according to Plutarch) responsible for the statesman's lofty rhetoric and character. Swept up in the political contests surrounding Pericles, he was tried for impiety in 437 and banished from Athens.[11] So Anaxagoras was directly involved in democratic politics, yet his world vision is not in any simple sense democratic. Anaxagoras envisions an original state in

7. Vernant 2006a; the quotations are on p. 207, 206, 230.

8. Vernant 2006b, 209; 2006a, 216; and 1982, 108. Cf. Vernant 1982, 131: "When philosophy arose at Miletus, it was rooted in the political thought whose fundamental preoccupations it expressed and from which it borrowed a part of its vocabulary."

9. Sassi 2007, 214; and Laks 2018, 59–62. Vernant's analysis is less avowedly causal than that of Lloyd (e.g. 1999, 258), but he approaches this in Vernant 2006b; and 1982, 49–68. It should give us pause that the diction of *mesotēs* and *isotēs*, which Vernant equates with the egalitarian polis, also occurs in Parmenides (B8/D8), whose solitary Being expressly excludes all collectivity or community. Sassi (2007) offers a careful critique of Vernant's interpretation of the philosophical sources. See also Seaford (2004, 175–89), rejecting a political explanation in favor of an economic.

10. This is especially clear in Vernant 1982, which traces the "double impulse toward democratization and disclosure" (51) that drives both the development of the polis and the evolution from mythic to scientific thought. Democracy is an even stronger point of reference in Vlastos 1947. Atack's (2019) survey of the political vicissitudes of the cosmos-polis analogy discredits any simple link between Presocratic cosmology and Athenian democracy.

11. Plut. *Per.* 4–6, 8. On the political background, see Filonik 2013. Clazomenae was probably a democracy of some sort after the Ionian revolt (Hdt. 6.43) but it is not clear exactly what sort and unlikely to have been the Athenian sort.

which all elements are reciprocally intermeshed and "everything is in everything." Into this egalitarian ur-community order is introduced by the quasi-tyrannical Nous (Mind or Thought) who holds *kratos* over the elements and distributes them into a perceptible cosmos. Nous's autocratic *diakosmēsis* seems incompatible with a democratic conception of the world.[12] Plutarch makes Nous a model for Pericles at his most arrogant and aristocratic, Pericles the "Olympian," under whose reign, as Thucydides said, Athens was "a democracy in name but in fact the *arkhē* of the first man."[13] Anaxagoras's ambivalent relation to democracy is neatly summed up by Herodotus, who seems to quote the philosopher twice in the Constitutional Debate in Book 3: once in Otanes's speech in favor of democracy and once in Megabyzos's speech against it.[14]

My aim in this chapter is not to situate Anaxagoras in relation to Athenian democracy, pro or con, nor to read his cosmology as an allegory for Athenian politics. Instead, I wish to consider his political thought on a more abstract level; that is, to approach him as a political philosopher thinking not about one specific historical *politeia* but about the nature of power more broadly and, in particular, about the absolute and unitary power we call sovereignty. Scholars of Greek political thought have argued that the concept of sovereignty, developed to explain the monarchical early modern nation state, is anachronistic when applied to the Greek polis. But Kinch Hoekstra proposes that the Athenians did have a concept of sovereignty and they represented it through the figure of the tyrant, who personified both absolute political power within the polis and the domination of one polis over others.[15] Raised in a subject state of the Athenian empire, later an intimate of that empire's architect, Anaxagoras would have had complex experience with sovereignty in both its imperial and domestic forms.[16] His Nous is not a cipher for imperial Athens nor for "Olympian" Pericles but a way of thinking about

12. Thus for Vlastos (1947, 175–78) Anaxagoras is an outlier among the Presocratics, the leader of an abortive reactionary revolt against egalitarianism that finally succeeded with Plato and Aristotle.

13. Thuc. 2.65; Plut. *Per.* 4.4: Anaxagoras was "Pericles's closest associate and the one who did most to invest him with a dignity and spirit more weighty than demagoguery." Cf. *Per.* 8.1–2: it was from the study of natural philosophy that Pericles acquired the loftiness of spirit that earned him the nickname Olympian.

14. Otanes: we should promote the *plēthos,* for all things are in the many (*en gar tōi pollōi eni ta panta,* Hdt. 3.80.6); Megabyzos: the *dēmos* is ignorant and "pushes affairs forward without *noos*" (Hdt. 3.81.2).

15. Hoekstra (2016), arguing against Ober (1996, 120–21). Sovereignty is closely linked conceptually to imperial power. Hardt and Negri (2017, 26) define sovereignty as "a kind of internal colonialism." Conversely, Thucydides represents Athens's empire as a tyranny: 1.124.3, 2.63.2, 3.37.2; Connor 1977. On the concept of sovereignty, see Bartelson 1995; and on sovereignty and indigeneity, Barker 2006.

16. Clazomenae was under Persian imperial rule in the sixth century; a member of the Delian League while Anaxagoras was living there, it revolted against Athens in 412 BCE but was quickly re-subjugated (Thuc. 8.14, 8.23). Lampsacus, where Anaxagoras settled after his exile from Athens, had a similar history of colonization. My thanks to Richard Neer for suggesting I consider the imperial implications of Anaxagoras's thought and to Ben Akrigg for bibliographic recommendations.

sovereign power in the abstract. Likewise, his original elements are neither democratic citizens nor indigenous communities; instead, I propose, they are an attempt to envision relations of power—both political and metaphysical—rendered invisible by sovereignty's distribution of the sensible.

At issue, then, is not a specific political formation but a broader question about the nature of power, *kratos*. Vernant understands *kratos* as the domination that emerges from the contest between opposing forces: "It is always a matter of opposing force to force, power to power, in order to conquer or dominate."[17] As such, *kratos* is immanent, agonistic, political. Against this agonistic *kratos* we can set Jacques Derrida's conception of "ipsocratic" power. An expression of what Derrida calls ipseity, this sovereign *kratos* is unitary and autotelic; determined by nothing but itself, it originates in itself, authorizes itself, it "*gives itself* its own law."[18] This dichotomy between immanent, agonistic *kratos* and ipsocratic *kratos* is not stable. In fact, as we shall see, the latter can be understood as a dissimulated form of the former.[19] But these competing conceptions of *kratos* can help us to approach the question of sovereignty in Anaxagoras. In the figure of Nous, I suggest, Anaxagoras articulates something like an ipsocratic sovereign power: he describes Nous as *autokrates* and predicates this autocratic power on Nous's ontological separation from the world he rules and exception to its laws. But that state of exception is achieved only by obscuring alternatives to Nous's supreme *auto-kratos* and erasing the political struggle by which he obtained and sustains his power.

Anaxagoras reveals that obscure genealogy and in the process imagines an alternative distribution of the sensible to Nous's cosmic ordering. This alternative political aesthetics is no sooner glimpsed than erased, and that erasure, as we shall see, is a condition of possibility of Anaxagoras's own cosmology, which operates through a generalization of Nous's omniscient gaze. The political alternatives repressed in the content of his philosophy persist, however, in the paratactic style of his prose, which refuses hierarchy in favor of a "flat ontology" and horizontal relations among equal elements.[20] The formal structure of Anaxagoras's text enacts an ongoing contest between two distributions of the sensible, revealing a history of struggle occluded by Nous's self-positing sovereignty and keeping open the question of the nature of his *kratos*. Politics emerge as a matter of aesthetics in multiple

17. Vernant 2006a, 216–23 (the quotation is on p. 217). See also Loraux 2002, 68–71.

18. Derrida 2005, 11 (original emphasis). Derrida himself mostly uses the term ipsocentric; ipsocratic is, he notes, "a pleonasm, for the idea of force (*kratos*), of power, and of mastery, is analytically included in the concept of ipseity" (17).

19. Derrida will go on to deconstruct the concept of ipseity, and Stocking (2023, 73–110) shows that such deconstruction is anticipated in the very passages of Homer and Hesiod on which Derrida bases his notion of sovereignty. I am grateful to Charles Stocking for sharing his then-unpublished work with me and for pointing me toward Derrida's *Rogues*. I follow him in setting Derrida's notion of ipsocentric power against an agonistic model of *kratos*.

20. Stimulating theorizations of flat ontology are offered by Garcia (2014) and Gabriel (2015, 252–62).

senses, and style not only has a politics but itself *is* a politics, part of a contest over the very principles of order and of the power, sovereign or otherwise, they sustain.

A COMMUNITY OF THINGS

The Ionian philosophers begin, as we said, with the search for an *arkhē*, the first principle of the cosmos: for Thales, it is water, for Anaximenes, air. Anaxagoras's *arkhē* is a collective, a collocation, a community. Fragment B1/D9 is the opening of his book:

> ὁμοῦ πάντα χρήματα ἦν, ἄπειρα καὶ πλῆθος καὶ σμικρότητα· καὶ γὰρ τὸ σμικρὸν ἄπειρον ἦν. καὶ πάντων ὁμοῦ ἐόντων οὐδὲν ἔνδηλον ἦν ὑπὸ σμικρότητος· πάντα γὰρ ἀήρ τε καὶ αἰθὴρ κατεῖχεν, ἀμφότερα ἄπειρα ἐόντα· ταῦτα γὰρ μέγιστα ἔνεστιν ἐν τοῖς σύμπασι καὶ πλήθει καὶ μεγέθει.
>
> All things were together (*homou*), unbounded both in amount and smallness, for the small, too, was unbounded. And since all things were together, nothing was manifest on account of smallness. For air and aether held down all things, both being unbounded, for these things are greatest among all things, both in amount and magnitude.

This original community is defined by a shared space (*homou*).[21] Like Anaximander, Anaxagoras imagines the cosmos as an infinite sphere, but its structure is importantly different from the political geometry traced by Vernant. For Vernant the spatial and political logic of the city is centralized and centripetal: power placed in the center is a virtual definition of the polis. But for Anaxagoras, the center is not a strong reference point. His cosmic motor is a vortex (the *perikhōrēsis*), so the order it eventually produces will be centrifugal; all the action happens at the periphery, and the diction of the *meson* is absent from the extant fragments.[22] For Anaximander *to apeiron* named both the singular ruling *arkhē* of the whole cosmos and the cosmic whole itself. In Vernant's reading, it is because *to apeiron* stands in the middle, equivalent to none of the individual elements, that they can be equal members of an egalitarian universe. But for Anaxagoras, *apeiron* is not an autonomous metaphysical governing principle but an immanent physical quality of the elements. If Anaxagoras uses the word in B1/D9 in allusion to Anaximander, he transfers its conceptual primacy from the whole to the parts, from the

21. Cf. B6/D25: "As in the beginning (*arkhēn*) so too now all things are together" (*einai kai nun panta homou*). Nancy (2000, 1–99), from whom the epigraph to this chapter is taken, conceptualizes being as a being-with-one-another or originary "co-ipseity" (44). See also Benjamin's (2010) interesting study of place, commonality, and being.

22. Earth and other heavy things are closer to the middle (B15/D30; cf. A1.28/≠LM, A42.2/D4.2, A88/≠LM) but only contingently, as a result of the physical force of rotation: see Curd 2007, 208.

cosmos to the things that constitute it, large and small alike, "for the small too was *apeiron*."[23] The things come first, and they are together and infinite.

So what are these things? In B1/D9, Anaxagoras calls them simply *khrēmata*. The word is prosaic, even plebeian. It is far from the ontological abstraction of Parmenides's *To Eon* or the technical specificity of Empedocles's *rhizōmata* or the atomists' *atoma*. An everyday Greek word for everyday things, *khrēmata* is material and mundane. If we hear the verb *khraomai* behind the noun, these humble *khrēmata* are functional, useful, perhaps even necessary things.[24] These "things" are the basic ingredients of Anaxagoras's universe. The first qualities we should notice about them are that they are plural and they are real.[25] The reiterated variations on "being together" (*homou panta khrēmata ēn*, B1/D9; *pantōn homou eontōn*, B4b/D12; *einai . . . panta homou*, B6/D25) lay equal stress on "being" and "together" and bind reality and plurality conceptually. This is in strong and probably pointed contrast to Parmenides, whose *To Eon*, as we saw in chapter 1, is insistently singular.[26] Like Parmenides's unitary Being, Anaxagoras's plural things have no birth or death (B17/D15): there is no time when they do not exist. No matter how small they may be they will never cease to exist (B3/D24), and there will never be more or fewer of them, but "they are all eternally equal" (*panta isa aei*, B5/D16). So Anaxagoras's things are ontologically basic: they are and cannot not be.

These *khrēmata* are the material basis of all the phenomenal *khrēmata* we use and need in ordinary life, again in marked contrast to Parmenides, for whom *To Eon* is rigorously segregated from the world of phenomena. The latter—also called *khrēmata* (B17/D15)—are for Anaxagoras compounds formed through *apokrisis*, a process of separation and combination driven by the vortex. Now, strictly speaking, this phenomenology could operate with a small number of initial elements, like Empedocles's four roots that compound through Love and Strife to produce all the objects in the world.[27] This makes it all the more noteworthy that Anaxagoras's

23. In B2/D10, the great surround (*periekhon*) of the cosmos is described as boundless (*apeiron*). Nous will also be *apeiron* at B12.1/D27. On the meaning of *apeiron* in Anaximander, see Kahn 1960, 231–39.

24. An eminently practical verb, *khraomai* can mean to need or desire; to borrow or lend; to use or experience. Virtually the first meaning of *khrēma* in the extensive LSJ entry is "a thing that one needs or uses." *Khrēmata* in classical Greek also means property or money. For the semantic range of the noun and interpretation of its sense (in relation to Protagoras B1/D9) see Van Berkel 2013, 39n6.

25. The forms of *einai* in B1/D9 are predicative, but see Kahn (1973) on the close connection between the predicative, existential, and veridical functions of the verb. The question of what exactly Anaxagoras includes among the primary elements is disputed, but I agree with Curd (2007, 153–77; cf. 1998, 131–41) that the *khrēmata* are not just the opposites (hot and cold, etc.) but all basic ingredients for future phenomena; contra, Marmodoro 2017, 11–43.

26. Curd (2007, 137–42; see also 1998, 131–54; 2002; 2008, 231–33; and Furley 1987, 61–78) sees Anaxagoras's theory of everything in everything as a means of reconciling Parmenides's theory of being with the empirically observed coming-to-be and passing-away of phenomena. Thus Graham (1999, 176) labels Anaxagoras an Eleatic pluralist; cf. Sisko 2003.

27. As Aristotle points out, *Cael.* 3.3 302a28–b5.

khrēmata are infinitely diverse and heterogeneous. Fragment B4a/D13 describes these "seeds of all things" as "many and all sorts" (*polla te kai pantoia*).[28] They have all sorts of forms or appearances (*ideas pantoias*), complexions or colors (*khroias*), and flavors or maybe even pleasures (*hēdonas*).[29] The things are diverse and have diverse perceptible forms; their world is rich and sensory, made up of all sorts of shapes, colors, and tastes. We get some examples of this diversity in B4b/D12: the wet and the dry, the hot and the cold, the bright and the dark. But these pairs are just exemplary. As the fragment goes on to say, the seeds are limitless (*apeirōn*) and in no way like one another (*ouden eoikotōn allēlois*). Anaxagoras repeats the point for emphasis: "For none of the other things was alike one to the other" (*oude gar tōn allōn ouden eoike to heteron tōi heterōi*).[30]

Aside from heterogeneity, the other quality these things seem to have in the beginning is size or number, but Anaxagoras is curiously casual about the distinction. In B1/D9 we are told that the *khrēmata* are boundless in *plēthos* and *smikrotēs*, and these two terms recur frequently throughout the fragments. But their precise measure is hard to reckon. *Plēthos*, which I have translated "amount," usually denotes a large number or multitude. In Anaxagoras, confusingly, the word seems at times to indicate a great number, at other times large mass or extent.[31] In the first sentence of B1/D9, coupled with *smikrotēs*, it could denote either magnitude (vs. smallness) or number (vs. size). The confusion is compounded by the ambiguity of

28. The relation between these *spermata* and the *khrēmata* is debated. Sider (2005, 94) identifies *kai spermata* in B4a/D13 as a *kai* of specification ("many and varied things, i.e. seeds"); cf. Vlastos 1950; and Schofield 1980, 121–33. Inwood (1986, 26) and Curd (2007, 171–77), by contrast, see *spermata* as a higher level of organization than the basic ingredients (cf. Raven 1954; Lanza 1966, 203–4; and Lewis 2000). Teodorsson (1982, 45–64) surveys views on the question; cf. Marmodoro 2017, 147–53. Diels-Kranz print B4, reconstructed from two related passages of Simplicius, as a single fragment, but most modern editors consider it to be two separate fragments, which I label 4a and 4b (= Laks-Most D13 and D12).

29. "Flavors" is a specialized meaning of *hēdonē* in the Ionian writers: LSJ s.v.; Diogenes B5/D10; cf. Arist. *Part. an.* 2.17 660b9; Theophr. *Hist. pl.* 4.4.7. *Pantoia* is emphasized through repetition in B4a/D13: it describes both the seeds themselves and their qualities. Later in the fragment it will also describe the *khrēmata* of our phenomenal world: "And the earth grows many and all sorts of things (*polla te kai pantoia*) for them, the most beneficial of which they gather into their houses and use (*khrōntai*)." Note the echo of *khrēmata* in *khrōntai*.

30. Cf. B12.27–28/D27: Nous is entirely the same (*pas homoios esti*) but nothing else is the same as anything else (*heteron de ouden estin homoion oudeni*). There is debate about how restrictively to understand the opposites (e.g. Schofield 1980, 107–21; Teodorsson 1982, 25–43; and Curd 2007, 153–71). I take them to be exemplary not exclusive.

31. Number seems implied in the reference to "seeds boundless in *plēthos*" (B4b/D12) and the "*plēthos* of things separated out" (B7/D23); size or extent, in B2/D10's description of the *periekhon* as "boundless in *plēthos*." In the final line of B1/D9, paired with *megethos* it would seem to mean number: "size" would make it pleonastic. In B6/D25 ("since the shares of the large and the small are equal [*isai*] in *plēthos*") it is uncertain whether we should take *plēthos* with "shares" (in which case it denotes number) or with "large and small" (in which case it suggests size). Every instance seems to me ambiguous. Inwood (1986, 32) comments, "This ambiguity of quantity terms . . . is an annoying feature of Anaxagoras's style." He understands *plēthos* as total amount, not countable number (23–27).

smikrotēs itself, which, as Aristotle already noted, seems to combine number (few) and size (small).[32] Patricia Curd proposes that Anaxagoras conflates the different measures and that *smikrotēs* and *plēthos* denote not absolute size or number, but a greater or lesser degree (respectively) of submergence of one thing in another. She and others accordingly imagine the things not as particulates of various sizes but as more like liquids that come in varying concentrations.[33] But this liquid model is hard to reconcile with the term *khrēma*, which usually names a discrete object, and Anaxagoras seems to imagine the *khrēmata* as discrete things, for example, at B12.28/D27: "No other thing is similar to anything else" (*heteron de ouden estin homoion oudeni*).[34] "None" (*ouden*) implies a "one" (*hen*) and suggests that the things are at least theoretically countable, even if Anaxagoras is unable—or unwilling—to count them.

Regardless of whether we view the things as liquids or particles, Curd seems right that large and small imply preponderance not absolute size. This means that these predicates are not essential differentiating qualities of the individual *khrēmata* but rather contingent effects of their interactions. Largeness indicates a higher degree of association of like elements; smallness, a lower degree. Largeness and smallness are thus relative terms. Anaxagoras says this expressly in B3/D24: there are no absolute degrees of largeness and smallness but "each thing is both large and small relative to itself" (*pros heauto de hekaston esti kai mega kai smikron*). This in turn suggests that while smallness and largeness form a binary, they do not form a hierarchy. Large and small are equal (*ison*, B3/D24, B6/D25) and both equally boundless.[35] The identity of the things is likewise relational and nonhierarchical. If, as we just saw, "no other thing is similar to anything else" (*heteron de ouden estin homoion oudeni*, B12.28/D27), each thing *is* a thing—a one—only in its relation of difference to each other thing. The things are both individual and

32. Arist. *Metaph.* 10.6 1056b28–30 (A60/≠LM): Anaxagoras "should have said paucity (*oligotēti*) instead of smallness (*mikrotēti*)." Further examples of Anaxagoras's bad math include the conflation of quality (*hopoia*) and quantity (*hosa*) at B12.17–19/D27, and the occasional substitution of "many" (*polla*) for "all" (*panta*) in the phrase "everything in everything," discussed below.

33. Curd 2007, 34, 178–91. For this "non-particulate view" see also Barnes 1982, 323–26; Inwood 1986; and Furley 1987, 67. Contra, Graham 1994, 101–12; and Sider 2005, 86–88. Schofield (1980, 68–79) considers both views and concludes that Anaxagoras may not have settled the question in his own mind.

34. *Khrēma* is used of goods or property, sacred objects, flocks, implements, and slaves. I can find no instance where it refers to a liquid. *Khrēmata* can of course occur *en masse:* in the plural the word can express "a great number or mass . . . a heap of" (LSJ II.3.b), but Anaxagoras does not use it in this way, and even as such it is still at least notionally countable.

35. Curd (2007, 40) believes this means that large and small are equally complex; cf. Lloyd 1970, 45; and Inwood 1986, 30–32. Porter (2016, 424) remarks that Anaxagoras's "mind-boggling calculus of infinite scales . . . nearly ruin[s] the coherence of 'scale.'"

equal in their difference from one another, their egalitarian diversity stressed by the polyptoton *ouden . . . oudeni.*[36]

If the qualities of the *khrēmata*, both their size/number and their heterogeneous identities, are fundamentally relational, they are meaningful only to the extent that the things exist all together: *homou panta khrēmata ēn* (B1/D9). What it actually means for all things to be together—the nature of this diverse community and the relations it entails—is explicated in B6/D25:

> καὶ ὅτε δὲ ἴσαι μοῖραί εἰσι τοῦ τε μεγάλου καὶ τοῦ σμικροῦ πλῆθος, καὶ οὕτως ἂν εἴη ἐν παντὶ πάντα· οὐδὲ χωρὶς ἔστιν εἶναι, ἀλλὰ πάντα παντὸς μοῖραν μετέχει. ὅτε τοὐλάχιστον μὴ ἔστιν εἶναι, οὐκ ἂν δύναιτο χωρισθῆναι, οὐδ' ἂν ἐφ' ἑαυτοῦ γενέσθαι, ἀλλ' ὅπωσπερ ἀρχὴν εἶναι καὶ νῦν πάντα ὁμοῦ. ἐν πᾶσι δὲ πολλὰ ἔνεστι καὶ τῶν ἀποκρινομένων ἴσα πλῆθος ἐν τοῖς μείζοσί τε καὶ ἐλάσσοσι.

> And since the shares (*moirai*) of the large and the small are equal (*isai*) in amount, in this way too all things would be in everything; nor is it possible to be separate, but all things have a share (*moiran metekhei*) of everything. Since it is not possible that there exist a least thing, it could not be separated nor come to be by itself, but just as in the beginning so too now all things are together. And in all things there are many things even of the things being separated off, equal (*isa*) in amount both in the greater ones and in the lesser.

"Everything in everything" (*en panti panta*) is Anaxagoras's mantra. He repeats it numerous times in even the few fragments we have, sometimes confusingly substituting *polla* (many) for *panta* (all), although apparently with no difference in meaning (another instance of arithmetic imprecision). The phrase encapsulates Anaxagoras's physics as a whole. Because the elements are eternal—they do not come into being or pass away, nor increase or decrease—even after they have been separated out in the *apokrisis*, every single element still contains at least some bit of every other single element. Anaxagoras may have developed this bizarre theory to explain how, for example, a child grows bigger by eating bread: there must be some bone and muscle and blood already in the bread.[37] So every thing in Anaxagoras's universe, no matter how small, contains all other things within it; and every thing, no matter how big, is in all other things. There can be no autonomous or pure element, apart by itself—with one supreme exception to which we will return shortly.

36. Cf. B4b/D12, again with polyptoton: "Of the other things none is alike one to another" (*tōn allōn ouden eoike to heteron tōi heterōi*). *Heteron* implies a closed and equal difference: one of two (comparable) things.

37. "For how can hair come to be from what is not hair and flesh from what is not flesh?" (B10/D21; cf. A46/D3). The authenticity of the quotation has been questioned by Schofield (1980, 133–43), but it is accepted as genuine by Mansfeld (1982); Curd (2007, 53–54); and Macé (2011). The details of Anaxagoras's physics are vigorously debated. Articulations of the problems and various attempts to solve them can be found in Cornford 1930; Vlastos 1950; Raven 1954; Stokes 1971; Kerferd 1974; Strang 1975; Schofield 1980; Furth 1991; and Graham 1994.

This physical theory is articulated in B6/D25 in strikingly political language. *Metekhein* ("to have a part") is the verb used to express political belonging: to be a citizen is *metekhein tēs poleōs* or *metekhein tēs koinōnias*. In a democracy, Aristotle comments, "everyone has a share of everything" (*metekhousi pantes pantōn*).[38] *Moira* (share or portion) is a word associated with distribution and distributive justice: *isai moirai* occurs in Homer for the distribution of *timē* (*Il.* 9.318) and of meat shared at the feast as a symbol of relative rank (*Od.* 20.282, 294).[39] This idea of distributed portions conforms to Vernant's geometry of *to meson*, as common goods are shared out among members of the group defined *as* members by virtue of receiving a share. The power relations behind this centralized distribution are clear if one thinks of Zeus in the *Theogony*, who after coming to power allots to the gods their various *moirai* and *timai* (Hes. *Th.* 348, 413, 544, 789).

Anaxagoras's *isai moirai* operate within a different economy and imply a different "distribution of the sensible." For *isai moirai* here denotes not equal portions the elements receive but instead the portions they are for everything else or they contain of everything else in the complete intermixing of *en panti panta*. Anaxagoras's language of partition indicates not a centralized, hierarchical distribution but rather a horizontal, multidirectional, and reciprocal interconnection of all things with each other. The *khrēmata* are not connected as equal parts of a whole that they share in common, like the equal citizens in Vernant's egalitarian polis. Instead they are connected in a reciprocal relation of part and whole such that every part is a whole for another part and every whole a part of another whole.

We get a quintessential formulation in B11/D26: "There is a share of everything in everything" (*panti pantos moira enesti*). *Moira* belongs equally to both "everythings," part *in* the first and part *of* the second; it is both the share everything has and the share everything is. The two everythings—again bound by the equalizing trope of polyptoton—are reciprocal and inseparable such that, as fragment B8/D22 says, they "have not been separated from one another nor chopped off with an ax." Their bond is material, literal, and direct. It is not mediated by a common connection to some determinate totality: note that it is *pan* indefinite not *to pan*, the whole. In fact, it is not even clear there could be a whole, since every whole is also a part, with no upper limit (B3/D24).[40] If there is a whole, it is nothing more

38. Arist. *Pol.* 7.9 1328b32–33. Aristotle's simple definition of the citizen is *metekhein kriseōs kai arkhēs* (*Pol.* 3.1 1275a22–24). Anaxagoras's elements can claim a share of the latter but the former is the preserve of Nous. *Metekhein* is also, incidentally, the word Plato will use for the participation of phenomena in the Forms.

39. Cf. Solon 34.8–9: "nor good men hold an equal share (*isomoiriēn ekhein*) of the rich earth of their fatherland to the bad." Vlastos (1947) examines *isomoiria* in early Greek philosophy, but the term is more rare than he suggests. The closest parallels are in Empedocles's use of *meros* (B17.29/D73.260, B22.1/D101.1, B26.1–2/D77b1–2); cf. Her. B20/D118, B25/D122b; Ps-Arch. B47.25/≠LM.

40. The only place where Anaxagoras suggests otherwise is B4b/D12: one must imagine all things to be in (*eneinai*) the total collective (*tōi sumpanti*). But that whole is nothing more than the *panta* that constitute it, as is suggested by the recurrence of the word in B1/D9 in the plural (*tois sumpasi*). In B8/

than the sum of the unmediated, reciprocal, and horizontal relations among the parts. This is what it means for *panta khrēmata* to be together, *homou*; it is not a *having* in common (as in Vernant's model) but a *being* in common: *en panti panta*. Through his novel redeployment of the language of partition—*metekhein* and *moira*—Anaxagoras posits a unique *partage du sensible*. In this initial state of things Anaxagoras imagines a radically egalitarian distribution of being; it is a *partage* in which every part has a part, since no thing can exist apart.

But all is not perspicuous in this distribution of the perceptible. B1/D9 says, "since all things were together, nothing was *endēlon* (visible, clear, manifest) on account of smallness." B4b/D12 reiterates the point: "Before these things were separated off because all things were together not even any color was manifest (*endēlos*), for the mixture of all things was preventing it" (*apekōlue gar hē summixis pantōn khrēmatōn*). The *summixis* of all things makes it impossible to discern anything. The concentrations of any given thing are too small to allow the perception of discrete colors, forms, flavors, or identities. Each thing is unique, like no other thing (B4b/D12, B12.28/D27). But if each thing contains everything else within it, sameness and difference are meaningless and the defining alterity of *heteron* and *heteron* is lost. As Aristotle observed, everything in everything means there can be nothing, properly speaking, no discrete entity with its own unique visible identity.[41] That is to say, this distribution of the perceptible leaves one thing *im*perceptible: identity, individuality, self-sameness, what Derrida terms ipseity.

But without ipseity, as Derrida stresses, there can be no politics.[42] For Rancière, too, politics require ipseity. This is precisely what is at stake in the question—which for him is *the* political question—of *who counts*: who is identifiable and thus has an identity within the regime of the perceptible. This question cannot be asked in Anaxagoras's original state, where everything has a part but nothing, properly, counts. Conflating size and number, his *plēthos* is, as we saw, innumerable. This bad math takes on specific historical significance when we remember that one of the most common meanings of *plēthos* in Anaxagoras's day was "the people," that population whose political excellence (as Aristotle says) lies in their numbers.[43] Politics, Rancière posits, begins with a miscount of the part for the whole and the

D22 Anaxagoras refers to "the one cosmos" (*en tōi heni kosmōi*). But *kosmoi* too are plural for him (B4a/D13), and the phrase perhaps differentiates our cosmos from the presumably infinite others.

41. Arist. *Metaph.* 4.4 1007b18–26: if everything is everything else (in contravention of the law of noncontradiction) then nothing is anything, "and we end up with the state Anaxagoras describes when he says that all things are together: the result is that nothing truly exists." Cf. Porter (2016, 425–26), who also connects this lack of identity to the impossibility of measurement.

42. Derrida (2005, 13) defines democracy as "the power and ipseity of the people (*dēmos*)." *Rogues* explores this paradox of a sovereign *kratos* at the heart of a regime defined by *différance*. On the tense relation between democracy and ipseity in Derrida's thought, see Brown 2009.

43. Arist. *Pol.* 3.15 1286a21–b3. In Herodotus and other contemporary authors, *plēthos* functions as a virtual synonym for *dēmos*. E.g. Hdt. 3.80.6: "the *plēthos* ruling holds the most beautiful name of all, *isonomia*."

demand of those who do not count to be taken into account.[44] But such a politically generative miscount is impossible in Anaxagoras's cosmology because the difference between many and all—between "many things in all things" (*en pasi de polla*, B6/D25; cf. B12.25/D27) and "everything in everything" (*en panti panta*, B6/D25)—is literally immeasurable.[45]

Without ipseity, then, the political possibilities implicit in Anaxagoras's initial state cannot be developed or, in his idiom, become manifest (*endēlon*). In B1/D9, for example, we hear that air and aether "held down (*kateikhen*) all things, both being unbounded, for these things are greatest (*megista*) among all things, both in amount (*plēthei*) and magnitude (*megethei*)." *Katekhein* can mean simply to cover or contain, but it can also connote domination or mastery, suggesting a proto-organization, even a proto-politics; in classical Greek the verb is used of a superior power seizing and occupying a domain.[46] But in the mixture of everything in everything, air and aether are only "semi-emergent," and their potential domination over the things remains unrealized.[47] Nor can the egalitarian potential of the relations between the things be realized, as I have suggested, for if "all things have a share of everything," then there can be no "part with no part" whose demand for inclusion initiates politics. If everything is both a part of and a whole for every other thing, there can be no representation (part for whole) or participation (part of a whole). Moreover, the *summixis* of everything in everything eliminates not just ipseity, but also alterity and with it the overt and contestable relations that are the basis of the polis. A being-*in* rather than being-*with*, the originary state of "all things together" remains a confused collocation, not a real political community. It is a virtual distribution of the perceptible, but one that cannot actually become manifest, *endēlon*.

NOUS AUTOKRATES

Everything changes with the arrival of Nous. Nous marks a rupture in the space-time of the cosmos and an exception to its fundamental laws. He inaugurates a new distribution of the sensible.[48] The key text is fragment B12/D27.

44. Rancière 1999, 6, 10. Rancière begins with Arist. *Pol.* 7.4 1326a, where the first question of political theory is the number and nature of the *plēthos*. On politics and/as enumeration, see further Derrida 1997, esp. 1–25, 101–2.

45. Rancière (1999, 10) takes a similar conflation of many and all—"for all things are in the many" (*en gar tōi pollōi eni ta panta*), Otanes's formula for democracy at Hdt. 3.80.6—as paradigmatic of "the fundamental miscount of politics."

46. E.g. Hdt. 5.15, 5.45, 5.72; Thuc. 4.2.4, 4.92.6, 4.110.1, 6.23.2; cf. Hdt. 5.91 for domination by a tyrant. At Thuc. 2.65.8 Pericles is said to have restrained (*kateikhe*) the majority (*plēthos*).

47. "Semi-emergent" is Curd's (2007, 35) description. Inwood (1986, 26–27) suggests that air and aether are only virtually present, in the sense that the elements to constitute them are present: cf. n. 70 below.

48. I refer to Nous as "he" because the noun is masculine and is defined (with a few exceptions discussed below) by masculine adjectives and relative pronouns. I capitalize the word to highlight Nous's

τὰ μὲν ἄλλα παντὸς μοῖραν μετέχει, νοῦς δέ ἐστιν ἄπειρον καὶ αὐτοκρατὲς καὶ μέμεικται οὐδενὶ χρήματι, ἀλλὰ μόνος αὐτὸς ἐπ' ἑωυτοῦ ἐστιν. εἰ μὴ γὰρ ἐφ' ἑαυτοῦ ἦν, ἀλλά τεωι ἐμέμεικτο ἄλλωι, μετεῖχεν ἂν ἁπάντων χρημάτων, εἰ ἐμέμεικτό τεωι· ἐν παντὶ γὰρ παντὸς μοῖρα ἔνεστιν, ὥσπερ ἐν τοῖς πρόσθεν μοι λέλεκται· καὶ ἂν ἐκώλυεν αὐτὸν τὰ συμμεμειγμένα, ὥστε μηδενὸς χρήματος κρατεῖν ὁμοίως ὡς καὶ μόνον ἐόντα ἐφ' ἑαυτοῦ. ἔστι γὰρ λεπτότατόν τε πάντων χρημάτων καὶ καθαρώτατον, καὶ γνώμην γε περὶ παντὸς πᾶσαν ἴσχει καὶ ἰσχύει μέγιστον· καὶ ὅσα γε ψυχὴν ἔχει καὶ τὰ μείζω καὶ τὰ ἐλάσσω, πάντων νοῦς κρατεῖ. καὶ τῆς περιχωρήσιος τῆς συμπάσης νοῦς ἐκράτησεν, ὥστε περιχωρῆσαι τὴν ἀρχήν. καὶ πρῶτον ἀπό του σμικροῦ ἤρξατο περιχωρεῖν, ἐπὶ δὲ πλέον περιχωρεῖ, καὶ περιχωρήσει ἐπὶ πλέον. καὶ τὰ συμμισγόμενά τε καὶ ἀποκρινόμενα καὶ διακρινόμενα πάντα ἔγνω νοῦς. καὶ ὁποῖα ἔμελλεν ἔσεσθαι καὶ ὁποῖα ἦν, ἅσσα νῦν μὴ ἔστι, καὶ ὅσα νῦν ἐστι καὶ ὁποῖα ἔσται, πάντα διεκόσμησε νοῦς, καὶ τὴν περιχώρησιν ταύτην, ἣν νῦν περιχωρέει τά τε ἄστρα καὶ ὁ ἥλιος καὶ ἡ σελήνη καὶ ὁ ἀὴρ καὶ ὁ αἰθὴρ οἱ ἀποκρινόμενοι. ἡ δὲ περιχώρησις αὐτὴ ἐποίησεν ἀποκρίνεσθαι. καὶ ἀποκρίνεται ἀπό τε τοῦ ἀραιοῦ τὸ πυκνὸν καὶ ἀπὸ τοῦ ψυχροῦ τὸ θερμὸν καὶ ἀπὸ τοῦ ζοφεροῦ τὸ λαμπρὸν καὶ ἀπὸ τοῦ διεροῦ τὸ ξηρόν. μοῖραι δὲ πολλαὶ πολλῶν εἰσι. παντάπασι δὲ οὐδὲν ἀποκρίνεται οὐδὲ διακρίνεται ἕτερον ἀπὸ τοῦ ἑτέρου πλὴν νοῦ. νοῦς δὲ πᾶς ὅμοιός ἐστι καὶ ὁ μείζων καὶ ὁ ἐλάττων. ἕτερον δὲ οὐδέν ἐστιν ὅμοιον οὐδενί, ἀλλ' ὅτων πλεῖστα ἔνι, ταῦτα ἐνδηλότατα ἓν ἕκαστόν ἐστι καὶ ἦν.

The other things have a share of everything, but Nous is unbounded and *autokrates* and has been mixed with no thing, but he is alone himself by himself. For if he were not by himself, but had been mixed with something else, he would have a share of all things, if he had been mixed with anything; for there is a share of everything in everything, as I have said before. And the things that were mixed together would prevent him from controlling any thing in the same way as he does being alone by himself. For he is lightest and purest of all things and he holds all knowledge about everything and has the greatest strength. And however many things have soul, both the greater and the lesser, Nous controls all of these. And Nous controlled the whole rotation so that it rotated to begin with. First it began to revolve from the small, then it revolves more, and it will revolve even more. The things that are mixed together and the things that are separated off and becoming distinct, Nous knew them all. And whatever sorts of things were going to be, and whatever sorts were that now are not, and however many are now and whatever sorts will be, all these things Nous set in order, and the rotation, in which now revolve the things being separated off: the stars and the sun and the moon and the air and the aether. The rotation itself created separation. And the dense is separated from the rare and the hot from the cold and the bright from the dark and the dry from the wet. There are many shares of many things. And nothing is separating off entirely nor becoming distinct, one from another, except Nous. Nous is entirely the same, both the greater and the lesser. But no other thing is similar to anything else, but whatever things predominate in something, these things are most manifestly what each thing is and was.

singularity, in contrast to the anonymous collective things. Line numbers in the quotation, added for ease of reference, are based on Diels-Kranz's layout. Laks-Most do not provide line numbers for their D27.

With the appearance of Nous, the world starts anew. We read in line 13: "Nous controlled (*ekratēsen*) the entire rotation so that it rotated to begin with (*tēn arkhēn*)."[49] Nous initiates a new *arkhē*, at once a new first element and a new ruling principle. This new *arkhē* introduces chronology into Anaxagoras's cosmology and allows us to see that the initial state of the *khrēmata* is a bygone era. The imperfects of *homou panta khrēmata ēn* and throughout the fragments we have been considering seemed on first reading like imperfects of description. But with Nous's new beginning we can see in retrospect that they actually mark a past tense defined in relation to the now of Nous. So time starts over, or perhaps for the first time, since without a mechanism of change the initial state could have no time. Nous introduces historical tense—he controlled (*ekratēsen*, 13), he came to know (*egnō*, 16), he ordered (*diekosmēse*, 18)—and sets time in motion. Himself eternal (*aei esti*, B14/D28), he orders a continuous sequence of past, present, and future: "And whatever sorts of things were going to be (*emellen esesthai*), and whatever sorts were (*ēn*) that now are (*esti*) not, and however many are (*esti*) now and whatever sorts will be (*estai*), all these things Nous set in order" (17–19).[50]

Nous's temporal rupture accompanies a spatial rupture. Nous comes out of nowhere—literally: Anaxagoras's universe is a plenum and it was already full up with "everything" before Nous arrived on the scene.[51] Nous thus appears as a supplement to everything; he is supernumerary and emphatically separate. We are told repeatedly that nothing can exist apart (*khōris*, B6/D25, B8/D22, cf. B12.26–28/D27), but Nous does. He is thus nowhere but also everywhere, all-pervasive in space as he is in time: "Nous, who is always, is most certainly even now where (*hina*) all the other things are, in (*en*) the surrounding magnitude and in (*en*) the things joined together and in (*en*) the things separated off" (B14/D28). We will return below to the question of what it means for Nous to be "in" everything, but it is clear that he is not in everything in the same way as everything else is in everything. He shares the things' space but not their collective being, for "there is a share of everything in everything except Nous" (B11/D26). Nous thus introduces a double spatial rupture, a rift not only in the original spatial disposition of the things (everything in everything) but in the very logic of space (the meaning of "in").[52]

49. Cf. B13/D29b: "and when Nous began (*ērxato*) to move things"; Arist. *De an.* 1.2 405a15 (< A55/R13): "Anaxagoras makes Nous especially the *arkhē* of all things."

50. Note also the insistence on temporal sequence at lines 13–15: after he imposed the *arkhē*, the rotation "began to revolve (*ērxato perikhōrein*) from the small, then it revolves (*perikhōrei*) more, and it will revolve (*perikhōrēsei*) even more."

51. Lucr. 1.843–44 (= A44/R29); Arist. *Cael.* 4.2 309a19–20, *Ph.* 4.6 213a22–24 (= A68/D59–60); Hippol. *Haer.* 1.8.3 (= A42/D4); Curd 2008, 233.

52. Nous's ubiquity raises the question of his materiality and corporeality, questions on which there is no consensus: see Lanza 1966, 222–24; Renehan 1980, 115–16; and Curd 2007, 200–4. Although he lacks the corporeal features of Xenophanes's *theos* (Xen. B23–26/D16–19), Nous does seem to occupy space. Later commentators like Simplicius (ad B14/D28) make Anaxagoras a dualist; so too, Sedley

Nous's arrival ruptures not only the original space-time of the cosmos but also its basic ontology. Nous is ontologically distinct from the *khrēmata* and an exception to the rules they live by. B12/D27 begins: "The other things have a share of everything, but Nous is unbounded and *autokrates* and has been mixed with no thing but he is alone himself by himself." The *men/de* construction sets Nous against the "other things" that used to be everything. Boundless like the things (*apeiron*, cf. B1/D9), he is, however, not one of them. Indeed, despite being "lightest and purest of all things" (a description to which we will return), Nous has a fundamentally different constitution from the things, as the end of the fragment explains. While everything else is radically heterogeneous, both externally (because no thing is like anything else) and internally (since everything contains a share of everything), Nous is only and entirely himself: "Nous is entirely the same" (*nous de pas homoios esti*, B12.27–28/D27). Unitary, singular, and homogenous, an exception to the basic laws of the universe, Nous is no-thing.

Nous's exceptional nature is the source of his exceptional power. He is *autokrates* (B12.2/D27): he rules by himself and for himself. *Autokrates* is a strong word. It appears nowhere before Anaxagoras and his usage seems to have been memorable. Plato recalls it when paraphrasing Anaxagoras in the *Cratylus* (413c). In classical Greek it denotes persons vested with the full legitimate authority of the polis; it is frequently used for plenipotentiary embassies.[53] It is also used of tyrants and other absolute rulers. Authorized by and answering to no political community, solitary and solipsistic, Nous is a cosmic tyrant. His *kratos* is autotelic: it derives from itself, inheres in itself, and refers only to itself. It is its own *arkhē*—its own ground or legitimation—and its own *telos*. Nous *autokrates* thus exemplifies the absolute and unconditional sovereignty that Derrida terms ipsocratic. Carl Schmitt famously defines the sovereign as "he who decides on the state of exception."[54] Anaxagoras's Nous is a literal exception, for as B11/D26 says, "there is a share of everything in everything except Nous" (*plēn nou*, cf. B12.27/D27). No wonder that later readers considered Nous a god (A48/P34).[55]

2008b, 8–25. It is worth noting that some scholars view the basic elements as immaterial, e.g. Furth 1991; and Marmodoro 2017, 17–24.

53. For generals, ambassadors: Andoc. *De myst.* 15, *De pace*, 6, 33, 34, 39; Ar. *Av.* 1595, *Lys.* 1010, *Pax* 359; Lys. 13.9. Of absolute rulers or magistrates with unlimited power: Thuc. 1.126, 6.72; Xen. *An.* 6.1.21; Pl. *Leg.* 875b, *Plt.* 299c; Dem. 18.235; Arist. *Pol.* 3.9 1285a8, 4.8 1295a12.

54. Schmitt 2005 (translation modified). As a violent suspension of the existing order, Schmitt's sovereign raises a political version of the Eleatic problem: "Looked at normatively, the decision emerges from nothingness" (31). Derrida (1992b) offers a meditation on this paradox. Cf. Agamben (2005), stressing the state of exception as a domain of lawlessness within the law.

55. Menn (1995) examines the concept of god as *nous*; as Porter (2016, 547–54) observes, in early Greek philosophy, matter at its most sublime gives way to the divine. See also Derrida (2009, 46–54) on the concealed "ontotheological" basis of sovereignty (barely concealed in Schmitt's treatment).

Mind's sovereignty both emerges from and eventuates in a new distribution of the sensible, a distribution at once physical, metaphysical, and political. Nous is *autokrates* because he is unmixed with the elements, as Anaxagoras explains in B12.1–8/D27: he dominates because he is separate. He also dominates through separation. His very presence introduces new divisions in the universe of the *khrēmata*. B11/D26 continues: "There is a share of everything in (*en . . . enesti*) everything except Nous, but there are things that Nous is also in (*eni*)." What it means for Nous to be "in" some things is debated, but commentators agree that the *eni* at the end of the sentence describes a different relation from the *enesti* in the first part, since it is nonreciprocal: Nous can be in some things but they cannot be in him. Now things are distinguished not only by the relative differences of color, shape, and size, but also by the apparently absolute difference of the presence or absence of Nous. The special things that contain Nous are presumably the same ones described in B12.11/D27 as "however many things have *psukhē*, both the greater and the lesser" and glossed in B4a/D13 as "humans and all other living things that have *psukhē*." Anaxagoras doesn't say whether this new division is hierarchical, but as a differential intimacy with the source of power it seems that it must be.[56] Nous thus reapportions the perceptible into a new hierarchy of being.

Division is the source of Mind's power and of his knowledge. Power and knowledge are closely linked for Nous, as his name might lead us to expect. In B12.10/D27 he "holds all knowledge about everything (*gnōmēn ge peri pantos pasan iskhei*) and has the greatest strength (*kai iskhuei megiston*)." The connection is reinforced by the aural repetition *iskhei/iskhuei*. Nous knows all things and dominates them by differentiating them, as B12.16–19/D27 explains: "The things that are mixed together and the things that are separated off and becoming distinct, Nous knew them all. And whatever sorts of things were going to be, and whatever sorts were that now are not, and however many are now and whatever sorts will be, all these things Nous set in order" (*diekosmēse*). This *diakosmēsis*—this ordering (*kosmos*) through division (*dia*)—is Nous's sovereign act and the fullest expression of his power/knowledge.[57] Sorting the ingredients by both quantity (*hosa*) and quality (*hopoia*), he separates (*apokrinomena*) and differentiates (*diakrinomena*) and in this way creates the universe as we know it, setting in motion the processes that will generate all the familiar phenomena of our world and all other possible worlds (B4a/D13).

Through his *diakosmēsis* Nous introduces a principle of visibility into a formerly opaque cosmos—again in keeping with his name, which was originally linked

56. As Aristotle drily notes, "It does not seem that *nous*, at least in respect to *phronēsis*, is similarly present in all animals, nor even in all human beings" (*De an.* 1.2 404b1–7 < A100/R12). He takes Anaxagoras to task for failing to differentiate *nous* and *psukhē* (*De an.* 1.2 405a13–19 < A55/R13).

57. Cf. B13/D29b's triple repetition of *diakrinō*. Laks (1993) associates Nous's *gnōmē* closely with his powers of *krisis;* contra, Lesher 1995.

to visual perception.[58] Where before there was just the undifferentiated chaos of everything in everything, a *summixis* in which no thing was manifest (*ouden endēlon ēn*, B1/D9; cf. B4b/D12), now things are separated and concentrated so that, as the last line of B12/D27 says, "whatever things predominate (*pleista*, literally, "are most") in something, these things are most manifestly (*endēlotata*) what each thing (*hen hekaston*) is and was." Visibility is the manifestation of discrete, numerable objects. In the original *summixis*, as we saw, it was impossible to measure the *plēthos* of elements or to count any individual element. But now one can discern which things are "most" (*pleista*) in anything and, as a result, can reckon the identity of "each one" (*hen hekaston*).[59] In one and the same moment, Nous introduces visibility, countability, and identity—in short, ipseity. In this way, as André Laks has argued, Nous remakes the things in his own image; himself an integer ("alone himself by himself," B12.3/D27), he separates the things into discrete identities the better to know and control them.[60] This brings us back to Nous's *auto-kratos*. The cosmos his *kratos* commands is the same (*auto*) as that *kratos* itself, a perfect ipsocentric circle.

Under the *arkhē* of Nous, Anaxagoras thus redistributes the sensible in the image of an autocratic sovereign. And yet on closer inspection it appears that Nous's *diakosmēsis* is incomplete and both his *autos* and his *kratos* curiously limited. Plato, in fact, remarks on this. In the *Phaedo* Socrates describes his initial excitement on finding that Anaxagoras made Nous the cause of everything. He expected that "ordering mind would order all things and establish each in the best possible way" (*Phd.* 97c4–6), so that by reading the philosopher he would discover not only how things are but also why it is best that they be that way (97e). He was bitterly disappointed, then, to discover "that the man makes no use (*khrōmenon*) of Nous and provides no causes for the *diakosmēsis* of things" (98b8–c1). In other words, Nous lacks *nous*; he causes the *diakosmēsis* but does not, in Plato's view, plan or intend it, betraying the etymology of his own name.[61]

Other readers wondered whether he even really caused it. Aristotle is acerbic: "Anaxagoras uses (*khrētai*) Nous as a contrivance (*mēkhanēi*) for producing cosmic order (*kosmopoiian*). He drags him on when he is at a loss for an explanation

58. Von Fritz (1943, 91) describes *noos* in Homer as "a mental vision, which not only penetrates deeper but also 'sees farther' both in space and in time than our eyes." He traces the evolution of the term from a sensory to a purely cognitive function (1945, 1946, with critique by Lesher [1994a, 3–10]). Compare Xenophanes's *theos*, which likewise brings together *nous* and sense perception: as a whole he sees, knows (*noei*), hears (B24/D17).

59. Inwood 1986, 27: "Only when the separation has occurred, *now* rather than *then*, can one refer to greatness or largeness. For the separation has produced discernible, countable bodies."

60. Laks 1993.

61. The example Plato gives highlights the noncentripetal design of Anaxagoras's cosmic geometry: Socrates expected that if Anaxagoras said that something is in the center (*en mesōi*) he would say why it was better for it to be in the center (*Phd.* 97e). On Socrates's critique, see Furley 1987; and on his broader engagement with Anaxagoras's ideas, Vasiliou 2021.

for some necessity; but otherwise he attributes the cause of generation to everything but Nous."[62] Nous is not the architect of *kosmopoiia*, but a mere device (*mēkhanē*), a *khrēma* the author uses (*khrētai*). Other ancient readers too thought Anaxagoras gives too much credit to the *perikhōrēsis*: Nous sets it in motion, but it is the mechanical rotation that actually creates the world.[63] In B12.13/D27, as we have seen, the inaugural act of Nous's *kratos* (*ekratēsen*, the first occurrence of the verb in a historical tense) is to inaugurate the rotation "so that it rotated to begin with" (*tēn arkhēn*). Mind's *kratos* is the *arkhē*. But in the next sentence the noun *arkhē* becomes a verb, *ērxato*, and *perikhōrēsis* is its subject.[64] So if Nous is the *arkhē*, he shares this honor with the mindless vortex. He also shares with it some of his power. In B9/D14 we are told that things as they revolve are separated out "by force and speed (*hupo biēs te kai takhutētos*); and the speed produces force." Traditionally, Biē stands next to Kratos as the twin attendants of Zeus and symbols of his sovereignty.[65] But here, the two are split up: Nous has *kratos*, but *biē* belongs to the centrifugal motion of vortex. It's worth noting that in Aristophanes's parody of Anaxagorian physics in *Clouds*, it is whirl (Dinos), not Nous, that unseats Zeus as cosmic sovereign (*Nub.* 379–81, 827–29, 1471–73).

So we have a *kratos* without force, an *arkhē* that is not really the *arkhē*, a Mind that lacks mind. Autocratic Nous is thus divided from himself: he is not self-same (*autos*), neither in his power nor in his being. Further, his power and his being are divided from one another. Nous is separate from everything else: that is essential to his exceptional being and sovereign power. But that separation also sets a limit on the very knowledge that defines him as Mind. We cannot reconstruct Anaxagoras's theory of cognition from the extant fragments, but if it followed a principle of opposites, as his theory of perception did (according to Theophrastus, A92/D70, 72, 73), then Nous can know the things but not himself or his own power. What is an *autokratos* that cannot know itself? If, conversely, cognition follows a principle of like affecting like, then we might wonder, as Aristotle did, "if Nous is simple and

62. *Metaph.* 1.4. 985a18–21 (A47/R10). The critique is echoed and extended by Silvestre (1988). Von Fritz (1964) sees in Anaxagoras a compromise between *nous* as a quasi-divine ordering principle and as a mechanical cosmogonic force, and thus between a teleological and antiteleological explanation of the cosmos. On the question of Mind's intent and Anaxagorean teleology, see Sedley 2008b, 20–25; Laks 2002b; and Louguet 2002.

63. Clem. Al. *Misc.* 2.14 (= A57/≠LM). Simplicius defends Anaxagoras against this charge at B13/D29b and A53/R32. It seems clear that Nous is not cosmogonic in a strict sense, since the basic ingredients of the world preexist him. As many scholars note, his powers are organizational rather than generative; thus Sedley (2008b, 23): "*Nous* is a farmer."

64. Contrast B13/D29b, where the *perikhōrēsis* merely continues the separation that Nous began. Note that Nous is absent from B15–17/D30, 31, 15, where the cosmogonic processes of separation and congealing proceed without his direction.

65. Hes. *Th.* 385; Solon 36.15–16; Aesch. *PV* 12; Stocking 2023, 87–90.

unaffected and shares nothing in common with anything, as Anaxagoras says, how it will think, if thinking means affecting something."[66]

Finally, it is not even clear that Nous ultimately succeeds in his *diakosmēsis*. If Nous's intention in the *apokrisis* is to separate the things into discrete identities so that he may know and control them, Laks observes that he fails in his goal, for as B6/D25 says, "just as in the beginning so too now all things are together. And in all things there are many things even of the things being separated off."[67] Even after Mind's *diakosmēsis*, everything remains in everything—perhaps even Nous himself. In B12.9–10/D27 we hear that he is "lightest and purest of all things" (*leptotaton te pantōn khrēmatōn kai katharōtaton*). The partitive genitive makes him conceptually part of "all things," and the adjectives are not masculine (as is usual for Nous) but neuter. Likewise, in the opening sentence of the fragment, even as Nous is "alone by himself" in the masculine forms (*monos autos*), he is described as *apeiron* and *autokrates* in the neuter.[68] Maybe Nous is just a *khrēma* after all, as Plato and Aristotle suggest when the former complains that Anaxagoras makes insufficient use (*khrōmenon*) of Nous and the latter, that he uses (*khrētai*) Nous as a *mēkhanē*, a contrivance or tool. But if Nous is just one thing among all the others, if he is not separate and exceptional, then what is the basis of his *kratos?* As Laks concludes, "Whatever the achievements of νοῦς [*nous*] are, the principle according to which 'everything is in everything' imposes an absolute limit to its power."[69]

Laks's formulation brings us back to the relation between Nous and the elements and invites us to think about it as a political relation. In Anaxagoras's

66. Arist. *De an.* 3.4 429b22–25; cf. 1.2 405b19–23. Simplicius poses a related conundrum (*in Cael.* 608, 23 < B7/≠LM; cf. Arist. *Ph.* 1.4 187b7–12): since knowledge delimits the thing known, then either the *khrēmata* must not be *apeira*, as Anaxagoras says in B1/D9, or, if they are, Nous must be unable to know them. By that logic, Nous, who is likewise *apeiron* (B12.1/D27), cannot know himself either. On Anaxagoras's epistemology and the problem of Mind's knowledge, see further Von Fritz 1964; Laks 1993, 2002b; DeFilippo 1993; Lesher 1995; Curd 1998, 141–47, 2007, 192–205; and Louguet 2002, 510–22. On Anaxagoras's theory of perception, see Warren 2007a.

67. Laks 1993, 32. Compare the end of B12/D27: even after Nous introduces number such that "each one" (*hen hekaston*) can be what it is, the principle of everything in everything still makes it impossible to distinguish many (*polla*) from all (*pantapasi*, B12.25/D27).

68. At B12.1/D27 Nous is contrasted to "the other things" (*ta men alla . . . nous de*), but is *alla* exclusive ("the other things") or inclusive ("the rest of the things")? Cf. B14/D28, where Nous "is most certainly even now where all the other things are" (*hina kai ta alla panta*). On the ambiguity of "lightest and purest of all things," see Schofield (1980, 11–12): does this mean that Nous is particularly fine matter or not matter at all? Curd (2007, 59) believes that "in using the superlatives . . . Anaxagoras is again calling attention to the fundamental difference between *Nous* and the ingredients in the mix." But see Derrida (2009, 256–65): the superlative makes the sovereign a member, albeit a superlative one, of the group to which he is compared.

69. Laks 1993, 32: "Complete separation is mind's wishful thinking" (33; cf. 2002b; contra, Lesher 1995).

account, Nous has no genesis. Even as his miraculous appearance is represented as a new beginning and a sharp break with what went before, he always exists (*aei esti*, B14/D28), and his eternal being transcends the rift between before and after. Indeed, to the extent that the murky pre-Nous past becomes visible (*endēlon*) only from the clarifying vantage point of the post-Nous present, there is no "before" of Nous. His sovereignty was implicit from the start and his *kratos* is without origin.[70] Or rather, it is its own origin: when he "controlled (*ekratēsen*) the whole rotation so that it rotated to begin with (*arkhēn*)" (B12.13/D27), his *kratos* generates the *arkhē* and the *arkhē* enacts his *kratos* in a closed circle of ipsocentric self-positing.[71]

Yet behind this vision of eternal sovereignty we can detect traces of an obscure genealogy of Nous's power, one that breaks its circle of self-legitimation. B12/D27 begins by introducing Nous as *autokrates*, his power pure and unconditional. But the sentences that follow show that Nous's power is not, in fact, unconditional; indeed, it is quite literally conditional.

> τὰ μὲν ἄλλα παντὸς μοῖραν μετέχει, νοῦς δέ ἐστιν ἄπειρον καὶ αὐτοκρατὲς καὶ μέμεικται οὐδενὶ χρήματι, ἀλλὰ μόνος αὐτὸς ἐπ' ἑωυτοῦ ἐστιν. εἰ μὴ γὰρ ἐφ' ἑαυτοῦ ἦν, ἀλλά τεωι ἐμέμεικτο ἄλλωι, μετεῖχεν ἂν ἁπάντων χρημάτων, εἰ ἐμέμεικτό τεωι· ἐν παντὶ γὰρ παντὸς μοῖρα ἔνεστιν, ὥσπερ ἐν τοῖς πρόσθεν μοι λέλεκται· καὶ ἂν ἐκώλυεν αὐτὸν τὰ συμμεμειγμένα, ὥστε μηδενὸς χρήματος κρατεῖν ὁμοίως ὡς καὶ μόνον ἐόντα ἐφ' ἑαυτοῦ. (B12.1–8/D27)
>
> The other things have a share of everything, but Nous is unbounded and *autokrates* and has been mixed with no thing, but he is alone himself by himself. For if he were not by himself, but had been mixed with something else, he would have a share of all things, if he had been mixed with anything; for there is a share of everything in everything, as I have said before. And the things that were mixed together would prevent him from controlling any thing in the same way as he does being alone by himself.

70. This self-positing explains a certain temporal circularity in Anaxagoras's discussion of the original state. Scholars have wondered, for instance, how in B1/D9 air and aether can be said to exist as discrete phenomena before their separation by the vortex and can predominate in that condition of total *summixis*. Inwood (1986, 26–27) notes the switch from the imperfect to the present tense at the end of the fragment ("for these are [*enestin*] greatest among all the things") and proposes that we can only understand the predominance of these elements from the perspective of the future, after they will have been separated out by Nous. Following Inwood, we could say that the things in the original state have a virtual identity that only becomes actual after it is discerned by Nous. Cf. Louguet (2002, 522–28), who argues that the things constitute the order of the cosmos in and of themselves; Nous merely makes that order manifest.

71. Derrida 2009, 67: "The concept of sovereignty will always imply . . . this autoposition of him who posits or posits himself as *ipse*, the (self-)same, oneself." It is this political *an-arkhē* that Schmitt (2005) designates the state of exception.

This is the only counterfactual condition in Anaxagoras's extant writings, and it is strikingly anomalous in a fragment that is otherwise content simply to assert Nous's existence, qualities, and activities in straightforward declarative statements.[72] The syntactical anomaly becomes all the more striking when we note that it is in this conditional sentence that Anaxagoras first extends Mind's *auto-kratos* to *kratos* over other things—or more precisely, over no other thing, *mēdenos khrēmatos kratein*. While Nous's *auto-kratos* was positively asserted (*nous de estin . . . autokrates*), his power over the *khrēmata* is introduced under negation, in a counterfactual imagination of his powerlessness.

This counterfactual exposes both a repressed history of political conflict and the textual strategies of its repression. If Nous were mixed with anything else—which of course he is not—he would be subject to the principle of everything in everything. If that were the case—which, Anaxagoras repeats, it is not—that very principle of *summixis* would prevent (*ekōluen*) Nous from ruling. We are invited to imagine—if only for a second and under safe syntactical conditions—a violent *agōn* between Nous and the *khrēmata*. In this instant, we are reminded of Vernant's definition of *kratos* as inherently agonistic: "a matter of opposing force to force, power to power, in order to conquer or dominate."[73] Nous's *auto-kratos* claims to be self-grounding: it has always existed, "alone itself by itself." But in this counterfactual we glimpse a different narrative, a repressed story of opposition, struggle, and conquest. In this narrative, Mind's power does not lie in his ontological separation from the *khrēmata*, as Anaxagoras insists, but instead emerges out of an agonistic relation to them. The *khrēmata* lost this struggle—hence Nous's *kratos*—but in another sense perhaps they won, for their very mention here mixes Nous up with them, implicating him in the *summixis* of everything in everything and thus declaring that his *kratos* is not, in fact, *autokrates*. He is not a sovereign exception but merely one (victorious) thing among others.

That possibility is immediately foreclosed. It is foreclosed, first, by the counterfactual syntax and the logical circularity that resecures the self-legitimation of Nous's autocracy. That circle of self-legitimation is emphasized in the triple repetition of *ep' heautou* (Nous is by himself . . . if he were not by himself . . . but he is by himself). It is sustained by the causal conjunctions that make the nature of physical reality the explanation for Nous's separation: "For (*gar*) there is a share of everything in everything." Finally, if grammar, logic, and verbal repetition are not enough, the author inserts himself ("as I have said before," *moi lelektai*)—again,

72. Schofield (1980, 6–10, building on Deichgräber 1933, 347–53) differentiates the two styles of B12/D27: the archaic "solemn predication" of most of the fragment and the more complex argumentation of this section; cf. Ugolini 1985, 326–27. The closest parallel to the conditional syntax of this section is at the end of B4a/D13 (well discussed by Fränkel [1955, 288–91]), describing the probability of other worlds.

73. Vernant 2006a, 217. *Kōluō* may have originally implied physical restraint if it is based on the noun *kōla* (limbs), but any sense of that etymology seems to have been lost early on.

an almost unparalleled phenomenon in the extant fragments, and one to which we will return in the next section. This is a reminder that the *kratos* of Nous is not, in point of fact, ipsocentric and self-positing. It is posited by the philosopher, constructed through his labored logic, secured through his repetitive rhetoric, and guaranteed through his authorial presence. Nous's sovereignty is the product of philosophical, not just political, struggle.

In observing these strategies of textual production and revealing the history of political contest they obscure, we glimpse a concealed genealogy of Nous's purportedly eternal *kratos* and, with it, political potentialities rendered invisible by Nous's *diakosmēsis*. We noted how in the original state of things when the *khrēmata* were all together, individual identities were said to be imperceptible (*oude . . . endēlos ēn oudemia*) "because the *summixis* of all things was preventing it" (*apekōlue gar hē summixis pantōn khrēmatōn*, B4b/D12). This is the same language that in B12.7/D27 describes the counterfactual possibility that the things mixed together would prevent (*ekōluen*) Nous from dominating as he does. Reading the two fragments together, we can discern here that contest over partition of the sensible that Rancière places at the heart of the political. In B4b/D12 the commingled *khrēmata* were preventing Nous from imposing his vision on the world—or if we take the imperfect as conative, they were trying to do so. Was this just an attempt at obfuscation? Or was it an effort to preserve the variegated visual regime that existed before Nous, that plenum of shapes and colors and pleasures, of *polla kai pantoia khrēmata*, none resembling any other? Infinitely varied and intermeshed, the initial state of things was a complex perceptible order with its own structuring rules and relations. It already had its own aesthetics.

Nous is blind to this rich cosmos of things. When it surveys this *summixis*, Mind's eye perceives only obscurity, a chaos in which there is, literally, nothing to see. But if that prior order is invisible to all-seeing Nous, it is because Anaxagoras obscures it in order to preserve Nous's exceptionality. The things lack identity, apparently by nature. But if Nous is eternal and there is no time before him, then his qualities were conceptually available from the start, and Anaxagoras's refusal to share them with the *khrēmata* is a deliberate choice. In other words, if the things are obscure and uncountable, it is not because Anaxagoras cannot see or count them but because he *will* not: he denies them ipseity so as to prevent them from becoming like Nous. In so doing he curtails the political potentialities implicit in the original state of things, preventing their collocality from becoming a political community or their immeasurable *plēthos* a *dēmos*. He forestalls the manifestation of a latent egalitarian politics in the name of a metaphysics of sovereign singularity. But in the process he also renders that sovereignty strangely powerless and self-contradictory, as we have seen. By insisting on his ontological singularity, Anaxagoras isolates Nous from the world he rules, limiting the knowledge that grounds that rule and that defines him as Mind. Anaxagoras hobbles both the *autos* and the *kratos* of *Nous autokrates* in order to preserve his exceptionality. We should recall that in Schmitt's definition the sovereign is not simply exceptional but "he who decides on the state of exception." By this definition, it is Anaxagoras who is the sovereign.

VISION OF THE OBSCURE

To suggest this is to point to Anaxagoras's ambivalent investment in the power of Nous. In Athens Anaxagoras was apparently nicknamed Nous, and as the mind that sees, knows, and organizes the world imagined in this text, the author has a special affinity for his protagonist.[74] Indeed, we might view Nous as the personification of the authorial mind within the text and a projection of its totalizing vision. The order of Mind's *diakosmēsis* is the cosmic order discerned and described by Anaxagoras, and Nous's knowledge is ultimately the author's own.

Aligning himself with Nous's omniscient gaze, Anaxagoras goes beyond the limitations of human perception to obtain a "vision of the obscure." Sextus Empiricus reports that Anaxagoras faulted the senses, saying that "because of their feebleness we are not able to distinguish the truth" (*krinein t'alēthes*, B21/D5). The proof of their unreliability is the mixing of colors. If we take two dyes, black and white, and pour one into the other drop by drop, our sight will not be able to differentiate (*diakrinein*) the minute changes, "although they truly exist in nature."[75] With our blunt vision we can see the gross phenomena created by the *apokrisis* but cannot discern the boundless *khrēmata* of which they are composed; we cannot see the everything in everything that constitutes "the truth" of physical reality. And yet for one who knows how to see, "appearances [or phenomena] are a vision of the obscure" (*opsis adēlōn ta phainomena*, B21a/D6).[76] The word *adēlōn* evokes the regime of visibility introduced by Nous, the new capacity to discern what each thing is "most manifestly" (*endēlotata*, B12.29/D27). Nous separated the imperceptible elements into visible phenomena; the fact that Anaxagoras uses the same word—*khrēma*—for both shows that the former things are still obscurely present in the latter.[77] David Sider notes the "amphiboly" of *opsis*, which is both subjective (seeing) and objective (something seen).[78] Anaxagoras's text mediates between the two. By allowing us to see with our minds the *khrēmata* we cannot see with our eyes, he allows us to grasp the objective reality of our world. In this way he lets us

74. Diog. Laert. 2.6 (< A1/P42); Plut *Per.* 4 (< A15/P43).

75. Only the first quotation is reported as Anaxagoras's own words, but the example is likely to be drawn from him. See Warren 2007a, 32–35.

76. Sextus quotes this fragment in the course of a discussion of Democritus, and it is possible that he, not Anaxagoras, is the author. Sider (2005, 165–66) believes it is Anaxagorian.

77. "No thing (*khrēma*) is born or dies but it is mixed together and distinguished out of the things that are" (*eontōn khrēmatōn,* B17/D15): the first *khrēma* denotes phenomena, the second the basic elements. At B12.16–17/D27, Nous knew both "the things that are mixed together and the things that are separated off and becoming distinct." To his panoptical eye, both the phenomena and the invisible things that compose them are equally manifest.

78. Sider 2005, 166–67: "The amphiboly seems intentional" (166).

see, as he does, through Nous's eyes, granting us too some share of Nous's discriminating power, his ability to discern the *khrēmata* within the *khrēmata* and thus to "distinguish the truth" (*krinein t'alēthes*, B21/D5).

That truth is both ontological and cosmological: it is a truth about the nature of the things around us today as well as about their primordial origin. Nous's perennial gaze forms the bridge between the two. It encompasses all things past, present, and future—"whatever sorts of things were going to be, and whatever sorts were that now are not, and however many are now and whatever sorts will be" (B12.17–18/D27)—and also discerns their fundamental identity over time. Thus Nous can see "most manifestly what each thing is and was" (*esti kai ēn*, B12.30/D27). This line encapsulates Anaxagoras's cosmogonic project and, indeed, the intellectual project of cosmogony as a whole, which explains what each thing is by revealing what it originally was. When the cosmologist writes "as in the beginning (*arkhēn*) so too now all things are together" (B6/D25), he adopts Nous's eternal gaze and he, like Nous, transcends time.[79]

This timeless vision lets the author see not only what Nous sees, but even further, for he sees the world before Nous existed and discerns the things that are unclear to Nous clearly enough to declare them unclear. If there is no "before" of Nous, as I suggested in the last section, that is because Anaxagoras retrojects Mind's principle of visibility and discrimination to a time before he exists. The author becomes omniscient in the figure of Nous, but Nous also becomes omniscient in the person of the author, able to see even what predates himself. If Nous is the projection of the author within the text—the eye with which he surveys and knows the world he has imagined—the authorial mind outstrips its own creation. It is Anaxagoras who "holds all knowledge about everything and has the greatest strength" (B12.10–11/D27).[80]

Anaxagoras, however, works to obscure this fact. He projects his cosmogonic power onto Nous and conceals himself behind his character. Let's return to B12/D27 and the counterfactual conditions from which Nous's sovereignty is born.

79. Other examples of the author's transtemporality are the shift from the past to the present tense at the end of B1/D9 (noted by Inwood [1986, 26–27]) and the shift in perspective in B12.17–18/D27 (noted by Sider [2005, 29]) from a vantage point in the cosmos's first moments ("whatever sorts of things were going to be") to one in our present ("whatever sorts were that now are not, and however many are now and whatever sorts will be").

80. Perhaps ancient readers intuited this: coins from ancient Clazomenae figure Anaxagoras holding or seated on a globe (A27/P49), and Aristotle relates that, when asked why one should choose to be born rather than not, Anaxagoras replied, "to view the heavens and the order in the entire cosmos" (*Eth. Eud.* 1.5 1216a10–14 < A30/P35). Similarly, his epitaph praised him for "reaching the furthest limit of truth of the heavenly cosmos" (Diog. Laert. 2.15 < A1/P46). Philosophy continues to identify with omniscient Mind: as Curd (2007, 89) observes, versions of the numismatic images appear in volume 3 of Diels-Kranz's *Fragmente der Vorsokratiker* and on the cover of volume 2 of Guthrie's *A History of Greek Philosophy* (1965).

> Nous is unbounded and *autokrates* and has been mixed with no thing, but he is alone himself by himself. For (*gar*) if he were not by himself, but had been mixed with something else, he would have a share of all things, if he had been mixed with anything; for (*gar*) there is a share of everything in everything, as I have said before (*hōsper en tois prosthen moi lelektai*). And (*kai*) the things that were mixed together would prevent him from controlling (*kratein*) any thing in the same way as he does being alone by himself. (B12.1–8/D27)

With its redundant hypotheticals and otiose causal connectives, this passage foregrounds its logical argumentation and draws attention to the mind behind this logic. That shadowy authorial presence is concretized by the sudden first-person intervention: "as I have said before" (*moi lelektai*).[81] In this instant the author appears only to retreat behind his own *logos*: the authorial *egō* declines to the dative (*moi*). That *logos*, furthermore, merely repeats the facts of the cosmos: "For there is a share of everything in everything." It is thus neither Anaxagoras himself nor his *logos* that sustains Nous's power but the physical law of everything in everything to which he is an exception. The circular logic of the passage and its repeated causal particles (*gar*) create an inferential loop in which the bare fact of Nous's *autokratos* is its own justification: he rules because he is exceptional and he must be exceptional because he rules. The author just reiterates this illogical logic, his creative force eclipsed by Nous's self-authorizing sovereignty.[82]

It thus appears that the world exists, and the author merely occupies it. We have seen how other Presocratic writers advertise the value of their teachings by opposing their own unique knowledge to the ignorance of others. Thus in his first fragment Heraclitus sets the incomprehension of mortals against his own *logos*, "such words and deeds as I expound, distinguishing each thing according to its nature and saying how it is" (Her. B1/D1).[83] Anaxagoras seems to do something similar in B17/D15 when he criticizes the Greeks, who "do not think rightly (*ouk orthōs nomizousin*) about birth and death, for (*gar*) no thing is born or dies but it is mixed together and distinguished out of the things that are. Thus they would correctly call (*houtōs an orthōs kaloien*) 'to be born' 'to be mixed together' and 'to die' 'to be distinguished.'" But Anaxagoras contrasts the ignorance of the Greeks not to his own philosophy but to the physical reality of the cosmos. Again the causal connectives create a logical circle in which the facts of the universe are their own justification: the physical law of combination and separation is the logical

81. The only other first-person authorial intervention is at the end of B4a/D13, in the same phrase: "These things have been said by me (*tauta men oun moi lelektai*) about the *apokrisis*." Anaxagoras is the only Presocratic philosopher to use this phrase (an apparent parallel in Thales B3/R44 is not *ipssisima verba*). Sider (2005, 30n17) contrasts Anaxagoras's retroactive use of the phrase to the variations of *moi dokei* that often come at the beginning of works, "staking out a claim and calling attention to the author's own contribution to knowledge."

82. Schofield (1980, 3–22) offers a subtle analysis of this fragment's logic (or lack thereof).

83. Cf. Parm. B6/D7, B8.38–41/D8.43–46, B8.50–61/D8.55–66; Emp. B2/D42, B4/D47, B11/D51; Alcmaeon B1/D4; Hecataeus FGH 1 F1. Schofield (1980, 36–40) notes the contrast in his discussion of the "impersonal" (39) style of the opening of Anaxagoras's book.

premise (*gar*); the conclusion (*houtōs*) follows. The fragment brings Greek *nomos* and nomenclature into alignment (*orthōs*) with physical reality, but also elides the author's role in that orthonomic process. The universe itself corrects the Greeks' error, without overt intervention from Anaxagoras.

This authorial self-effacement is generalized throughout Anaxagoras's text by his idiosyncratic use of logical connectives. Anaxagoras uses *gar* frequently, almost always—as in the instances we have just seen—to reiterate physical facts of the cosmos. Often there seems to be little difference in semantic force between *gar* (for) and *kai* (and), explanation and description.[84] Thus a construction that might normally work to assert the presence of the author in his text, offering explanations and drawing out causal inferences, instead makes the description of the universe its own logical support. The philosopher merely follows the logic of his world; he does not produce it. The same is true of another favorite construction, the use of the genitive absolute as a connective.[85] B4a/D13 begins: "These things being so, it is necessary to believe (*khrē dokein*) that there are many and all sorts of things in everything." In the logic of this passage, a posited reality generates its own argumentative necessity. The reader must believe not because the author tells her to but because this is simply how it is; the author falls out of the equation. We get a similar construction in B5/D16: "These things having been separated out in this way, it is necessary to know (*ginōskein khrē*) that . . . all things are equal." In place of belief (*dokein*) we are here enjoined to knowledge (*ginōskein*) and the same kind of knowledge said to be held by Nous, who "holds all knowledge (*gnōmēn*) about everything" (B12.10/D27; cf. *egnō*, B12.16/D27). Reading the text, following its logic and accepting its necessary conclusions, we come to know what Nous knows: reality in its totality. The discursive effort that produces that knowledge is, in the process, erased.

In a text dominated by tropes of visibility, the author thus renders his own creative force invisible, *adēlon*.[86] By effacing himself, Anaxagoras sustains Nous

84. Schofield 1980, 97: "Despite the inferential particles . . . Anaxagoras is not arguing with his reader in the manner of a Plato or Aristotle. . . . He is just explaining the way things are." See, e.g., B9/D14, where the logic seems causal but phrases are linked by *kai*; or B12/D27, where the *gars* of the first nine lines then yield to *kai*, with no apparent shift in argumentative force. I count fifteen instances of *gar* in the extant fragments. Of these, only three are anything other than a bare assertion of the physical facts as Anaxagoras sees them: the counterfactual at B12.3/D27 and the theoretical premises in B3/D24 and B5/D16 ("for it is impossible for what is not to be"; "for it is impossible to be more than all"). In some cases the causality is ostentatiously circular, e.g., in B4b/D12: "Seeds boundless in amount, none like to one another; for (*gar*) of the other things none was alike one to another."

85. E.g., B1/D9: "All things were together . . . and all things being together, nothing was manifest." Equivocating between circumstance and cause, the genitive absolute poses as a neutral description of reality: circumstance *as* cause. Ugolini (1985) shows how the interplay of expository and exegetical structures Anaxagoras's sentences. The genitive absolute also occurs in the first and last sentence of B4b/D12 and in B13/D29b; the grammar of the genitives in B7/D23 and B9/D14 is ambiguous.

86. Thus he is an exception to the text's totalizing world vision. Again, this exceptionality marks his sovereignty. Compare Foucault's reading of Velasquez's *Las Meninas*, where the unseen sovereign

as autonomous, self-authorizing, and self-authoring. The same dynamic would seem to explain the most characteristic feature of Anaxagoras's style, its predominantly paratactic structure.[87] Laying each point side by side, parataxis promises total visibility. Every element can be accounted for and the whole surveilled at a glance. Surveillance and the spatial distribution that facilitates it are a familiar technique of both imperial and domestic power and are especially appropriate for a power so intimately associated with vision as Nous.[88] The visibility effect of parataxis is reinforced by polysyndeton. Anaxagoras not only lays clauses side by side, but emphasizes that distribution with abundant connective and coordinating conjunctions that link the individual items even as they set them off: X *and* Y *and* Z. This combination of polysyndeton and parataxis sets textual objects out on a horizontal plane, each one discrete and identifiable. In doing so, it reiterates the differentiating *kratos* of Nous: every item can be seen, known, and counted.

An example comes in B12/D27, soon after the conditional sentences that both recount and repress the contested genealogy of Nous's *kratos*. That *kratos* is introduced as a hendiadys of power and knowledge: "He holds all knowledge about everything and (*kai*) has the greatest strength" (*gnōmēn ge peri pantos pasan iskhei kai iskhuei megiston*, B12.10–11/D27). The objects of this power/knowledge are then laid out over the next ten lines through paratactic accretion and polysyndetic accumulation: and (*kai*) Nous controls everything with soul, both (*kai*) the larger and (*kai*) the smaller; and (*kai*) he commanded the *perikhōrēsis*; and (*kai*) he knew all the things mixed together and (*te* . . . *kai*) the things separated out and (*kai*) the things distinguished, and so on. The only hypotactic constructions in this section (the result clause in line 13 and the relative clause in line 19) describe the transfer of Nous's force to the *perikhōrēsis*, where it continues: and (*kai*) the *perikhōrēsis* began to revolve, and (*de*) it revolved more, and (*kai*) it will revolve more. Through the *perikhōrēsis* Nous sets out each phenomenon and quality, identifying each one and putting it in array next to the others: the stars and (*te kai*) the sun and (*kai*) the moon and (*kai*) the air and (*kai*) the aether revolve; and

is the invisible organizing point of the painting (1970, 3–16). Anaxagoras, coincidentally, is said to have theorized the laws of perspective (A39/D97).

87. The extent fragments do, of course, contain hypotactic structures: see the subtle analysis of Ugolini (1985). But even where there is subordinating syntax, the subordination tends to be shallow: we rarely find the multiple layers of nested subordinate clauses that we see in Anaxagoras's contemporary Empedocles or, for that matter, in his predecessor Parmenides. Fränkel (1955, 40–96) emphasizes the "serial style" of archaic Greek literature as an immediate presentation of the facts of the world as they are perceived. This connects the construction to Anaxagoras's use of *gar* and the genitive absolute, discussed above. Compare Auerbach's famous study of Homeric style, emphasizing the full presence and visibility of every detail and relationship (1953, 3–23).

88. The classic work is Foucault 1977, 141–49, 195–228. Mourelatos (2008b, 316) connects parataxis to *noein* as "mental vision" but not specifically to Anaxagoras's Nous. Cf. Dewald (1987, 169–80): parataxis in Herodotus offers readers a god's-eye view of the overarching patterns of history, although there, she argues, the construction foregrounds the author's intervention.

(*kai*) the thick is separated out from the thin and (*kai*) the hot from the cold and (*kai*) the bright from the dark and (*kai*) the dry from the wet. The effect of distribution is reinforced by Anaxagoras's use (here and throughout) of neuter adjectives or participles with the substantivizing definite article (the hot, the cold, etc.) for a "thingification" of abstractions. Thus the syntax performs the *diakosmēsis* that makes all things *endēlotata*. It mimetically reproduces that process but also simply instantiates it as each thing—each concept, each noun—is laid out in order, discrete and discernible.

So from this perspective, the structure of Anaxagoras's prose supports the surveilling power/knowledge of Nous and reinforces the author's alignment with that all-seeing mind.[89] And yet there is another way to look at the lists of B12/D27 and the politics of Anaxagoras's parataxis in general. In his analysis of Hölderlin's paratactical structures, Theodor Adorno treats parataxis as an "antiprinciple" that resists the synthesizing operations of "a dominating Logos" to "evade the logical hierarchy of a subordinating syntax."[90] The political affordances of this "antiprinciple" have been developed by scholars of Indigenous narratives. Jared Dahl Aldern shows how parataxis in North Fork Mono storytelling undoes the bond between knowledge and power by fostering multiple, open-ended connections among ideas and "sustains a worldview of equivalence, reciprocity, and balance."[91] This narrative mode decenters settler power and levels its hierarchies, as Timothy Donahue argues in his reading of the narratives of the Great Basin, "because the relational and deconstructive thinking afforded by parataxis is antithetical to the unitary form of nation-state sovereignty."[92]

From this perspective we might view Anaxagoras's parataxis not as a stylistic tool of Nous's sovereign power/knowledge but instead as a formal alternative to it.[93] Willfully anachronistic, Anaxagoras's parataxis harkens back to a "premodern" distribution of the sensible; it evokes a time before Nous's *arkhē* and refuses the *telos* he imposes on the cosmos. The refusal of a *telos* is, in fact, a defining feature of the "strung-together style" (*lexis eiromenē*) of parataxis, according to Aristotle

89. Again that gaze extends even to the time before Nous: thus the long list of heterogeneous elements in the *summixis* in B4b/D12—and (*kai*) the moist and (*kai*) the dry and (*kai*) the hot and (*kai*) the cold and (*kai*) the bright and (*kai*) the dark and (*kai*) earth and (*kai*) countless seeds—surveils them retrospectively, discerning each element in order to identify it as indiscernible and unidentifiable.

90. Adorno 1992, 140, 131.

91. Aldern 2013, 9. He takes this narrative structure as a model for both ecological and cultural interactions. See further Kroeber (2004, 4–5) on the paratactic style of Native American narratives.

92. Donahue 2019, 24. "Parataxis at once foregrounds the relations between entities and deconstructs conventional hierarchical conceptions of those relations" (24); it is a form of "unsettlement" (33).

93. Lesher (1995, 126) hints at this when he remarks that "the archaic paratactic style which characterizes much of B12 obscures how Mind's powers of control relate to the 'discerning judgment' or 'knowledge.'" Lesher implies that Anaxagoras's formal primitivism evinces a failure to align with Mind's discrimination, but we might rather see it as resistance to such an alignment.

(*Rh.* 3.9 1409a29–b8). He finds the construction "unpleasant" (*aēdes*) because, he says, it is "unbounded" (*apeiron*) and "has no *telos* in itself but only stops when the content does." For Aristotle, as for Adorno, parataxis is a kind of anti-form, in contrast to the clearly defined periods of hypotaxis, "which has a beginning (*arkhēn*) and end (*teleutēn*) in itself and an easily seen magnitude (*megethos eusunopton*)" and is easier to remember "because it has number (*arithmon*) by which it can be measured (*metreitai*)." Without *arkhē* and *telos*, parataxis is *apeiron*—unbounded, indistinct—and immeasurable. In this it evokes less the boundless (*apeiron*, B12.1/D27) rule of Nous than the boundless (*apeira*, B1/D9) and countless *khrēmata* of the original state. Its refusal of subordination and emphasis on egalitarian relationality—each thing laid out side by side on a level syntactical plane—recalls their horizontal interrelations. Is parataxis the indigenous language of the things all together, the linguistic structure of their original communality?[94]

Recuperating the original collectivity of the things, parataxis, I propose, represents an alternative distribution of the sensible to Nous's solipsistic sovereignty. This formal alignment with the things is supported by other aspects of Anaxagoras's style as well. For instance, his use of the definite article to "thingify" an adjective or participle, which we earlier considered as a tool of Nous's distribution and surveillance, might instead be seen as a way of giving "an equal ontological dignity to each individuated thing," the large and the small alike.[95] Or we might think of Anaxagoras's use of simile and metaphor—or rather his non-use. Metaphor, as we discussed in chapter 1, is the master trope of an idealist metaphysics. Transferring the concrete to the conceptual, metaphor turns things into ideas (creating difficulties, as we saw in the last chapter, for Empedocles's materialist aesthetics). Anaxagoras eschews metaphor and sticks with the things.[96] Fragment B8/D22 offers a case in point: "They have not been separated from one another, the things in the one

94. Mourelatos (2008b) sets the "*logos*-textured world" of Plato against a "naive metaphysics of things" in which "each thing will be complete by itself, and the plurality of things will form a whole . . . in which all relations are external and explicit" (316). He posits a historical progression from this ontological parataxis (316) to Plato's hypotactic logic, with Anaxagoras marking a "relapse" (331). But the philosopher's choice of this archaic construction gestures not toward an earlier moment in Greek thought, in my view, but to an earlier moment in his own cosmology, and the opposition between a "naive metaphysics of things" and a "*logos*-textured world" is less a matter of intellectual progression than of political contestation. Cf. the discussion in the Conclusion.

95. The quotation is from Garcia (2014, 4), describing flat ontologies. Sider (2005, 32) notes Anaxagoras's use of this feature of Greek.

96. Of course he cannot avoid metaphor altogether (language itself being fundamentally metaphoric) but I can identify no word in Anaxagoras that *must* be understood metaphorically. Political diction like *moira* and *metekhein* can be interpreted metaphorically, but I have argued above for taking it literally. If Nous is considered immaterial, then the language of space ("in some things," "separate," "where the other things are") would have to be taken metaphorically when used of him; likewise the description of Nous as "lightest and purest of all things" (B12.9/D27). But to assume this is to concede Nous's metaphysical victory twice over: his ontological separation from the *khrēmata* and the attendant separation of concept from thing.

cosmos, nor have they been chopped off with an ax (*oude apokekoptai pelekei*), neither the hot from the cold nor the cold from the hot." Since the fragment describes a time before there could be such an object as an ax, the language is assumed to be figurative. Laks identifies it as the only metaphor in the extant fragments.[97] But it is not explicitly phrased as such. We don't get a simile where we expect one—even where we possibly have one.

The resistance to simile marks a problem with similitude more broadly. B9/D14 describes the speed of the vortex: "Their speed (*takhutēs*) was similar in speed (*takhutēta*) to no thing of the things that exist now among men, but it is many times as fast (*takhu*)." Speed is compared to speed in respect to speed only to declare the simile insufficient; the polyptoton (*takhutēs, takhutēta, takhu*) underlines the failure of the comparison even as the repetitions slow the line down, form pulling against content.[98] As tropes of substitution, simile and metaphor rest on ipseity, the discrete identity that enables the equation of one thing to another. At once absolutely dissimilar ("no other thing is similar to anything else," B12.28/D27) and materially the same (since everything is composed of everything else), the things resist such one-for-one equivalence. Instead their relation is fully metonymic, not a vertical substitution of one for another but the horizontal contiguity among interconnected parts.[99]

97. Laks 1993, 32; cf. Lanza 1966, 218; and Sider 2005, 117. It is an open question whether Anaxagoras imagined hot and cold as material things that could be chopped. In B19/D55, the apparently metaphorical proposition that the rainbow is a "sign (*sumbolon*) of a storm" is likely the scholiast's words, not Anaxagoras's, as Solmsen (1963) argues. Note too the antifigurative thrust of B22/D92: "What is called bird's milk is egg white" (if the fragment is by Anaxagoras and if that is the right reading; see Brennan 1995; and Sider 2005, 169–70). That the absence of metaphor in the treatise is deliberate is suggested by the report that Anaxagoras was the first to read Homer allegorically (Diog. Laert. 2.11): he was clearly capable of metaphoric thinking.

98. Perhaps the ultimate example of Anaxagoras's resistance to similitude is the fact that he posits multiple worlds but imagines them as "just like ours" (B4a/D13, the structure of which collapses the very difference it introduces: Louguet 2002, 528). This peculiar replication may be a byproduct of the mechanics of his universe, but for Vlastos (1975) the ramifications for Mind's discrimination are reason enough to reject the theory: "It is not likely that Mind would choose to engage in cosmic mass-production" (359; cf. Schofield 1996, 8: such a mind "forfeits its claim to *be* a mind."). Again (cf. n. 93 above), we can ask whether the lack of differentiation is Mind's failure or Anaxagoras's refusal to accede to his success. For various positions on the multiple-world theory and its implications for Nous's *diakosmēsis*, see Fränkel 1955, 284–93; Mansfeld 1980; Schofield 1996; Louguet 2002; and Curd 2007, 212–22.

99. See Jakobson and Halle (2002, 69–96), whose definition of metonymy reads like a linguistic gloss on Anaxagoras's everything in everything. It is only under the differentiating regime of Nous that one discrete object could stand in metaphorically for another. But even then the abiding rule of everything in everything complicates the situation. Thus B21a/D6 (*opsis adēlōn ta phainomena*) both is and isn't a metaphor. On the one hand, the visible objects around us offer a perceptible analogy to the invisible mechanics of the cosmos, a tangible substitute for the intangible things. On the other hand, though, those objects simply are the things, and in looking at them we actually see their unseen components.

The avoidance of metaphor thus reinforces the paratactical structure, and both contribute to a flat textual ontology that reiterates the horizontal relations among the things, keeping their original communality alive even after the ascension of Nous. This paratactic distribution of the sensible not only recuperates and preserves that archaic order, but develops it, realizing its incipient political potential. In the original state, as we saw, there could be no politics properly speaking. Without ipseity there could be no accounting for those who do not count; with everything in everything there could be neither identity nor alterity, and thus no explicit relations between things. Parataxis, I have suggested, is the syntactical form of "all things together" (*homou panta khrēmata*), but with a significant difference, because parataxis is not everything *in* everything but everything *next to* (*para*) everything. In laying each thing side by side on a single ontological plane, parataxis grants each its own visibility and identity, its own ipseity: this thing and that thing and the other thing. Stringing each discrete thing together like beads on a thread (in Aristotle's image), parataxis preserves their ontological equality and egalitarian interconnectedness but makes the connections between them explicit. This overt relationality is reinforced by Anaxagoras's polysyndetic *kai*, which stresses connection but leaves its nature vague.[100] Ubiquitous but underdetermined, the relations between the things become open to interpretation and contestation. That is, they become political.

Thus a politics of horizontality that is, at most, obscurely adumbrated in Anaxagoras's cosmological theory is made fully manifest—*endēlotata*—in his paratactical style. Form pushes thought, enacting a new distribution of the sensible and opening new political possibilities. This reading of the politics of parataxis does not negate the reading that sees it as part of Nous's surveillance. In actuality, there is no way to decide between these two hermeneutic perspectives, between Nous's sovereign gaze and a formal community of equal things. How could one decide, for instance, whether Anaxagoras's substantivized adjectives represent the nomination and distribution of sovereign power/knowledge or the ontological leveling that bestows dignity on each individual thing? That undecidability is not a contingent feature of the theory, the result of its fragmentary condition or intellectual incoherence. Instead, it is a necessary entailment both of the openness of the form—the underdetermined nature of paratactic connections—and of the nature of *kratos*, which in the final reckoning is never self-positing and *autokrates*, for all it may claim to be, but is always the effect of political contest.

In Anaxagoras's cosmos, Nous wins that contest. Indeed, as we saw, he has always already won and *has* to have won, for his victory is the enabling condition

100. As a supremely general and generic copular conjunction, *kai* reinforces the openness of paratactical connections: see Trenker 1960, 30–60. Cf. Hayles 1990, 398: "Parataxis does not necessarily mean that there is no relation between the terms put into juxtaposition. Rather the relation, unspecified except for proximity, is polysemous and unstable."

of cosmology as a philosophical endeavor. But the competition decisively concluded in the physical theory carries on in the aesthetic form of the text. Anaxagoras's prose is a site of permanent struggle, where alternative visions of power play out without ever being decided. The style is thus political in the most active sense: it makes politics possible and is politics in action. Politics are aesthetic, a matter of visibility and invisibility, the disposition of elements in, under, or next to one another. Aesthetics are also political, as Rancière says: "The aesthetic experience—as a refiguration of the forms of visibility and intelligibility of artistic practice and reception—intervenes in the distribution of the sensible."[101] Anaxagoras's deceptively simple style gives us a vision of what is all but invisible in his cosmology. By making manifest a distribution of the sensible rendered imperceptible by Nous's *diakosmēsis* it preserves the possibility of an alternative politics that endures, obscurely, within that metaphysical sovereignty, for "just as in the beginning so too now all things are together" (B6/D25).

101. Rancière 2009b, 5; cf. 2009a, 25.

5

Democritus and the Poetics of (N)othing

I have nothing to say
and I am saying it *and that is*
poetry

—JOHN CAGE

ONTOLOGY'S SECRET STOWAWAY

In this final chapter we circle back, in good Presocratic fashion, to where we began: the aporetic relation, intrinsic to ontology, between *logos* and *to on*. Parmenides, as we saw in chapter 1, sustains a precarious unity between language and being by rigorously excluding nonbeing from both: Is Not is not and must not be (Parm. B2.5/D6.5, B6.2/D7.2, B7.1/D8.1, B8.17–18/D8.22–23); accordingly it cannot be thought or named (B8.17/D8.22), known or spoken (B2.7–8/D6.7–8). Nonbeing strains the relation between language and being to the breaking point. How does one speak of nonbeing without granting it being, rendering one's own *logos* self-negating and nonsensical? The sophist Gorgias poses this question in his treatise "On Nonbeing." What is not surely does not exist, for if it did, it would be and not be at the same time, which is absurd (Gorg. B3.67/D26b.67). To try to speak of nothing is immediately to feel the tension between *logos* and *to on*; the fundamental grammar of existentiality and predication makes it impossible to say what nothing is or even *that* nothing is. It stands to reason that "to say nothing" in ancient Greek (*ouden legein*) meant to talk nonsense. Nothing is the ultimate aporia of ontology.[1]

Epigraph: From "Lecture on Nothing," by John Cage. In *Silence: Lectures and Writings by John Cage.* Middletown, Conn., Wesleyan University Press, 109. Copyright © 1961 by the John Cage Trust. Used by permission.

1. John Cage muses on this aporia in his "Lecture on Nothing." The typography is original; the line ends "and that is poetry as I need it." "Is not" is as complicated a philosophical question as "is." It is explored at length not only in Gorgias's "On Nonbeing," but also by Plato at *Prm.* 160b5–166c5; *Soph.* 237a–39c, 255e–261a. Thom (2002) examines the problem of nonbeing and how ancient philosophers

Democritus does not seek to circumvent this aporia but rather embraces it and around it constructs a novel poetics of being. He encompasses nonbeing within his *logos* while still preserving its character as unspeakable. He does not do this by making space for the void. The void figures nonbeing as a real and positive entity, the ontological equal of the atom, as Democritus makes clear in his most famous fragment: "By convention sweet and by convention bitter, by convention hot, by convention cold, by convention color, but in reality atoms and void" (*eteēi de atoma kai kenon*, B9/D14).[2] Instead, Democritus incorporates nonbeing into his ontology by inventing a new lexeme, one that does not so much signify nonbeing as embody it within language. That lexeme is *den*. *Den* is a neologism formed from the Greek word *mēden* or *ouden*, "nothing," which was itself originally a combination of the compound negative adverb (*oude* in statements of fact, *mēde* in subjective statements, both meaning "not even") and the neuter singular adjective *hen* ("one"). *Den* is produced by a false division of *ouden* or *mēden* such that the *de*, originally part of the negation, is treated as if it were part of the adjective *hen*. That is, instead of *mēd-hen*, "nothing" is erroneously parsed as *mē-den*. Translators trying to render the term in English have proposed "'othing."[3]

The *den* appears only obliquely within Democritus's discourse. Aristotle mentions it in a list of synonyms for the atom (A37/D29); likewise Galen, who in quoting B9/D14 glosses atoms and void as *den* and *ouden* (A49/D23b). Plutarch reports Democritus as saying that "the 'othing (*den*) exists no more than the nothing (*mēden*), calling the body *den* and the void *mēden*, on the grounds that this too has a certain nature and its own existence" (*Adv. Col.* 1109A = B156/D33). Diels-Kranz consider this a verbatim quotation, but Laks-Most think that only the words *den* and *mēden* are Democritus's own. These scanty citations point up one of the signal difficulties of working on Democritus. The text of the atomists is bedeviled, even

---

addressed it, but does not discuss Democritus. On the contribution of the atomists, see Laks 2004, 14–20.

2. The fragment is quoted by Sextus Empiricus (*Math.* 7.135) and repeated in slightly abbreviated form by Galen (B125, A49/D23a, b) and Diogenes Laertius (B117/D24). Diels-Kranz's fragment B9 combines two Democritean sentences quoted in this passage of Sextus. When I cite B9 I am referring to this sentence; I refer to the second (Laks-Most's D15) as B9a.

3. Diels translates it *das Ichts;* Cassin (2017, 34) proposes *ien* (from *rien*) or *iun* (from *ni un*). Other translators dodge the issue: Taylor 1999b; Graham 2010: "thing"; Laks-Most: "something"; Luria 2007: "l'essere." On the etymology, see Moorhouse 1962, 236; Luria 2007, 967–68; and Cassin 2020, 102–6 (~ 2017, 29–31). That the false etymology is deliberate and designed to be noticed is suggested by the only other occurrence of the word in Greek literature, in Alcaeus fr. 320 L-P: "And nothing (*ouden*) would come from 'othing (*den*)" (*kai k'ouden ek denos genoito*). The phrase probably means something like "anything can come to nought." It expresses this by way of a complex linguistic joke, deriving *ouden* from *den* by addition of the negation (rather than the reverse): etymology is made to replicate semantics as something (*den*) produces nothing (*ouden*) twice over. But the "something" that produces "nothing" is itself produced from "nothing," so in fact etymology reverses semantics. Democritus seems to have arrived at the term independently from Alcaeus (Moorhouse 1962, 238).

by the low transmission standards of early Greek philosophy. There are virtually no remaining verbatim fragments of Leucippus, the founder of atomic theory, and not much more of Democritus, who developed and disseminated the theory.[4] The few words of theirs we do have are buried within great masses of doxographical testimony aiming to explicate the atomists' thought. Discerning the text of the Presocratic philosophers is never straightforward, as we have seen throughout, but with Democritus the project comes up against its limits, and we are often dealing with what is not there as much as what is. The challenge is to interpret the status of this not-there: to differentiate the absence of Democritus's text from the absence within Democritus's text, the contingent void of transmission from the essential void within Democritus's own thought.

These two voids overlap in the *den*. Barbara Cassin, reading Democritus with Lacan, argues that the radical nature of the *den* has been obscured by the doxographic tradition, in particular by Aristotle.[5] Aristotle assimilates the *den* to the atom, which he views as a tiny fragment of Parmenidean being, glittering against the empty background of the void. Atoms and void alike have a positive being; together they constitute a physics and metaphysics of unadulterated presence. Aristotle thus treats Democritus as a material positivist, the philosopher of atomic reality. But in so doing, Cassin charges, Aristotle evades the challenge of the *den*. Cassin draws on Heinz Wismann's brilliant study of Democritus, which argues for the primacy of nonbeing in his thought: producing something by subtraction from nothing, the *den*, he proposes, renders being "a privative state of nonbeing, its positivity just a lure."[6] Being is literally less than nothing.

For Wismann and Cassin, the *den* thus names a fundamentally different kind of being from Parmenides's *To Eon*. Whereas the latter is eternal, ungenerated, and undying, with the *den*, being comes *into* being out of nonbeing. Dependent on and derivative of nonbeing, being is no longer autonomous and self-grounding as it was for Parmenides; nor is it pure and homogeneous, for the *d'* of *den* preserves a remnant of *mēden* within it. So *den* cannot simply be assimilated to the atom as positive body, *pace* Aristotle, Plutarch, and Galen, but instead figures the atom as a negated negativity. Nor can it be assimilated to void as the positive place of the atom's nonpresence, for *den* identifies a nonpresence (*mēden*)

4. Diels-Kranz's division of Leucippus (DK 67) from Democritus (DK 68) and the difficulty with both authors of segregating A fragments from B fragments make their edition of the atomists particularly unsatisfying. I have profited from other editions, including Taylor 1999b and Luria 2007, but especially Laks and Most 2016, vol. 7, whose judgment I generally follow as to which fragments are verbatim. I refer here to Democritus but, following current practice, I make no attempt to distinguish his thought from that of Leucippus (for such an attempt see Bailey 1964; and Graham 2008a). Diels-Kranz numbers refer to Democritus unless otherwise specified.

5. Cassin 2017, 28–29, 34–36; cf. Wismann 2010, 6–9, 28–36, 60–62.

6. Wismann 2010, 65. The key ideas were first published in "Atomos Idea," *Neue Hefte für Philosophie* 15/16 (1979), 34–52. Wismann stresses the speculative nature of the atomist's materialism. He is surprisingly uninterested in the *den*, which he mentions only in passing (48, 65, 84).

within the atom itself. Thus while void can stand alongside atoms in a positive (Parmenidean) ontology, both equally real, the *den* poses a more radical challenge to that ontology. It suggests that an account of reality is not fully exhausted by "is" and "is not." Instead, it must be able to accommodate something that is simultaneously being and nonbeing and to conceptualize the atom (in Wismann's apt phrase) as an "avatar of the void."

Cassin, along with Mladen Dolar and Slavoj Žižek, recuperates the *den* as a way of thinking beyond the binarisms that have structured Western philosophy: not only being and nonbeing, presence and absence, but *morphē* and *hulē*, idealism and materialism, male and female, sense and non-sense.[7] For these theorists, the *den* points not to physical reality but to the Lacanian Real, that register that exceeds the symbolic order of language and knowledge. The Real cannot be spoken or represented: it manifests in the symbolic only in the form of what Lacan terms the *objet a*. A bone of the Real that "remains stuck in the gullet of the signifier," the *objet a*, while unpronounceable in itself, engenders the circumlocutions and displacements that constitute the syntax of the symbolic.[8] In this way, it shapes, even as it eludes, discourse. Lacan himself drew a connection between his *objet a* and Democritus's *den* in his essay "L'Étourdit." In the *den*, he proposes, Democritus smuggles the Real into discourse as "a stowaway" (*passager clandestin*).[9] Indeed, *den* is a stowaway twice over: as something derived from nothing it smuggles nonbeing into being; as the marker of this (non)being it smuggles the Real into language. The secret bearer of nonbeing within both *to on* and the *logos* about it, *den* is, as Dolar puts it, an "ontological scandal."[10]

Cassin, Dolar, and Žižek track the trajectory of that *passager clandestin* within the history of Western philosophy, from Aristotle to Hegel to Lacan. But *den* is

7. Cassin 2017, 2020, 93–125; Dolar 2013a, 2013b; and Žižek 2012, 58–60. For Cassin, the *den* belongs to language as "ab-sense" (neither sense nor its simple negation) and to a "sophistic" tradition that rejects Aristotle's reduction of language to univocal meaning. Dolar (2013a, 22–26, 2013b, 233–38) takes atomism's binary of atoms and void as the ancestor of Hegel's dialectic of being and nonbeing and sees the *den* as a (non)entity that escapes that binary. While for Dolar the *den* highlights the contrast between Hegel and Lacan, for Žižek (2012, 58–60, cf. 495, 957) it marks their convergence, prefiguring the "Hegelian-Lacanian" conception of the Real as divided and incomplete.

8. Lacan 1977, 270. Over the course of his career Lacan used different terms for this marker of the Real within the symbolic: *objet a*, the unary trait, the phallic signifier, the Thing. In the later seminars he turned to the matheme, on the theory that "mathematization alone reaches a real" (1998, 131). Formed through subtraction and governing (as we shall see) a calculus of nonequation, *den* might be considered a Democritean matheme. Badiou (2005, 9) proposes that Lacan saw in the Presocratics' poetic form "a grandiose anticipation of the matheme" (see Conclusion, n. 15), but does not discuss the *den*. Lucid accounts of the Lacanian Real are offered by Fink (1995, 24–31); and Eyers (2012).

9. Lacan 1973, 51: "Démocrite en effet nous fit cadeau de l'ἄτομος, du réel radical, à en élider le pas (μή). . . . Moyennant quoi le δέν fut bien le passager clandestin dont le clam fait maintenant notre destin." Lacan also links the *den* to the Real in his discussion of Aristotle's *tukhē* and *automaton* (1977, 53–64) as the object that gives thought access to negativity.

10. Dolar 2013a, 25 (~ 2013b, 236). Žižek 2012, 60: "*Den* lies outside the scope of the unity of *logos* and being."

also a stowaway within Democritus's own thought. Authoritative studies of Democritus by specialists such as C. C. W. Taylor or Solomon Luria generally view the atomist through the same lens as Aristotle. They interrogate every aspect of atomic theory except the *den*.[11] No scholar of ancient philosophy, as far as I can tell, has engaged with the readings of Cassin, Dolar, and Žižek, who in turn rarely cite these scholars and whose interest in Democritus is limited almost exclusively to the *den*.[12] This striking noncommunication in modern readings of Democritus produces a parallax view of his thought: look at him from one perspective and you see the reality of atoms and void; approach him from the other and you see the radical Real of the *den*.[13]

This chapter seeks to bring these two interpretive schools into dialogue. It does not discount or dispute the traditional (Aristotelian) view of Democritus but challenges it by juxtaposing a view from the angle of the *den*. It is, in this sense, an experiment in parallactic reading. I draw on the insights of Cassin, Dolar, and Žižek, but take them back to the text of Democritus in an attempt to understand how the *den* appears—or significantly fails to appear—within the atomist's own thought. With the *den* Democritus brings nonbeing into ontology, but in a form that does not allow for explicit theoretical articulation. He invents the word but does not put it to work within his discourse. He does not offer an account of the *den*. Instead, he gives us a theory of atoms and void. If the *den* is a stowaway from the Real, atomic theory is an account of reality ("in reality atoms and void," B9/D14). Democritus presents this as "an account of all things," a *logos peri tōn xumpantōn*, and indeed it boasts a comprehensiveness and coherence unsurpassed until Aristotle. But in elaborating this totalizing theory, it is as if Democritus "forgot" that he himself had invented the *den*. The *den* thus appears within Democritus's system precisely as its exclusion, that which doesn't fit and eludes its totalizing reach. Democritus's philosophy is a theory of everything and of nothing but not of 'othing.

And yet if the *den* does not (or cannot) receive theoretical elaboration, it does exert a latent force on Democritus's thought, like some philosophical dark matter

11. The *den* is barely mentioned in many seminal or synoptic treatments of atomism, including Bailey 1964, 118; Barnes 1982, 342–77; Kirk, Raven, and Schofield 1983, 402–33; Taylor 1999b; and Berryman 2023.

12. This despite the fact that Cassin is herself a scholar of ancient philosophy (and was a student of Wismann). Wismann's own status is symptomatic of the split: he is credited by Cassin and Dolar but his study of Democritus does not appear in the bibliographies of Furley 1987 or Taylor 1999b, nor in Palmer's *Oxford Bibliographies Online* entry for Democritus.

13. Dolar 2013a, 26 (~ 2013b, 238). Žižek (2006) theorizes the parallax as two closely connected perspectives between which, however, there can be no synthesis or mediation. Žižek's critical intervention is to show how the difference between the two perspectives reinscribes a difference within each perspective. Thus we will see how the divergence in the reception history reproduces a gap or void within Democritus's own theory, an opacity marked by the *den*. In a way, then, Democritus anticipates his own future reception.

that can be observed only in its distorting effects.[14] Noticing those effects produces a radically unfamiliar vision of ancient atomism. This chapter traces the impact of the *den* on Democritus's physics, where it renders the atom heterogeneous and unstable, destabilizing in turn the physical laws predicated on it; and on his ethics, where the self-sufficient ethical subject—the subject as atom—is shown to be structured around a psychic void. We will also trace the *den*'s effects on Democritus's *logos*. A point of opacity within a philosophical language that aims for transparency and an omission within a theoretical discourse that aims for universality, the *den* marks the limits of Democritus's discourse and the atomic reality it purports to reveal. In so doing, it sets that discourse in a particular relation to truth and knowledge that, as I will suggest at the end, characterizes it—more than any superficial similarity to modern atomic physics—as a science. In this way, *den* figures the aporia within ontology as a philosophical and discursive project that has been one of the central themes of this book. Situated at the asymptotic nonconvergence between *onta* and *logos*, the *den* encapsulates both the impossibility of bringing being into language and the generative force of that impossibility.

ATOMS, VOID, AND THE INDIFFERENT PHYSICS OF THE *DEN*

The atomists start from a double *arkhē*, as Aristotle explains in the *Metaphysics*.

> Λεύκιππος δὲ καὶ ὁ ἑταῖρος αὐτοῦ Δημόκριτος στοιχεῖα μὲν τὸ πλῆρες καὶ τὸ κενὸν εἶναί φασι, λέγοντες τὸ μὲν ὂν τὸ δὲ μὴ ὄν, τούτων δὲ τὸ μὲν πλῆρες καὶ στερεόν, τὸ ὄν, τὸ δὲ κενὸν καὶ μανόν, τὸ μὴ ὄν (διὸ καὶ οὐθὲν μᾶλλον τὸ ὂν τοῦ μὴ ὄντος εἶναί φασιν, ὅτι οὐδὲ τὸ κενὸν ⟨ἔλαττον⟩ τοῦ σώματος), αἴτια δὲ τῶν ὄντων ταῦτα ὡς ὕλην. (*Metaph.* 1.4 985b4–10 < 67A6/D31 [Diels-Kranz's text])
>
> Leucippus and his associate Democritus say that the basic elements are the full and the empty, meaning what is (*to on*) and what is not (*to mē on*). Of these the former is full and solid, what is, and the latter empty and sparse, what is not (and for this reason they also say that what is exists no more than what is not, because the void [exists] no less than the body), and these are the causes of the things that exist, comprising their material.

In the form of atoms and void, what is (*to on*) and what is not (*to mē on*) occupy the same ontological footing: nonbeing exists no less than being, and the two share top billing as the origins and primary elements (*stoikheia*) of the atomists' cosmology.[15]

14. This is the dynamic of the Lacanian Real, which is not some "real thing" beyond the symbolic, but, as Eyers (2012, 61–93) stresses, a projection of the symbolic's lack (incompleteness, incoherence), an external cause retroactively posited on the basis of its effects within signification.

15. See further Diog. Laert. 9.44 (< A1/D13); Simpl. *in Phys.* 28.15 (< A38/D32); 67A8/D32, 67A12/≠LM, 67A14/D61, A44/≠LM, A46/≠LM.

In *On Generation and Corruption*, Aristotle explains this dual *arkhē* as an attempt to reconcile Parmenides's unitary, unchanging being with the empirical experience of plurality and change.

> ὁμολογήσας δὲ ταῦτα μὲν τοῖς φαινομένοις, τοῖς δὲ τὸ ἓν κατασκευάζουσιν ὡς οὐκ ἂν κίνησιν οὖσαν ἄνευ κενοῦ τό τε κενὸν μὴ ὂν καὶ τοῦ ὄντος οὐθὲν μὴ ὄν, φησιν εἶναι τὸ κυρίως ὂν παμπλῆρες ὄν, ἀλλ' εἶναι τὸ τοιοῦτον οὐχ ἕν, ἀλλ' ἄπειρα τὸ πλῆθος καὶ ἀόρατα διὰ σμικρότητα τῶν ὄγκων. ταῦτα δ' ἐν τῶι κενῶι φέρεσθαι (κενὸν γὰρ εἶναι), καὶ συνιστάμενα μὲν γένεσιν ποιεῖν, διαλυόμενα δὲ φθοράν. (*Gen. corr.* 1.8 325a25–32 = D30/67A7 [Laks-Most's text])

> Agreeing in this respect with the phenomena, but agreeing with those who maintain of the one that there could not be change without void, that the void does not exist and that nothing that does not exist pertains to being, he [Leucippus] says that what properly exists is entirely full, but that such a being is not one, but they are boundless in number and invisible because of the smallness of their mass. These travel in the void (for the void exists) and by coming together they cause generation and by separating, destruction.

"Little beings (*mikrai ousiai*) boundless in number," atoms are ungenerated and eternal, unchanging, indivisible, and homogeneous: as "what properly exists" (*to kuriōs on*), they are Parmenides's *To Eon* miniaturized and pluralized.[16] These tiny beings combine and separate to produce all the phenomena in our world. This positive ontology of atomic being also positivizes nonbeing in the form of the void. Void is understood as the physical vacuity (*kenon*) that enables atoms to move, join, and separate.[17] "An interval in which there is no perceptible body," as Aristotle says (*diastēma en hōi mēden esti sōma aisthēton, Ph.* 4.6 213a28–29), the void enables the atom's presence: *atoma* can only "be there" because the *kenon* provides a place for them to be. Likewise void sustains the atom's atomic identity: an atom can only be an individual because it is separated from other atoms by void, and it can only be indivisible because it contains no void within it and therefore cannot be cut.[18] So, on the one hand, void as what is not functions as a support for what is. On the other hand, in void nonbeing is granted a positive (albeit empty) being of its own, equally real as the atom, "for the void exists" (*kenon gar einai*).[19]

16. *Mikrai ousiai*: Arist. *Dem.* fr. 208 Rose (= A37/D29). Mourelatos (2004) lays out clearly the ways in which the atom meets (and fails to meet) the "Parmenidean requirements" for being. On Democritus as a response to the Eleatics, see Von Fritz 1938, 15–17; Stokes 1971, 218–36; Furley 1974; Wardy 1988; Curd 1998, 180–216; Sedley 2008a; and Clarke 2019, 146–66; and as a mediation between monism and pluralism, Bailey 1964, 69–76.

17. Cf. Arist. *Ph.* 4.6 213b3–22 (< 67A19/D39): void receives; it contracts and compresses; it absorbs. Simplicius explains that void "is yielding and does not resist" the atoms that move through it (*in Phys.* 1318.31–19.2 < A58/D36). On the relation of void to atomic motion, see Berryman 2002; and Mourelatos 2004, 52–53.

18. Curd 1998, 184–88, 201–3; cf. Stokes 1971, 218–22.

19. Serres 2018, 83: "The void is the zero state of matter; the atom is the minimum state." Sedley (1982, 179) believes Aristotle got it wrong, and the atomists understood void not as empty space but

In this conception of atoms and void, the atomists' double *arkhai* work together to affirm the positivity of being. Together they provide an exhaustive description of reality: atoms and void are what is and they are all that is.

Exegetes both ancient and modern have largely followed Aristotle in viewing Democritus as a material positivist and have worked to reconstruct the details of his atomic physics, to understand the nature of the atom and the principles governing its movement and interactions in the void.[20] But in so doing, as Cassin argues, they sidestep the most challenging aspect of Democritus's theory, the inextricability of being and nonbeing formalized in the *den*. For Aristotle, followed by Galen and Plutarch, the *den* is simply a synonym for the atom as positive substance: "He calls each of the substances (*tōn ousiōn*) by these names: the *den*, the compact, what is (*to on*)."[21] But *to den*, as Cassin stresses, implies a very different ontology from the atom and cannot be reduced to Parmenides's *To Eon* under a new name. What would Democritean physics look like if we viewed it, not from the familiar angle of atoms and void—those double *arkhai* of presence—but from the parallactic perspective of the *den?*

First, the physics of the *den* splits the atom. The word "atom" comes from the adjective *atomos*, meaning "unable to be cut." The *den*, by contrast, is the product of an ostentatious and artificial cut, the incomplete excision of *mēden*. If one point of calling atoms uncuttable is to signal that they are completely homogeneous, with no parts that can be separated off, the atom as *den* is intrinsically heterogeneous, a compound of *-de* and *hen*. As *den*, the atom not only could be divided; it would have to be divided in order to become a positive autonomous one (*hen*).[22] In this scission, what is is generated out of what is not. Parmenides decreed that something cannot come from nothing, but the *den* does just that: it is something—a word, at a minimum, but also the (non)entity it names—generated out of (the word and [non]substance) nothing. Moreover, it retains that nothing within its being, for in the false division of *mēden*, the excision of the negative is incomplete: the *d'* is a shard of the nothing (*mēden*) left in the one (*hen*). This means that

as the negative substance that occupies it; cf. Kirk, Raven, and Schofield 1983, 415–16; contra, Furley (1987, 117–22), for whom void is "not anything in particular," the negation of the properties of what is. Attempts have been made to differentiate *mēden* from *ouden* as different types of nonexistent (Bailey 1964, 118–19; Cassin 2017, 29–30), but the ancient testimonia use both terms for the void and the Greek rules of negation militate against overinterpreting the difference.

20. For a clear synopsis of the physics of atoms see Taylor 1999b, 69–90, 160–95 (abbreviated at 1999a, 181–85).

21. Arist. *Dem.* fr. 208 Rose = A37/D29. Cf. Gal. *Elem. Hipp.* 1.2 (= A49/D23b); Plut. *Adv. Col.* 1109A (= B156/D33). "If the *den* ends up being a 'stowaway,' [as Lacan says] it is because Aristotle forbade it the first-class deck—the open field of 'philosophy'" (Cassin 2017, 5 ~ 2020, 101).

22. There is a telling variation in Galen's gloss on fragment B9/D14: "In reality all things are *den* and *mēden,* for he has also said this, naming the atoms *den* and the void *mēden*" (A49/D23b). *Den* here is an editorial correction for the manuscripts' *hen:* someone, whether Galen himself or a later copyist, thought of atoms as "one" and an antonym of nothing. *Den* complicates that antimony. The *de-* of *mēde/oude* emphasizes the negation of the one: not *even* one.

the division between being and nonbeing is internal to being itself. Thus in place of the positive ontology of atoms and void, we have in *den* a being derived from nonbeing and bearing nonbeing within it. Neither atom nor void but merging aspects of both, a thing that is also nothing, *den* is "the parasite of ontology."[23]

Blurring the fundamental distinction between is and is not, the *den* introduces something like a quantum indeterminacy into Democritus's physics. Seen from this angle, the atom oscillates weirdly between matter and immateriality. In B9/D14 ("in reality atoms and void") atoms are *atoma*, the neuter plural form of the adjective agreeing, the doxographers suggest, with an implied noun *sōmata* (bodies).[24] Corporeality is also suggested by another Democritean term for atoms, *ta nasta*, "compact things" (A37/D29, A47/D37), and by their possession of shape, size, and (according to some testimonia) weight.[25] But alongside the neuter *ta atoma* we also find the feminine, *hai atomoi*, for which Plutarch supplies the noun *ideai* (forms).[26] Are atoms form or matter? Are they somehow both at once, as Galen suggests when he writes, apparently without sensing a contradiction, "*hai atomoi* [sc. *ideai*], being all small *sōmata*, are without qualities" (A49/≠ LM)? The atom as *den* oscillates between *hulē* and *morphē*, as Dolar observes, posing a challenge to Aristotle's hylomorphism *avant la lettre.*[27]

23. Cassin 2020, 107; cf. 2017, 34.

24. B9/D14 contains the only direct reference to atoms in the text considered verbatim by Laks-Most, and thus, if they are correct, the only form we can confidently attribute to Democritus himself (cf. A49/D63, B117/D24, B125/D23a, all quotations of this fragment). *Sōmata* is supplied at 67A1/D80a, 67A6/D31, 67A13/R95, 67A14/D61, 67A15/D45, 67A16/R42, A43/≠LM, A47/D37, R94, A49/D43, A58/D36, A101/D130, B156/D33. Even if the neuter adjective stands alone as a substantive, it substantivizes the atom.

25. *Nasta:* see further 67A8/D32, 67A14/≠LM, A46/≠LM, A125/≠LM. Atoms are frequently characterized in the testimonia as *sterea* (solid): 67A6/D31, 67A7/R18, A45/≠LM, A60/D40, D68, A135§82/R59. Whether atoms had weight was disputed: see A58/D36, A47/D50–51, A60/D48, A61/D49. O'Brien (1981, 330–47) argues that they did; cf. Furley 1983. Some of the diction of their interactions suggests the collision of massy bodies (e.g. *allēlotupia,* A47/D53; *plēgē,* A47/D54), but Democritean atoms do not fall downward, as Epicurean atoms do: see Furley 1987, 150–51; O'Keefe 1996; Salem 1996, 89–95; and Taylor 1999b, 179–84.

26. *Adv. Col.* 1111A (A57/D34). This supplement may be supported by the fact that Democritus wrote a treatise entitled *Peri Ideōn* (B6/D5). Other possible feminine nouns are *phuseis* (A58/D36) and *ousiai* (A37/D29). Imagined as forms, the atoms could have conceptual shape and size without physical mass, and their indivisibility could be theoretical, as argued by Furley (1974, 1987, 125–31); contra, Barnes 1982, 352–60. This might explain the mysterious possibility of an atom the size of a cosmos (A47/D62). But the question is debated: see Alfieri 1979, 199–204; Konstan 1982; Sorabji 1983, 354–57; Makin 1989; Hasper 2006; and Sedley 2008a.

27. Dolar 2013a, 20. Wismann goes so far as to speculate that the famous materialists were in fact idealists (2010, 51–66). Cf. Hegel 1975b, 144, 1955, 303; Lacan 1973, 51, 1977, 64; Alfieri 1979, esp. 59–60; and Joly 1984, 262. This ambivalence is partly what makes Democritus attractive to thinkers, from Nietzsche and Marx to Dolar and Žižek, rethinking both materialism and idealism. On Nietzsche's

This atomic indeterminacy is generalized as a universal law in the so-called indifference principle that operates across Democritus's system.[28] The indifference principle takes the form *mē mallon ē*: "not more X than Y." This principle governs Democritus's physics. Atoms combine in the ways they do because of the infinite diversity of their shapes, "since nothing is more one sort of thing than another" (Simpl. *in Phys.* 28.15 < A38/D32). It also governs his metaphysics, as Aristotle suggests in the passage of the *Metaphysics* quoted at the start of this section: the atomists "say that what is exists no more than what is not, because the void [exists] no less than the body."[29] Plutarch puts it pithily: "He declares that the *den* exists no more than the *mēden*" (*mē mallon to den ē to mēden einai*).[30] The formula was clearly striking. Simplicius repeats it four times in the space of two paragraphs (twice in reference to the heterogeneity of atomic shapes and twice to the equality of being and nonbeing), and it was apparently parroted by Democritus's disciples.[31]

The indifference principle is generally understood as a negative corollary of the principle of sufficient reason, which C. C. W. Taylor takes to be the atomists' primary logical axiom. While that principle dictates that nothing can be true without a reason for it being so and not otherwise, the indifference formula posits that in the absence of such a reason, one thing is no more true than its alternatives.[32] But if the *mē mallon* formula reaffirms the general hegemony of the law of sufficient reason, it also marks off a terrain on which it does not function, a terrain where the insufficiency of reason is itself an operative principle. Structured as a negated comparison, the phrase asserts the irreducibility of difference even as it

early fascination with Democritus, see Porter 2000, 82–126; for Marx's views on atomism, see Marx 2006; and McCarthy 1990, 19–56.

28. Makin (1993, 8–14, 49–97) believes Democritus's physical and epistemological theories arose out of his interest in this mode of argument, which he adapted from Zeno. On the role of the principle in Democritus's thought, see the clear and helpful discussion of Curd (1998, 188–98).

29. Arist. *Metaph.* 1.4 985b4–8 (< 67A6/D31). *Elatton* is supplied by Zeller and accepted by Diels. The manuscripts' reading (without the supplement) makes void exist no more than body, contradicting the preceding clause.

30. Plut. *Adv. Col.* 1108F–1109A (B156/D33). Diels takes this as the original Democritean formulation. On the formula in Plutarch's *Against Colotes*, see Matson 1963; and Kechagia 2011, 313–21. In that treatise, Colotes (the "he" in the sentence quoted) interprets Democritus's use of the formula along epistemological lines as a kind of Protagorean relativism, while Plutarch argues for an ontological interpretation. As Kechagia points out, both can be right and simply focused on different parts of Democritus's theory.

31. Simpl. *in Phys.* 28.4–27 (67A8, A38/D32). Sen. *Ep.* 88.43 (B4/R74) attributes it to Nausiphanes. The same principle is adduced to explain the variations in sense perception: one person's perception is no more accurate than another's (Arist. *Metaph.* 4.5 1009b10 [A112/R52]). Cf. Sext. Emp. *Pyr.* 1.213 (R106/≠DK), who distinguishes Democritus's use of the phrase from the Skeptics'; see DeLacy 1958.

32. Taylor 1999b, 162, 166–67, 189–93. Both principles have many permutations, analyzed by Makin (1993).

ostensibly levels it. It is a comparison that declines to compare and an equation that doesn't really equate: instead of a simple identity (X = Y) we get an approximate equivalence (X≈Y) in the form of a nonaddition (not more) that is also a nonsubtraction (not less), as Aristotle implies when he conflates the positive version of the formula ("what is exists no more than what is not") with the negative ("the void exists no less than the body").

This equivocal equation reiterates the incomplete subtraction of the *den* and generalizes its logic. Etymologically, *den* is literally no more than *mēden*. Thus to write, as Plutarch does, "the *den* exists no more than the *mēden*" is both a truth and a tautology. Both *mē mallon* and *den* subtract difference but do not eliminate it so as to produce a singular one, identity or the *hen*. For Parmenides Is and Is Not are binary and mutually exclusive, 1/0. But with the *den* that difference becomes a matter of indifference, formalized in the indifference principle. The distinction between being and nonbeing is irreducible but cannot be posed in binary or even comparative terms. It is a difference that makes no clear difference.

The principle of indifference governs the atomic interactions that produce the phenomenal world. Atoms are in constant motion, their rhythms, rotations, and contacts determined by their shape.[33] That shape, however, is indifferent: "The number of shapes in the atoms is boundless because nothing is more one sort of thing than another" (Simpl. *in Phys.* 28.9–10 < 67A8, A38/D32). This means that atomic motion lacks sufficient, to say nothing of necessary, reason. In this it goes against the atomists' general emphasis on *anankē* (necessity), a term that appears frequently in the extant fragments and seems to denote not strict determinism but rather an insistence on a cause or sufficient reason. As Leucippus wrote in one of his only surviving verbatim fragments, "No thing comes about at random (*matēn*), but everything for a reason (*ek logou*) and by necessity (*hup' anankēs*)" (67B2/D73).[34] Aëtius, our source for this fragment, equates the atomists' *anankē* specifically with atomic interaction.[35] But if those interactions are determined by the

33. Democritus's terms for atomic movement are *rhusmos* (rhythm), *diathigē* (touching), and *tropē* (rotation) (67A6/D31, A38/D32). As Von Fritz notes (1938, 25–28, followed by Wismann [2010, 7–9, 29–32, 60–61]; Cassin [2017, 37]; and Dolar [2013a, 24]), these terms suggest a flux and dynamism that Aristotle fixes into static ontological states with his translation of the three terms as *skhēma* (shape), *taxis* (order), and *thesis* (position) (*Metaph.* 1.4 985b15–19 < 67A6/D31). See the discussion by Mourelatos (2004).

34. Aristotle praises the atomists for proposing "that nothing happens by *tukhē*, but that there is some determinate cause (*aition*) for everything we say happens spontaneously or by chance" (*Ph.* 2.4 195b36–96a3 = A68/D76a; cf. A36/R28), although he observes that they failed to offer an *aition* for motion (Arist. *Metaph.* 1.4 985b19–20; cf. *Metaph.* 12.6 1071b31–34 = 67A18/R37, 67A6/R38, A67/R31). For assessments of Aristotle's critique, see Balme 1941; Barnes 1982, 429–32; Hirsch 1990; and Johnson 2005, 104–12.

35. Aët. 1.26.2 < A66/D75. See also Arist. *Dem.* fr. 208 Rose (= A37/D29): atomic aggregates hold together until "some stronger necessity (*anankē*) from the environment" disperses them. That necessity can only be the impact of other atoms. Diogenes Laertius associates *anankē* closely with the

shapes of atoms, and atomic shapes are a matter of indifference—no more likely to be of one sort than another—then there is a fundamental contingency within causal necessity. This *tukhē* is not merely epistemological, the scientist's acknowledgment of the limits of his knowledge of natural causes, as Taylor suggests.[36] Instead, it marks a more fundamental ontological indeterminacy. Insufficient reason is not a lack of known cause, it *is* the cause. To that extent, contingency is *anankē* and the sufficient/insufficient cause of atomic motion.

By positing contingency at the primary causal level of the cosmos, the *mē mallon* principle introduces a swerve at the heart of Democritus's physics. In *The Birth of Physics*, Michel Serres draws a strong line between the early atomists and Epicurus who, Serres proposes, revolutionized atomic theory with the introduction of the *clinamen*, the swerve, the minimal difference from the rigid parallel fall of gravity without which there could be no atomic interaction and hence no generation.[37] For Serres the *clinamen* represents an openness and contingency within Epicurean physics that Democritus failed to grasp. Yet if, as Serres says, the *clinamen* is a minimal deviation from perpetual self-sameness—"to exist rather than," as he puts it—there could hardly be a more precise formulation of this idea than Democritus's indifference principle.[38] Moreover, *mē mallon* locates the *clinamen* not just within atomic motion (as in Epicurus) but within the atom itself. No more likely to be one shape than another, no more likely to *be* than what is not, the atom as *den* is intrinsically swervy.[39]

---

vortex (*dinē*), which comes into being during the course of cosmogenesis and determines the subsequent direction of atomic movement (Diog. Laert. 9.45 < A1/D13, 9.33 < 671A1/D80). On the atomists' conception of necessity, see Guthrie 1965, 414–19; Edmunds 1972; Alfieri 1979, 97–120; Barnes 1984; Taylor 1999b, 188–95, 1999a, 185–89; Morel 2000, 16–37; and Johnson 2009.

36. Taylor 1999a, 187: events only appear to happen by chance when we do not know the cause. Cf. Bailey 1964, 138–43; Edmunds 1972, 353–54; and Salem (1996, 77–89), who remarks that this makes chance a "sobriquet" for necessity.

37. Serres 2018. Dolar (2013a, 16–22, 2013b, 228–33) notes the recent fad for the *clinamen* and examines its treatment by Badiou and Deleuze. The dichotomy between Democritean necessity and the freedom of the swerve is present already in Marx (2006, 112–18).

38. Serres 2018, 40. Serres does credit Democritus with understanding the mathematical principles underpinning the physics of the *clinamen* (28–30, 126–28, 130–31) and even speculates that Democritus may have developed a "fluid mechanics" in his lost works (29–30). He also notes that Democritus discovered the vortex, which is a perpetual *clinamen* (24, 25, 29, 104, 114). Schmidt (2007, 77–117) examines Epicurus's rethinking of Democritus's theory of atomic motion.

39. Serres's (2018) "to exist rather than" sheds a different light on the description of atoms as "full" (*plēres*) and void as "empty" (*kenon*) or "sparse" (*manon*). In the *Metaphysics* passage quoted at the start of this section, Aristotle offers the full and the empty as Leucippan synonyms for *to on* and *to mē on*. Recalling the homogenous plenitude of Parmenidean Being (which "is all full of being," B8.24/D8.29), this formulation figures *plēres* and *kenon* as absolutes. But full and empty are relative terms, and relative precisely to one another. This is hinted at in the second Aristotle passage quoted above, from *On Generation and Corruption*: Leucippus differentiated the atom from the void, saying that "what properly exists is entirely full" (*to gar kuriōs on pamplēres on*). The existence of nonbeing requires Leucippus to assert a being surcharged with existence: *pamplēres* is a *hapax legomenon* and *to kuriōs on* nearly so. The

Atomic physics imagines atoms combining in the void to produce the phenomena around us. The atom's positive being grants phenomena a solid, though impermanent, reality. But what is the ontology of phenomena in the physics of the *den?* Like the *den*, phenomena too stand in an indeterminate relation to form and matter. This is most manifest in the case of the so-called *eidōla. Eidōla* (or *deikela*, as Democritus also calls them, B123/D146) are the images of phenomena by which we perceive them. As Theophrastus explains, every object gives off an atomic efflux (*aporrhoē*) that produces an impression on the air. This shaped air, which has solidity and color, then impresses itself on the moist surface of the eye.[40] An ancient etymologist glosses the *eidōlon* as "an efflux that is similar in form to things" (*kat' eidos homoia tois pragmasin aporrhoia*, B123/D146); they are not real things but merely their formal likeness. These airy images would seem to be paradigmatically immaterial.[41] But in fact *eidōla* are atomic aggregates and to that extent every bit as material as the objects that emit them. Theophrastus uses the material diction of stamping, carving, or casting (*tupoō*) to describe the process by which the image is produced in the air and says Democritus compared it to molding wax (*Sens.* 51 < A135/R57). Not just material, the *eidōla* are corporeal. Theophrastus worries about potential traffic jams of *eidōla* in the air when there are multiple objects in the same field of vision; he objects that the air would be so crowded with images (including those we ourselves emit) that we would be unable to see anything (Theophr. *Sens.* 53 < A135/R57). This suggests that *eidōla* are not merely likenesses of bodies but bodies themselves, at least corporeal enough to impede one another's path and block the viewer's line of sight.

These quasi-corporeal beings exhibit quasi-intelligence and quasi-agency, "a share of perception and impulsion," as Plutarch puts it (*Quaest. conv.* 682F < A77/D153). He explains that the *eidōla* "not only possess molded similarities of shape to the body . . . but also receive impressions of the motions and decisions of each person's soul and his habits and emotions which they carry along with them and, with these things, when they meet someone they speak like living beings and announce to those who receive them the opinions, arguments, and desires of those who sent them."[42] Since soul atoms are part of the atomic efflux that we are always

superlative underlines the problem of the comparative, even as it seems to solve it, for if an atom can be "entirely full" it can also be less than entirely full, "sparse" or even (relatively) "empty." In the striking diction of this passage we may sense anxiety about a comparative ontology in which the difference between is and is not is a matter not of all-or-nothing but of more-or-less.

40. Theophr. *Sens.* 50 < A135/D147. Rudolph (2016, 49–52) offers a succinct synopsis of the mechanics of Democritean vision.

41. The question of whether air is matter or immaterial (a live question at this period) reiterates rather than resolves the problem of the *eidōla*'s status. Renehan (1980, 111–12) suggests that air provided a means of conceptualizing the immaterial before Plato invented the relevant technical vocabulary.

42. *Quaest. conv.* 735A–B < A77/D152. Cf. *Quaest. conv.* 682F–683A < A77/D153: the *eidōla* emitted by jealous and malicious individuals are themselves jealous and malicious and a constant torment to

shedding, it makes sense that our *eidōla* would possess psychological as well as physical qualities.[43] As bearers of affect, ethical traits, speech, will, and desire, the *eidōla* take on a quasi-autonomous existence, separate from the subjects who emit them: they are no more likeness than real being. By the same token, in the transitive logic of indifference, phenomena themselves (including the human subject) are no more real beings than their likenesses; they are both materially and theoretically continuous with their ghostly doubles. Moreover, if Taylor is right in supposing that the atomic efflux of different objects can merge in the air to form a joint *eidōlon* (for instance, horse atoms and man atoms combining to form the *eidōlon* of a centaur), then really existent things could produce a nonexistent thing, which nonetheless exists materially (atomically) no less than they.[44] Hovering between matter and form, something and nothing, the *eidōla* exhibit the same indifferent existence as the *den* and generalize its equivocal (non)being to phenomenal reality as a whole.[45]

As Theophrastus's detailed exposition suggests, ancient commentators found *eidōla* explicable within the terms of atomic theory, and it seems likely that Democritus explained them in those terms, not in terms of the *den*. Indeed, the *den* appears manifestly in no verbatim statement of Democritus's physical theory. This is not, I think, just an effect of the lacunose state of the evidence. Nor is it, as Cassin proposes, solely the result of Aristotle's determination to overwrite the weird physics of the *den* with the binarism of atoms and void. Democritus never had an explicit theory of the *den*. And how could he? As an entity that is both/neither atom and void, there is literally no space for the *den* in a physics that is all and only atoms and void ("but in reality atoms and void," B9/D14). And yet if the *den* cannot appear manifestly in Democritus's account of the cosmos, it leaves symptomatic traces in that account: in the atom's oscillation between matter and immateriality; in the contingency within atomism's causal necessities and the indifferent ontology of its phenomena. These traces let us sense, beneath or beyond the reality of atoms and void, those twin *stoikheia* of a positivist physics, the latent Real of nonbeing within being. The *den* is not only a *passager clandestin* within the later exegesis of atomism; it is there from the *arkhē*.

their originals. Two testimonia suggest that these autonomous *eidōla*, or perhaps a particularly striking subset of them, are the origin of belief in the gods (B166/D154, A74/D209).

43. Cf. Taylor 1999b, 207: inasmuch as *psukhē* is the source of animacy, this also means "that *eidōla* of living things are themselves alive."

44. Taylor 1999b, 206.

45. Joly (1984) emphasizes the double nature of the *eidōla* as matter and form. The same ontological gray zone is occupied by the dead. Because life is itself atomic (based on the presence of *psukhē* atoms, A117/D140) one can be more or less alive (cf. A160/D141, 142): see Warren 2002a; Taylor 2007a. Perhaps this explains Democritus's interest in accounts of the dead coming back to life, apparently collected in his work "About Hades" (*Peri tou Haidou*). Žižek (2012, 60) associates the *den* with the living dead, nonbeings thought within the space of living beings.

KNOW THYSELF AND NOTHING IN EXCESS

The existence of the *eidōla* means that the individual cannot be imagined as an atomic unit, bounded and whole; she is always surrounded by a penumbra of more-or-less selves that are a part of herself and exist "no less than" she does. This has implications for Democritus's ethical theory. From one angle of the parallax, Democritus's ethical prescriptions seem to follow atomic principles, aiming to maintain psychic equilibrium amid the dynamic interchange of atomic influences and effluences. But from another angle, Democritus's ethics, like his physics, exhibit the pull of the *den*, which voids the autonomy and self-mastery of the human subject, complicating the Delphic maxim "Know Thyself" and giving new meaning to "Nothing in Excess."

We can start with fragment B9/D14: "By convention (*nomōi*) sweet and by convention bitter, by convention hot, by convention cold, by convention color, but in reality (*eteēi*) atoms and void." The fragment is quoted by Sextus Empiricus along with seven others selected to show that Democritus denies the veracity of sense perceptions: "He says that none of the phenomena appears according to truth (*kat' alētheian*) but only according to opinion (*kata doxan*)."[46] Setting faulty human perception against atomic reality, these fragments seem to define the Democritean self by way of a Parmenidean antithesis between *doxa* and *alētheia*. But for Democritus the antithesis between *nomos* and *eteos* is not as clear-cut as it initially appears, for the senses that divide us from atomic reality also participate directly in it. Perception, as we saw with the *eidōla*, is a process of material transformation. As Theophrastus explains, there is no sweet or bitter, but these are merely the changes that different shapes and configurations of atoms produce on our sense organs.[47] So sense perceptions and atomic reality are not mutually exclusive alternatives, as B9/D14 might suggest. Sweet may be sweet by convention but it is also

46. Sext. Emp. *Math.* 7.135 = B9/R108. The fragments are B6–11/D14–21. Laks-Most give the whole passage of Sextus at R108; see the detailed analysis by Sedley (1992). Cf. Gal. *Exper. Med.* 15.7.5 = B125/D23a; Diog. Laert. 9.72 = B117/D24. The ancient testimonia are divided over whether Democritus was a Skeptic who rejected the evidence of the senses entirely or a subjectivist who accepted nothing but that evidence. See the helpful discussion of Taylor (1999b, 216–22) and judicious review of the testimonia by Lee (2005, 181–250). The extent and nature of Democritus's skepticism is much debated; see further Bailey 1964, 177–85; Guthrie 1965, 454–65; Taylor 1967, 16–24; Sassi 1978, 207–13, 227–36; Barnes 1982, 559–64; McKim 1984; Furley 1987, 131–35, 1993; Sedley 1992; Salem 1996, 157–70, 2007; O'Keefe 1997; Ganson 1999; Morel 2000, 93–105; Curd 2001; Wismann 2010, 36–49, 67–91; and the provocative suggestion of Hacking (1983, 140–42) that Democritus was the first to differentiate between representation and reality, thus introducing reality as we know it.

47. Sweet is produced by round atoms of moderate size and bitter by small, curved ones: Theophr. *Sens.* 63–66 < A135/D64–65. Color too is produced by atoms of specific shapes (*Sens.* 73–78 < A135/D66), as is temperature (*Sens.* 63 < A135/D64). See further A49/D63, A120/D57, A129/D160. On Democritus's theory of perception and cognition, see Von Fritz 1946, 24–30; Bicknell 1968; Baldes 1975; Burkert 1977; Couloubaritsis 1980; Taylor 1999b, 208–11; Rudolph 2016, 49–52; and especially the detailed study of Sassi (1978).

sweet "in reality," and to taste sweetness is to experience that atomic reality directly on the tongue: *nomos* is *eteos*.[48]

In perceiving we are thus enacting the reality of atoms and void. This material continuity is suggested in the very fragments Sextus cites to illustrate the opposite. Right after fragment B9/D14 he quotes another passage that he claims shows Democritus condemning the senses: "In reality (*tōi men eonti*) we know nothing accurately (*atrekes*), but something that changes (*metapipton*) according to the disposition (*diathēkēn*) of the body and of what enters and repels" (*tōn epeisiontōn kai tōn antistērizontōn*, B9a/D15). Like B9/D14, this fragment seems to set our unreliable sensory experience against a stable knowledge based on ontic (*tōi eonti*) reality. But that experience is characterized in the technical terminology of atomic motion.[49] To that extent it is, in fact, accurate (*atrekes*) even if we don't recognize it. Another fragment Sextus quotes asserts that "in reality (*eteēi*) we know nothing about anything, but opinion (*doxis*) is a rhythmic afflux (*epirhusmiē*) for each person" (B7/D18). Again we seem to have a Parmenidean antithesis between atomic *alētheia* and erroneous human *doxis*. But the *epirhusmiē* that constitutes that *doxis* refers to atomic shape.[50] The polarity between atomic truth and human beliefs again breaks down: our senses are a direct experience of the very reality of which we are ignorant, the reality of atoms and void.

This means that the split these fragments describe is in fact all in our heads. That is, the rift lies not between us and atomic reality but within ourselves. As Karl Marx observed in his dissertation on Democritus and Epicurus, "Democritus makes sensuous reality into subjective semblance; but the antinomy, banned from the world of objects, now exists in his own self-consciousness, where the concept of the atom and sensuous perception face each other as enemies."[51] This "enmity" is staged as a psychic wrestling match in a passage quoted by Galen.

> τοῦτο καὶ Δ. εἰδώς, ὁπότε τὰ φαινόμενα διέβαλε, 'νόμωι χροιή, νόμωι γλυκύ, νόμωι πικρόν', εἰπών, 'ἐτεῇι δ' ἄτομα καὶ κενόν', ἐποίησε τὰς αἰσθήσεις λεγούσας πρὸς τὴν διάνοιαν οὕτως· 'τάλαινα φρήν, παρ' ἡμέων λαβοῦσα τὰς πίστεις ἡμέας καταβάλλεις; πτῶμά τοι τὸ κατάβλημα'. (*Med. Exper.* 15.7.5 Schöne = B125/D23a)

48. This is how I understand Aristotle's report that because the atomists equate thought (*phronēsis*) with sense perception (*aisthēsis*) and attribute the latter to atomic alterations, "they say that that which appears with respect to sense perception is necessarily true" (*alēthes*, *Metaph.* 4.5 1009b12–17 = A112/R53). Cf. *Metaph.* 4.5 1010b1–4, *Gen. corr.* 1.2 315b9, *De an.* 1.2 404a27–31; and the nuanced discussion of Couloubaritsis (1980).

49. For *metapiptein* see A135§63/D64, B191/D226. *Antistērizein* is cognate with *stereos*, a common qualifier of the atom. If we read *diathigē* for *diathēkē* here (as Menzel proposed) there is further resonance with 67A6/D31 and A38/D32; *diathigē* or *diathēgē* is a technical term for the disposition of an atom in relation to others. I take *tōi eonti* as equivalent to *eteēi* and a reference to atomic reality: *to on* is another synonym for the atom.

50. Taylor 1999b, 11–12n4. "Rhythmic afflux" is Laks-Most's translation. On *rhusmos*, cf. below, n. 88.

51. Marx (2006, 98), commenting on Democritus's views on the relation between thought and reality.

> Democritus knew this [the importance of evidence] and whenever he slandered appearances, saying "by convention color, by convention sweet, by convention bitter, but in reality atoms and void," he made the sense perceptions reply to thought as follows: "Wretched mind (*phrēn*), you get your evidence from us and then you overthrow us? That overthrow is your downfall."

In this vivid little drama, the external division between atomic reality and sense perception becomes an internal division between thought and sensation, but an illusory one, as the senses argue. It is a matter of false consciousness on the part of the *phrēn*, since as the psychological enactment of atomic dynamics, they are the mind's direct conduit to reality. Indeed, they might have pushed their claim further, for thought too is an atomic process for Democritus.[52] Thus "wretched mind" has no right to vaunt over the senses: both alike operate by means of changing configurations of atoms. Our problem, this fragment implies, is not that we cannot know the reality of atoms and void, since at the most basic level "to know" (to perceive, to think) simply *is* that reality. The problem is that we do not know that we know it. Our wretched minds fail to recognize the atomic nature of our psychic makeup, sensory and cognitive alike. In other words, it is not atoms and void we do not know; it is ourselves.

The *agōn* of B125/D23a projects the possibility that mind and senses will reconcile to form a harmonious psychic whole. But another fragment quoted by Sextus suggests that the split is irreparable and, as such, basic to our identity as human beings. "There are two forms of knowledge (*gnōmēs*), one legitimate (*gnēsiē*) and the other obscure (*skotiē*). And all these things belong to the obscure one: sight, hearing, smell, taste, touch. The other is legitimate and separated from this one" (B11/D20). Here the *agōn* between intellection and sensation is staged not as a wrestling match but as an inheritance dispute. The adjective *gnēsios* connotes legitimate birth or lineage; in classical Athens it is the legal term for a legitimate heir. *Skotios* is used for literal darkness but also for clandestine unions and the offspring they produce.[53] Knowledge is split between the two. That split is not managed by a contentious distribution of psychic capacities within a subjective whole, as in Galen's wrestling match. As subjects of bifurcated knowledge, we are intrinsically split. We are simultaneously legitimate heir and bastard, our filiation to truth fundamentally ambiguous.

The self that emerges from these fragments is divided by its non-knowledge of the cosmos and of itself. Further, if "man is a small universe" (*tōi anthrōpōi mikrōi kosmōi onti*), as B34/D225 has it, those two ignorances are one. Since our

52. As Aristotle complains, Arist. *De an.* 1.2 404a27 < A101/D133. Cf. Theophr. *Sens.* 58 < A135/D134: "It is clear that he attributes thinking to the mixture of the body, which is consistent with his making the soul a body." See Taylor 1999b, 200–208. Galen's internal wrestling match is repeated in a juridical idiom in the body's prosecution of the soul for mistreatment, in a fragment quoted by Plutarch (*Libid. et Aegrit.* 2 = B159/D233a; cf. B159/D233b).

53. *Skotios* in this sense is poetic, however, not juridical (LSJ s.v.). For discussion of this fragment, see Sassi 1978, 213–21.

bodies, senses, and thoughts are atomic through and through, to know ourselves would be to know the nature of the universe and vice versa. But we are ignorant of both, an ignorance that defines us, as we read in another fragment quoted by Sextus: "It is necessary to recognize man [or for man to recognize] by this criterion, that he is separated from reality" (*gignōskein te khrē . . . anthrōpon tōide tōi kanoni, hoti eteēs apēllaktai*, B6/D17). To know man is to recognize his non-knowledge of atomic reality, even as that reality is the material basis of his knowledge. That recognition is self-recognition if we take *anthrōpon* as the subject rather than the object of the infinitive *gignōskein*.[54] The fragment thus functions as a form of the Delphic imperative *Gnōthi Seauton*, drawing out the maxim's implicit split in the self as both subject and object of knowledge and supplementing it with the split in knowledge itself.

Self-knowledge as the recognition of our non-knowledge installs a negativity within the human subject at the heart of our self-relation. "Indeed, this *logos* too reveals that in reality we know nothing about anything/nothing (*eteēi ouden ismen peri oudenos*), but opinion (*doxis*) is a rhythmic afflux for each person" (B7/D18). The second *ouden* in this fragment is usually translated positively ("anything"), in accordance with the normal Greek rule of negation that a compound negative (*ouden*) following another negative confirms the negative force of the former. But the sophistication of Democritus's play with negation encourages us to read the phrase more literally: "we know nothing about 'nothing.'" Read this way, *ouden* names the ignorance that constitutes our self-knowledge. This negativity reiterates the logic of the *den*. Our thought and sense perception connect us to atomic reality, but the nature of that connection is negative, a minus sign: we do not know our own atomic nature and we do not know that we do not know it. That double negation does not produce a positive but at best an imperfect subtraction from nothing: *~~ou~~den*. *Ich* is *~~N~~ichts*.

Democritus does not try to fill in that hole of non-knowledge; instead, he establishes it as the basis of his ethical theory. This theory is set out in more than two hundred ethical maxims preserved in two late antique anthologies, one by Stobaeus and attributed to Democritus, the other an anonymous collection of "Sayings of Democrates," presumably a corruption of "Democritus." These fragments present special difficulties, not only of authorship (most are assumed to be inauthentic) but also of interpretation.[55] To put it bluntly, these maxims are exceptionally banal.

54. *Kanoni* could be taken with "recognize" (Diels-Kranz, Taylor) or "separated" (Luria, Laks-Most). In the latter construction it refers to man's ignorance; in the former, to Democritus's *logos* about it. A third translation would take the final clause in apposition to *kanoni*, making separation from reality the criterion for recognizing man. I keep all three possibilities in play. *Kanones* is the title of a Democritean treatise (B11/D6). Luria 2007, 986: *kanōn* is "il principio metodico fondamentale."

55. The Democrates collection is generally considered less secure than the Stobaeus collection, but Laks-Most (vol. 7, 5) may be right to consider both as part of Democritus's reception rather than his original text. Contra, Johnson 2020. My discussion rests heavily on B191/D226, one of the few

Their cheery prescriptions for contentment were clichéd already by Democritus's day. Temperance increases satisfaction (B211/D244); justice conduces to happiness (B174/D320); ill-gotten wealth is pernicious (B78/D261, B218/D263); it is better to speak the truth (B225/D347a). The eye glazes over.

Scholars have sought a connection between Democritus's atomic physics and his ethical theory. Gregory Vlastos argues that the well-being (*euestō*) that is the goal of Democritean ethics refers to a stable condition of atoms in the body and soul that can be regulated through education.[56] He homes in on fragment B33/D403: "Nature (*phusis*) and teaching (*didakhē*) are similar. For teaching changes a man's configuration (*metarhusmoi*) and, in changing his configuration, makes his nature (*phusiopoiei*)." *Metarhusmos* is Democritus's term for atomic reconfiguration, as Vlastos notes; thus the idea that we can rearrange our atomic natures through learning builds a tight "nest of interconnections between physics and ethics."[57] Those interconnections are traced in a rich and comprehensive study by Cynthia Farrar. Building on Vlastos's insight, Farrar proposes that the novelty of Democritean ethics lies in the autonomy it grants the individual subject, who can achieve the ideal moral-material balance through his own capacity for rational self-reflection.[58] The ethical fragments, as she reads them, are "injunctions to men to understand that they are causes, that their world is to a very large extent mind-dependent."[59] The sole source of his own well-being and master of his interactions with the world, the subject is characterized by both freedom and control; he is a positive law unto himself, as she says: "Man is literally *autonomos*."[60] For Farrar, the

fragments accepted as authentic. On the authenticity of the ethical fragments, see further Leszl 2007, 64–76. Democritus's originality as an ethical thinker is defended by Annas (2002) and Johnson (2020).

56. Vlastos 1945, 582–85, 1946. Also arguing for a connection between the ethics and physics: Natorp 1893, 88–121; Sassi 1978, 236–40; Curd 2001; Johnson 2009. Arguing against: Bailey 1964, 186–89; Taylor 1967 (with partial reconsideration at 1999b, 32–34); Barnes 1982, 530–35; and Salem 1996, 325–31. Kahn (1985, 11) and Warren (2002b, 58–64, 71–72) remain agnostic, though the latter proposes an intriguing physical mechanism for interpersonal harm via the *eidōla* (2007b).

57. Vlastos 1946, 56. *Metarhusmos* and related terms are found at 67A6/D31, 67A28/D132, A33X/D2bX, A38/D32, B7/D18, B51, B8a/D2bV, B139/D38, B197/D297, B266/D363.

58. Farrar 1988, 192–264. Both Vlastos and Farrar presuppose the unique nature of the human mind as irreducible to its atomic makeup and capable of reflecting critically on it. See esp. Vlastos 1946, 57; Farrar 1988, 227–29, 244–48. Farrar's use of the masculine pronoun reflects that of Democritus. There is no theoretical reason why the atomic subject should be normatively male; nonetheless, for Democritus it is, implicitly and sometimes explicitly (*anēr*, B35/≠LM, B68/≠LM, B70/≠LM, B236/D296, B247/D354). See further his maxims on the place and virtue of women (B111/D391, B273–74/D328–29).

59. Farrar 1988, 231. Johnson (2020, 230–32) also emphasizes the importance of autonomy in Democritus's ethics.

60. Farrar 1988, 238. Farrar's autonomous subject more closely resembles the modern liberal subject than the corporate subject of classical Greece (on which see Anderson 2018, 193–207). Farrar recognizes the similarity (257–58) but does not explain how it complicates the critique of the liberal democratic self that frames her study (4–5). In modern Greek άτομο means "individual."

ethical subject is not only composed of atoms; whole, unitary, and self-contained, he is himself a psychic and social atom.

This vision of the subject as an atomic being is compelling, and it makes good sense of the maxims' obsessive injunction to *autarkeia* (self-sufficiency) and *metriotēs* (moderation) as the goals of ethical practice and the keys to living well. Human beings possess the source of their health and happiness, as well as their misfortune, within themselves (*en heautois*, B234/D240; cf. B146/D245, B149/D267). They do not need to rely on the unstable gifts of fortune because their nature is self-sufficient: *phusis de autarkēs* (B176/D252; cf. B246/D254, B209/D255). This autarky is achieved through "moderation (*metriotēti*) of pleasure and proportion (*summetriēi*) in life" and a reduction of the changes that disturb the soul (B191/D226; cf. B210/D277). Learning to be satisfied with what one has (*arkeesthai*, the verb from which *autarkeia* is derived) instead of grasping for what one doesn't have, being contented with what is possible rather than longing for more (*mēketi pleionōn epithumeonti*), the individual will achieve the psychic and physical homeostasis that constitutes well-being (*euestō*, B191/D226; cf. B3/D228, B211/D244, B231/D253, B233/D246, B286/D278).

The ethical fragments thus seem to subscribe to a familiar Greek normativity of regulated desires and moderate self-mastery. But what if we shift our view and imagine the Democritean subject not as an atom—an autonomous positive being—but as an avatar of the *den?* This perspective reveals something beyond this homeostatic principle, or rather within it, a pervasive negativity at work within Democritus's upbeat prescriptions that hollows out their contentment.[61] *Euestō*, the cheerful self-sufficiency for which Democritean ethics aims, is achieved by setting one's sights on the ever-present prospect of lack. In the fragments' ubiquitous language of measure (*metriotēs, summetria*), ethical moderation should be calculated according to the yardstick of lack and need.[62] Fragment B285/D256 is typical: "It is necessary to recognize (*gignōskein*) that human life is feeble and short and mixed together with many diseases and difficulties, so that one should concern oneself with moderate (*metriēs*) possessions, and misery should be measured (*metrētai*) based on necessities." As in B6/D17, to recognize (*gignōskein*) an individual is to acknowledge a definitional negativity, but here that negativity grounds a positive regimen of the self: lack is the *kanōn* by which an ethical life is measured. Self-sufficiency accordingly means not only being satisfied with what little you

61. In labeling this principle homoestatic I am alluding to Freud's (1955) pleasure principle. Derrida (1987) shows how the death drive operates within the pleasure principle and "hollows it out" (304) from within.

62. Morel 2000, 59: "Pour Démocrite, la téléologie morale est d'abord une téléologie négative." Forms of *metrios* occur at B70/≠LM, B233/D246, B285/D256, B286/D278, A167/D231. We also might note the driving force of want and lack in Democritus's anthropology: Diod. Sic. 1.8.5–6, 1.8.9 (< B5/D202): "On the whole need (*khreian*) itself was men's teacher in all things" (1.8.9). Cole (1990) reconstructs Democritus's anthropology.

have but scaling back your desires so that little becomes enough: "If you do not desire many things, few will seem many to you, for a small appetite makes poverty equal to wealth" (B284/D259). Through one's ethical efforts, a little becomes equal to a lot: *autarkeia* is learning to be satisfied with a loaf of barley bread and a bed of straw (B246/D254). Nothing makes something look like everything.

Hence the constant reminder to consider the suffering of others—not so as to alleviate it, but so as to use it as a benchmark against which to measure one's own relative comfort. Fragment B191/D226, by far the longest of the ethical fragments and widely viewed as authentic, is often cited as evidence for an ethics of atomic autarky. It opens: "Contentment (*euthumiē*) comes from moderation (*metriotēti*) of pleasure and proportion (*summetriēi*) in life." The fragment teaches a lesson in achieving this psychic measure through the reduction of stimulus (*kinēsis*) and limitation of desire (*epithumia*).[63] "Look at the lives of the miserable, reflecting on their great suffering in order that what is present and available to you (*ta pareonta soi kai huparkhonta*) will seem great and enviable, and you will no longer suffer in your soul because you desire more (*pleionōn epithumeonti*)." The *metriotēs* that brings happiness is here defined as a median between two lacks: desire for what one doesn't have and the imagined loss of what one does. The former is insatiable—it produces only greater desire, suffering, and ultimately crime—and should be remembered only in order to be forgotten: "Have little memory of what you envy and admire and do not dwell on them in your thoughts." Forget desire. Focus your attention not on your own lack but on others': "Compare your life to that of those who are worse off and consider yourself blessed thinking about what they suffer and how much better you are faring and living than they." By gazing at those who lack what we have, we will come to appreciate what is present for us (*tois pareousin, ta pareonta*) through visualizing its absence. The ethical subject is thus formed between two nothings: the wealth one will never obtain and should not even think about and the poverty one must hold always before one's eyes.

In this fragment *euthumia* is achieved through an imaginative subtraction that reiterates the logic of the *den*. You think what you have is nothing; but someone else has less than that: look to that less than nothing and your nothing will look like something. Contentment with what is present (*tois pareousin arkeesthai*) is the elimination of desire for what is absent: *~~mē~~den* (cf. B231/D253). A similar psychic arithmetic is at work throughout the ethical fragments. Subtraction becomes a form of addition: "If you do not desire many things, few will seem many to you, for a small appetite makes poverty equal (*isosthenea*) to wealth" (B284/D259); "the most infrequent pleasures please the most" (*malista*, B232/D247); and temperance "makes pleasure even greater" (*epimeizona*, B211/D244). Less is always

63. For good discussion of B191/D226 see Warren 2002b, 44–64. Kahn (1985, 17–19) stresses desire as lack in Democritus. On the ethical dangers posed by desire for Democritus, see Holmes 2010, 216–22.

more. Conversely, addition produces loss: "If someone exceeds the right measure (*huperballoi to metrion*) the most pleasurable things (*epiterpestata*) become most unpleasurable" (*aterpestata*, B233/D246); "desire for more (*tou pleonos epithumiē*) destroys what is present" (B224/D251). Through a kind of ethical repetition compulsion, excess (*ta pleona, ta meizona, ta huperballonta*)—desire as the desire for more (*epi-thumia*)—is conjured over and over again in order to be nullified.[64] In this way, Democritus reworks the Delphic maxim "Nothing in Excess" (*Mēden Agan*) such that excess yields nothing and nothing is the measure of *metriotēs*.[65]

Subtracting lack on both sides—the excess one wants and the destitution one fears—the ethical subject is less than nothing. That subject is structured not like an autonomous atom but like the *den*. An ethics of atomic autarky (such as Farrar proposes) circles around a real void, the void of the Real. Thus we read in B176/D252: "The gift of *tukhē* is great but insecure, but nature is *autarkēs*; therefore by means of the lesser but secure, it conquers the greater thing that belongs to hope [or the thing greater than hope]" (*tukhē megalodōros, all' abebaios, phusis de autarkēs; dioper nikāi tōi hēssoni kai bebaiōi to meizon tēs elpidos*). Man's *autarkēs phusis* triumphs over (*nikāi*) the extravagant gift of *tukhē*. The logic of security through diminution (*hēssoni kai bebaiōi*) that enables its victory is the subtractive logic of Democritean well-being. *Tukhē* menaces this homeostatic logic with its simultaneous threat of annihilation (*abebaios*) and its hope for something more than satisfaction and more even than hope—not a stable, present contentment, but an exorbitant, inaccessible *jouissance*.[66] The object of that hope-beyond-hope is what Lacan calls the *objet a* and what Democritus labels the *den*, a something-that-is-nothing in excess of desire and its satisfaction, the fantasy that fills a subjective void that can never be filled. The autarkic subject, formed through the prohibited longing for this impossible object, carries its negated negativity in its very *phusis*.

Within this ethics of the *den*, the indifference principle of the physics is converted into a positive principle of ethical preference. Many of the ethical fragments advocate an ethical choice that could be expressed in the formula of indifference, *mē mallon ē*: desire wealth no more than poverty (B210/D277, B219/D257,

64. "Greater appetites produce greater needs" (B219/D257). A contented person should not "choose what is beyond (*huper*) his capability and nature" nor "try to grasp more (*pleō*) than what is possible" (B3/D228). Those who exceed proper measure (*huperbeblēkotes ton kairon*) get only brief satisfaction and greater need (B235/D248). B191/D226 opens with the repudiation of both lack (*ta elleiponta*) and excess (*huperballonta*). That fragment is structured by the move from desire (*epithumia*) via contemplation (*enthumia*) to contentment (*euthumia*), but the drive for more insists in the fragment's repetition of *epi-* (more, addition).

65. Warren (2002b, 54) relates B235/D248 to the Delphic maxim in a more straightforward manner: "Excess leads to painful after-effects." Likewise, Johnson 2020, 226.

66. Zupančič 2000, 242: *jouissance* is neither the satisfaction of lack nor something added to it; "instead, it is that which *subtracts itself from the lack*" (original emphasis). For Lacan (1977, 53–64), *tukhē* names the missed encounter with the Real that disrupts the pleasure principle. His discussion of *tukhē* ends with a reference to Democritus's *den*.

B286/D278); care for body no more than for soul (B187/D236); cherish what you want no more than what you have (B191/D226, B231/D253); feel shame before others no more than before yourself (B244/D336, B264/D386).[67] This ethical indifference turns contentment into a condition of negative affect: Diogenes Laertius explains *euthumiē* as "not the same as pleasure . . . but the state in which the soul abides calmly and steadily, disturbed by no fear or superstition or any other affection" (Diog. Laert. 9.45 < A1/D229). This psychic indifference culminates in an indifference to life itself: value your life no more than death.[68] Life is to be enjoyed (B200/D283, B201/D284), but not out of a fearful preference to death: "Thoughtless people live as if hating to live through fear of Hades" (B199/D286, cf. B205/D285). The preference of life to death recoils on itself: to fear death is to pursue it (B203/D288). To truly live—to live well and wisely—is to embrace death no less than life, one's being no more than one's nonbeing.

In these two hundred trite maxims, Democritus erects a positive ethics of temperance, contentment, and cheerfulness upon the Real of negativity within being, lending a decidedly different tenor to the laugh of this notorious "laughing philosopher."[69] This unspeakable Real takes the form of a psychic void within the self: the lack that structures, even as it annuls, the subject's autarkic contentment, hollowing out its temperate pleasures with an inaccessible hope-beyond-hope; the internal schism that constitutes ethical subjects even as it alienates them from both reality and themselves, preventing them from ever fully cohering into autonomous, "atomic" individuals. Nonbeing casts a shadow over Democritus's ethical subject, but it also gives a different shade to his entire ethical discourse, "for *logos* is a shadow of *ergon*, according to Democritus" (B145/D338). This final maxim encapsulates the parallactic appearance of the *den* within the text of Democritean ethics. Read from one perspective it is a hackneyed (and hence self-confirming) adage about the primacy of deeds over words. Viewed from another, it adumbrates without being able to elucidate the Thing (*ergon*) obscured by *logos*, the very matter of the Real of which Democritus's cheery precepts are but the shadow.[70]

67. Accordingly, happiness is comparative: B191/D226 begins by promising contentment (*euthumiē*) but in the end delivers only relative contentment ("you will live more contentedly," *euthumoteron*).

68. On the indifference to death in Democritean (and Epicurean) atomism, see Warren 2002a.

69. This moniker is often assumed to derive from Democritus's emphasis on cheerfulness (e.g. Berryman 2023), but the ancient biographical tradition associates it rather with madness: the testimonia are gathered by Laks-Most (P46–48). See further the discussion of Luria (2007, 932–36), who believes the characterization reflects Democritus's mockery of fools and their empty hopes.

70. That is, *das Ding* or *objet a*, material remnant of the Real within the symbolic. Lacan defines ethics as the subject's assumption of responsibility for his or her relation to the Real, the commitment to an impossible truth that, in its impossibility, orients the subject's fantasy, desire, and actions (1992, 11, 20, 76; cf. Zupančič 2000, esp. 234–45).

SIGNIFYING NOTHING

The shadowy force of the *den* is formative not only for Democritus's ethics but also for his poetics, and indeed for his philosophical discourse as a whole. The signifier of something/nothing that cannot by its nature be signified, the *den* can appear only as an abyss—a true void—within the text of Democritus's philosophy. His *logos peri phuseōs* is woven around and covers over that abyss without ever filling it, and its indistinct presence as an absence will simultaneously define and defy the truth of that *logos*. If, as Alenka Zupančič writes, "reality is constituted in the loss of a little bit of the Real," *den* marks that little bit of the Real, the loss of which constitutes both Democritus's atomic reality and his science of it.[71] Ancient atomism is sometimes viewed as an antecedent to modern atomic theory, and a direct line drawn from Leucippus and Democritus to Rutherford, Bohr, and Heisenberg.[72] But if Democritus's *logos* is a science, I will suggest, what makes it so is not his "discovery" of the atom but the relation he sustains, by means of the *den*, to the impossible Real.

The word *den*, as we have seen, appears only in the paraphrases of the doxographers, where it is listed as a simple synonym for the atom. We never hear the word spoken in Democritus's own voice, as it were. This absence is especially striking in a discourse that boasts a godlike totality. The *Mikros Diakosmos* may have opened with the proclamation, "I say the following concerning all things" (*legō tade peri tōn xumpantōn*), a claim so grandiose as to verge on hubris, as Sextus snidely remarks in quoting the line: Democritus spoke "likening himself to the voice of Zeus" (< B165/P44b).[73] And indeed, Democritus does seem to have aimed for a truly Olympian universality. The catalog of his lost works substantiates the claim to speak about "all things," encompassing anthropology, eschatology, ethics and psychology, astronomy and meteorology, botany and biology, geometry, medicine, aesthetics, and land management, as well as a Small World-System (*Mikros Diakosmos*) and a Great World-System (*Megas Diakosmos*).[74] One characteristic

71. Zupančič 2000, 240.

72. Barnes 1982, 342: "We are all atomists now." Cf. Furley 1987, 123; and Zilioli 2020. Barnes goes on to enumerate the differences (cf. Gregory 2020), but also to posit a Heisenberg principle of ancient atomism (561–64; cf. Kirk, Raven, and Schofield 1983, 433). On the (question-begging) question of whether the Presocratic *phusikoi* were scientists, see Algra 1999, 60–63.

73. The verb *legō* appears in the participial form in Sextus but Cicero quotes the line in the indicative: "*haec loquor de universis*" (< B165/P44a). Democritus assumes this Jovian perspective in part by effacing himself as author: the first-person singular is extremely rare in the extant fragments, and for the most part the author disappears behind the authoritative force of his own text: "This *logos* reveals" (B7/D18); "it has been revealed" (B10/D16). I find only two first-person pronouns in the text considered authentic by Laks-Most (although Apollonius Dyskolos cites the author's use of *emeu* and *emeo* [B13/R3a] so there may well have been more): *dokei de moi* in A151/D179 and *me* in B116/P22a. The latter speaks directly to the author's anonymity: "I came to Athens and no one recognized me."

74. Thrasyllus apparently called Democritus "a real pentathlete in philosophy" (Diog. Laert. 9.37 < A1/P42) and Philodemus praised him as unrivaled in his intellectual curiosity (B144/P43). On the

often taken to define Presocratic philosophy, as I noted in the Introduction, is its claim to *legein peri tōn xumpantōn*, "to give a universalist account . . . to take everything—the world as a whole—as the subject of inquiry."[75] That universalizing ambition reaches its apotheosis, as it were, in Democritus's Jovian world-systems.

This comprehensive discourse is unified by a finite set of operating principles. The attraction of like-to-like, for instance, governs not just the aggregation (*sustēma*) of atoms into celestial elements (Diog. Laert. 9.44 < A1/D13), but also the consolidation (*sustēma*) of earth and other planets (Diog. Laert. 9.30 < 67A1/D80b), and the assembling (*sustēma*) of human beings into tribes (Diod. Sic. 1.8.4 < B5/D202).[76] Fragment B164/D55 describes this universal and universalizing principle, which acts equally on the large and the small, the animate and inanimate, the artificial and the natural:

> καὶ γὰρ ζῶια . . . ὁμογενέσι ζώιοις συναγελάζεται ὡς περιστεραὶ περιστεραῖς καὶ γέρανοι γεράνοις καὶ ἐπὶ τῶν ἄλλων ἀλόγων ὡσαύτως. ⟨ὣς⟩ δὲ καὶ ἐπὶ τῶν ἀψύχων, καθάπερ ὁρᾶν πάρεστιν ἐπί τε τῶν κοσκινευομένων σπερμάτων καὶ ἐπὶ τῶν παρὰ ταῖς κυματωγαῖς ψηφίδων· ὅπου μὲν γὰρ κατὰ τὸν τοῦ κοσκίνου δῖνον διακριτικῶς φακοὶ μετὰ φακῶν τάσσονται καὶ κριθαὶ μετὰ κριθῶν καὶ πυροὶ μετὰ πυρῶν, ὅπου δὲ κατὰ τὴν τοῦ κύματος κίνησιν αἱ μὲν ἐπιμήκεις ψηφῖδες εἰς τὸν αὐτὸν τόπον ταῖς ἐπιμήκεσιν ὠθοῦνται, αἱ δὲ περιφερεῖς ταῖς περιφερέσιν ὡς ἂν συναγωγόν τι ἐχούσης τῶν πραγμάτων τῆς ἐν τούτοις ὁμοιότητος. (B164/D55)
>
> For animals . . . herd together with animals of the same species, such as doves with doves and cranes with cranes and likewise with the other irrational creatures. So too for the inanimate things, as one can see with seeds being sifted and pebbles on the beach. In the first case, because of the rotation (*dinon*) of the sieve, lentils are arrayed separately with lentils and barley with barley and wheat with wheat. In the second case, because of the movement of the wave, oblong pebbles are pushed into the same place with oblong ones and round pebbles with round, as if the intrinsic similarity of the things exerted some force of attraction.

The use of *dinos* (whirl) to describe the winnowing process might suggest that this is an illustrative analogy. The cosmopoetic *dinē* is said to separate elements

---

extent of his polymathy in its historical context, see Patzer 2006, 149–53; and Gemelli Marciano 2007. The titles are collated by Laks-Most at D2–9 and assessed fully by Leszl (2007). The *Mikros Diakosmos* was probably by Leucippus (67B1a, but see also A31/D3, A33.III/≠LM). Schofield (2019) believes the *Megas Diakosmos* dealt with the plurality of worlds at the cosmological level; the *Mikros Diakosmos* with arrangements of atoms at the microscopic level.

75. Long 1999b, 10 and see the references in the Introduction, n. 57.

76. Other examples of like-to-like movement include the attraction of magnet and iron (A165/D126), the differential sorting of animals to the element most like them (B5/D129), acoustics (A128/D156). Other general principles are the *rhusmos* (fluid configuration) that operates within physics (67A6/D31, A38/D32, B139/D38), aesthetics (67A6/D31, B8a/D2b.V, A33X/D2bX), ethics (B33/D403, B197/D297, B266/D363) and psychology/epistemology (67A28/D132, B7/D18, B33/D403); and the indifference principle which, I proposed, governs ontology, atomic motion, sense perception, and ethical choice.

out like-to-like in a process Diogenes likens to winnowing (*hōsper diattōmena*, Diog. Laert. 9.31 < 67A1/D80b). But despite its empirical tone ("as one can see"), this fragment does not offer herding animals or sifted grains as visible analogies to unobservable cosmic aggregation. Nor does it present these everyday phenomena as the visible effect of unobservable atomic aggregation. Instead, it hypothesizes a general law that operates across these different registers: it is "as if" there were some universal law of attraction. The support for the hypothesis lies in the diversity of phenomena it explains. The universality of the system is its own proof.

Language is a part of this system. The orderly taxonomy of the passage's structure mimetically reproduces its content: first animals (*zōia*), subdivided into doves and cranes; then inanimate things (*apsukha*), subdivided into grains and pebbles, the former further subdivided into lentils, barley, and wheat, the latter into long pebbles and round ones. Words are themselves sorted like-to-like through Democritus's jostling jumble of plosives, his use of repetition (*kai epi tōn, meta*) and polyptoton (*peristerai peristerais, geranoi geranois*, etc.). Language not only describes atomic principles but directly instantiates their effects.

This fragment points to the ambiguous status of language in relation to Democritus's atomic system: it is simultaneously grounded in his theory of matter and encompasses it as an Olympian metalanguage. On the one hand, language follows and demonstrates the physical principles of atomism. Aristotle explains the atomists' phenomenology by comparing atoms to letters: different combinations and configurations of atoms (*stoikheia*) produce different phenomena, just as letters (*stoikheia*) do words.[77] Building on the double meaning of *stoikheion* as element and letter, James Porter reconstructs a "*stoikheion* theory of language" by which Democritus generalized the analytic model of atomism to linguistics and aesthetics. In this atomic theory of language, the relation between atoms and letters, like that between birds, beans, and pebbles in B164/D55, is more than simple analogy: as *stoikheia*, Porter argues, letters are both abstract units within an integrated system and material elements. Linguistic expression is not just an illustration of atomic processes but is itself a material process "decisively determined by, and in the extreme case reducible to, the properties of some non-linguistic physical substrate."[78] In the fundamental dichotomy of B9/D14, language would seem to

77. "For they say that what is differs only by *rhusmos, diathigē*, and *tropē*. Of these, *rhusmos* is shape, *diathigē* order, and *tropē* position. For A differs from N in shape, AN from NA in order, and Z from N in position" (Arist. *Metaph.* 1.4 985b15–19 < 67A6/D31). Cf. Arist. *Gen. corr.* 1.2 315b14–15 < 67A9/D56. Porter (2010, 217) believes the letter analogy was Democritus's own; cf. 1989, 168–69n107; Von Fritz 1938, 25; Burkert 1959; Barnes 1982, 368; and Wismann 2010, 11. Linguistic theory was part of Democritus's omniscient purview: he wrote treatises "On poetry," "On rhythms and harmony," "On euphonious and cacophonous letters," and "On the beauty of words." On these works and Democritus's aesthetic theory more broadly, see Brancacci 2007.

78. Porter 2010, 213–39; the quotation is on p. 225. See also Porter 1989. If for Porter letters work like atoms, for Wismann (2010, 11–15, 29–32, 50, 60–62) atoms are like letters. Extrapolating from this analogy, Wismann argues that Democritus's physical theory is, at base, "une physique du fonctionnement

stand—counterintuitively—on the side not of *nomos* but of *eteos*, the physical reality of atoms and void.

On the other hand, language is not only *etic*, as it were, but also thetic. Proclus tells us Democritus viewed names as arbitrary: they are not inherent to the thing they name but posited (*thesei*) and thus belong "not to nature (*phusei*) but to chance" (*tukhēi*, B26/D205).[79] He based this view, Proclus says, on the fact of verbal ambiguity: homonymy (*polusēmon*), polyonymy (*isorropon*), changes of name (*metōnumon*), and things without names (*nōnumon*) would be impossible, he reasoned, if names existed by nature. He demonstrates the posited nature of language by himself positing new words for these very linguistic phenomena (*polusēmon, isorropon, metōnumon*, and *nōnumon*), coinages that simultaneously illustrate the theory and ward off linguistic ambiguity through their immediate legibility.[80]

These same qualities of artificiality and legibility characterize Democritus's lexical practice as a whole. In chapter 3 we looked at Empedocles's extravagant verbal creativeness, his free invention of new words and exotic repurposing of familiar words. Democritus too was famous in antiquity for his linguistic invention. Callimachus wrote a catalog of his "rare words and constructions," and the Hellenistic grammarian Hegesianax composed a book on his diction (*lexis*, A32/R2).[81] In comparison to the flamboyant artistry of Empedocles, however, Democritus's inventions may strike us as disappointingly plain. Despite Cicero's praise for the "brilliant verbal ornament" that made Democritus's work like a poem without meter (*Orat.* 20.67 < A34/R6), his linguistic borrowings tend to come not from archaic poetry (like those of Empedocles) but from contemporary medical writing, such as his use of *skēnos* (tent, hut) to refer to the human body, a usage derived

du langage" (2010, 12, 15). See also Cassin 2017, 36: "To say that atomism is a physical representation of discourse is to say that discourse is the proper object of physics or even that the *logos* is the *phusis* that needs to be described."

79. The artificial nature of language is also suggested by Democritus's artisanal metaphors—the gods' names are their "speaking statues" (B142/D206); Homer "built (*etektēnato*) an order of all sorts of verses" (B21/D221)—by his wordplay (e.g. on *gunē/gonē* in B122a/D167), and by his analysis of the evolution of human communication (Diod. Sic. 1.8.1–9 < B5/D202): posited by convention, language is one of the *tekhnai* men learned through need and experience (1.8.3, 1.8.9). Brancacci (1986) argues that Proclus misrepresents Democritus's theory of language, which he believes takes aim at the Parmenidean unity of words and being. Cf. Piergiacomi 2017.

80. As Cicero remarks, "Heraclitus is very obscure, Democritus not at all" (*Div.* 2.133 < A34/R7). Only *isorropon* (for different names applied to the same thing) is not immediately comprehensible. Its base meaning is "equally weighted"; here it seemingly indicates the precise equivalence between words. *Metōnumon* is supplied by Diels. The fragment offers as an example of name change Theophrastus (formerly Tyrtamus). If this refers to the Peripatetic philosopher, he postdated Democritus; some thus question the attribution of the fragment.

81. Plutarch deems his diction "divine and magnificent" (*daimoniōs, megaloprepōs*, A77/R9). Many examples of Democritus's coinages are helpfully collected at Laks-Most R4. On Democritus's style, see Norden 1915, 22–23; Von Fritz 1938, 24–38; Patzer 2006, 155–58; and Hose 2016, 242.

from, or at least shared with, Hippocrates.[82] There are few overtly poetic words in the extant fragments.[83] The bulk of his coinages are minor variations on everyday Greek vocabulary, new but proximate forms of familiar words (like *doxis* for *doxa* in B7/D18) or new words produced following regular patterns of Greek word formation (like *apatēton*, "untrodden," a *hapax legomenon* formed normally from the verb *pateō*, B131/R3f).[84]

Indeed, his linguistic inventions are so minor one might wonder why he even bothered. For instance, he calls hearing "a receptacle for words" (*ekdokheion muthōn*, A126a/D155). *Ekdokheion* is unparalleled in classical Greek but is easily derived from *ekdekhomai* (to receive).[85] There were other words available in Greek to express the idea of a receptacle: why did Democritus go out of his way to invent this word? Not for poetic effect: the metaphor is faded and unambitious; it doesn't evoke a particularly strong image or carry an affective valence. Instead, the point of these coinages seems to be to construct a technical language that is immediately legible but also noticeably distinct from normal language and in which the true meaning of words—artificial but unambiguous—is ultimately determined by

82. Other words that occur only or mainly in medical writings include *apoplēxiē* and *epilēpsia* (B32/D163a–b), *eurous* (A162/D201), *humēn* (B5/D129, A93/D117), *ambē* (B29/R4b), *palmos* (A47/D52). See Vlastos 1945, 587; and Holmes 2010, 202–5, 216–27. The line of influence may run in the opposite direction: the Suda reports that Democritus taught Hippocrates (A10/P28). See Salem 1996, 220–63; Gemelli Marciano 2007, 213–24; and Damiani 2020.

83. Among them we might list the "honeycombed" bones of bulls' horns (*tenthrēniōdes*, A155/D192) and the "wave-like" motion of worms (*kumatoeidōs*, B126/D196), with their metaphor and strong visual imagery; or the description of a cylinder as a "rolling mass" (*olooitrokhon*, B162/D215), a word that repurposes Homeric vocabulary (e.g. *Il.* 13.137). At B168/D36 the description of atoms "sprinkled about" in the void (*peripalassesthai*, if Diels's emendation is correct) might also have a Homeric feel. In general, there are very few metaphors in the extant fragments, and they tend to be so weak that it is hard to determine whether they are really metaphors at all. For instance, when Democritus speaks of the *kanōn* by which mortals are measured in B6/D17, it seems doubtful that a fifth-century Greek would automatically think of a carpenter's rule. Where we do find lively similes for atomic action—crowds of people in a public square (Sen. *QNat.* 5.2.1 = A93a/D118) or dust motes in a sunbeam (Arist. *De an.* 1.2 403b31–404a9 = 67A28/D132)—there is no evidence that these are original to Democritus. Interestingly, some of Democritus's most vivid language describes the violent process of sexual reproduction (B32/D163, A151/D179).

84. Hesychius flags *apatēton* as irregularly compounded (B131/R3f), but see Chantraine 1968, 863. Likewise, the various compounds with *ameipsi*– (*ameipsikhron*, changing color, B139a/R4c; *ameipsikosmiē*, changing order, B138/D83b; *ameipsirhusmein*, changing configuration, B139/D38) are all *hapax legomena* but easily derived from *ameibō*. Cf. *askalēnes* (equilateral, B132/R4f) from *skalēnos* (uneven); *brōkhmōdēs* (moist, B133/R4g) from *brekhō* (to wet); *lapathous* (pits, B122/R4k) from *lapassō* (to empty); *sous* (impulse, A62/D125) from *seuō* (to rush). *Enkatabussousthai*, which at A77/D152 describes the deep penetration of images into the pores of perceivers, is a *hapax*, but the combination of the two prefixes and *bussos* (a variant of *buthos*) easily yields the meaning.

85. *Ekdokheion* is found in later Greek: Josephus uses it for a reservoir or water tank. Cf. *dexamenai*, receptacles for fluids (B135/D182). Other available options included other forms of the same root (*hupodokhē, dokhē, dokheion, dexamenē*) or separate words like *angeion*.

the discourse itself.[86] For example, Democritus supplies our only classical instance of the noun *deikelon*, a minor variation on *deikēlon*, meaning a representation, exhibition, or image.[87] The meaning of *deikelon* (derived from *deiknumi*, to show) seems obvious, but the unexpected vowel quantity marks it and alerts us to the possibility of a special meaning: the ancient commentator who quotes it defines the word as "an efflux similar in form to things" (B123/D146), a *terminus technicus* within Democritus's atomic theory of perception. The same may be said for the various permutations on the common noun *rhusmos* (the Ionic form of *rhuthmos*, meaning measured motion, rhythm, symmetry or order). Democritus coins the novel forms *epirhusmiē* (B7/D18), *metarhusmoō* (B33/D403), and *ameipsirhusmia* (B8a/D2b.V) as terms of art for his atomic configurations, appropriating an everyday word and transforming it, by way of minor morphological tweaks, into a series of technical terms.[88] He does the same with many other common words, including *tropē* (for atomic position, 67A6/D31, A38/D32, A123/D72), *metapiptein* (for atomic motion, B9/D15, B101/≠LM, A135/D64, B191/D226), even *atoma* and *kenon*.

Through this precise and understated linguistic innovation, Democritus creates a new technical language for his new world-system, one in which meaning is determined primarily by the system itself as a feature of its metadiscursive totalization. At once natural and constructed, etic and thetic, this *logos* enables Democritus to "speak concerning all things," giving each one a name that will be unique and specific. By positing a language of reality that is itself real—a direct enactment of atomic physics—and translating that reality into *nomos* through his subtle variations on conventional parlance, Democritus appears to span B9/D14's gulf between *nomos* and *eteos*, convention and atomic reality, so as to forge a metadiscourse that is transparent, universal, and real.

Within this universal discourse one thing, however, remains unspoken: the *den*. Democritus speaks of atoms and void; he speaks of something and of nothing. But he does not speak of 'othing. He invents this word, but he cannot put it to work within his totalizing world-system. As an ostentatious linguistic invention, *den* would seem to exemplify the posited nature of words for Democritus. It is manifestly the artifact of *thesis* not *phusis*. But unlike his other coinages, *den*

86. Patzer 2006, 164: "Demokrit ist recht eigentlich der Erfinder der *wissenschaftlichen* Prosa." This is a feature of all technical, including philosophical, discourse: compare, e.g. Lacan's Symbolic and Real. On ancient Greek technical writing, see further Thesleff 1966; Havelock 1983, 20–41; Van der Eijk 1997; Asper 2007, 11–56; Schironi 2010; and Fögen 2016.

87. *Deikēlon* (with an eta) is used as early as Herodotus (2.171). *Deikelon* (with an epsilon) is not found again until the *Anthologia Graeca* in epigrams attributed to late authors Paulos Silentiarios (5.260.2) and Agathios Skholastikos (9.153.4, 16.332.2).

88. Aristotle considers *rhusmos* a term of art for atomic configuration (67A6/D31, A38/D32; cf. B139/D38). Democritus wrote treatises "On changes of configuration" (*Peri ameipsirhusmiōn*) and "On different configurations" (*Peri tōn diapherontōn rhusmōn*). *Ameipsirhusmein* shows up at Hippoc. *Epist.* 18.10, but the others are unparalleled.

is neither transparent nor univocal, as the doxographers' efforts to gloss it demonstrate. It can be made to signify only when translated as *atomon*, but that, as we have seen, is a mistranslation. If the *den* denotes the atom as the negation of nothing, it seems not to *signify* that concept so much as to materially instantiate it in its own morphological formation.[89] In that sense perhaps it exemplifies Porter's understanding of Democritean words as material *stoikheia*. As a linguistic element, however, the *den* is inert: it resists combination within larger semantic or syntactical units of meaning. Atoms, linguistic and physical, combine to produce all the things of the world and the words that name them. But the *den* exists in isolation. It bears linguistic relation to no words other than those it contains within itself, *hen* and *mēden*, and it cannot arrange these in such a way as to produce a coherent meaning. A nonexistent word, a meaningless signifier with no obvious signified, *den* seems to belong to language not as the vehicle of lucid communication but, as Cassin argues, as a system characterized by ambiguity, obscurity, non-sense.[90]

Den thus seems to be the exception to Democritus's Olympian discourse and to mark the limits of its totalizing vision. "In reality atoms and void." But atoms and void—what is and what is not, *to on* and *to mē on*—do not provide an exhaustive description of reality. There is something left over, something that is neither atom nor void but also somehow both. A less-than-nothing that is more-than-everything, the *den* exceeds Democritus's *logos peri tōn xumpantōn* and reveals that *logos* to be incomplete, not-all. In so doing, it speaks to the status of knowledge and truth in Democritus's philosophy and the nature of this philosophy as a science. Let us return one final time to B9/D14: "By convention sweet and by convention bitter, by convention hot, by convention cold, by convention color, but in reality (*eteēi*) atoms and void." This fragment implicitly promises us a knowledge of reality in its entirety: atoms and void really are and are all that really is; knowing them we know everything. But the expression of that truth is oddly limiting. Sextus Empiricus, as we have seen, assimilates Democritus's *eteos* to Parmenides's *alētheia*, explaining, "he means that none of the phenomena appears according to truth (*kat' alētheian*) but only according to opinion" (*kata doxan, Math.* 7.135 < B9/R108). Parmenides's terminology was available to Democritus, but he pointedly avoids it. His binary of *nomos* vs. *eteos*—a coupling found nowhere else in Greek literature—conflates Parmenides's dichotomy of *doxa* vs. *alētheia* with contemporary sophistic debates over *nomos* vs. *phusis* in a way that distances him from both.

89. Eyers (2012) differentiates the "signifier-in-relation" (which produces meaning through differential relation to other signifiers) from the "signifier-in-isolation," which "designates the signifier as Real, isolated in its material element away from the networks of relation that render it conducive to meaning" (38). The latter describes well the linguistic qualities of the *den*.

90. See Cassin 2020, 106–9. She thus considers *den* "the signifier that signifies the signifier" (2020, 102), both in its genesis out of difference and in its refusal of a univocal meaning; cf. 2017, 37–39. Ambiguity is built into the very definition: the LSJ entry (*deis-denos*) gives as the first definition "no one or thing" and as the second, "something." On the contradictory entry in Chantraine, cf. Cassin 2017, 26.

Instead of either *phusis* (the physical nature of reality) or *alētheia* (the truth about that reality), we get *eteos*.[91] This word, which occurs in five of the eight fragments quoted by Sextus, is a curious choice. It is not a philosophical word: it appears nowhere else in philosophical prose of the archaic or classical period, and was uncommon enough that scholiasts felt the need to gloss it (they invariably understand it as *alēthes*).[92] Galen, in his exegesis of B9/D14, suggests that Democritus invented the word.[93] But in fact the adjective appears frequently in Homer in regard to prophetic signs and human speech. Its most common usage is in conditional clauses to verify claims (if that is true, as you say) or beliefs (if that is true, as it seems).[94] In Aristophanes it occurs only in questions: "Is that really true?"[95] In Hippocrates, it names the hallucinations of the mad, who "cry although nothing is harming or hitting them, fear what is not fearful, are bothered by things they should not be, and perceive nothing really (*eteēi*) as sane men should" (*De diaeta* i–iv 35.60–61). In contemporary usage, then, *eteos* seems to mark an unsure relation between human knowledge and reality. It functions more as a question mark than an anchor point of truth.[96]

91. Galen (*Elem. Hipp.* 1.2 = A49/D23b) simply conflates the three terms, in a single sentence (quoted in n. 93 below) glossing *eteos* as both *phusis* and *alēthes*. *Phusis* might have been expected here: it was part of Democritus's lexicon and perhaps even one of his terms for the atom (A58, B168/D36; cf. B26/D205, B21/D221, B33/D403, B176/D252). Treatises *Peri phuseōs*, *Peri anthrōpou phusios*, and *Peri phuseōs kosmou* are attributed to Democritus, but these rather generic titles may have been assigned to the works later. On the title *Peri Phuseōs*, see Naddaf 2005, 16–35; and on Democritus's multifarious use of the word *phusis*, Morel 2007; Taylor 2007b, 2–9.

92. The only two exceptions are Epimenides fr. 22.1 and Phaenias fr. 11.25, both passages with strong Homeric influence. It is worth noting that *eteēi* in Sextus's quotations is an emendation. The manuscript has *aitiē* (and in one case the nonsensical *toiē*). *Aitiē* is agrammatical and clearly wrong, but the correction suggests that *eteos* was an uncommon word and the copyist replaced it with one with a more respectable philosophical pedigree.

93. Gal. *Elem. Hipp.* 1.2 = A49/D23b: "*Nomōi* means the same thing as 'conventionally' and 'for us,' not in accordance with the *phusis* of things themselves; the latter in turn he calls *eteēi* from *eteon*, which means *alēthes*, having invented the word." It is unclear whether Galen is claiming Democritus invented the adjective or merely its dative form.

94. Of prophecy: *Il.* 2.300, 12.217. Of truthful human speech: *Il.* 7.359, 12.233, 14.125, 15.53, 20.255. Verifying claims: *Il.* 8.423–24, 13.375; *Od.* 19.215–17, 23.35–36, 24.258–59. Verifying impressions: *Il.* 18.305; *Od.* 13.328, 23.107–108, 24.352. It is also used of the correct interpretation of divine will (*Il.* 5.104, 13.153; *Od.* 16.320) and of legitimate paternity (*Od.* 3.120–23, 9.528–9, 16.300–301). Of the twenty-two occurrences in Homer, the only two that do not follow *ei* also occur in contexts of uncertainty: *Il.* 2.300: "wait until we know whether Calchas prophesies truly or not"; *Il.* 20.255: "many things true and not."

95. E.g. "Who are you *eteon?*" (*Eq.* 733, *Vesp.* 184); "What is this *eteon?*" (*Nub.* 93, *Vesp.* 836). Cf. *Eq.* 32, 1246, 1392; *Eccl.* 376; *Nub.* 35, 820, 1502; *Vesp.* 8; and *Ach.* 322, 609. Aeschylus associates it with true naming at *Sept.* 830.

96. Hesiod's Muses famously contrast "lies resembling real things" (*pseudea . . . etumoisin homoia*) to "truths" (*alēthea, Theog.* 27–28). If, as Snell (1975) and Krischer (1965) suggest, in archaic Greek *alēthes* denoted veracity (true communication) and *etumos* ontic reality, Democritus, I am claiming, reverses the relation and problematizes the latter. But these terms were ambiguous already in Homer and Hesiod (Tor 2017, 65–72) and shifted over time (Cole 1983).

Eteos thus collapses back into *nomos*, rendering Democritus's reality—the truth his philosophy offers—uncertain. Whereas Parmenides's *alētheia* is the singular passage (*poros*) out of the ignorance of *doxa* to an absolute and ultimate truth, Democritus's *eteos* leaves us in aporia: "In reality to recognize what each thing is is in aporia" (*eteēi hoion hekaston gignōskein en aporōi esti*, B8/D19). The same non-knowledge that divides the ethical subject thus forms a void within reality itself. It is not simply that we know nothing *about* reality (which would thereby be left whole and perfect beyond our knowledge) but that we know nothing *in* reality, and reality is defined by that non-knowledge.[97] *Eteos*—reality itself as well as Democritus's revelation of it—is incomplete and riven by negativity. Truth, exiled from reality, can appear only as a negative projection in an inaccessible beyond: "In reality we know nothing, for *alētheia* is in an abyss" (*eteēi de ouden idmen; en buthōi gar hē alētheia*, B117/D24).[98]

Within the closed circuit between *nomos* and *eteos*, Democritus's *logos* circles around that abyss without ever actually speaking it, and it is constituted by that futility. "This *logos* demonstrates (*dēloi*) that in reality we know nothing about anything" (*eteēi ouden ismen peri oudenos*, B7/D18). Unable to illuminate the abyssal *alētheia* of the Real, Democritus's *logos* can only demonstrate the non-knowledge that characterizes reality, and it does so over and over again: "That in reality (*eteēi*) we do not comprehend what each thing is or is not has been demonstrated (*dedēlōtai*) in many ways" (B10/D16). That is all it has done and all it ever will do: "And yet it will be clear (*dēlon estai*) that in reality (*eteēi*) to recognize what each thing is is in aporia" (*en aporōi*, B8/D19). Democritus's *logos* is nothing but the reiterated demonstration of this aporia.

Thus Democritus's entire philosophical project is structured like the *den*, the subtraction of a non-knowledge of non-knowledge (*a-poria*) that yields truth as the negation of a negation (*a-lētheia*). *Den*, "forgotten" within Democritus's text, is the material remainder and reminder of that unforgettable truth. A solipsistic signifier that cannot be assimilated into an atomic symbolic order, embodying (not signifying) an ontology that cannot be articulated within that order, *den* is exorbitant to Democritus's philosophical discourse and his *logos peri tōn xumpantōn*. And yet, this universalizing discourse encompasses even what eludes

97. This is, in essence, the point of Barad (2007) in regard to quantum physics, which she argues marks a revolution not merely in epistemology (Heisenberg) but in ontology (Bohr). In her terms, the *den* means that knowledge of reality is always attended by non-knowledge (Heisenberg's uncertainty principle) and, further, that such non-knowledge is a feature of reality itself (Bohr's indeterminacy principle).

98. Wismann (2010, 14–15, 49–50) understands *alētheia* similarly as a real beyond representation of which atoms are just the linguistic trace. The abyss figures in B172/D268 (one of the Stobaean fragments and therefore of questionable authenticity) as an example of things that are sources of both good and evil: "Deep water is useful for many things but also, conversely, an evil, for there is a danger of drowning. So a solution was discovered: teach people to swim." We could say that Democritus's *logos*, unable to plumb the depths of the Real, teaches us how to swim around it.

it and communicates even what it cannot say, for if we have any inkling of the *den* as what exceeds Democritus's *logos* it is because it has stowed away, scandalously, within that *logos.*

It is this, in the end, and not merely his intuition of the atom, that makes Democritus a scientist. True science, as Lacan defines it, incorporates the Real into its own discourse as the internal limit of its knowledge and as the acknowledgment of its own incompleteness.[99] Bruce Fink, in explicating this definition, offers as an example Werner Heisenberg who, by setting a limit on science's ability to determine the precise state of the elementary particle at any moment, introduced the Real into physics in the form of quantum indeterminacy. Physics, Fink writes, "when carried out in a truly scientific spirit, is ordained and commanded by the real, that is, by that which does not work, by that which does not fit."[100] Heisenberg himself rejected Democritus as a direct predecessor because (following Aristotle) he understood Democritean atoms as stable and unchanging material bodies: he knew only the reality (*eteos*) of Democritus's atomic theory, not the truth (*alētheia*) of the *den* as "that which does not fit" within that theory and that challenges it from within.[101] In the *den*, Democritus brings the Real into atomic theory as its internal limit and constitutive aporia, and into his universal *logos* as the (n)othing it cannot say. In saying it, Democritus is a true scientist.

99. Lacan 2006. Lacan associates science with the hysteric's discourse: see Fink 1995, 132–35, 138–46; and Conclusion, n. 11.

100. Fink 1995, 134–35.

101. Heisenberg 1958, 69–75, cited by Wismann (2010, 24). See also Barad (2007, 138), likewise differentiating the "atomistic metaphysics" of Democritus from the essentially indeterminate (quantum) metaphysics of Bohr. I hope to have shown that indeterminacy was a feature of the metaphysics of atomism from the beginning.

Conclusion

The Prose of the World

It is precisely because he was a poet that Parmenides says what he has to say to us in the least stupid of manners. Otherwise, the idea that being is and that nonbeing is not, I don't know what that means to you, but personally I find that stupid.

—JACQUES LACAN

This book has traced the productive aporia between *logos* and *onta* at the heart of early Greek ontology. It has argued that for the Presocratics, that aporia is both inescapable and generative. As the sophist Gorgias said, "The things that exist and that are (*ta onta*) are not speech (*logos*)" (Gorg. B3.84/D26b.84). If they were, there would be nothing to say about being, inasmuch as world and word would be identical. The Presocratics have a great deal to say about being, and they say it with exceptional innovation and artistry. Their approach to the nonidentity of language and being is a defining feature of their philosophy. The sophists, when faced with the schism between *logos* and *onta*, throw in their lot with the former. For Gorgias, this schism means that all *logos* can speak is *logos*, and it is irrational (*alogon*) to try to say otherwise. Thus being becomes an effect of language, and ontology essentially a *logos* about *logos*.[1] Plato, by contrast, takes up the banner of *onta*. His theory of the Forms fixes and reifies being, preserving it both from the vagaries of phenomenal becoming and from language, which is relegated to the sphere of the secondary and simulacral.

Epigraph: From *On Feminine Sexuality: The Limits of Love and Knowledge (1972–73); Encore: The Seminar of Jacques Lacan, Book XX,* by Jacques Lacan, translated by Bruce Fink, 22.

1. "We do not reveal what is (*ta onta*) to those near us, but *logos,* which is different from existing things" (Gorg. B3.84/D26b.84). Cassin characterizes the sophists' ontology as a logology (1995, 23–117; 2000, 961–64). She sets the sophists against Plato and Aristotle as (anti)philosophers of equivocal *logos* against the latter's philosophy of univocal being and meaning. The Presocratics get lost in this dichotomy, despite Cassin's brilliant work on Parmenides and Democritus.

If the sophists opt for *logos* and Plato for *onta*, the Presocratics sustain the aporia between the two, and this is one of the motors driving their thought. We have seen how each author attempts to resolve the tension between words and world, bringing the two into alignment. But in each case we have also noticed a resistance to such ontological closure: again and again, these authors reopen the gap between language and being and reproduce the tension between them. Parmenides, as we saw in chapter 1, attempts to purify language of its doxic ambiguities so that, as he says, "a single utterance of road is still left: that Is" (B8.1–2/D8.6–7). He dreams of a transparent *logos* of "Is." But he sustains that dream through metaphors: the metaphor of Necessity's bonds required to bind his vision of Being also exposes its boundedness precisely by language. Heraclitus seems to conflate language and being with a *logos* that names the structure of both. For him, as I argued in the second chapter, the *homologia* between the cosmic *logos* and his own produces a universe of exceptional unity and coherence. And yet even as he works to sustain that unity, he does not fully eliminate incoherence; instead he preserves it as a space of difference within his cosmos, an interval that is the enabling condition both of his philosophical project and of human life.

Like Parmenides and Heraclitus, Empedocles creates a *logos* of being—not by forging a language of being but by positing the material being of language: *logos* is a thing, composed of the same root elements as any other thing. Empedocles attempts to write this rhizomatic ontology from within it, but in doing so reinscribes a stable authorial self that reopens the schism between *logos* and *onta* that the theory seems to close. The author himself marks the point on the Möbius strip where the two cross without meeting. The tension between the desire to resolve the aporia of ontology and the desire to sustain it that we observed in the first three chapters has a politics that became evident in the fourth. Anaxagoras's Nous at once organizes the cosmos (in that sense making it a *kosmos* to begin with) and renders it visible and representable, imposing a rational order (*logos*) on the things that are (*ta onta*). Anaxagoras is complicit with Nous, and that complicity, I argued, is the condition of possibility of his cosmological project. But he also resists Nous's sovereign logic of being: his paratactic style, encoding an alternative to Nous's order of things, exposes both its costs and its contingency, political and philosophical.

Democritus, finally, would seem to bring not only being but also nonbeing under the rule of *logos* with his construction of a transparent and universal discourse "concerning all things." And yet, once more aporia is introduced in the form of the *den*. A rock of the Real within the symbolic order, the *den* would seem to embody the unity of word and thing of which Parmenides dreamed with his *Esti*. But *den* unites a (non)word with a (no)thing, its indeterminacy vitiating the identitarian logic of a "correspondence theory of truth." The unspeakable name of an impossible being, *den* exceeds both *logos* and *onta*, revealing the limits of both; it is the "parasite of ontology."[2]

2. Cassin 2020, 107.

The rift between language and being is thus generative for the Presocratics. Whereas the sophists and Plato both move past this crossroads in one direction or the other, the Presocratics linger at the impasse. They embrace this aporia as a creative resource (*poros*) for thought and build it into their theories, and their ambivalent response to it forms the very substance of their philosophy. This is because, for these thinkers, language is never supplementary nor purely mimetic but is always part of the world it describes. For Empedocles that is literally true: words are things and they "run through" other things, flowing, combining and separating, entering the listener to produce meaning. The material being of language makes it impossible to differentiate the metaphorical from the literal or the author's artistry from words' own actancy. When we read that Philotēs, "inborn in their joints (*arthrois*)" causes mortals to "think dear (*phila*) thoughts and accomplish conjoint (*arthmia*) deeds" (*emphutos arthrois, tēi te phila phroneousi kai arthmia erga telousi*, B17.22–23/D73.253–54), is this a skillful verbal representation of Philotēs's influence or is it simply the manifestation of that influence? In speaking of Harmonia, the signifier is in harmony with its signified, and that linguistic harmony both explicates her effect and enacts it directly in the internal rhyme of *phroneousi* and *telousi* and the homophony of *arthrois* and *arthmia*, both from the same linguistic "root." Describing Love, Empedocles's words fall under its sway. For Empedocles and for all the authors we have discussed, language is vitally rooted in life. Thus even when they composed in meter, the Presocratics wrote a "prose of the world" in both senses of the genitive—theirs is a discourse about the world that belongs in a fundamental way to that world.[3]

Heraclitus, like Empedocles, harmonizes world and words: *logos* is both the structure of the cosmos and its linguistic articulation. Thus Alexander Mourelatos views Heraclitus as a precursor to Plato in creating a "*logos*-textured world," the world characterized by discursive mediation and conceptual abstraction in which we still live today.[4] Nietzsche, by contrast, praises Heraclitus for his refusal to elevate concepts over things, divorcing metaphysics from physics.[5] Heraclitus enables both interpretations and fully conforms to neither. His bow and lyre are at once signifiers of underlying principles and a material instantiation of those principles. His cosmic fire will burn your finger, and every bedside candle is a spark of the eternal flame. Physics metaphysics, metaphysics physics: a perfectly Heraclitean paradox. Thus the "worldliness" of their prose and verse does not mean that the

3. *The Prose of the World* was the working title of an unfinished work by Merleau-Ponty (1973, xiii), which was to present a phenomenological theory of truth. It is also the title of the second chapter of Foucault's *The Order of Things* (1970), where it denotes the system of resemblances that makes the world both legible and in need of reading. Both take the phrase from Hegel's *Aesthetics*, where it describes "a world of finitude and mutability, of entanglement in the relative, of the pressure of necessity from which the individual is in no position to withdraw" (1975a, 150; cf. 245, 259, 566, 598: "the common prose of life").

4. Mourelatos 2008b, 299.

5. Nietzsche 1962, 51.

Presocratics were "premetaphysical" or incapable of metaphysical thought.[6] Even the most thoroughgoing materialists among them are metaphysicians: for Democritus atoms and void are all there is, but atoms and void, as Hegel observed, are conceptual objects, and their interactions constitute a metaphysical principle.[7] Rather, metaphysical principles are so thoroughly immersed in the physical world that their status in relation to that world is undecidable. Are Empedocles's Love and Strife higher forces that organize the root elements or do they simply name the immanent relations between those elements? Is Anaxagoras's sovereign Nous ontologically separate from the things he rules or is he merely a thing himself? Even Parmenides, the most metaphysical of the Presocratics (as Nietzsche charged), does not fully leave behind the sublunary realm of phenomenal becoming in his journey toward Being. The conundrum of the relation between his Aletheia and Doxa stands as the ultimate symptom of the conceptual inextricability of the two.[8] Metaphysical truths for the Presocratics are thus never beyond the physical world (*meta*) but always stand with or within it (*meta*).

This immanent metaphysics is far from naive. If the Presocratics' world is not fully "*logos*-textured," no more is it (in Mourelatos's dichotomy) a "naive metaphysics of things," in which each thing appears in its own "is-ness," without mediation or abstraction.[9] Indeed, these authors reflected in sophisticated ways on the very idea of abstraction and on the relation between physics and what claims to succeed and supersede it. Anaxagoras's Nous may seem to represent the apotheosis of abstraction, the triumph of Mind over matter. But his rise, as we saw, was not uncontested, including by Anaxagoras himself. For Anaxagoras, the relation between physics and metaphysics is a power relation. The move from the former to the latter is not an intellectual progression at once natural and triumphant, but rather the contingent outcome of political and discursive contest between two different "distributions of the sensible" and understandings of reality.

Anaxagoras's reflection on the relation between physics and metaphysics was carried out, as we saw, not only through language but *in* language, in the structure

6. *Pace* Heidegger and Fink 1993, 65, 74–76; cf. Heidegger 2018. Longing for a "before" of metaphysics is often taken to motivate Nietzsche's interest in the Presocratics, but Porter (2000, 21) argues that Nietzsche's studies of pre-Platonic philosophy in fact "reveal the *inescapability* of metaphysical thinking." As Nietzsche (1962, 83) comments on Parmenides's concept of Being, "Through words and concepts we shall never reach beyond the wall of relations, to some sort of fabulous primal ground of things."

7. Hegel 1975b, 144: "The atom, in fact, is itself a thought; and hence the theory which holds matter to consist of atoms is a metaphysical theory." Likewise, Lacan 1998, 71: "The atom is simply an element of flying signifierness." Cf. chapter 5, n. 78, on the atom as signifier.

8. Simplicius *in Cael.* 556.25–30 (< Parm. A14/R7): Parmenides and Melissus are rightly called *phusikoi* and their works titled *Peri Phuseōs,* for the nature of what is (*tēn tōn ontōn phusin*) is also part of *phusis,* and these authors speak not just of what is *huper phusin* but also of *ta phusika.*

9. Mourelatos 2008b, 316. Cf. Merleau-Ponty 1973, 4: "We all secretly venerate the ideal of a language which in the last analysis would deliver us from language by delivering us to things."

of his sentences. Speculations on *logos* and *to on* necessarily take place within both: there is no metalinguistic position from which to examine language, nor a meta-ontological vantage on being. That means that in the course of working through the paradoxes of ontology, these thinkers inevitably reproduce them. The tension between being and language that generates their thought also recurs within it, creating certain incoherences within their theories. These incoherences within the work, like the ontological aporia that produces them, are both irreducible and generative. They arise out of the primary desires and commitments that motivate the text, and they provide its fundamental architecture. Parmenides wants both to subordinate language to *To Eon* and to bind *To Eon* within language. Those two goals are incompatible, and the tension between them structures his entire text in the competing geometries of road and circuit, in the schism between the Aletheia and Doxa, in the two-way mimesis between a circular poem and the sphere of Being. In Heraclitus, the unresolvable tension between a drive to synthesis (what differs *agrees*) and the preservation of difference within sameness (what *differs* agrees) is felt at every level, from the nonclosure of the cosmic cycle to the slightest arrhythmia in his symmetrical aphorisms. Empedocles's every word vibrates with the tension between the mobile ontology he presents and the fixed position from which he must present it, while Anaxagoras's competing commitments to Nous and to the things organize both his cosmos and his cosmology. His irreconcilable fantasies of a totalizing discourse and of something that exceeds it create a parallax not just in the reception of Democritus's atomic theory but also within that theory itself. In each case, opposing lines of force within the author's thought form the "back-turned harmony" that structures both that thought and its expression. To attempt to reduce or reconcile them would be to unstring the work as a whole.

It is at the crux between these competing forces that we encounter the author within his text. One way in which readers have traditionally sought to reconcile a work's tensions and eliminate incoherences is by appeal to an all-knowing author, for whom any apparent inconsistency is actually deliberate and intended.[10] In the texts we have been discussing, however, the authorial persona does not appear in the guise of an all-knowing, all-intending subject. Instead it appears as an embodiment of the text's structuring contradictions. This may seem a counterintuitive claim for works that boast divine inspiration (Parmenides) or even authorship (Empedocles), in which the authorial *egō* claims understanding beyond all other mortals (Heraclitus), a vision of the invisible (Anaxagoras), or an Olympian knowledge of all things (Democritus). But in fact in each case study, the authorial "I" emerges at the point of maximum torsion within the theory.

10. Foucault 1984, 119: "The author is therefore the ideological figure by which one marks the manner in which we fear the proliferation of meaning." By "the author," I mean not the historical author, whose intentions are unrecoverable, but the author function, the position or persona of the author projected by and within the text. The author function is a retroactive effect of interpretation, but, as Foucault remarks (112), it is not pure projection, any more than the interpretation itself.

In chapter 3 we saw how Empedocles's poetics and physics of the roots reached their limit with the figure of the poet himself: Empedocles, he of "stable glory," emerged as the singular exception to the unstable ontology he expounds and the site of an incurable schism within his philosophy. Likewise, when Heraclitus says, "listen not to me but to the *logos*," his own *logos* becomes audible at the very moment it articulates a doubleness in the unitary *logos* that underwrites the wisdom that "all things are one" (Her. B50/D46). In Parmenides, the gap between three levels of enunciation—the goddess who reveals the path of Truth, the young initiate who relays her teaching, and the poet who recites their journey—opens the closed circle of the poem's mimesis, leaving the discursive and ontological boundedness of his Being in doubt. Similar tensions mark the authorial position in Anaxagoras and Democritus, the former in the problem of locating the cosmologist's position within his own cosmology, the latter in the problem of speaking the unspeakable within a totalizing world system. In each of these cases, the authorial *egō* emerges not as the stabilizing origin of his own philosophy, securing its meaning by supplying a masterful intent, but instead as a symptom of the aporias that both structure his thought and mark its internal limits.[11]

Such aporias may be considered as failings within an Aristotelian tradition that makes philosophy the pursuit of a univocal truth carried out under the law of noncontradiction. If the definition of truth is, as Aristotle says, "to say of what is that it is and of what is not that it is not" (*to men gar legein . . . to on einai kai to mē on mē einai alēthes, Metaph.* 4.7 1011b26–27), the Presocratics, in troubling the relation between *legein* and *einai*, demand a more capacious definition of truth and an appreciation of the multifarious ways of speaking it. They themselves, as we have seen, found myriad ways of speaking it: in prose and in verse, in metaphors and metonymies, through exposition or imagery, logical argumentation or epic allusion, even through paradox. Thus truth for Heraclitus might be to say of what is that it is and that it is not simultaneously, while the truth of Democritus's *den* might be closer to saying of what is that it is not and of what is not that it is. Paradox and contradiction, then, are not necessarily failures of thought. On the contrary, they can be modes of thought, as well as modes of expression, and can speak a different kind of truth.

This different mode of truth-telling situates the Presocratics at an oblique angle to the Aristotelian definition of philosophy. It may even make them

11. This is to say that the author within these texts speaks the discourse of the hysteric, in Lacan's terms, not that of the master or the university. In the hysteric's discourse, the split subject ($) addresses herself (the hysteric being paradigmatically female) to the master signifier (S_1), showing it to be lacking; in this way she produces knowledge (S_2) and the real (*a*) as the unacknowledged truth of that knowledge (Lacan 2007, 31–38, 94–98, 175–76). The Presocratic philosopher, a subject presumed not to know ($), addresses himself to ontology (S_1), showing it incoherent, inconsistent, contradictory; in doing so he produces his own philosophy as a totalizing system (S_2) and also the truth of that system's gaps and paradoxes (*a*).

antiphilosophers. Antiphilosophers, in Badiou's term, throw down the gauntlet to philosophy by demonstrating that it concerns itself only with truth as the evaluation of statements (i.e., *logos*), not with the "truest" aspect of being that those statements cannot speak.[12] "This," Badiou writes, "is precisely where antiphilosophy deposes philosophy: by showing what its theoretical pretension has missed and which in the end is nothing less than the real."[13]

The Presocratics, even as they aim to offer a *logos peri tōn xumpantōn*, also hint at what that account has missed. In this way they acknowledge the incompleteness of their own discourse and of any totalizing discourse of being. At the same time they gesture to a being inaccessible to *logos*, that unspeakable and senseless (*alogon*) remainder of all ontological inquiry that Lacan calls the Real. We glimpsed this most clearly in the case of Democritus's obscure *den*. A supplement to everything, the *den* shows that the description of reality is not fully exhausted by what is and what is not. There is something left over, a something that, exceeding both meaning and being, is necessarily nothing. In their gaps and aporias, their stutters and incoherences, the Presocratics speak not propositional truths about reality but the Real, which structures those truths but cannot be expressed by them. In this oblique form, they install the Real within their texts as what escapes the compass of their ontological inquiry. That Real appears not as a mystical plenitude of pure being, to be accessed by a ladder of language that, once ascended, is cast away.[14] Rather, the Real as it appears in these texts is itself aporetic, a surplus of both meaning and being produced by the noncongruity of the two.

The Presocratics articulate this paradoxical Real through their poetics, as Lacan suggests in the quotation that serves as an epigraph to this Conclusion.[15] Faced with being, *logos* is reduced to stupidity, Aristotle's vacuous proposition that being is and nonbeing is not. Poetry, Lacan suggests, offered the Presocratics a way of speaking that goes beyond truth as the univocal proposition of an unequivocal being and touches on the Real. To say this is to reiterate the central claim of this book: for the Presocratics, poetics are not extrinsic or secondary to their thought, at best an ornamentation (and at worst an obfuscation) of the reiterated statement that being is and nonbeing is not. Instead, they are a different means of speaking the truth and a means of speaking a different truth. In their poetics, something

12. Badiou 2011, 80: "The antiphilosophical act consists in letting what there is show itself, insofar as 'what there is' is precisely that which no true proposition can say."

13. Badiou 2011, 95.

14. Cf. the discussion in the Introduction and chapter 1.

15. Lacan 1998, 22. Badiou (2005, 9) quotes this passage and argues that for Lacan the Presocratics' poetry prefigures his own attempt to articulate the Real through mathemes. Likewise, Badiou (2011, 137) himself defends philosophy from the antiphilosophers by promoting mathematics as philosophy's language of the Real (cf. Badiou 2014; Badiou 2018, 27–37; and Meillassoux 2009). The recourse to mathematics may seem to align these continental philosophers with the algebraism of analytic philosophy, but for the latter (as Badiou would argue) mathematical formulas express propositional truths, whereas for the former they articulate something beyond such propositions.

speaks through their language rather than being spoken by it. In Democritus's impossible neologism and Anaxagoras's archaizing syntax, in the radical vibrancy of Empedocles's verbiage, in Heraclitus's cosmic symmetries and syncopations and Parmenides's wayward metaphors, we see these writers coming up to the edge of their own thought and going beyond the limits of their own *logos* to articulate a paradoxical truth that remains, as Democritus puts it, "in an abyss" (B117/D24). Their poetics are, in this very *real* sense, their (anti)philosophy.

BIBLIOGRAPHY

Adorno, T. W. 1992. "Parataxis: On Hölderlin's Late Poetry." In *Notes to Literature, Volume II*, edited by T. W. Adorno, translated by S. W. Nicholsen, 109–49. New York.

Agamben, G. 2005. *State of Exception*. Translated by K. Attell. Chicago.

Alcocer Urueta, R. 2023. "The Verb Εἰμί and Its Benefits for Parmenides' Philosophy." *Rhizomata* 11: 140–88.

Aldern, J. D. 2013. "Making Space for North Fork Mono (Nium) Narrative: Land, Learning, Parataxis, Policy, and Water in Central California." *Occasion: Interdisciplinary Studies in the Humanities* 5: 1–23.

Alfieri, V. E. 1979. *Atomos idea: l'origine del concetto dell'atomo nel pensiero greco*. Galatina.

Algra, K. 1999. "The Beginnings of Cosmology." In Long 1999a, 45–65.

Algra, K., and J. Mansfeld. 2001. "Three Thētas in the 'Empédocle de Strasbourg.'" *Mnemosyne* 54: 78–84.

Allen, R. E., and D. J. Furley, eds. 1975. *Studies in Presocratic Philosophy. Vol. II: The Eleatics and Pluralists*. London.

Anderson, G. 2018. *The Realness of Things Past: Ancient Greece and Ontological History*. New York.

Annas, J. 2002. "Democritus and Eudaimonism." In Caston and Graham 2002, 169–81.

Année, M. 2020. "Héraclite, fr. 52 D.-K.: jeux de mots ou nécessité linguistique d'une composition en αἰών majeur?" In Bouvier and Dasen 2020, 47–73.

Asper, M. 2007. *Griechische Wissenschaftstexte: Formen, Funktionen, Differenzierungsgeschichten*. Stuttgart.

Atack, C. 2019. "Tradition and Innovation in the *Kosmos*-Polis Analogy." In Horky 2019, 164–87.

Auerbach, E. 1953. *Mimesis: The Representation of Reality in Western Literature*. Translated by W. R. Trask. Princeton.

Badiou, A. 2005. "Lacan and the Pre-Socratics." In *Lacan: The Silent Partners*, edited by S. Žižek, 7–16. London.

Badiou, A. 2007. *Being and Event*. Translated by O. Feltham. London.

Badiou, A. 2011. *Wittgenstein's Antiphilosophy*. Translated by B. Bosteels. London.

Badiou, A. 2014. *Parménide: L'Être 1, figure ontologique, 1985–1986*. Paris.

Badiou, A. 2018. *Lacan: Anti-Philosophy 3*. Translated by K. Reinhard and S. Spitzer. New York.

Bailey, C. 1964. *The Greek Atomists and Epicurus*. New York. First published 1928.

Baldes, R. W. 1975. "Democritus on Visual Perception: Two Theories or One?" *Phronesis* 20: 93–105.

Ballew, L. 1979. *Straight and Circular: A Study of Imagery in Greek Philosophy*. Assen.

Balme, D. M. 1941. "Greek Science and Mechanism: II. The Atomists." *Classical Quarterly* 35: 23–28.

Baltussen, H. 2005. "The Presocratics in the Doxographical Tradition: Sources, Controversies, and the Current Research." *Studia Humaniora Tartuensia* 6: 1–26.

Barad, K. M. 2007. *Meeting the Universe Halfway: Quantum Physics and the Entanglement of Matter and Meaning*. Durham.

Barker, J., ed. 2006. *Sovereignty Matters*. Lincoln, NE.

Barnes, J. 1982. *The Presocratic Philosophers*. London.

Barnes, J. 1983. "Aphorism and Argument." In Robb 1983a, 91–109.

Barnes, J. 1984. "Reason and Necessity in Leucippus." In Benakis 1984, 141–58.

Barrett, J. 2004. "Struggling With Parmenides." *Ancient Philosophy* 24: 267–91.

Bartelson, J. 1995. *A Genealogy of Sovereignty*. Cambridge.

Becker, O. 1937. *Das Bild des Weges und verwandte Vorstellungen im frühgriechischen Denken*. Berlin.

Benakis, L., ed. 1984. *Proceedings of the First International Congress on Democritus*. Athens.

Benjamin, A. 1988. "Time and Interpretation in Heraclitus." In *Post-Structuralist Classics*, edited by A. Benjamin, 106–31. London.

Benjamin, A. 2010. *Place, Commonality and Judgment: Continental Philosophy and the Ancient Greeks*. New York.

Benveniste, E. 1937. "Expression indo-européenne de l'*éternité*." *Bulletin de la Société de Linguistique de Paris* 38: 103–12.

Bernabé, A. 2009. "Expresiones polares en Heráclito." In Hülsz Piccone 2009, 103–37.

Berryman, S. 2002. "Democritus and the Explanatory Power of the Void." In Caston and Graham 2002, 183–91.

Berryman, S. 2023. "Democritus." *The Stanford Encyclopedia of Philosophy* (Spring 2023 Edition), edited by E. N. Zalta and U. Nodelman. https://plato.stanford.edu/archives/spr2023/entries/democritus.

Betegh, G. 2006. "Eschatology and Cosmology: Models and Problems." In *La costruzione del discorso filosofico nell'età dei Presocratici*, edited by M. M. Sassi, 27–50. Pisa.

Betegh, G. 2009. "The Limits of the Soul: Heraclitus B 45 DK. Its Text and Interpretation." In Hülsz Piccone 2009, 391–414.

Betegh, G. 2013. "On the Physical Aspect of Heraclitus' Psychology." In Sider and Obbink 2013, 225–61.

Bicknell, P. 1968. "The Seat of the Mind in Democritus." *Eranos* 66: 10–21.
Bignone, E., ed. 1916. *Empedocle. Studio critico; traduzione e commento delle testimonianze e dei frammenti.* Turin.
Billings, J. 2021. *The Philosophical Stage: Drama and Dialectic in Classical Athens.* Princeton.
Blanchot, M. 1993. *The Infinite Conversation.* Translated by S. Hanson. Minneapolis.
Blank, D. L. 1982. "Faith and Persuasion in Parmenides." *Classical Antiquity* 1: 167–77.
Böhme, R. 1986. *Die verkannte Muse: Dichtersprache und geistige Tradition des Parmenides.* Berlin.
Bollack, J. 1965. *Empédocle, 1: Introduction à l'ancienne physique.* Paris.
Bollack, J., ed. 1969. *Empédocle, 3: Les origines (commentaires 1 et 2).* Paris.
Bollack, J., ed. 2003. *Les Purifications: Un projet de paix universelle.* Paris.
Bollack, J. 2005. "Empedocles: Two Theologies, Two Projects." In Pierris 2005, 45–72.
Bollack, J. 2006. *Parménide: De l'étant au monde.* Lagrasse.
Bollack, J. 2016. *The Art of Reading: From Homer to Paul Celan.* Translated by C. Porter and S. Tarrow. Washington, DC.
Bollack, J., and H. Wismann. 1972. *Héraclite ou la séparation.* Paris.
Bollack, J., and H. Wismann. 1974. "Le moment théorique." *Revue des sciences humaines* 154: 203–12.
Bossi, B. 2009. "Acerca del significado del fragmento B 62 (DK) de Heráclito." In Hülsz Piccone 2009, 285–314.
Boudouris, K. J., ed. 1989. *Ionian Philosophy.* Athens.
Bouvier, D., and V. Dasen, eds. 2020. *Héraclite: Le temps est un enfant qui joue.* Liège.
Bowra, C. M. 1937. "The Proem of Parmenides." *Classical Philology* 32: 97–112.
Brancacci, A. 1986. "Les mots et les choses: la philosophie du langage chez Démocrite." In *Philosophie du langage et grammaire dans l'antiquité*, edited by H. Joly, 9–28. Brussels.
Brancacci, A. 2007. "Democritus' *Mousika.*" In Brancacci and Morel 2007, 181–205.
Brancacci, A., and P.-M. Morel, eds. 2007. *Democritus: Science, the Arts, and the Care of the Soul.* Leiden.
Bredlow, L. A. 2011. "Parmenides and the Grammar of Being." *Classical Philology* 106: 283–98.
Bremer, D. 1980. "Aristoteles, Empedokles und die Erkenntnisleistung der Metapher." *Poetica* 12: 350–76.
Brennan, T. 1995. "The Text of Anaxagoras Fragment DK 59 B22." *American Journal of Philology* 116: 533–37.
Brooks, C. 1949. *The Well Wrought Urn: Studies in the Structure of Poetry.* London.
Brown, W. 2009. "Sovereign Hesitations." In *Derrida and the Time of the Political*, edited by P. Cheah and S. Guerlac, 114–32. Raleigh.
Bryan, J. 2012. *Likeness and Likelihood in the Presocratics and Plato.* Cambridge.
Bryan, J. 2018. "Reconsidering the Authority of Parmenides' Doxa." In *Authors and Authority in Ancient Philosophy*, edited by J. Bryan, R. Wardy, and R. Warren, 20–40. Cambridge.
Bryan, J. 2020. "The Pursuit of Parmenidean Clarity." *Rhizomata* 8: 218–38.
Buchheim, T. 2005. "Feuer und Flüsse: Überlegungen zum Prinzip des Lebens nach Heraklit." In *Frühgriechisches Denken*, edited by G. Rechenauer, 174–202. Göttingen.
Burkert, W. 1959. "ΣΤΟΙΧΕΙΟΝ: Eine semasiologische Studie." *Philologus* 103: 167–97.

Burkert, W. 1969. "Das Proömium des Parmenides und die 'Katabasis' des Pythagoras." *Phronesis* 14: 1–30.

Burkert, W. 1977. "Air-Imprints or Eidola: Democritus' Aetiology of Vision." *Illinois Classical Studies* 2: 97–109.

Cage, J. 1961. "Lecture on Nothing." In *Silence: Lectures and Writings by John Cage*, 109–27. Middletown, CT.

Calame, C. 1995. *The Craft of Poetic Speech in Ancient Greece*. Translated by J. Orion. Ithaca, NY.

Cambiano, G. 2006. "Unité du savoir et pluralité des savoirs en Grèce ancienne." In *Figure, macchine, sogni: Saggi sulla scienza antica*, edited by G. Cambiano, 1–20. Rome.

Carson, A. 1999. *Economy of the Unlost: Reading Simonides of Keos With Paul Celan*. Princeton.

Cassin, B. 1995. *L'effet sophistique*. Paris.

Cassin, B., ed. 1998. *Parménide: Sur la nature ou sur l'étant. La langue de l'être?* Paris.

Cassin, B. 2000. "Sophists." In *Greek Thought: A Guide to Classical Knowledge*, edited by J. Brunschwig and G. E. R. Lloyd, translated by E. Rawlings and J. Pucci, 957–76. Cambridge, MA.

Cassin, B. 2014. *Sophistical Practice: Toward a Consistent Relativism*. New York.

Cassin, B. 2017. "Ab-Sense, or Lacan From A to D." In *There's No Such Thing as a Sexual Relationship: Two Lessons on Lacan*, by A. Badiou and B. Cassin, translated by S. Spitzer and K. Reinhard, 3–43. New York.

Cassin, B. 2020. *Jacques the Sophist*. Translated by M. Syrotinski. New York.

Caston, V., and D. W. Graham, eds. 2002. *Presocratic Philosophy: Essays in Honour of Alexander Mourelatos*. Aldershot.

Chantraine, P. 1968. *Dictionnaire étymologique de la langue grecque: histoire des mots*. Paris.

Cherniss, H. F. 1935. *Aristotle's Criticism of Presocratic Philosophy*. Baltimore.

Cherubin, R. 2001. "Λέγειν, Νοεῖν, and Τὸ Ἐὸν in Parmenides." *Ancient Philosophy* 21: 277–303.

Cherubin, R. 2004. "Parmenides' Poetic Frame." *International Studies in Philosophy* 36: 7–38.

Cherubin, R. 2005. "Light, Night, and the Opinions of Mortals: Parmenides B8.51–61 and B9." *Ancient Philosophy* 25: 1–23.

Cherubin, R. 2017. "Mortals Lay Down Trusting To Be True." *Epoché* 21: 251–71.

Cherubin, R. 2018. "Parmenides, Liars, and Mortal Incompleteness." *Proceedings of the Boston Area Colloquium of Ancient Philosophy* 33: 1–21.

Cherubin, R. 2019. "Sex, Gender, and Class in the Poem of Parmenides: Difference Without Dualism?" *American Journal of Philology* 140: 29–66.

Chitwood, A. 2004. *Death By Philosophy: The Biographical Tradition in the Life and Death of the Archaic Philosophers Empedocles, Heraclitus, and Democritus*. Ann Arbor.

Ciampa, C. R. 2021. "Eschatological Visions in Pindar and Empedocles." In *Eschatology in Antiquity: Forms and Functions*, edited by H. Marlow, K. Pollmann, and H. Van Noorden, 131–43. New York.

Ciampa, C. R. 2023. "Between Poetry, Philosophy and Medicine: Body, Soul and Dreams in Pindar, Heraclitus and the Hippocratic *On Regimen*." *Rhizomata* 11: 55–76.

Clarke, T. 2019. *Aristotle and the Eleatic One*. Oxford.

Claus, D. B. 1981. *Toward the Soul: An Inquiry Into the Meaning of Ψυχή Before Plato*. New Haven.

Cole, T. 1983. "Archaic Truth." *Quaderni urbinati di cultura classica* 13: 7–28.

Cole, T. 1990. *Democritus and the Sources of Greek Anthropology*. Atlanta.
Colvin, M. 2007. "Heraclitean Flux and Unity of Opposites in Plato's *Theaetetus* and *Cratylus*." *Classical Quarterly* 57: 759–69.
Comay, R., and F. Ruda. 2018. *The Dash—The Other Side of Absolute Knowing*. Cambridge, MA.
Connor, W. R. 1977. "Tyrannis Polis." In *Ancient and Modern: Essays in Honor of G. F. Else*, edited by J. H. D'Arms and J. Eadie, 95–109. Ann Arbor.
Cook, A. 1975. "Heraclitus and the Conditions of Utterance." *Arion* 2: 431–81.
Coope, U. 2005. *Time for Aristotle: Physics IV.10–14*. Oxford.
Cordero, N.-L. 1979. "Les deux chemins de Parménide dans les fragments 6 et 7." *Phronesis* 24: 1–32.
Cordero, N.-L. 2004. *By Being, It Is: The Thesis of Parmenides*. Las Vegas.
Cornford, F. M. 1930. "Anaxagoras' Theory of Matter." *Classical Quarterly* 24: 14–30, 83–95.
Cornford, F. M. 1952. *Principium Sapientiae: The Origins of Greek Philosophical Thought*. Cambridge.
Cosgrove, M. R. 2011. "The Unknown 'Knowing Man': Parmenides, B1.3." *Classical Quarterly* 61: 28–47.
Couloubaritsis, L. 1980. "Considérations sur la notion de Noûs chez Démocrite." *Archiv für Geschichte der Philosophie* 62: 129–45.
Couloubaritsis, L. 1989. "La notion d'*aion* chez Héraclite." In Boudouris 1989, 104–13.
Couloubaritsis, L. 2008. *La pensée de Parménide*. Brussels.
Coxon, A. H. 1968. "The Manuscript Tradition of Simplicius' Commentary on Aristotle's *Physics* I–IV." *Classical Quarterly* 18: 70–75.
Coxon, A. H., ed. 2009. *The Fragments of Parmenides: A Critical Text With Introduction and Translation*. Las Vegas. First published 1986.
Curd, P. 1991. "Knowledge and Unity in Heraclitus." *The Monist* 74: 531–49.
Curd, P. 1992. "Deception and Belief in Parmenides' *Doxa*." *Apeiron* 25: 109–33.
Curd, P. 1998. *The Legacy of Parmenides: Eleatic Monism and Later Presocratic Thought*. Princeton.
Curd, P. 2001. "Why Democritus Was Not a Skeptic." In *Essays in Ancient Greek Philosophy VI: Before Plato*, edited by A. Preus, 149–69. Albany, NY.
Curd, P. 2002. "The Metaphysics of Physics: Mixture and Separation in Empedocles and Anaxagoras." In Caston and Graham 2002, 139–58.
Curd, P. 2005. "On the Question of Religion and Natural Philosophy in Empedocles." In Pierris 2005, 137–62.
Curd, P., ed. 2007. *Anaxagoras of Clazomenae: Fragments and Testimonia*. Toronto.
Curd, P. 2008. "Anaxagoras and the Theory of Everything." In Curd and Graham 2008, 230–49.
Curd, P. 2016. "Powers, Structure, and Thought in Empedocles." *Rhizomata* 4: 55–79.
Curd, P., and D. W. Graham, eds. 2008. *The Oxford Handbook of Presocratic Philosophy*. Oxford.
Damiani, V. 2020. "The Reception of Atomism in Ancient Medical Literature." In Zilioli 2020, 39–60.
Dasen, V. 2020. "La royauté de l'enfant: À propos d'Héraclite et de pratiques ludiques enfantines en Grèce ancienne." In Bouvier and Dasen 2020, 97–123.

DeFilippo, J. G. 1993. "Reply to André Laks on Anaxagoras' ΝΟΥΣ." *The Southern Journal of Philosophy* 31: 39–48.

Deichgräber, K. 1933. "Hymnische Elemente in der philosophischen Prosa der Vorsokratiker." *Philologus* 88: 347–61.

Deichgräber, K. 1958. *Parmenides' Auffahrt zu Göttin des Rechts*. Mainz.

Deichgräber, K. 1963. *Rhythmische Elemente im Logos des Heraklit*. Mainz.

DeLacy, P. 1958. "Οὐ μᾶλλον and the Antecedents of Ancient Scepticism." *Phronesis* 3: 59–71.

Deleuze, G. 1990. *The Logic of Sense*. Translated by M. Lester. New York. First published 1969.

Deleuze, G. 1994. *Difference and Repetition*. Translated by P. Patton. London. First published 1968.

Deleuze, G. 1997. "He Stuttered." In *Essays Critical and Clinical*, translated by D. W. Smith and M. A. Greco, 107–14. London.

Deleuze, G. 2006. *Nietzsche and Philosophy*. Translated by H. Tomlinson. New York. First published 1962.

Deleuze, G., and F. Guattari. 1983a. "What is a Minor Literature?" Translated by R. Brinkley. *Mississippi Review* 11: 13–33. First published 1975.

Deleuze, G., and F. Guattari. 1983b. *Anti-Oedipus: Capitalism and Schizophrenia*. Translated by R. Hurley, M. Seem, and H. R. Lane. Minneapolis. First published 1972.

Deleuze, G., and F. Guattari. 1986. *Kafka: Toward a Minor Literature*. Translated by D. Polan. Minneapolis. First published 1975.

Deleuze, G., and F. Guattari. 1987. *A Thousand Plateaus: Capitalism and Schizophrenia*. Translated by B. Massumi. Minneapolis.

Deleuze, G., and F. Guattari. 1994. *What is Philosophy?* Translated by H. Tomlinson and G. Burchell. New York.

De Man, P. 1979. "Autobiography as De-Facement." *Comparative Literature* 94: 919–30.

Denyer, N., ed. 2001. *Plato: Alcibiades*. Cambridge.

Derrida, J. 1982a. "Tympan." In *Margins of Philosophy*, translated by A. Bass, ix–xxix. Chicago.

Derrida, J. 1982b. "White Mythology: Metaphor in the Text of Philosophy." In *Margins of Philosophy*, translated by A. Bass, 207–71. Chicago. First published 1971.

Derrida, J. 1987. *The Post Card: From Socrates to Freud and Beyond*. Translated by A. Bass. Chicago.

Derrida, J. 1992a. "Aphorism Countertime." In *Acts of Literature*, edited by D. Attridge, translated by N. Royle, 414–33. New York.

Derrida, J. 1992b. "Force of Law: The 'Mystical Foundation of Authority.'" In *Deconstruction and the Possibility of Justice*, edited by D. Cornell, M. Rosenfeld, and D. G. Carlson, translated by M. Quaintance, 3–67. New York.

Derrida, J. 1997. *Politics of Friendship*. Translated by G. Collins. London.

Derrida, J. 2005. *Rogues: Two Essays on Reason*. Translated by P.-A. Brault and M. Naas. Stanford.

Derrida, J. 2009. *The Beast and the Sovereign*. Vol. 1. Translated by G. Bennington. Chicago.

Detienne, M. 1996. *The Masters of Truth in Archaic Greece*. Translated by J. Lloyd. New York.

Detienne, M., and J. P. Vernant. 1978. *Cunning Intelligence in Greek Culture and Society*. Translated by J. Lloyd. Atlantic Highlands, NJ.

Dewald, C. 1987. "Narrative Surface and Authorial Voice in Herodotus' *Histories*." *Arethusa* 20: 147–70.
Dewald, C. 2005. *Thucydides' War Narrative: A Structural Study*. Berkeley.
Dickie, M. W. 1976. "On the Meaning of Ἐφήμερος." *Illinois Classical Studies* 1: 7–14.
Diels, H. 1929. *Doxographi Graeci*. Berlin.
Diels, H. 1969. "Über die Gedichte des Empedokles." In *Kleine Schriften zur Geschichte der antiken Philosophie*, edited by W. Burkert, 127–46. Hildesheim. First published 1898.
Diels, H. 2003. *Parmenides Lehrgedicht*. Sankt Augustin. First published 1897.
Diels, H., and W. Kranz, eds. 1951. *Die Fragmente der Vorsokratiker*. Vol. 1. Zurich. First published 1903.
Diels, H., and W. Kranz, eds. 1952. *Die Fragmente der Vorsokratiker*. Vol. 2. Zurich. First published 1903.
Dilcher, R. 1995. *Studies in Heraclitus*. New York.
Dilcher, R. 2005. "Im-Fluß-sein (Heraklit, B 12)." In *Frühgriechisches Denken*, edited by G. Rechenauer, 203–16. Göttingen.
Dolar, M. 2013a. "The Atom and the Void—From Democritus to Lacan." *Filozofski vestnik* 34: 11–26.
Dolar, M. 2013b. "Tyche, Clinamen, Den." *Continental Philosophy Review* 46: 223–39.
Donahue, T. 2019. "Styles of Sovereignty: Parataxis, Settler-Indigenous Difference, and the Transnationalisms of the Great Basin." *American Literary History* 32: 22–45.
Dover, K. 1997. *The Evolution of Greek Prose Style*. Oxford.
DuBois, P. 1995. *Sappho is Burning*. Chicago.
Edmunds, L. 1972. "Necessity, Chance, and Freedom in the Early Atomists." *Phoenix* 26: 342–57.
Egli, F. 2003. *Euripides im Kontext zeitgenössischer intellektueller Strömungen: Analyse der Funktion philosophischer Themen in den Tragödien und Fragmenten*. Munich.
Ellis, R. 2020a. "Beyond the Human Condition: Duration and Virtuality in Heraclitus." *Ramus* 49: 41–69.
Ellis, R. 2020b. "Ludic Philosophy and Heraclitus' Playing Children." In Bouvier and Dasen 2020, 125–45.
Emlyn-Jones, C. J. 1976. "Heraclitus and the Identity of Opposites." *Phronesis* 21: 89–114.
Evans, M. 2021. "The Work of Justice in Parmenides B 8." *Oxford Studies in Ancient Philosophy* 60: 1–43.
Eyers, T. 2012. *Lacan and the Concept of the 'Real'*. New York.
Fantino, E., U. Muss, C. Schubert, and K. Sier, eds. 2017. *Heraklit im Kontext*. Berlin.
Farrar, C. 1988. *The Origins of Democratic Thinking: The Invention of Politics in Classical Athens*. Cambridge.
Ferella, C. 2024. *Reconstructing Empedocles' Thought*. Cambridge.
Festugière, A. J. 1949. "Le sens philosophique du mot ΑΙΩΝ." *La parola del passato* 4: 172–89.
Feynman, R. 2013. *The Feynman Lectures on Physics*. Vol. 1. Los Angeles.
Filonik, J. 2013. "Athenian Impiety Trials: A Reappraisal." *Dike* 16: 11–96.
Fink, B. 1995. *The Lacanian Subject: Between Language and Jouissance*. Princeton.
Finkelberg, A. 1988. "Parmenides' Foundation of the Way of Truth." *Oxford Studies in Ancient Philosophy* 6: 39–67.
Finkelberg, A. 1998. "On the History of the Greek ΚΟΣΜΟΣ." *Harvard Studies in Classical Philology* 98: 103–36.

Finkelberg, A. 1999. "Being, Truth and Opinion in Parmenides." *Archiv für Geschichte der Philosophie* 81: 233–48.

Finkelberg, A. 2009. "The Cosmic Cycle, a Playing Child, and the Rules of the Game." In Hülsz Piccone 2009, 315–36.

Finkelberg, A. 2013. "Heraclitus, the Rival of Pythagoras." In Sider and Obbink 2013, 147–62.

Finkelberg, A. 2017. *Heraclitus and Thales' Conceptual Scheme: A Historical Study*. Leiden.

Floyd, E. D. 1992. "Why Parmenides Wrote in Verse." *Ancient Philosophy* 12: 251–65.

Fögen, T. 2016. "Technical Literature." In *A Companion to Greek Literature*, edited by M. Hose and D. Schenker, 266–79. Malden, MA.

Folit-Weinberg, B. 2022. *Homer, Parmenides, and the Road to Demonstration*. Cambridge.

Ford, A. L. 2002. *The Origins of Criticism: Literary Culture and Poetic Theory in Classical Greece*. Princeton.

Foucault, M. 1970. *The Order of Things: An Archaeology of the Human Sciences*. New York.

Foucault, M. 1977. *Discipline and Punish: The Birth of the Prison*. Translated by A. Sheridan. New York.

Foucault, M. 1984. "What is an Author?" In *The Foucault Reader*, edited by P. Rabinow, translated by J. V. Harari. 101–20. New York.

Fränkel, H. 1946. "Man's 'Ephemeros' Nature According to Pindar and Others." *Transactions of the American Philological Association* 77: 131–45.

Fränkel, H. 1955. *Wege und Formen frühgriechischen Denkens: literarische und philosophiegeschichtliche Studien*. Munich.

Fränkel, H. 1975. "Studies in Parmenides." In Allen and Furley 1975, 1–48. Translated by R. E. Allen and D. J. Furley. First published 1930.

Freud, S. 1955. "Beyond the Pleasure Principle." In *The Standard Edition of the Complete Psychological Works of Sigmund Freud*, edited and translated by J. Strachey, 18: 1–64. London. First published 1920.

Furley, D. J. 1956. "The Early History of the Concept of Soul." *Bulletin of the Institute of Classical Studies* 3: 1–18.

Furley, D. J. 1974. "The Atomists' Reply to the Eleatics." In Mourelatos 1974, 504–26.

Furley, D. J. 1983. "Weight and Motion in Democritus' Theory." *Oxford Studies in Ancient Philosophy* 1: 193–209.

Furley, D. J. 1987. *The Greek Cosmologists*. Vol. 1, *The Formation of the Atomic Theory and Its Earliest Critics*. Cambridge.

Furley, D. J. 1993. "Democritus and Epicurus on Sensible Qualities." In *Passions and Perceptions: Studies in Hellenistic Philosophy of Mind*, edited by J. Brunschwig and M. C. Nussbaum, 72–94. Cambridge.

Furth, M. 1991. "A 'Philosophical Hero'? Anaxagoras and the Eleatics." *Oxford Studies in Ancient Philosophy* 9: 95–129.

Gabriel, M. 2015. *Fields of Sense: A New Realist Ontology*. Edinburgh.

Gagné, R. 2021. *Cosmography and the Idea of Hyperborea in Ancient Greece: A Philology of Worlds*. Cambridge.

Gallop, D. 1979. "'Is' or 'Is Not'?" *The Monist* 62: 61–80.

Gallop, D., ed. 1984. *Parmenides of Elea, Fragments: A Text and Translation*. Toronto.

Gallop, D. 1989. "The Riddles of Heraclitus." In Boudouris 1989, 123–35.

Ganson, T. S. 1999. "Democritus Against Reducing Sensible Qualities." *Ancient Philosophy* 19: 201–15.

Garani, M. 2007. *Empedocles Redivivus: Poetry and Analogy in Lucretius*. New York.

Garcia, T. 2014. *Form and Object: A Treatise on Things*. Translated by M. A. Ohm and J. Cogburn. Edinburgh.

Garin, M. 2017. "Le sage dans la pénombre: Masques de l'énonciateur et de ses destinataires dans les fragments B 5 et B 42 d'Héraclite d'Éphèse." In Fantino, Muss, Schubert, and Sier 2017, 269–86.

Gemelli Marciano, M. L. 1990. *Le metamorfosi della tradizione: Mutamenti di significato e neologismi nel* Peri Physeos *di Empedocle*. Bari.

Gemelli Marciano, M. L. 2002. "Le contexte culturel des Présocratiques: Adversaires et destinataires." In Laks and Louguet 2002, 83–114.

Gemelli Marciano, M. L. 2007. "Le Démocrite technicien: Remarques sur la réception de Démocrite dans la littérature technique." In Brancacci and Morel 2007, 207–38.

Gemelli Marciano, M. L. 2008. "Images and Experience: At the Roots of Parmenides' *Aletheia*." *Ancient Philosophy* 28: 21–48.

Gheerbrant, X. 2017. *Empédocle: Une poétique philosophique*. Paris.

Gheerbrant, X. 2022. "Addressees, Knowledge, and Action in Hesiod and Empedocles." In Iribarren and Koning 2022, 263–93.

Gianvittorio, L. 2017. "Der Klang prophetischer Stimmen: Kassandra und die Sibylle in *Performance*." In Fantino, Muss, Schubert, and Sier 2017, 343–71.

Gigon, O. 1935. *Untersuchungen zu Heraklit*. Leipzig.

Goldhill, S. 2002. *The Invention of Prose*. Oxford.

Goldin, O. 1991. "Heraclitean Satiety and Aristotelian Actuality." *The Monist* 74: 568–78.

Graham, D. W. 1988. "Symmetry in the Empedoclean Cycle." *Classical Quarterly* 38: 297–312.

Graham, D. W. 1994. "The Postulates of Anaxagoras." *Apeiron* 27: 77–121.

Graham, D. W. 1999. "Empedocles and Anaxagoras: Responses to Parmenides." In Long 1999a, 159–80.

Graham, D. W. 2002. "Heraclitus and Parmenides." In Caston and Graham 2002, 27–44.

Graham, D. W. 2006. *Explaining the Cosmos: The Ionian Tradition of Scientific Philosophy*. Princeton.

Graham, D. W. 2008a. "Leucippus's Atomism." In Curd and Graham 2008, 333–52.

Graham, D. W. 2008b. "Heraclitus: Flux, Order, and Knowledge." In Curd and Graham 2008, 169–88.

Graham, D. W. 2009. "Representation and Knowledge in a World of Change." In Hülsz Piccone 2009, 75–91.

Graham, D. W., ed. 2010. *The Texts of Early Greek Philosophy: The Complete Fragments and Selected Testimonies of the Major Presocratics*. Cambridge.

Graham, D. W. 2013. "Once More Into the Stream." In Sider and Obbink 2013, 303–20.

Granger, H. 2004. "Argumentation and Heraclitus' Book." *Oxford Studies in Ancient Philosophy* 26: 1–17.

Granger, H. 2008. "The Proem of Parmenides' Poem." *Ancient Philosophy* 28: 1–20.

Grant, B. 2016. *The Aphorism and Other Short Forms*. New York.

Graziosi, B. 2002. *Inventing Homer: The Early Reception of the Epic*. Cambridge.

Gregory, A. 2020. "Early Ancient Atomism: Similarities and Differences." In Zilioli 2020, 23–38.

Gurd, S. A. 2016. *Dissonance: Auditory Aesthetics in Ancient Greece*. New York.

Guthrie, W. K. C. 1962. *A History of Greek Philosophy*. Vol. 1, *The Earlier Presocratics and the Pythagoreans*. Cambridge.

Guthrie, W. K. C. 1965. *A History of Greek Philosophy*. Vol. 2, *The Presocratic Tradition From Parmenides to Democritus*. Cambridge.

Guthrie, W. K. C. 1974. "Flux and *Logos* in Heraclitus." In Mourelatos 1974, 197–213.

Hacking, I. 1983. *Representing and Intervening: Introductory Topics in the Philosophy of Natural Science*. Cambridge.

Haraway, D. J. 2016. *Staying With the Trouble: Making Kin in the Chthulucene*. Durham.

Hardie, A. 2013. "Empedocles and the Muse of the *Agathos Logos.*" *American Journal of Philology* 134: 209–46.

Hardt, M., and A. Negri. 2017. *Assembly*. Oxford.

Hasper, P. S. 2006. "Aristotle's Diagnosis of Atomism." *Apeiron* 39: 121–56.

Havelock, E. A. 1958. "Parmenides and Odysseus." *Harvard Studies in Classical Philology* 63: 133–43.

Havelock, E. A. 1963. *Preface to Plato*. Cambridge, MA.

Havelock, E. A. 1966. "Pre-Literacy and the Pre-Socratics." *Bulletin of the Institute of Classical Studies* 13: 44–67.

Havelock, E. A. 1983. "The Linguistic Task of the Presocratics." In Robb 1983a, 7–81.

Hayles, N. K. 1990. "Postmodern Parataxis: Embodied Texts, Weightless Information." *American Literary History* 2: 394–421.

Hegel, G. W. F. 1955. *Lectures on the History of Philosophy*. Translated by E. S. Haldane and F. H. Simson. London. First published 1840.

Hegel, G. W. F. 1975a. *Aesthetics: Lectures on Fine Art*. Vol. 1. Translated by T. M. Knox. Oxford. First published 1835.

Hegel, G. W. F. 1975b. *Logic*. Translated by W. Wallace. Oxford. First published 1830.

Heidegger, M. 1975. *Early Greek Thinking*. Translated by D. F. Krell and F. A. Capuzzi. New York.

Heidegger, M. 2018. *Heraclitus: The Inception of Occidental Thinking and Logic: Heraclitus' Doctrine of the* Logos. Translated by J. G. Assaiante and S. M. Ewegen. London. First published 1979.

Heidegger, M., and E. Fink. 1993. *Heraclitus Seminar*. Translated by C. H. Seibert. Evanston, IL.

Heisenberg, W. 1958. *Physics and Philosophy: The Revolution in Modern Science*. New York.

Herbrechter, S. 2012. "Posthumanism, Subjectivity, Autobiography." *Subjectivity* 6: 327–47.

Hershbell, J. P. 1968. "Empedocles' Oral Style." *Classical Journal* 63: 351–57.

Hershbell, J. P. 1972. "Parmenides and *Outis* in *Odyssey* 9." *Classical Journal* 68: 178–80.

Hirsch, U. 1990. "War Demokrits Weltbild mechanistisch und antiteleologisch?" *Phronesis* 35: 225–44.

Hoekstra, K. 2016. "Athenian Democracy and Popular Tyranny." In *Popular Sovereignty in Historical Perspective*, edited by R. Bourke and Q. Skinner, 15–51. Cambridge.

Holland, E. W. 1999. *Deleuze and Guattari's Anti-Oedipus: Introduction to Schizoanalysis*. New York.

Holmes, B. 2010. *The Symptom and the Subject: The Emergence of the Physical Body in Ancient Greece*. Princeton.

Holmes, B. 2016. "Michel Serres's Non-Modern Lucretius: Manifold Reason and the Temporality of Reception." In *Lucretius and Modernity*, edited by J. Lezra and L. Blake, 21–37. New York.

Holmes, B. 2019. "Bios." *Political Concepts* 5. https://www.politicalconcepts.org/bios-brooke-holmes.

Hölscher, U. 1968. *Anfängliches Fragen: Studien zur frühen griechischen Philosophie*. Göttingen.

Hölscher, U. 1974. "Paradox, Simile, and Gnomic Utterance in Heraclitus." In Mourelatos 1974, translated by M. R. Cosgrove and A. P. D. Mourelatos, 229–38.

Horky, P. S., ed. 2019. *Cosmos in the Ancient World*. New York.

Hose, M. 2016. "Philosophical Writing: Treatise, Dialogue, Diatribe, Epistle." In *A Companion to Greek Literature*, edited by M. Hose and D. Schenker, 235–55. Malden, MA.

Hülsz Piccone, E., ed. 2009. *Nuevos ensayos sobre Heráclito: Actas del segundo Symposium Heracliteum*. Mexico City.

Hülsz Piccone, E. 2013. "Heraclitus on *Logos*: Language, Rationality and the Real." In Sider and Obbink 2013, 281–301.

Hussey, E. 1972. *The Presocratics*. London.

Hussey, E. 1982. "Epistemology and Meaning in Heraclitus." In *Language and Logos: Studies in Ancient Greek Philosophy*, edited by M. Schofield and M. C. Nussbaum, 33–59. Cambridge.

Hussey, E. 1991. "Heraclitus on Living and Dying." *The Monist* 74: 517–30.

Hussey, E. 1999. "Heraclitus." In Long 1999a, 88–112.

Immerwahr, H. R. 1966. *Form and Thought in Herodotus*. Cleveland.

Ingold, T. 2007. *Lines: A Brief History*. New York.

Ingold, T. 2011. *Being Alive: Essays on Movement, Knowledge and Description*. New York.

Ingold, T. 2015. *The Life of Lines*. New York.

Inwood, B. 1986. "Anaxagoras and Infinite Divisibility." *Illinois Classical Studies* 11: 17–33.

Inwood, B., ed. 2001. *The Poem of Empedocles: A Text and Translation with an Introduction*. Rev. ed. Toronto.

Inwood, B. 2007. "Who Do We Think We Are?" In *The Virtuous Life in Greek Ethics*, edited by B. Reis, 230–43. Cambridge.

Irby-Massie, G. 2008. "Prometheus Bound and Contemporary Trends in Greek Natural Philosophy." *Greek, Roman, and Byzantine Studies* 48: 133–57.

Iribarren, L. 2018. *Fabriquer le monde: Technique et cosmogonie dans la poésie grecque archaïque*. Paris.

Iribarren, L., and H. H. Koning, eds. 2022. *Hesiod and the Beginnings of Greek Philosophy*. Leiden.

Jacobs, D. C. 1999. *The Presocratics After Heidegger*. Albany, NY.

Jaeger, W. 1945. *Paideia: The Ideals of Greek Culture*. Vol. 1, *Archaic Greece, the Mind of Athens*. Translated by G. Highet. New York.

Jakobson, R., and M. Halle. 2002. *Fundamentals of Language*. Berlin. First published 1956.

Jameson, G. 1958. "'Well-Rounded Truth and Circular Thought in Parmenides." *Phronesis* 3: 15–30.

Johansen, T. K. 2016. "Parmenides' Likely Story." *Oxford Studies in Ancient Philosophy* 50: 1–29.

Johnson, M. R. 2005. *Aristotle on Teleology*. Oxford.

Johnson, M. R. 2009. "Spontaneity, Democritean Causality and Freedom." *Elenchos* 30: 5–52.

Johnson, M. R. 2020. "The Ethical Maxims of Democritus of Abdera." In *Early Greek Ethics*, edited by D. C. Wolfsdorf, 211–42. Oxford.

Johnstone, M. 2014. "On 'Logos' in Heraclitus." *Oxford Studies in Ancient Philosophy* 47: 1–29.

Joly, H. 1984. "Sur quelques significations 'ontologiques' et 'épistémologiques' de l'εἴδωλον Démocritéen." In Benakis 1984, 247–64.

Journée, G. 2012. "Lumière et nuit, féminin et masculin chez Parménide d'Elée: Quelques remarques." *Phronesis* 57: 289–318.

Kahn, C. H. 1960. *Anaximander and the Origins of Greek Cosmology*. New York.

Kahn, C. H. 1973. *The Verb "Be" in Ancient Greek*. Dordrecht.

Kahn, C. H. 1974. "Religion and Natural Philosophy in Empedocles' Doctrine of the Soul." In Mourelatos 1974, 426–56. First published 1960.

Kahn, C. H. 1979. *The Art and Thought of Heraclitus*. Cambridge.

Kahn, C. H. 1983. "Philosophy and the Written Word: Some Thoughts on Heraclitus and the Early Greek Use of Prose." In Robb 1983a, 110–24.

Kahn, C. H. 1985. "Democritus and the Origins of Moral Psychology." *American Journal of Philology* 106: 1–31.

Kahn, C. H. 2003. "Writing Philosophy: Prose and Poetry From Thales to Plato." In *Written Texts and the Rise of Literate Culture in Ancient Greece*, edited by H. Yunis, 139–61. Cambridge.

Kahn, C. H. 2009. *Essays on Being*. Oxford.

Kamtekar, R. 2009. "Knowing By Likeness in Empedocles." *Phronesis* 54: 215–38.

Kechagia, E. 2011. *Plutarch Against Colotes: A Lesson in History of Philosophy*. Oxford.

Keizer, H. 2000. "Eternity Revisited: A Study of the Greek Word *Aion*." *Philosophia Reformata* 51: 53–71.

Kerferd, G. B. 1974. "Anaxagoras and the Concept of Matter Before Aristotle." In Mourelatos 1974, 489–503.

Kingsley, K. S. 2024. *Herodotus and the Presocratics: Inquiry and Intellectual Culture in the Fifth Century BCE*. Cambridge.

Kingsley, P. 1995. *Ancient Philosophy, Mystery, and Magic: Empedocles and Pythagorean Tradition*. Oxford.

Kingsley, P. 1999. *In the Dark Places of Wisdom*. Inverness, CA.

Kingsley, P. 2002. "Empedocles for the New Millennium." *Ancient Philosophy* 22: 333–413.

Kingsley, P. 2003. *Reality*. Inverness, CA.

Kirk, G. S., ed. 1954. *Heraclitus: The Cosmic Fragments*. Cambridge.

Kirk, G. S. 1974. "Natural Change in Heraclitus." In Mourelatos 1974, 189–96.

Kirk, G. S., J. E. Raven, and M. Schofield, eds. 1983. *The Presocratic Philosophers: A Critical History With a Selection of Texts*. Cambridge. First published 1957.

Konstan, D. 1982. "Atomism and Its Heritage: Minimal Parts." *Ancient Philosophy* 2: 60–75.

Korab-Karpowicz, W. J. 2016. *The Presocratics in the Thought of Martin Heidegger*. Frankfurt.

Kotwick, M., and C. Moore, eds. Forthcoming. *Public Philosophy in Classical Greece: 470–370 BCE: A Sourcebook*. Cambridge.

Kouremenos, T. 1993. "Parmenidean Influences in the 'Agamemnon' of Aeschylus." *Hermes* 121: 259–65.

Kranz, W. 1938. "Gleichnis und Vergleich in der frühgriechischen Philosophie." *Hermes* 73: 99–122.

Krischer, T. 1965. "ΕΤΥΜΟΣ und ΑΛΗΘΗΣ." *Philologus* 109: 161–74.

Kroeber, K. 2004. *Native American Storytelling: A Reader of Myths and Legends.* Malden, MA.

Kronick, J. G. 2000. "Philosophy as Autobiography: The Confessions of Jacques Derrida." *Modern Language Notes* 115: 997–1018.

Kurke, L. 1999. *Coins, Bodies, Games, and Gold: The Politics of Meaning in Archaic Greece.* Princeton.

Kurke, L. 2011. *Aesopic Conversations: Popular Tradition, Cultural Dialogue, and the Invention of Greek Prose.* Princeton.

Lacan, J. 1973. "L'étourdit." *Scilicet* 4: 5–52.

Lacan, J. 1977. *The Four Fundamental Concepts of Psycho-Analysis: The Seminar of Jacques Lacan, Book XI.* Edited by J.-A. Miller. Translated by A. Sheridan. New York. First published 1973.

Lacan, J. 1992. *The Ethics of Psychoanalysis: The Seminar of Jacques Lacan, Book VII.* Edited by J.-A. Miller. Translated by D. Porter. London. First published 1986.

Lacan, J. 1998. *On Feminine Sexuality: The Limits of Love and Knowledge (1972–73); Encore: The Seminar of Jacques Lacan, Book XX.* Edited by J.-A. Miller. Translated by B. Fink. New York. First published 1975.

Lacan, J. 2006. "Science and Truth." In *Écrits*, edited and translated by B. Fink, 726–45. New York. First published 1965.

Lacan, J. 2007. *The Other Side of Psychoanalysis: The Seminar of Jacques Lacan, Book XVII.* Edited by J.-A. Miller. Translated by R. Grigg. New York. First published 1991.

Lackeit, C. 1916. *Aion: Zeit und Ewigkeit in Sprache und Religion der Griechen.* Königsberg.

Laks, A. 1993. "Mind's Crisis: On Anaxagoras' ΝΟΥΣ." *The Southern Journal of Philosophy* 31: 19–38.

Laks, A. 1999. "Soul, Sensation, and Thought." In Long 1999a, 250–70.

Laks, A. 2001. "Écriture, prose, et les débuts de la philosophie grecque." *Methodos* 1: 131–51.

Laks, A. 2002a. "'Philosophes présocratiques': Remarques sur la construction d'une catégorie de l'historiographie philosophique." In Laks and Louguet 2002, 17–38.

Laks, A. 2002b. "Les fonctions de l'intellect: À propos, derechef, du *Nous* d'Anaxagore." *Methodos* 2: 7–31.

Laks, A. 2002c. "Reading the Readings: On the First Person Plurals in the Strasburg Empedocles." In Caston and Graham 2002, 127–37.

Laks, A. 2004. *Le vide et la haine: Éléments pour une histoire archaïque de la négativité.* Paris.

Laks, A. 2005. "Some Thoughts About Empedoclean Cosmic and Demonic Cycles." In Pierris 2005, 265–82.

Laks, A. 2007. *Histoire, doxographie, vérité: Études sur Aristote, Théophraste et la philosophie présocratique.* Louvain-la-Neuve.

Laks, A. 2010. "Hystéron protéron? Des *Origines* aux *Purifications.*" In *La philologie au présent: Pour Jean Bollack*, edited by C. König and D. Thouard, 19–26. Villeneuve d'Ascq.

Laks, A. 2015. "Sommeils présocratiques." In *Le sommeil: approches philosophiques et médicales de l'Antiquité à la Renaissance*, edited by V. Leroux, N. Palmieri, and C. Pigné, 29–50. Paris.

Laks, A. 2018. *The Concept of Presocratic Philosophy: Its Origin, Development, and Significance.* Translated by G. W. Most. Princeton.

Laks, A., and C. Louguet, eds. 2002. *Qu'est-ce que la philosophie présocratique? What is Presocratic Philosophy?* Villeneuve d'Ascq.

Laks, A., and G. W. Most, eds. 2016. *Early Greek Philosophy*. 9 vols. Cambridge, MA.

Lanza, D., ed. 1966. *Anassagora: Testimonianze e frammenti*. Florence.

Last, H. 1924. "Empedokles and His Klepsydra Again." *Classical Quarterly* 18: 169–73.

Latona, M. J. 2008. "Reining in the Passions: The Allegorical Interpretation of Parmenides B Fragment 1." *American Journal of Philology* 129: 199–230.

Lebedev, A. V. 2017. "The Metaphor of *Liber Naturae* and the Alphabet Analogy in Heraclitus' *Logos*-Fragments (With Some Remarks on Plato's 'Dream Theory' and the Origin of the Concept of Elements)." In Fantino, Muss, Schubert, and Sier 2017, 231–67.

Lee, M.-K. 2005. *Epistemology After Protagoras: Responses to Relativism in Plato, Aristotle, and Democritus*. Oxford.

Lesher, J. H. 1983. "Heraclitus' Epistemological Vocabulary." *Hermes* 111: 155–70.

Lesher, J. H. 1984. "Parmenides' Critique of Thinking." *Oxford Studies in Ancient Philosophy* 2: 1–30.

Lesher, J. H., ed. 1992. *Xenophanes: Fragments*. Toronto.

Lesher, J. H. 1994a. "The Emergence of Philosophical Interest in Cognition." *Oxford Studies in Ancient Philosophy* 12: 1–34.

Lesher, J. H. 1994b. "The Significance of Κατὰ Πάντ' Ἄ<σ>τη in Parmenides Fr. 1.3." *Ancient Philosophy* 14: 1–20.

Lesher, J. H. 1995. "Mind's Knowledge and Powers of Control in Anaxagoras DK B12." *Phronesis* 40: 125–42.

Leszl, W. 2007. "Democritus' Works: From Their Titles to Their Contents." In Brancacci and Morel 2007, 11–76.

Lewis, E. 2000. "Anaxagoras and the Seeds of a Physical Theory." *Apeiron* 33: 1–23.

Lilja, S. 1968. *On the Style of the Earliest Greek Prose*. Helsinki.

Lloyd, G. E. R. 1970. *Early Greek Science: Thales to Aristotle*. New York.

Lloyd, G. E. R. 1992. *Polarity and Analogy: Two Types of Argumentation in Early Greek Thought*. Indianapolis. First published 1966.

Lloyd, G. E. R. 1995. *The Revolutions of Wisdom: Studies in the Claims and Practice of Ancient Greek Science*. Berkeley.

Lloyd, G. E. R. 1996. *Aristotelian Explorations*. Cambridge.

Lloyd, G. E. R. 1999. *Magic, Reason, and Experience: Studies in the Origins and Development of Greek Science*. Indianapolis. First published 1979.

Lloyd, G. E. R. 2002. "Le pluralisme de la vie intellectuelle avant Platon." In Laks and Louguet 2002, translated by A. Laks, 39–53.

Long, A. 2007. "Wisdom in Heraclitus." *Oxford Studies in Ancient Philosophy* 33: 1–17.

Long, A. 2017. "Immortality in Empedocles." *Apeiron* 50: 1–20.

Long, A. A. 1966. "Thinking and Sense-Perception in Empedocles: Mysticism or Materialism?" *Classical Quarterly* 16: 256–76.

Long, A. A. 1974. "Empedocles' Cosmic Cycle in the Sixties." In Mourelatos 1974, 397–425.

Long, A. A. 1975. "The Principles of Parmenides' Cosmogony." In Allen and Furley 1975, 82–101.

Long, A. A. 1992. "Finding Oneself in Greek Philosophy." *Tijdschrift voor Filosofie* 54: 255–79.

Long, A. A. 1996. "Parmenides on Thinking Being." *Boston Area Colloquium in Ancient Philosophy* 12: 125–62.

Long, A. A., ed. 1999a. *The Cambridge Companion to Early Greek Philosophy*. Cambridge.
Long, A. A. 1999b. "The Scope of Early Greek Philosophy." In Long 1999a, 1–21.
Long, A. A. 2013. "Heraclitus on Measure and the Explicit Emergence of Rationality." In Sider and Obbink 2013, 201–23.
Long, H. S. 1949. "The Unity of Empedocles' Thought." *American Journal of Philology* 70: 142–58.
Longrigg, J. 1963. "Philosophy and Medicine: Some Early Interactions." *Harvard Studies in Classical Philology* 67: 147–75.
Longrigg, J. 1989. "Presocratic Philosophy and Hippocratic Medicine." *History of Science* 27: 1–39.
Loraux, N. 2002. *The Divided City: On Memory and Forgetting in Ancient Athens*. Translated by C. Pache with J. Fort. New York.
Louguet, C. 2002. "Note sur le fragment B4a d'Anaxagore: pourquoi les autres mondes doivent-ils être semblables au nôtre?" In Laks and Louguet 2002, 497–530.
Luria, S., ed. 2007. *Democrito: Raccolta dei frammenti, interpretazione e commentario*. Milan. First published 1970.
Macauley, D. 2005. "The Flowering of Environmental Roots and the Four Elements in Presocratic Philosophy: From Empedocles to Deleuze and Guattari." *Worldviews* 9: 281–314.
Macé, A. 2011. "Une science athénienne de la nature: La promesse et le testament d'Anaxagore." *Méthexis* 24: 21–43.
Macé, A. 2019. "Ordering the Universe in Speech: *Kosmos* and *Diakosmos* in Parmenides' Poem." In Horky 2019, 42–61.
Macé, A. 2020. "Platon et Héraclite, le jeu des cinq lignes (*pente grammai*) comme analogie du destin." In Bouvier and Dasen 2020, 207–23.
Mackenzie, M. M. 1982. "Parmenides' Dilemma." *Phronesis* 27: 1–12.
Mackenzie, M. M. 1988. "Heraclitus and the Art of Paradox." *Oxford Studies in Ancient Philosophy* 6: 1–37.
Mackenzie, T. 2016. "The Contents of Empedocles' Poem: A New Argument for the Single-Poem Hypothesis." *Zeitschrift für Papyrologie und Epigraphik* 200: 25–32.
Mackenzie, T. 2017. "Parmenides and Early Greek Allegory." *Materiali e discussioni per l'analisi dei testi classici* 79: 31–59.
Mackenzie, T. 2020. "Empedocles, Personal Identity, and the Narrative of the Fallen *Daimōn*." *Phoenix* 74: 111–30.
Mackenzie, T. 2021a. *Poetry and Poetics in the Presocratic Philosophers: Reading Xenophanes, Parmenides and Empedocles as Literature*. Cambridge.
Mackenzie, T. 2021b. "A Heraclitean Allusion to the *Odyssey*." *Classical Quarterly* 71: 71–76.
Mackenzie, T. 2022. "Rationality and Presocratic Cosmology in Sophocles' *Antigone*." *Journal of Hellenic Studies* 142: 30–48.
Makin, S. 1989. "The Indivisibility of the Atom." *Archiv für Geschichte der Philosophie* 71: 125–49.
Makin, S. 1993. *Indifference Arguments*. Oxford.
Mansfeld, J. 1964. *Die Offenbarung des Parmenides und die menschliche Welt*. Assen.
Mansfeld, J. 1967. "Heraclitus on the Psychology and Physiology of Sleep and on Rivers." *Mnemosyne* 20: 1–29.
Mansfeld, J. 1980. "Anaxagoras' Other World." *Phronesis* 25: 1–4.
Mansfeld, J. 1982. "Review of M. Schofield, *An Essay on Anaxagoras*." *Mnemosyne* 35: 360–67.

Mansfeld, J. 1995. "Insight By Hindsight: Intentional Unclarity in Presocratic Proems." *Bulletin of the Institute of Classical Studies* 40: 225–32.

Mansfeld, J., and D. T. Runia. 1997. *Aëtiana: The Method and Intellectual Context of a Doxographer*. Leiden.

Marcovich, M. 1966. "On Heraclitus." *Phronesis* 11: 19–30.

Marcovich, M., ed. 1967. *Heraclitus*. Merida.

Marmodoro, A. 2017. *Everything in Everything: Anaxagoras's Metaphysics*. New York.

Marsden, J. 2006. "Nietzsche and the Art of the Aphorism." In *A Companion to Nietzsche*, edited by K. A. Pearson, 22–37. London.

Martin, A., and O. Primavesi, eds. 1999. *L'Empédocle de Strasbourg (*P. Strasb. gr. *Inv. 1665–1666): Introduction, édition et commentaire*. Berlin.

Martin, R. P. 1989. *The Language of Heroes: Speech and Performance in the* Iliad. Ithaca, NY.

Martin, R. P. 1998. "The Seven Sages as Performers of Wisdom." In *Cultural Poetics in Archaic Greece: Cult, Performance, Politics*, edited by C. Dougherty and L. Kurke, 108–28. New York.

Marx, K. 2006. "The Difference Between the Democritean and Epicurean Philosophy of Nature." In *The First Writings of Karl Marx*, edited and translated by P. M. Schafer, 84–184. Brooklyn. First published 1841.

Mason, R. 1988. "Parmenides and Language." *Ancient Philosophy* 8: 149–66.

Matson, W. I. 1963. "Democritus, Fragment 156." *Classical Quarterly* 13: 26–29.

Maurizio, L. 2012. "Technopaegnia in Heraclitus and the Delphic Oracles: Shared Compositional Techniques." In *The Muse at Play: Riddles and Wordplay in Greek and Latin Poetry*, edited by J. Kwapisz, D. Petrain, and M. Szymański, 100–120. Berlin.

McCarthy, G. E. 1990. *Marx and the Ancients: Classical Ethics, Social Justice, and Nineteenth-Century Political Economy*. Savage, MD.

McKim, R. 1984. "Democritus Against Scepticism: All Sense-Impressions Are True." In Benakis 1984, 281–89.

McKirahan, R. D. 2005. "Assertion and Argument in Empedocles' Cosmology or, What Did Empedocles Learn From Parmenides?" In Pierris 2005, 163–88.

McKirahan, R. D. 2008. "Signs and Arguments in Parmenides B8." In Curd and Graham 2008, 189–221.

McKirahan, R. D., ed. 2010. *Philosophy Before Socrates: An Introduction with Texts and Commentary*. Indianapolis. First published 1994.

Meillassoux, Q. 2009. *After Finitude: An Essay on the Necessity of Contingency*. Translated by R. Brassier. London.

Menn, S. 1995. *Plato on God as* Nous. Carbondale, IL.

Merleau-Ponty, M. 1973. *The Prose of the World*. Translated by J. O'Neill. Evanston, IL.

Miller, M. 2006. "Ambiguity and Transport: Reflections on the Proem to Parmenides' Poem." *Oxford Studies in Ancient Philosophy* 30: 1–47.

Moore, C. 2019. *Calling Philosophers Names: On the Origin of a Discipline*. Princeton.

Moorhouse, A. C. 1962. "ΔEN in Classical Greek." *Classical Quarterly* 12: 235–38.

Morel, P.-M. 2000. *Atome et nécessité. Démocrite, Épicure, Lucrèce*. Paris.

Morel, P.-M. 2007. "Démocrite et l'objet de la philosophie naturelle: À propos des sens de φύσις chez Démocrite." In Brancacci and Morel 2007, 105–24.

Morgan, K. A. 2000. *Myth and Philosophy From the Presocratics to Plato*. Cambridge.

Morgan, K. A. 2022. "Parmenides and the Language of Constraint." In Iribarren and Koning 2022, 221–38.

Morrison, J. S. 1955. "Parmenides and Er." *Journal of Hellenic Studies* 75: 59–68.

Morson, G. S. 2012. *The Long and Short of It: From Aphorism to Novel*. Stanford.

Most, G. 1999. "The Poetics of Early Greek Philosophy." In Long 1999a, 332–62.

Most, G. 2007. "Ἄλλος δ' ἐξ ἄλλου δέχεται: Presocratic Philosophy and Traditional Greek Epic." In *Literatur und Religion 2: Wege zu einer mythisch-rituellen Poetik bei den Griechen*, edited by A. Bierl, R. Lämmle, and K. Wesselmann, 271–302. Berlin.

Mouraviev, S. N. 2002. *Héraclite d'Éphèse*. Vol. 3.3.a, *Les fragments du livre d'Héraclite: Le langage d'obscur: Introduction à la poétique des fragments*. Sankt Augustin.

Mouraviev, S. N., ed. 2006. *Héraclite d'Éphèse*, Vol. 3.3.b, *Les fragments du livre d'Héraclite: Les textes pertinents*. Sankt Augustin.

Mouraviev, S. N. 2008. "Héraclite: Les fragments du fleuve: F 12: Le contexte: T 261." *Revue de philosophie ancienne* 26: 3–39.

Mourelatos, A. P. D., ed. 1974. *The Pre-Socratics: A Collection of Critical Essays*. Princeton.

Mourelatos, A. P. D. 2004. "Intrinsic and Relational Properties of Atoms in the Democritean Ontology." In *Metaphysics, Soul, and Ethics in Ancient Thought: Themes from the Work of Richard Sorabji*, edited by R. Salles, 39–63. Oxford.

Mourelatos, A. P. D. 2008a. "Determinacy and Indeterminacy, Being and Non-Being in the Fragments of Parmenides." In Mourelatos 2008c, 333–49. First published 1975.

Mourelatos, A. P. D. 2008b. "The Naive Metaphysics of Things." In Mourelatos 2008c, 299–332. First published 1973.

Mourelatos, A. P. D. 2008c. *The Route of Parmenides*. Las Vegas. First published 1970.

Mourelatos, A. P. D., and M. Pulpito. 2018. "Parmenides and the Principle of Sufficient Reason." In *Ways to Think: Essays in Honour of Néstor-Luis Cordero*, edited by M. Pulpito and P. Spangenberg, 121–41. Bologna.

Naddaf, G. 2005. *The Greek Concept of Nature*. Albany, NY.

Nancy, J.-L. 2000. *Being Singular Plural*. Translated by R. D. Richardson and A. E. O'Byrne. Stanford.

Natorp, P. 1893. *Die Ethika des Demokritos*. Marburg.

Neer, R. T. 2002. *Style and Politics in Athenian Vase-Painting: The Craft of Democracy, ca. 530–460 B.C.E.* Cambridge.

Nehamas, A. 2002. "Parmenidean Being/Heraclitean Fire." In Caston and Graham 2002, 45–64.

Nestle, W. 1942. *Vom Mythos zum Logos: Die Selbstentfaltung des griechischen Denkens von Homer bis auf die Sophistik und Sokrates*. Stuttgart.

Nietzsche, F. 1962. *Philosophy in the Tragic Age of the Greeks*. Translated by M. Cowan. New York. First published 1873.

Nietzsche, F. 1989a. "On Truth and Lying in an Extra-Moral Sense." In *Friedrich Nietzsche on Rhetoric and Language*, edited and translated by S. L. Gilman, C. Blair, and D. J. Parent, 246–57. Oxford. First published 1873.

Nietzsche, F. 1989b. *Beyond Good and Evil*. Translated by W. Kaufmann. New York. First published 1886.

Nietzsche, F. 1998. *Twilight of the Idols*. Translated by D. Large. Oxford. First published 1889.

Nightingale, A. W. 1995. *Genres in Dialogue: Plato and the Construct of Philosophy*. Cambridge.

Nooter, S. 2023. *Greek Poetry in the Age of Ephemerality*. New York.
Norden, E. 1915. *Die antike Kunstprosa vom VI Jahrhundert v. Chr. bis in die Zeit der Renaissance*. Vol. 1. Leipzig.
Noutopoulos, J. A. 1949. "Parataxis in Homer: A New Approach to Homeric Literary Criticism." *Transactions of the American Philological Association* 80: 1–23.
Nünlist, R. 1998. *Poetologische Bildersprache in der frühgriechischen Dichtung*. Stuttgart.
Nünlist, R. 2005. "Poetological Imagery in Empedocles." In Pierris 2005, 73–92.
Nussbaum, M. C. 1972a. "ΨΥΧΗ in Heraclitus, I." *Phronesis* 17: 1–16.
Nussbaum, M. C. 1972b. "ΨΥΧΗ in Heraclitus, II." *Phronesis* 17: 153–70.
Nussbaum, M. C. 1990. "Form and Content, Philosophy and Literature." In *Love's Knowledge: Essays on Philosophy and Literature*, 3–53. Oxford.
Obbink, D. 1993. "The Addressees of Empedocles." *Materiali e discussioni per l'analisi dei testi classici* 31: 51–98.
Ober, J. 1996. *The Athenian Revolution: Essays on Ancient Greek Democracy and Political Theory*. Princeton.
O'Brien, D. 1969. *Empedocles' Cosmic Cycle: A Reconstruction From the Fragments and Secondary Sources*. Cambridge.
O'Brien, D. 1970. "The Effect of a Simile: Empedocles' Theories of Seeing and Breathing." *Journal of Hellenic Studies* 90: 140–79.
O'Brien, D. 1980. "Temps et intemporalité chez Parménide." *Les études philosophiques* 3: 257–72.
O'Brien, D. 1981. *Democritus, Weight and Size: An Exercise in the Reconstruction of Early Greek Philosophy*. Leiden.
O'Brien, D. 2001. "Empedocles: The Wandering Daimon and the Two Poems." *Aevum Antiquum* 1: 79–179.
O'Brien, D. 2016. "Empedocles on the Identity of the Elements." *Elenchos* 37: 5–32.
O'Connell, E. 2005. *Heraclitus and Derrida: Presocratic Deconstruction*. New York.
O'Keefe, T. 1996. "Does Epicurus Need the Swerve as an *Archē* of Collisions?" *Phronesis* 41: 305–17.
O'Keefe, T. 1997. "The Ontological Status of Sensible Qualities for Democritus and Epicurus." *Ancient Philosophy* 17: 119–34.
Olney, J. 1980. "Some Versions of Memory/Some Versions of *Bios*: The Ontology of Autobiography." In *Autobiography: Essays Theoretical and Critical*, 236–67. Princeton.
Onians, R. B. 1951. *The Origins of European Thought About the Body, the Mind, the Soul, the World, Time, and Fate*. Cambridge.
Osborne, C. 1987a. "Empedocles Recycled." *Classical Quarterly* 37: 24–50.
Osborne, C. 1987b. *Rethinking Early Greek Philosophy: Hippolytus of Rome and the Presocratics*. London.
Osborne, C. 1998. "Was Verse the Default Form for Presocratic Philosophy?" In *Form and Content in Didactic Poetry*, edited by C. Atherton, 23–35. Bari.
Osborne, C. 2005. "Sin and Moral Responsibility in Empedocles's Cosmic Cycle." In Pierris 2005, 283–308.
Osborne, C. 2006. "Was There an Eleatic Revolution in Philosophy?" In *Rethinking Revolutions through Ancient Greece*, edited by S. Goldhill and R. Osborne, 218–45. Cambridge.

Owen, G. E. L. 1960. "Eleatic Questions." *Classical Quarterly* 10: 84–102.

Owen, G. E. L. 1974. "Plato and Parmenides on the Timeless Present." In Mourelatos 1974, 271–92.

Owens, J. 1979. "Knowledge and *Katabasis* in Parmenides." *The Monist* 62: 15–29.

Palmer, J. 2009. *Parmenides and Presocratic Philosophy*. Oxford.

Palmer, J. 2013. "Revelation and Reasoning in Kalliopeia's Address to Empedocles." *Rhizomata* 1: 308–29.

Papamichael-Paspalides, E. 2005. "The Concept of One in Heraclitus." *Revue de philosophie ancienne* 23: 41–54.

Patzer, A. 2006. *Wort und Ort: Oralität und Literarizität im sozialen Kontext der frühgriechischen Philosophie*. Freiburg.

Pellikaan-Engel, M. E. 1974. *Hesiod and Parmenides: A New View on Their Cosmologies and on Parmenides' Proem*. Amsterdam.

Perry, B. E. 1937. "The Early Greek Capacity for Viewing Things Separately." *Transactions of the American Philological Association* 68: 403–27.

Picot, J.-C. 1998. "Sur un emprunt d'Empédocle au *Bouclier* hésiodique." *Revue des études grecques* 111: 42–60. Reprinted in Picot 2022, 15–32.

Picot, J.-C. 2000. "L'Empédocle magique de P. Kingsley." *Revue de philosophie ancienne* 18: 25–86. Reprinted in Picot 2022, 33–79.

Picot, J.-C. 2022. *Empédocle sur le chemin des dieux*. Paris.

Piergiacomi, E. 2017. "Naming the Principles in Democritus: An Epistemological Problem." *Apeiron* 50: 435–48.

Pierris, A. L., ed. 2005. *The Empedoclean Κόσμος: Structure, Process and the Question of Cyclicity*. Patras.

Popper, K. R. 1992. "How the Moon Might Throw Some of Her Light Upon the Two Ways of Parmenides." *Classical Quarterly* 42: 12–19.

Porter, J. I. 1989. "Philodemus on Material Difference." *Cronache Ercolanesi* 19: 149–78.

Porter, J. I. 2000. *Nietzsche and the Philology of the Future*. Stanford.

Porter, J. I. 2010. *The Origins of Aesthetic Thought in Ancient Greece: Matter, Sensation, and Experience*. Cambridge.

Porter, J. I. 2016. *The Sublime in Antiquity*. Cambridge.

Porter, J. I. 2020. "Living on the Edge: Self and World *in Extremis* in Roman Philosophy." *Classical Antiquity* 39: 225–83.

Porter, J. I. 2023. "How Ideal is the Ancient Self?" In *Ideas and Idealism in Philosophy: New Studies in the History and Historiography of Philosophy*, edited by J. Simoniti and G. Kroupa, 3–26. Berlin.

Porter, J. I. 2024. "Life Cycles Beyond the Human: Biomass and Biorhythms in Heraclitus." *Classical Antiquity* 43: 50–96.

Porter, J. I. 2025. "Love, Strife, and the Roots of All Things: Empedoclean Cosmopoetics." *Representations* 169: 11–27.

Postclassicisms Collective. 2020. *Postclassicisms*. Chicago.

Primavesi, O. 2008. "Empedocles: Physical and Mythical Divinity." In Curd and Graham 2008, 250–83.

Primavesi, O. 2013. "Empedokles." In *Die Philosophie der Antike, Band I: Frühgriechische Philosophie*, edited by H. Flashar, D. Bremer, and G. Rechenauer, 667–739. Basel.

Pucci, P. 1982. "The Proem of the *Odyssey*." *Arethusa* 15: 39–62.

Raaflaub, K. A. 2017. "Shared Responsibility for the Common Good: Heraclitus, Early Philosophy, and Political Thought." In Fantino, Muss, Schubert, and Sier 2017, 103–28.

Ramelli, I., and D. Konstan. 2007. *Terms for Eternity: Aiônios and Aïdios in Classical and Christian Texts*. Piscataway, NJ.

Ramnoux, C. 1968. *Héraclite ou l'homme entre les choses et les mots*. Paris.

Rancière, J. 1999. *Disagreement: Politics and Philosophy*. Translated by J. Rose. Minneapolis.

Rancière, J. 2006. "The Distribution of the Sensible: Politics and Aesthetics." In *The Politics of Aesthetics: The Distribution of the Sensible*, edited and translated by G. Rockhill, 12–19. London.

Rancière, J. 2009a. *Aesthetics and Its Discontents*. Translated by S. Corcoran. Cambridge.

Rancière, J. 2009b. "The Aesthetic Dimension: Aesthetics, Politics, Knowledge." *Critical Inquiry* 36: 1–19.

Rancière, J. 2010. *Dissensus: On Politics and Aesthetics*. Translated by S. Corcoran. New York.

Rankin, H. D. 1995. "Heraclitus on Conscious and Unconscious States." *Quaderni urbinati di cultura classica* 50: 73–86.

Ranzato, S. 2015. *Il* kouros *e la verità: Polivalenza delle immagini nel poema di Parmenide*. Pisa.

Rapp, C. 2017. "His Dearest Enemy: Heraclitus in the Aristotelian Oeuvre." In Fantino, Muss, Schubert, and Sier 2017, 415–38.

Rashed, M. 2008. "Le proème des *Catharmes* d'Empédocle: Reconstitution et commentaire." *Elenchos* 29: 7–37.

Rashed, M. 2018. *La jeune fille et la sphère: Études sur Empédocle*. Paris.

Raven, J. E. 1954. "The Basis of Anaxagoras' Cosmology." *Classical Quarterly* 4: 123–37.

Reinhardt, K. 1959. *Parmenides und die Geschichte der griechischen Philosophie*. Frankfurt am Main. First published 1919.

Renehan, R. 1980. "On the Greek Origins of the Concepts Incorporeality and Immateriality." *Greek, Roman, and Byzantine Studies* 21: 105–38.

Robb, K., ed. 1983a. *Language and Thought in Early Greek Philosophy*. La Salle, IL.

Robb, K. 1983b. "Preliterate Ages and the Linguistic Art of Heraclitus." In Robb 1983a, 153–206.

Robb, K. 1986. "'Psyche' and 'Logos' in the Fragments of Heraclitus: The Origins of the Concept of Soul." *The Monist* 69: 315–51.

Robbiano, C. 2006. *Becoming Being: On Parmenides' Transformative Philosophy*. Sankt Augustin.

Robbiano, C. 2016. "*Being* is Not an Object: An Interpretation of Parmenides' Fragment DK B2 and a Reflection on Assumptions." *Ancient Philosophy* 36: 263–301.

Robinson, T. M. 1991. "Heraclitus and Plato on the Language of the Real." *The Monist* 74: 481–90.

Robinson, T. M. 2009. "Heraclitus and *Logos*—Again." In Hülsz Piccone 2009, 93–102.

Rohde, E. 1925. *Psyche: The Cult of Souls and the Belief in Immortality Among the Greeks*. Translated by W. B. Hillis. New York.

Rosenfeld-Löffler, A. 2006. *La poétique d'Empédocle: Cosmologie et métaphore*. Bern.

Rosetti, L. 2010. "La structure du poème de Parménide." *Philosophie antique* 10: 187–226.

Rösler, W. 1983. "Der Anfang der *Katharmoi* des Empedokles." *Hermes* 111: 170–79.

Rousseau, P. 1970. "Le sommeil de la vie et la veille de la mort: Héraclite, fragment 26 DK." *Les études philosophiques* 4: 499–506.

Rowett, C. 2013. "Literary Genres and Judgements of Taste: Some Remarks on Aristotle's Remarks about the Poetry of Empedocles." In *Argument und literarische Form in antiker Philosophie*, edited by M. Erler and J. E. Heßler, 305–14. Berlin.

Rowett, C. 2016. "Love, Sex and the Gods: Why Things Have Divine Names in Empedocles' Poem, and Why They Come in Pairs." *Rhizomata* 4: 80–110.

Rowett, C. 2017. "On Being Reminded of Heraclitus By the Motifs in Plato's *Phaedo*." In Fantino, Muss, Schubert, and Sier 2017, 373–414.

Rowett, C. 2020. "Analytic Philosophy, the Ancient Philosopher Poets and the Poetics of Analytic Philosophy." *Rhizomata* 8: 158–82.

Rudolph, K. 2016. "Sight and the Presocratics: Approaches to Visual Perception in Early Greek Philosophy." In *Sight and the Ancient Senses*, edited by M. Squire, 36–53. New York.

Salem, J. 1996. *Démocrite: Grains de poussière dans un rayon de soleil*. Paris.

Salem, J. 2007. "Perception et connaissance chez Démocrite." In Brancacci and Morel 2007, 125–42.

Sandywell, B. 1996. *Presocratic Reflexivity: The Construction of Philosophical Discourse c. 600–450 BC*. New York.

Sassi, M. M. 1978. *Le teorie della percezione in Democrito*. Florence.

Sassi, M. M. 2002. "La naissance de la philosophie de l'esprit de la tradition." In Laks and Louguet 2002, 55–81.

Sassi, M. M. 2007. "Le paradigme de la cité." *Philosophie antique* 7: 191–215.

Sassi, M. M. 2018. *The Beginnings of Philosophy in Greece*. Translated by M. Asuni. Princeton.

Scapin, N. 2020. *The Flower of Suffering: Theology, Justice, and the Cosmos in Aeschylus'* Oresteia *and Presocratic Thought*. Berlin.

Šćepanović, S. 2022. "Thinking About Time and Eternity—From Hesiod and the Presocratics to Plato and Aristotle." In Iribarren and Koning 2022, 139–58.

Schädler, U. 2020. "'Le temps un enfant qui joue'—mais à quoi? La perspective ludographique." In Bouvier and Dasen 2020, 147–57.

Schironi, F. 2010. "Technical Languages: Science and Medicine." In *A Companion to the Ancient Greek Language*, edited by E. J. Bakker, 338–53. Oxford.

Schmidt, E. A. 2007. *Clinamen: Eine Studie zum dynamischen Atomismus der Antike*. Heidelberg.

Schmitt, C. 2005. *Political Theology: Four Chapters on the Concept of Sovereignty*. Translated by G. Schwab. Chicago. First published 1922.

Schofield, M. 1970. "Did Parmenides Discover Eternity?" *Archiv für Geschichte der Philosophie* 52: 113–35.

Schofield, M. 1980. *An Essay on Anaxagoras*. Cambridge.

Schofield, M. 1991. "Heraclitus' Theory of Soul and Its Antecedents." In *Companions to Ancient Thought 2: Psychology*, edited by S. Everson, 13–34. Cambridge.

Schofield, M. 1996. "Anaxagoras' Other World Revisited." In *Polyhistor: Studies in the History and Historiography of Ancient Philosophy*, edited by K. Algra, P. W. Van der Horst, and D. T. Runia, 3–20. Leiden.

Schofield, M. 2019. "*Diakosmēsis*." In Horky 2019, 62–73.

Schreckenberg, H. 1964. *Ananke: Untersuchungen zur Geschichte des Wortgebrauchs*. Munich.

Schubert, C. 2017. "Heraklit und die ionischen Isonomien." In Fantino, Muss, Schubert, and Sier 2017, 129–50.

Schwabl, H. 1956. "Empedokles Fr. B 110." *Wiener Studien* 69: 49–56.

Schwabl, H. 1963. "Hesiod und Parmenides: zur Formung des parmenideischen Prooimions (28 B 1)." *Rheinisches Museum für Philologie* 106: 134–42.

Seaford, R. 2004. *Money and the Early Greek Mind: Homer, Philosophy, Tragedy*. Cambridge.

Seaford, R. 2013. "Aeschylus, Herakleitos, and Pythagoreanism." In *Tragedy and Archaic Greek Thought*, edited by D. L. Cairns, 17–38. Swansea.

Sedley, D. N. 1982. "Two Conceptions of Vacuum." *Phronesis* 27: 175–93.

Sedley, D. N. 1989. "The Proems of Empedocles and Lucretius." *Greek, Roman, and Byzantine Studies* 30: 269–96.

Sedley, D. N. 1992. "Sextus Empiricus and the Atomist Criteria of Truth." *Elenchos* 13: 19–56.

Sedley, D. N. 1999. "Parmenides and Melissus." In Long 1999a, 113–33.

Sedley, D. N. 2005. "Empedocles' Life Cycles." In Pierris 2005, 331–71.

Sedley, D. N. 2008a. "Atomism's Eleatic Roots." In Curd and Graham 2008, 305–32.

Sedley, D. N. 2008b. *Creationism and Its Critics in Antiquity*. Berkeley.

Serres, M. 2018. *The Birth of Physics*. Translated by D. Webb and W. Ross. London. First published 1977.

Serres, M., and B. Latour. 1995. *Conversations on Science, Culture, and Time*. Translated by R. Lapidus. Ann Arbor.

Sider, D. 1985. "Textual Notes on Parmenides' Poem." *Hermes* 113: 362–66.

Sider, D. 1989. "Word Order and Sense in Heraclitus: Fragment One and the River Fragment." In Boudouris 1989, 363–68.

Sider, D., ed. 2005. *The Fragments of Anaxagoras*. Sankt Augustin.

Sider, D. 2013. "Heraclitus' Ethics." In Sider and Obbink 2013, 321–34.

Sider, D., ed. Forthcoming. *Parmenides: A Commentary on His Poem*.

Sider, D., and D. Obbink, eds. 2013. *Doctrine and Doxography: Studies on Heraclitus and Pythagoras*. Berlin.

Silk, M. 2010. "The Language of Greek Lyric Poetry." In *A Companion to the Ancient Greek Language*, edited by E. J. Bakker, 424–40. Oxford.

Silvestre, M. L. 1988. "Significato e ruolo del *nous* nella filosofia di Anassagora." *Il contributo* 12: 29–52.

Sisko, J. E. 2003. "Anaxagoras' Parmenidean Cosmology: Worlds Within Worlds Within the One." *Apeiron* 36: 87–114.

Snell, B. 1926. "Die Sprache Heraklits." *Hermes* 61: 353–81.

Snell, B. 1953. *The Discovery of the Mind: The Greek Origins of European Thought*. Translated by T. Rosenmeyer. Oxford.

Snell, B. 1975. "ΑΛΗΘΕΙΑ." *Würzburger Jahrbücher für die Altertumswissenschaft* 1: 9–17.

Solmsen, F. 1963. "Anaxagoras B 19 Diels-Kranz." *Hermes* 91: 251–52.

Solmsen, F. 1967. "Ζωρός in Empedocles." *Classical Review* 17: 245–46.

Solmsen, F. 1975. "Eternal and Temporary Beings in Empedocles' Physical Poem." *Archiv für Geschichte der Philosophie* 57: 123–45.

Sorabji, R. 1983. *Time, Creation, and the Continuum: Theories in Antiquity and the Early Middle Ages*. Ithaca, NY.

Stamatellos, G. 2007. *Plotinus and the Presocratics: A Philosophical Study of Presocratic Influences in Plotinus'* Enneads. Albany, NY.

Stehle, E. 2005. "The Addressees of Empedokles, *Katharmoi* Fr. B112: Performance and Moral Implications." *Ancient Philosophy* 25: 247–72.

Stocking, C. 2023. *Homer's* Iliad *and the Problem of Force*. Oxford.

Stokes, M. C. 1971. *One and Many in Presocratic Philosophy*. Washington, DC.

Strang, C. 1975. "The Physical Theory of Anaxagoras." In Allen and Furley 1975, 361–80.

Tarán, L., ed. 1965. *Parmenides*. Princeton.

Tarán, L. 1979. "Perpetual Duration and Atemporal Eternity in Parmenides and Plato." *The Monist* 62: 43–53.

Tarán, L. 1986. "The First Fragment of Heraclitus." *Illinois Classical Studies* 11: 1–15.

Tarán, L. 1999. "Heraclitus: The River-Fragments and Their Implications." *Elenchos* 1: 9–52.

Taylor, C. C. W. 1967. "Pleasure, Knowledge and Sensation in Democritus." *Phronesis* 12: 6–27.

Taylor, C. C. W. 1999a. "The Atomists." In Long 1999a, 181–204.

Taylor, C. C. W., ed. 1999b. *The Atomists: Leucippus and Democritus*. Toronto.

Taylor, C. C. W. 2007a. "Democritus and Lucretius on Death and Dying." In Brancacci and Morel 2007, 77–86.

Taylor, C. C. W. 2007b. "*Nomos* and *Phusis* in Democritus and Plato." In *Freedom, Reason, and the Polis: Essays in Ancient Greek Political Philosophy*, edited by D. Keyt and F. D. Miller, 1–20. Cambridge.

Teodorsson, S.-T. 1982. *Anaxagoras' Theory of Matter*. Göteborg.

Thesleff, H. 1966. "Scientific and Technical Style in Early Greek Prose." *Arctos: Acta Philologica Fennica* 4: 89–113.

Thom, P. 2002. "On the Pervasiveness of Being." In Caston and Graham 2002, 293–301.

Tor, S. 2016. "Heraclitus on Apollo's Signs and His Own." In *Theologies of Ancient Greek Religion*, edited by E. Eidinow, J. Kindt, and R. Osborne, 89–116. Cambridge.

Tor, S. 2017. *Mortal and Divine in Early Greek Epistemology: A Study of Hesiod, Xenophanes, and Parmenides*. Cambridge.

Tor, S. 2023a. "Empedocles the Wandering *Daimōn* and Trusting in Mad Strife." *Phronesis* 68: 1–30.

Tor, S. 2023b. "Language and Doctrine in Parmenides' *Way of Reality*." *Journal of Hellenic Studies* 143: 250–75.

Traglia, A. 1952. *Studi sulla lingua di Empedocle*. Bari.

Trenker, S. 1960. *Le style* KAI *dans le récit attique oral*. Assen.

Trépanier, S. 2003. "'We' and Empedocles' Cosmic Lottery: 'P. Strasb. gr. Inv. 1665–1666,' Ensemble A." *Mnemosyne* 56: 385–419.

Trépanier, S. 2004. *Empedocles: An Interpretation*. New York.

Trépanier, S. 2014. "From Wandering Limbs to Limbless Gods: Δαίμων as Substance in Empedocles." *Apeiron* 47: 172–210.

Trépanier, S. 2017. "From Hades to the Stars: Empedocles on the Cosmic Habitats of Soul." *Classical Antiquity* 36: 130–82.

Ugolini, G. 1985. "Appunti sullo stile di Anassagora." *Elenchos* 6: 315–32.

Van Berkel, T. A. 2013. "Made to Measure: Protagoras' *Metron*." In *Protagoras of Abdera: The Man, His Measure*, edited by J. M. Van Ophuijsen, M. Van Raalte, and P. Stork, 37–67. Leiden.

Van der Ben, N., ed. 1975. *The Proem of Empedocles'* Peri Physios. Amsterdam.

Van der Eijk, P. J. 1997. "Towards a Rhetoric of Ancient Scientific Discourse." In *Grammar as Interpretation*, edited by E. J. Bakker, 77–129. Leiden.

Van Groningen, B. A. 1960. *La composition littéraire archaïque grecque*. Amsterdam.

Van Groningen, B. A. 1971. "Empédocle, poète." *Mnemosyne* 24: 169–88.

Vasiliou, I. 2021. "Mixing Minds: Anaxagoras and Plato's *Phaedo*." In *Brill's Companion to the Reception of Presocratic Natural Philosophy in Later Classical Thought*, edited by C. Harry and J. Habash, 404–28. Leiden.

Vegetti, M. 1999. "Culpability, Responsibility, Cause: Philosophy, Historiography, and Medicine in the Fifth Century." In Long 1999a, 271–89.

Verdenius, W. J. 1966. "Der Logosbegriff bei Heraklit und Parmenides." *Phronesis* 11: 81–98.

Vernant, J. P. 1982. *The Origins of Greek Thought*. Ithaca, NY.

Vernant, J. P. 1991. "A 'Beautiful Death' and the Disfigured Corpse in Homeric Epic." In *Mortals and Immortals: Collected Essays*, edited by F. I. Zeitlin, translated by A. Szegedy-Maszak, 50–74. Princeton. First published 1982.

Vernant, J. P. 2006a. "Geometric Structure and Political Ideas in the Cosmology of Anaximander." In *Myth and Thought among the Greeks*, translated by J. Lloyd and J. Fort, 213–33. New York. First published 1968.

Vernant, J. P. 2006b. "Geometry and Spherical Astronomy in Early Greek Cosmology." In *Myth and Thought among the Greeks*, translated by J. Lloyd and J. Fort, 197–211. New York. First published 1963.

Vieira, C. 2013. "Heraclitus' Bow Composition." *Classical Quarterly* 63: 473–90.

Vlastos, G. 1945. "Ethics and Physics in Democritus (Part 1)." *The Philosophical Review* 54: 578–92.

Vlastos, G. 1946. "Ethics and Physics in Democritus (Part 2)." *The Philosophical Review* 55: 53–64.

Vlastos, G. 1947. "Equality and Justice in Early Greek Cosmologies." *Classical Philology* 42: 156–78.

Vlastos, G. 1950. "The Physical Theory of Anaxagoras." *The Philosophical Review* 59: 31–57.

Vlastos, G. 1955. "On Heraclitus." *American Journal of Philology* 76: 337–68.

Vlastos, G. 1975. "One World or Many in Anaxagoras?" In Allen and Furley 1975, 354–60.

Voigtländer, H.-D. 1995. "Sprachphilosophie bei Heraklit." *Hermes* 123: 139–55.

Von Fritz, K. 1938. *Philosophie und sprachlicher Ausdruck bei Demokrit, Plato und Aristoteles*. New York.

Von Fritz, K. 1943. "*Noos* and *Noein* in the Homeric Poems." *Classical Philology* 38: 79–93.

Von Fritz, K. 1945. "ΝΟΥΣ, ΝΟΕΙΝ, and Their Derivatives in Pre-Socratic Philosophy (Excluding Anaxagoras): Part I. From the Beginnings to Parmenides." *Classical Philology* 40: 223–42.

Von Fritz, K. 1946. "ΝΟΥΣ, ΝΟΕΙΝ, and Their Derivatives in Pre-Socratic Philosophy (Excluding Anaxagoras): Part II. The Post-Parmenidean Period." *Classical Philology* 41: 12–34.

Von Fritz, K. 1964. "Der ΝΟΥΣ des Anaxagoras." *Archiv für Begriffsgeschichte* 9: 87–102.

Wardy, R. B. B. 1988. "Eleatic Pluralism." *Archiv für Geschichte der Philosophie* 70: 125–46.

Warren, J. 2002a. "Democritus, the Epicureans, Death, and Dying." *Classical Quarterly* 52: 193–206.

Warren, J. 2002b. *Epicurus and Democritean Ethics: An Archaeology of Ataraxia*. Cambridge.
Warren, J. 2007a. "Anaxagoras on Perception, Pleasure, and Pain." *Oxford Studies in Ancient Philosophy* 33: 19–54.
Warren, J. 2007b. "Democritus on Social and Psychological Harm." In Brancacci and Morel 2007, 87–104.
Warren, J. 2007c. *Presocratics: Natural Philosophers Before Socrates*. Berkeley.
Wedin, M. V. 2014. *Parmenides' Grand Deduction: A Logical Reconstruction of the Way of Truth*. New York.
Wiggins, D. 1982. "Heraclitus' Conceptions of Flux, Fire and Material Persistence." In *Language and Logos: Studies in Ancient Greek Philosophy*, edited by M. Schofield and M. C. Nussbaum, 1–32. Cambridge.
Wilamowitz-Moellendorff, U. von. 1929. "Die Καθαρμοί des Empedokles." *Sitzungsberichte der Preußischen Akademie der Wissenschaften* 27: 626–61.
Wilamowitz-Moellendorff, U. von. 1930. "Lesefrüchte." *Hermes* 65: 245–50.
Wilberding, J. G. 2016. "Eternity in Ancient Philosophy." In *Eternity: A History*, edited by Y. Y. Melamed, 14–55. Oxford.
Wilcox, J. 1991. "Barbarian *Psyche* in Heraclitus." *The Monist* 74: 624–37.
Willi, A. 2008. *Sikelismos: Sprache, Literatur und Gesellschaft im griechischen Sizilien (8.–5. Jh. v. Chr.)*. Basel.
Williams, B. 1993. *Shame and Necessity*. Berkeley.
Wismann, H. 2010. *Les avatars du vide: Démocrite et les fondements de l'atomisme*. Paris.
Wittgenstein, L. 2001. *Tractatus Logico-Philosophicus*. Translated by D. Pears and B. McGuinness. London. First published 1921.
Wohl, V., ed. 2014. *Probabilities, Hypotheticals, and Counterfactuals in Ancient Greek Thought*. Cambridge.
Wohl, V. 2020. "The Sleep of Reason: Sleep and the Philosophical Soul in Ancient Greece." *Classical Antiquity* 39: 126–51.
Wohl, V. 2024. "Heraclitus Stuttered." In *Radical Formalisms: Reading, Theory, and the Boundaries of the Classical*, edited by S. Nooter and M. Telò, 138–52. London.
Wohlfart, G. 1991. *'Also sprach Herakleitos': Heraklits Fragment B 52 und Nietzsches Heraklit-Rezeption*. Freiburg.
Wöhrle, G. 1993. "War Parmenides ein schlechter Dichter? Oder: zur Form der Wissensvermittlung in der frühgriechischen Philosophie." In *Vermittlung und Tradierung von Wissen in der griechischen Kultur*, edited by W. Kullmann and J. Althoff, 167–80. Tübingen.
Worman, N. 2015. *Landscape and the Spaces of Metaphor in Ancient Literary Theory and Criticism*. Cambridge.
Wright, M. R., ed. 1981. *Empedocles: The Extant Fragments*. New Haven.
Zatta, C. 2017. *Interconnectedness: The Living World of the Early Greek Philosophers*. Sankt Augustin.
Zatta, C. 2018. "Aristotle on 'the Sweat of the Earth' (DK 31 B55)." *Philosophia* 48: 55–70.
Zeitlin, F. I. 1996. *Playing the Other: Gender and Society in Classical Greek Literature*. Chicago.
Zeller, E. 1881. *A History of Greek Philosophy: From the Earliest Period to the Time of Socrates*. Vol. 2. Translated by S. F. Alleyne. London.

Zeller, E. 1923. *Die Philosophie der Griechen in ihrer geschichtlichen Entwicklung.* Leipzig. First published 1880.
Zilioli, U., ed. 2020. *Atomism in Philosophy: A History From Antiquity to the Present.* London.
Žižek, S. 2006. *The Parallax View.* Cambridge, MA.
Žižek, S. 2012. *Less Than Nothing: Hegel and the Shadow of Dialectical Materialism.* London.
Zuntz, G. 1971. *Persephone: Three Essays on Religion and Thought in Magna Graecia.* Oxford.
Zupančič, A. 2000. *Ethics of the Real: Kant, Lacan.* London.

INDEX

Founded in 1893,
UNIVERSITY OF CALIFORNIA PRESS
publishes bold, progressive books and journals on topics in the arts, humanities, social sciences, and natural sciences—with a focus on social justice issues—that inspire thought and action among readers worldwide.

The UC PRESS FOUNDATION
raises funds to uphold the press's vital role as an independent, nonprofit publisher, and receives philanthropic support from a wide range of individuals and institutions—and from committed readers like you. To learn more, visit ucpress.edu/supportus.

www.ingramcontent.com/pod-product-compliance
Ingram Content Group UK Ltd.
Pitfield, Milton Keynes, MK11 3LW, UK
UKHW010858240725
461140UK00001B/1